W9-BLG-783

The Shaping of the West Indian Church
1492–1962

The Shaping of the West Indian Church 1492–1962

Arthur Charles Dayfoot

The Press University of the West Indies
Barbados • Jamaica • Trinidad and Tobago

University Press of Florida
Gainesville • Tallahassee • Tampa • Boca Raton • Pensacola •
Orlando • Miami • Jacksonville

Published by The Press University of the West Indies
1A Aqueduct Flats   Mona
Kingston 7 Jamaica
ISBN 976-640-061-X (paper)

Published simultaneously in the United States of America by
University Press of Florida
15 NW 15th Street, Gainesville, FL 32611
ISBN 0-8130-1626-6 (cloth)

03 02 01 00 99   5 4 3 2 1

CATALOGUING IN PUBLICATION DATA (UWI)

Dayfoot, Arthur Charles.
   The shaping of the West Indian church, 1492–1962 / Arthur Charles Dayfoot.
   p. cm.
   Includes bibliographical references and index.
   ISBN 976-640-061-X
   1. Christianity – Caribbean, English-speaking – History.
   I . Title.
   BR640.D38 1999   279.972'9

03 02 01 00 99   5 4 3 2 1

LIBRARY OF CONGRESS CATALOGUING IN PUBLICATION DATA (UPF)

Dayfoot, Arthur Charles.
   The shaping of the West Indian church, 1492–1962 / Arthur Charles
   Dayfoot.
   p. cm.
   Includes bibliographical references and index.
   ISBN 0-8130-1626-6 (cloth)
   1. Protestant churches—West Indies, British—History. 2. West Indies,
   British—Church history. 3. Protestant churches—Caribbean,
   English-speaking—History. 4. Caribbean, English-speaking—Church
   history. I. Title.
   BR640.D38   1999
   280'.4'097290917521—dc21   98-17620

Set in Trident
Book design by Errol Stennett
Cover photograph, Spanish Town Cathedral by Herbie Gordon
The cathedral is built near the site of the sixteenth century
"Red Church" of St Jago de la Vega.

Dedicated to the memory of

Idris Hamid (1934–1981)
David I. Mitchell (1921–1988)
James F. Seunarine (1921–1991)
Bishop S. U. Hastings (1916–1991)
Roy G. Neehall (1928–1996)

and to the many other Caribbean scholars and Christian leaders, most still living,
whose help and friendship have inspired this study

Contents

Illustrations and Maps

Illustrations

Maps

Foreword

Howard K. Gregory
President
United Theological College of the West Indies

In writing this foreword I am immediately reminded of the preface to Luke's gospel in which he dedicates his work to Theophilus and acknowledges the contribution of many others who have previously recorded their experiences and perspectives on the events that form the core of the gospel. He then sets out to indicate the basis for the unique contribution that he is about to make, as follows:

> Forasmuch as many have taken in hand to set forth in order a declaration of those things which are most surely believed among us,
> Even as they delivered them unto us, which from the beginning were eyewitnesses, and ministers of the word;
> It seemed good to me also, having had perfect understanding of all things from the very first, to write unto thee in order, most excellent Theophilus,
> That thou mightest know the certainty of those things, wherein thou hast been instructed.
>
> (Luke 1:1–4)

Arthur Dayfoot's book, *The Shaping of the West Indian Church*, attempts to provide an ecclesiastical history of the Caribbean which covers a period of five centuries from 1492. As a text covering the history of the Church in the Caribbean it is by no means the first such work since it takes its place among a collection of works which have been written primarily from a missionary or denominational perspective. Indeed, various subjects and themes have been covered by monographs written by various scholars and church historians.

To simply lump Dayfoot's work along with earlier works without taking cognizance of its uniqueness would be a great disservice to the author and to the character and scholarly work which this presentation typifies.

In the best of the classical historical tradition, Dayfoot not only tells a story about the Church through a focus on the various expressions of "Christ centred worship, proclamation, teaching, fellowship, pastoral help and social concern", but he locates the Church and its historical development in the wider context of Caribbean history and life. Hence, he examines the impact of the Church on the social, political and religious environment and vice versa. To that extent this work not only tells a history that transcends the paternalism and incestuous engagement which has characterized missionary and denominational works. This work will therefore excite both the enquiring Church member and the scholar of West Indian history who will find here a presentation of the history of the Caribbean Church which reflects the unique character of Caribbean society and history.

This work is distinguished by the perspective of the author and the scope of the material covered in it. Although aligned with one of the religious traditions represented among the players in this historical drama, Dayfoot can truly be said to have taken a nondenominational and ecumenical approach in his examination and treatment of the subject matter. If the author is to be accused of bias it can only be located in the prominence given to the southern Caribbean and the cross-cultural encounters between East Indian and Christian religious traditions. Given the author's experience of life and work in this context for nearly three decades, then the focus is understandable.

One element which will delight the reader of this work is the range and scope of the material covered, ranging from Spanish Roman Catholicism of the fifteenth century to North American Pentecostal incursions of the twentieth century. Dayfoot's citations of bibliographical data, hitherto unknown to many, and his treatment of subjects and events previously available in sketchy and fragmentary ways, have served to add scholarship and interest to the work. To this extent it is anticipated that his work will not become a terminus in the field of Caribbean Church history but a vantage point from which to view the new horizons that invite further research and exploration.

Having cited Luke and the preface to his gospel earlier, one needs only recall that Luke felt it necessary to give his unique perspective on the gospel. In like manner, Dayfoot has given us a historical work that is unique and that will enrich the life of the Caribbean Church and the reader. Having read Luke's gospel we not only know the gospel he has presented but we believe that we have come to know something of the person behind the gospel.

It seems appropriate that I should say something about Arthur Dayfoot the person who in the role of historian has given us this important work. Dayfoot was not born in the Caribbean but came as an ordained minister of the United Church of Canada to serve in the Presbyterian Church in Trinidad from 1952 to 1974. During this time he became a player within the drama that constitutes the life of the Caribbean Church but also developed a deep interest in the history of the Caribbean Church. This interest brought him into contact with some of the leading historians of the region and opened to him bibliographical data hitherto unexplored by church historians of the Caribbean. This interest has mushroomed and after forty years has come to fruition in this work.

At an age when many have retired and are given to a sedentary life of rest and recreation, Dayfoot has given himself to the pursuit of this enterprise. Serious illness has complicated the process for him but he has never lost his commitment and focus where this project was concerned.

The United Theological College of the West Indies stands to benefit from this work and offers a sincere expression of gratitude to Arthur Dayfoot and his family for the commitment to his work and its dedication to the college. We note with gratitude that his association with the institution began in the 1960s when its establishment as an ecumenical theological college was being negotiated. We know that his work will form an integral part of the historical studies in this institution and will be required reading as part of the formation process in the life of our students.

It is my opinion that readers of the book will find it a scholarly, engaging and vital work for those who seek to understand the West Indian Church and the unique forces and factors that have shaped it into the reality it is today.

Preface

This book arises out of a felt need for an answer to the question: How did Christianity come to take the form that it has in the English-speaking Caribbean? The writer again and again enquired whether there was a book that would respond to this need, or at least some Caribbean scholar working on it. Finding no answer, I began to gather materials, during twenty-two years of residence in the West Indies (including furloughs in Canada) to put the story together, and to confer with others who recognized the need. Much advice and encouragement were received from Caribbean scholars and others to persist in this quest.

The period 1492–1870 was dealt with in a doctoral thesis ("The Shaping of the West Indian Church") for Emmanuel College and the Toronto School of Theology (1982). Quite a few revisions have been made, together with an additional chapter to bring the story up to the 1960s.

My chief desire is that this book will be of service to readers, in the Caribbean and elsewhere, and especially to those who may wish to explore further the history of the Church in the West Indies.

Let me emphasize that this study is limited to an attempt to trace the origins and development of the Christian community in the West Indies during the colonial period. It is for Caribbean Church historians both to write their own account of those centuries, and to continue the story into the decades since Independence.

Since independence Caribbean scholars and church people have responded to the opportunity of refashioning the Church to meet the needs of the new era and the challenge of the future. In doing so they will wish to break with some regrettable traditions of the past. This account of the colonial period will provide data to assist in that process. It may also offer inspiring episodes worth remembering, and using in the celebration of Caribbean Church history and in the task of defining a Caribbean theology.

Within the English-speaking territories, Christian denominational pluralism is now very great. This is in contrast to the unitary form of Christianity which prevailed at first in the Caribbean (including Jamaica and Trinidad): that is, the Spanish Catholic Church. However, although the Commonwealth Caribbean today remains politically divided, there are many common historical elements to justify our speaking of "the West Indian Church".

For reasons explained in chapter 1, the traditional term "the West Indies" is used as a brief alternative for the more ponderous "English-speaking Caribbean".

The Church history of this region deserves comparison with that of two other English-speaking areas of the Western hemisphere which emerged earlier from colonialism, that is, the United States and Canada. Church histories of those countries were written by various scholars from an ecumenical viewpoint some time ago (see chapter 1 below, note 3). Readers interested in comparing such histories – and indeed those of Latin America – with that of the West Indies, may find here a starting point, but space forbids such comparative study in the present book.

It is impossible also for me to attempt to compare the shaping of Christianity here with that in Africa and in India, which in some ways hold family resemblances.

It goes without saying that this book, covering almost five centuries and many territories, depends largely upon printed sources. Many of these sources contain contemporary and first-hand material. Primary sources (or microfilms of them) were consulted when possible. Except for chapter 11, the sources are listed with fuller detail in the bibliography of the 1982 above-mentioned thesis (volume 2, pp. 539–727). This is available in theological libraries in Trinidad, Barbados and Jamaica, in Emmanuel College, Toronto, and in Queen's Theological College, Birmingham, England. A bibliography on "West Indian Church History", divided by territory, denomination and other categories, compiled by myself and the late Revd Roscoe Pierson, is in preparation.

The select bibliography included in the present work consists mainly of those references that have been quoted more than once in the notes, and that are accordingly of outstanding importance. Items cited only once have their details included in that citation.

Toronto, Canada
July 1998

Acknowledgments

It is impossible to name individually the many people who contributed in various ways to the gathering of the sources, facts and interpretations in the following pages. I wish to thank them all nevertheless. Special gratitude is due to my thesis director at Emmanuel College, Dr John Grant; to my employer, the United Church of Canada (Division of World Outreach); and to the Presbyterian Church in Trinidad with which I served as a "fraternal worker" from 1952 to 1974. I am grateful also to several historians of the University of the West Indies in Jamaica and Trinidad, to faculty members of the United Theological College of the West Indies, and colleagues at St Andrew's Theological College, Trinidad. Special thanks are due to Dr Brinsley Samaroo of the University of the West Indies, Trinidad, and Dr Patrick Taylor of York University, Toronto, whose advice recently during the revising of the manuscript has been invaluable.

I owe many thanks to my wife Bessie for support and assistance through forty years of research and writing. Several other family members have given valuable assistance in getting this work ready for publication, including Nancy and Lawrence Gordon, and Yasmin and Angus Müller. Catherine Müller, in particular, has assisted greatly over the years with secretarial work, proofreading and candid comments on the text.

I appreciate also the efforts of the staff, past and present, of The Press University of the West Indies who have looked after the publication of this book, despite the many problems presented by time and distance.

Abbreviations

ACMS American Christian Missionary Society
AME African Methodist Episcopal
BMS Baptist Missionary Society
CADEC Christian Action for Development in the Eastern Caribbean
CCC Caribbean Conference of Churches
CCJCA Caribbean Council for Joint Christian Action
CECD Caribbean Ecumenical Consultation for Development
CGSRS Caribbean Group for Social and Religious Studies
CJPWI Church in Jamaica in the Province of the West Indies
CM Canadian Mission
CMS Church Missionary Society
CPWI Church in the Province of the West Indies
CSPC *Calendar of State Papers, Colonial*
CWBM Christian Woman's Board of Missions
HMPEC *Historical Magazine of the Protestant Episcopal Church*
JBMS Jamaica Baptist Missionary Society
JBU Jamaica Baptist Union
JNH *Journal of Negro History*
LMS London Missionary Society
MCCA Methodist Church of the Caribbean and the Americas
NLJ National Library of Jamaica
SES *Social and Economic Studies*
SPCK Society for Promoting Christian Knowledge
UCJCI United Church of Jamaica and the Cayman Islands
UCJGC United Church of Jamaica and Grand Cayman
USPG United Society for the Propagation of the Gospel
UTCWI United Theological College of the West Indies
UTS Union Theological Seminary.
UWI University of the West Indies
WCC World Council of Churches

1

Introduction

The decade of the 1960s marked the end of the colonial era for the English-speaking islands and coastlands of the Caribbean region. The two most populous territories – Jamaica, and Trinidad and Tobago – became independent in 1962. Guyana and Barbados followed in 1966, and nearly all of the Leeward and Windward Islands, as well as the Bahamas and Belize, later moved on to full autonomy.

Emergence from colonial status introduces a new period in the life of the Church. Ecclesiastical history is inevitably influenced by such a major political change. Church organizations, already at various stages of indigenous adaptation, self-government and self-support, are spurred on to greater initiative. This was seen, for example, in the United States in the 1780s, in the years following Confederation in Canada (1867), and in the younger churches of Africa and Asia since World War II.

In addition, in 1962 the beginning of the Second Vatican Council and the merging of the International Missionary Council with the World Council of Churches facilitated new developments in ecumenical co-operation, including the formation of the Caribbean Conference of Churches in 1973. Other new social, liturgical and theological movements provide further evidence of a major turning point in Caribbean Christian history.

This book, therefore, looks back to see how the pattern of church life had been formed under colonial conditions. There is no attempt to survey the whole field of West Indian church history, which would be too large a task. It is instead to outline the response of Christianity to its environment, and the "shaping" of the organized Church in its social, political and religious circumstances.

Attention is concentrated on the major historical factors which give distinctive character to the ecclesiastical scene. Note will be taken of the overseas origins of the various traditions that have converged here, their denominational development, and their local (that is, Caribbean) features. We will bear in mind the special problems of the area related to its tropical setting, its plantation economy, the social and racial composition of its communities, the effect of various imperial connections and mingling of cultures, and the changes in religious attitudes and ecclesiastical organization which took place through the centuries. Specially important are certain of the more specifically religious and ecclesiastical topics such as the social characteristics of different branches of the Church, church-state relations, religious toleration, the growth of the Church, lay participation in church life, theological thinking and social concern, and the relationship of pluralistic tendencies to unitive or "ecumenical" aspirations.

The Caribbean, as part of the Western hemisphere, shares important sociological, cultural, political and religious characteristics of "the New World".[1] There is much in common in terms of pioneer settlement, transplantation from the "Old World" (Europe, Africa and Asia), conflict and adjustment with indigenous peoples, colonial dependence, and resistance to imperial domination.[2] Similarities and also differences may be seen between the Church in the West Indies and that of the two other major English-speaking regions: the United States and Canada.[3]

Although the New World and colonial ethos predominates in this account, the Caribbean Church is a part of the worldwide Christian community. It is not simply an extension of European (and North American) Christianity but has an important kinship especially with the Church in Africa and Asia, because of cultural and racial connections. In the twentieth century African and Black Studies and also Asian and Amerindian research have demonstrated the importance of these connections.[4] They have often been examined from the standpoint of sociology, with reference to religious groups which are on or beyond the fringe of orthodox Christianity. Less singular but also important is the distinctiveness of the West Indian Church. Comparison and contrast with the Black Church in the United States, with African Church history, or with parts of church life in India are possible. But since independence, contemporary scholars have begun the significant task of reflecting upon their Church and its society, past, present and future, from a Caribbean point of view. Since this book is about the formation of the Church in the colonial period, it does not try to encompass these later and broader perspectives, important as they are.[5]

The Church and the Churches

The title of this book speaks of "the West Indian Church" – in the singular. In fact, "the Church", as the term is used here, is not so much institution as movement – one that has visible expression, both in the form of communication and co-opera-tion (and indeed controversy) among believers in Christ, and also as a variety of

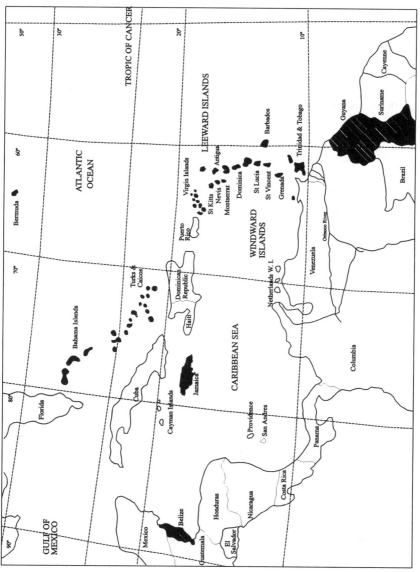

The Caribbean Area

ecclesiastical institutions. Wherever we can identify Christ-centred worship, proclamation, teaching, fellowship, pastoral help and social concern, the Church is recognized, whatever form of ecclesiastical organization there may be. This definition is intended to be a historical description rather than a theological doctrine. But it does imply a faith in the essential unity of the Church, and a viewpoint that may be described as unitive or "ecumenical".

Against this description, it may be objected that the number of organized churches, or "denominations", in the West Indies is very large, especially in recent times. They range from the monolithic Spanish Catholic state-church in the sixteenth century Caribbean (including Spanish Jamaica and Trinidad) to the modern multiplicity of small and poorly organized groups, even single congregations, whose outstanding characteristic seems to be a love of separate identity. With such diverse data it would be difficult, not to say controversial, to adopt some ecclesiastical or doctrinal criterion to determine which groups belong to "the West Indian Church" and which should be left outside it.

Indeed, why speak of the Church rather than of religion, or religions? Judaism has been in the West Indies from early days, and there are important Asian religions, Hinduism and Islam, especially in the southern Caribbean (Trinidad, Guyana and Suriname). Other religious groups, although borrowing Christian and biblical language, are clearly beyond the borderline of orthodox Christianity. Some of these, such as the Jehovah's Witnesses, are of North American origin. Others, such as Shango, Pocomania and the Rastafarians, stand closer to African religion.[6]

Primary attention is given to those churches which lay claim to traditional Christian orthodoxy. Our main purpose is to discover common elements and an overall pattern in the history of the Christian movement, or "Church" as defined above. This purpose would be obscured if we were to include, except in some peripheral way, bodies which directly or indirectly deny basic beliefs of worldwide Christianity.

Another objection to using "the Church" in the singular might be that it tends to perpetuate the common historical fallacy of making sweeping generalizations. For example, "the Church" is said to have been aligned with the propertied classes, or to have condoned slavery. The fact is that within the Church, and within the individual churches, there were different attitudes to vested interests, including slave ownership, as there were to the European treatment of the Amerindians, the exploitation of free labour, and to many other issues down to the present day. These attitudes appear among the clergy and the laity, leaders and nominal church members, within most if not all denominational groups. It is important to recognize both the reactionary elements and also the prophetic voices within the various communions. Such diversities within the churches are as important as the differences between the denominations themselves. The Dominican monk

Bartolomé de las Casas, the Anglican minister James Ramsay, and nonconformist missionaries John Wray and William Knibb are separated by historical circumstances and no doubt by doctrine, but they are brothers in the faith. Conversely every communion has had its leaders and members who supported or at least remained silent about the social injustices of the time.

In speaking of the Church, then, it must be remembered that this movement of people who profess Christian faith is not united in their understanding of that faith, still less of its social implications. The "shaping" of the Church through the centuries has to do with the impact of changing conditions and new insights upon all the churches together, as well as with the fortunes of rival denominations in building the allegiance of their people.

Therefore we do not simply speak of "churches". Attention will be given, of course, to the origins and comparative growth of one tradition or another in a given place or time. For this is important in the development of the Church. But there are common factors which deliniate a larger pattern, overlapping denominational and territorial divisions, requiring us to speak of the West Indian Church.

The English-Speaking Caribbean

"The West Indies" includes the islands in the Caribbean Sea which long were British colonies. Closely associated with these are the Atlantic islands of the Bahamas and the two mainland territories of Guyana and Belize. Certain "fringe" areas – for example the Danish (now American) Virgin Islands and even Bermuda – will be mentioned at times because of historical church connections of some kind.

In the era of independence the term "Caribbean" has come to be preferred to "the West Indies". There is difficulty, however, when a limited definition is required. For frequent usage, "English-speaking Caribbean", "anglophone Caribbean" or "English Caribbean", are cumbersome. Moreover since this book deals with the colonial period, it seems appropriate to employ the term which was common usage in that era. Therefore, "West Indies" and "West Indian" are retained in this book, with "Caribbean" as an alternative where the context admits of no ambiguity.

2

New World and
Old World Backgrounds

The history of Christianity in the Caribbean begins with the arrival of the Spaniards, in the last decade of the fifteenth century, bringing with them the faith of late medieval Christendom in the form which had emerged in the Iberian Peninsula. Here these Europeans met with the Amerindian inhabitants who, of course, had never had prior contact with the Christian religion.

The Amerindians survive in the West Indies only in Guyana, Belize and Dominica, with a tiny remnant in Trinidad. The English-speaking Caribbean is now otherwise populated by the descendants of the "Old World" of Europe, Africa and Asia who have moved here since 1492. In order to understand the shaping of the Church the earlier history of these diverse groups of people may be noted, in particular their connection, or the reasons for their lack of connection, with the Christian faith.

The character of the Church in the Caribbean was also determined, in part, by the long history of the Church through the first fifteen centuries of the Christian era. This development took place in various parts of the Old World, principally Europe. One important question is how the peaceable and sometimes persecuted Church of New Testament times came to be transformed into an instrument of Spanish imperial state policy. Subsequent chapters will indicate ecclesiastical characteristics of other nations which later exerted influence on the Caribbean scene, especially France, England and the United States.

Pre-Columbian Caribbean Peoples

Many varieties of culture and religion developed among the Amerindians of North and South America during the thousands of years of their spread through two continents and adjacent islands. Our concern is with two main types: the communities of the Caribbean islands and north-eastern South America, including the present Guyana, and the more hierarchical civilization of the Mayas who lived in Central America, including Belize.

At the time of Columbus the aboriginal inhabitants were the Arawaks who occupied the Greater Antilles, the Bahamas and Trinidad, and the Caribs in the Lesser Antilles. The latter were overrunning and supplanting the Arawaks, as far as eastern Puerto Rico.[1]

Most of the surviving Arawaks perished through mistreatment by the Spaniards, and by European diseases. The Caribs fiercely defended their liberty, and when English and French later began to settle the Lesser Antilles they met and fought with them.[2] Both Arawaks and Caribs remained however in parts of north-eastern South America, along with other "Tropical Forest Tribes" such as the Warrau, the Acawai and the Wapishana. They are important in the society and culture of the present Guyana.

Something of the early religion of the island Arawaks and Caribs can be known through archaeological evidence, and through early Spanish and French writers such as Ramón Pane and Raymond Breton.[3] The modern mainland Amerindians in Guyana and neighbouring regions also bear witness to their traditions, although allowance has to be made for influences from contact with Christianity.[4]

The predominant element in the religion of the Arawakan and Cariban tribes, and also of the Warrau and Wapishana, was belief in nature spirits, related to the plant and animal world. Various hunting and fertility rites resulting from this belief were practised.[5] The shamans (priest-doctors) were believed to draw power from these spirits in a state of trance. In the Antilles however the Arawak *cacique* (chief) did the work of the shaman.[6]

Expectation of survival after death and reverence for ancestors were also found. In the time of Columbus, indeed, Spaniards were able to entice many Lucayans from the Bahamas into slavery by promising to take them to meet the spirits of their ancestors.[7]

Belief in a powerful but remote Supreme Being seems to have been widespread among Cariban, Arawakan and Warrau peoples. This deity was not, however, to be worshipped, though he was believed to be governor, or even creator, of the world. Many myths are told concerning the origin of the universe.[8]

The Taino (Arawaks of the Greater Antilles) had images of stone, wood, textiles or other materials, called *zemis*, which played a part in their religious life, both tribal and domestic. Among other purposes, these sacred objects were believed to have influence with the supreme God.[9]

The island Caribs had a doctrine of human souls, some of which after the death of the body became evil spirits (*maboya*) which could cause damage on the sea or in the woods.[10]

Quite different from these tribal cultures was the developed civilization of the Maya Indians in the immediate vicinity of Belize, in the Petén (modern Guatemala and western Belize) and the Yucatán peninsula (just north of the Belizean border in Mexico).

By the time the Spaniards encountered the Mayas in the sixteenth century, their high civilization after hundreds of years of glory had been in decline for several decades, since the fall of Mayapán in 1441. Unfortunately their written records were largely destroyed by the invaders, so that our knowledge of them is limited.[11]

Their religion inspired great architectural achievements including pyramids, and their priests had enough scientific knowledge to produce a complicated calendar. The Mayas had many gods, although it has been claimed that their religion was more dualistic than polytheistic.[12] They also practised human sacrifice. This, with other rites regarded as superstitious and idolatrous, seemed to the Spaniards to justify the destruction of religious objects during their conquest of the area in the 1540s and afterwards. Much of what is known of pre-Columbian Maya religion and culture has been learned from three surviving manuscript volumes of the Maya themselves and also from the writings of Spanish priests such as Fray Diego de Landa who as a Franciscan Inquisitor was responsible for some of this very destruction, and who later became the first bishop of Mérida in Yucatán.[13]

Descendants of the ancient Maya live today in the interior parts of Belize as well as in Guatemala and Mexico. They still speak their ancestral language, and some Spanish as well. They are mostly Roman Catholic but some survivals of Maya belief and religious ceremony have been syncretized with their Christianity.[14]

Certain other Central American peoples are of interest because mission work was later undertaken among them by churches of the West Indies: the Moskitos and Sumus on the coast of Nicaragua, by the Anglicans and the Moravians, and the Guaymies or Valientes of Panama, by the Methodists.[15] Another people with historical connection to the Methodists are the Black Caribs who arose from intermixture of Caribs and escaped African slaves in St Vincent. They were transported at the end of the eighteenth century to the Bay Islands, and many of them later moved to Belize.[16]

The Church in the Old World: Asia, Europe and Africa

The Christian Church began with three hundred years of spontaneous expansion before any government offered favour to it, and at times in the face of persecution by the state. Personal witnessing, preaching and social service were the principal means of winning new adherents. By the beginning of the fourth century, churches were to be found in the continent of Asia from Palestine, Asia Minor and Arabia in the west to Armenia, Mesopotamia and possibly (if tradition be correct) India in the east. In Europe they spread throughout the Roman Empire, and in Africa along the north coast, especially in Egypt and what is now Tunisia.[17]

In the ancient world – and indeed everywhere until the coming of the modern secular state – religion was usually associated with the rulers of government, providing one source of social and political unity. As the new faith spread, Armenia, possibly Edessa, and then the Roman Empire began to favour Christianity. The emperor Constantine by the Edict of Milan (313 A.D.) granted toleration, and recognition along with the official state cult. As time went on, emperors increasingly favoured the Church, and interfered in its affairs. Under Justinian in the eastern Roman Empire a new kind of church organization emerged, on what came to be known in modern times as the Erastian pattern. In this Byzantine Empire the state dominated the Church, and in the western empire the bishop of Rome came to have growing political influence. With the barbarian invasions, new rulers such as the Vandals, Visigoths and Franks adopted Christianity and followed the practice of patronizing the Church and governing many of its affairs.[18]

Three important consequences from this conjunction of church and state – which had effects in the Caribbean centuries later – appeared in the course of the Middle Ages: (i) a long struggle for power between the two partners; (ii) interference, from both sides, with religious freedom; and (iii) the employment of military means for the conversion of non-Christians, and for a counterattack against Islam.

(i) A power struggle took place between the Church hierarchy on the one hand and lay rulers on the other. The issues concerned the principles of the priority of "spiritual authority" in the minds of churchmen, and the independence and rights of lay rulers in the rising nation-states from the viewpoint of these rulers and their advisers. In England the contest had its climax in the murder of Archbishop Thomas Becket in 1170, an event which touched deeply the English people. In spite of this the kings of England continued to hold much authority in ecclesiastical matters, and when England later became a colonial power, the government took for granted this privileged position. France too had its conflict between King Philip the Fair and Pope Boniface VIII at the beginning of the fourteenth century. The "Gallican" or national church tradition, although (unlike the English) remaining loyal to the Roman connection, formed the background of Church affairs in the French Antilles later on.[19]

(ii) On the issue of religious freedom, lay power, although feuding periodically with the ecclesiastical hierarchy, usually joined with it in a policy of religious coercion. What was judged to be heresy by the Church was felt by statesmen as a threat to political unity, and so became a crime. In England the fourteenth century Wyclifite or Lollard movement encountered this tendency. The stream of nonconformity which trickled forth at this time later became a flood in England and Scotland (but not in Eire), overflowing to the New World. Wyclif's influence was felt by John Huss and his followers in Bohemia and Moravia, among a people whose initial conversion to Christianity came from teachers sent from Constantinople by the Greek Church. They had encouraged a liturgy in the people's own Slavonic language. Persecution followed from a German hierarchy that insisted on the Latin rite and strict Roman Catholic doctrine. Huss was burned at the stake in 1415 and from his supporters emerged the *Unitas Fratrum* (United Brethren) that endured oppression for centuries, ultimately inspiring the "Moravian" settlement in Saxony from which came the first evangelical missionaries to the West Indies.[20]

(iii) In the medieval period the use of military force to advance religio-political ends became common. For example, missionary work in Frisia (Holland) was backed by Frankish military power before and during the time of the emperor Charlemagne. The people of the Netherlands, while finally accepting Christianity, maintained an independent spirit which reappeared in the sixteenth century in political and religious resistance to the Spanish Empire both in their own country and in the Caribbean. They became pioneers also in the practice of religious freedom.[21]

The consequences, in terms of the militarization of religion, of the long struggle between Christian and Islamic powers in Asia, Africa and Europe were felt throughout Christendom but especially in the Iberian Peninsula, and indirectly in the Caribbean later. After the death of Mohammed in 632 A.D., Muslim armies had conquered Palestine, Syria, Persia, Egypt and North Africa. In 711 A.D. they invaded what we know as Spain and Portugal and were stopped in southern France. For hundreds of years armies of Arab, Moorish and Turkish powers seemed to threaten the survival of the Christian world. European Christians remained cut off from communication with fellow Christians in Africa (Nubia and Ethiopia) and Asia (India) by a ring of Islamic countries. Hostility toward "the infidels" reached a climax from the eleventh to the thirteenth centuries, with the assault on the Near East known as the Crusades and the counterattack in the Iberian Peninsula known as the Reconquest. Warfare aggravated economic greed. The notion grew that faith could be promoted by the sword.[22]

Medieval crusading ideals were still widely influential at the time of the discovery of the New World. Columbus seriously hoped to become wealthy enough through his discoveries to finance a Crusade to rescue Jerusalem from the infidels. He and others dreamed of extending Christendom to new lands. In particular "the Great Khan", emperor of "Cathay", was believed to have asked the pope for Christian teachers. If Islam stood in the way of responding eastward, perhaps a westward approach could be made.[23]

While warlike methods of spreading the faith were admired by many, there was another approach. The monastic movement was adapted to missionary purposes. The Franciscan and Dominican orders founded in the thirteenth century led in the evangelizing of new areas since they were bands of ascetics in the world rather than in the cloister. When the time came for missionary activity in the New World, the followers of Francis and Dominic, and later the new order of the Jesuits, took the lead in Spanish and French colonies. On the other hand in England the monastic orders had declined in the fifteenth century and were dissolved by Henry VIII. When

England began to be involved in overseas settlement there were no missionary monks available.[24]

Christianity, Islam and Traditional Religion in Africa

Christianity, already established in Egypt, had been carried to Ethiopia early in the fourth century. The country became predominantly Christian, with its own Church related to the Egyptian Coptic Church.[25] Ethiopia's long Christian tradition holds a great fascination and inspiration for many in modern times, both in Africa and among people of African descent in the New World. In the sixth century Nubia also, in the Nile valley between Egypt and Ethiopia, was won to Christianity. For centuries the churches in Egypt, Nubia, and Ethiopia maintained their life in north-eastern Africa, although because of differences in doctrine they were somewhat isolated from European churches. However the advance of Islam in the seventh century reduced the Egyptian Coptic Church to a struggling minority, and finally overran much of Nubia in the fourteenth and early fifteenth centuries. The ancient kingdom of Ethiopia was saved for its Christian rulers only with the help of a Portuguese army in 1541–43.[26]

After the Islamic conquest of North Africa, Muslim merchants cultivated trans-Saharan trade with West Africa. Northern salt was exchanged for southern gold and slaves. The traders took their religion with them and by the eleventh century it began to be embraced by some rulers and people of the great empires on the south side of the desert, notably Tekrur, Mali, Songhai and Kanem-Bornu.[27] West Africa had little contact with Christian north-east Africa.[28] Accordingly for centuries such relations as this region had with the outside world were with Muslim North Africa. Among the Africans later brought to the Caribbean by the slave trade was a small minority of Muslims.

The religion of the great majority, however – coming from the forest areas nearer the Gulf of Guinea, where Islam had not penetrated to any great extent – consisted of the traditional religious beliefs and practices of the region.

African Traditional Religion is a modern term to describe the faith of many millions of African people south of the Sahara, which has also had a wide influence in tropical America. Since it does not have written scriptures, creeds, historical founder figures or a unified organization, its history is not easy to trace, but oral tradition, art, music, proverbs, myths, prayers, ritual formulas and ceremonies, and basic consistency of ideas, point to its long ascendency in villages and national areas.[29]

Two main features have characterized this religion for centuries: (i) a spiritual worldview in which there is a continuum between sacred and secular – between everyday living and an omnipresent world of spirits that impinge upon earthly existence; and (ii) an awareness of the corporate oneness of life in family, clan, tribal and national communities, without which the individual would have no meaning.[30]

This spiritual world which surrounds community life includes, for most Africans, a good supreme being or god who was creator of man, animals, plants and other objects. This god is now somewhat removed from his creation so that he is not usually worshipped, and yet is omniscient and omnipresent and may be appealed to in time of need.[31] There is also a company of lesser divinities or spiritual powers, associated with natural forces, which are corporately worshipped in particular regions: for example the Yoruban thunder-god Shango.[32]

The most intimate relationships are with the spirits of departed ancestors – "the living dead" as they are called by one writer. These spirits communicate with the living in dreams, oracles and rituals, and sometimes take an active part in family affairs, to help or rebuke the surviving members. After a few generations these spirits take their place in a less personal kind of existence, somewhat like that of the divinities mentioned above.[33]

In contact with this world of spirits, there live within the community a variety of sacred specialists such as priests, kings, rainmakers, medicine men, herbalists, mediums and diviners. They act as intermediaries to protect people from danger and to bring benefits, or, in the case of sorcerers, to do harm.[34]

An important part of religious life is a series of family rituals connected with birth, puberty, marriage, death and the afterlife. These rites express and transmit the religious beliefs of the community.[35]

Some Asian Religious Backgrounds

In Asia the Syrian Christian Church had connections eastward. By the end of the fifth century or perhaps earlier, a group of Christians with a Syriac liturgy were established on the Malabar coast of India. They maintained their minority position in the largely Hindu environment, but were unable to make extensive growth.[36]

In the fifteenth century, Europeans believed that there were many Christians beyond the Islamic nations, and that they had a rich prince named "Prester John". The location of this mythical Christian ruler was said to be in "the Indies", or "India", inexact terms meaning almost any region east and south of the familiar Mediterranean neighbourhood. One of the motives for the Portuguese endeavour to travel around Africa by sea was the hope of meeting Prester John and joining forces with him against the Muslims.[37] In addition, the Portuguese hoped to do missionary work in Africa and beyond. Papal bulls encouraged them in this purpose, promising ecclesiastical patronage over churches established in lands discovered "all the way to the Indians".[38] This expansionist movement led to the founding of the colony of Goa in India in 1510. However the Christian community in Goa, like the one in Malabar, was not in the part of India which three centuries later sent indentured workers to the Caribbean. There were likewise few such immigrants among the later converts of Protestant missionary societies (in the nineteenth and early twentieth centuries), although some of the indentured people had had contact with Christian schools and hospitals.[39]

An important number of Indian Muslims did come to the Caribbean. These were descendants of people, mainly in northern India, who were converted to Islam after Arab armies first reached what is now Pakistan in the eighth century. Believing in one God, Allah, and Mohammed as his prophet, they acknowledged as scripture the Qur'an, in its original Arabic. Muslims in India spoke Urdu, a variety of the Hindustani language written in Arabic characters.[40]

The greatest number of Indo-Caribbean migrants brought with them their Hindu religious traditions, which were those of the vast majority of the people of India from ancient times. These traditions include a wide variety of liturgical practices, beliefs and philosophies, found in the sacred writings (the *Vedas*, the *Upanishads*, and the highly regarded *Bhagavad-Gita*). Particularly important for the common people were the stories of the gods in epic poems (the *Ramayana* and the *Mahabharata*) and the customs and forms of worship which did not require extensive philosophical knowledge, and which were flexible enough to adapt to a new environment.

Some Chinese immigrants were of the Buddhist faith, but this was not widely observed in the Caribbean.

The Lebanese (usually referred to as "Syrians") who came to the West Indies in the late nineteenth and the twentieth centuries were mostly Maronite Christians. This church traces its origins to the time of the Crusades.

Iberian Expansion and Religion to 1492

The peninsula later known as Spain and Portugal had been under Arab and Moorish rulers from the eighth to the thirteenth centuries. These Muslim governments usually recognized the Church and gave religious freedom to Christians, and at times relations between the two religions were friendly and co-operative. Moreover the Arabs brought a high civilization to the area. Nevertheless the desire for independence drove the subject people of Iberia to revolt and finally to launch the "Reconquest".[41] In these wars for independence they found their focus of identity in religion. Small Christian kingdoms in the north grew stronger and they had the encouragement of the papacy. Portugal achieved independence in 1185. When in 1489 Isabella of Castile and Ferdinand of Aragon were married, their two kingdoms were drawn together.[42]

Spain, which finished the Reconquest in 1492 with the acquisition of Granada, was deeply marked by this struggle of seven centuries. In the light of this history can be understood the Spanish Church with its intense Catholicism combined with royal domination, its intolerance, its acceptance of rigid feudal structures and military arbitrament – and at the same time its zeal, its readiness for reformation and self-criticism within the Catholic framework, even its willingness to listen to a Las Casas, the crusader for social justice and humanity.

After the Reconquest, the many Muslims and Jews who remained within the peninsula presented a challenge to the missionary zeal of the Church.[43] The challenge was also a political one. In a day when religion was so closely allied to government it was thought dangerous to have what the twentieth century would call a "fifth column" within the country. To deal with the problem the Inquisition was introduced in Spain, on the authority of a papal bull but under royal control. This system of examining accused "heretics" by torture, and punishing them by imprisonment, confiscation of property or burning at the stake, shows the intolerance and violence of the age during which the New World was encountered.[44] The Inquisition was later introduced into Spanish America, although it did not play an important part in the Caribbean islands.

The eventful year 1492 brought the expulsion of the Jews from Spain, except for those who had submitted to baptism. A few years later the same policy was applied to the Muslims.[45] Thus the Spanish rulers made Catholic orthodoxy one of the foundations of national life.

Although orthodoxy acknowledged the pope as head of the Church, the Spanish crown achieved extensive control, by the *patronato real* (royal patronage) over ecclesiastical affairs in Spain and later in its colonies in America. When Christian kings in the north began to reconquer territory from the Muslims they had resumed the earlier royal tradition of appointing bishops and managing church affairs. When they built churches in newly conquered territories, or turned mosques into churches, the pope showed his gratitude by granting the right to appoint ecclesiastics to man them. This became a hereditary right of the king as "patron" of these particular religious establishments.[46]

With the growth of national policy under Ferdinand and Isabella, they put pressure upon the pope for further concessions. A bull of Innocent VIII, during the war for Granada, granted patronage over all benefices in the conquered area.[47] Another precedent for the patronato was found in ecclesiastical controls earlier given to Portugal after its explorations along the coast of Africa, with the promise of missionary work in that continent.[48]

While Africa was being explored, advances in the art of navigation had also made possible the settlement, and rule from the mainland, of the Canary Islands (1402), Madeira (1420), the Azores (1431) and the Cape Verde Islands (1456). The

Canaries were assigned to Spain, the others to Portugal. Missionaries and churchmen from the Franciscan order were associated with the colonizing expeditions.[49]

In the Canaries an important indigenous population resisted Spanish occupation. These islands in the fifteenth century provided a kind of dress rehearsal for the later tragic drama of the New World. The political and social system of feudal Europe was imposed, serfdom being the lot of the conquered people. They were assigned to their new lords by encomienda grants in the same way as the conquered Moors in Spain itself had been assigned during the Reconquest, and as Amerindians were later granted to Spanish settlers in the Caribbean. Slave traders also raided the islands for galley-slaves.[50] Several bishops protested against exploitation of the indigenous people and Pope Benedict XIII intervened on their behalf, withdrawing certain favours to one ruler of the time, Jean de Bethencourt, in an attempt to persuade him to treat them better. At first the churchmen appealed to the popes, then to the Spanish monarchs. From both they received sympathetic attention. But in the Canaries, as in America later, the prophets achieved only a mitigation of the evils they denounced. The encomienda system remained in force.[51]

A type of exploitation still more fateful for the Caribbean had its beginnings in the 1440s when West African slaves were first obtained by Portuguese explorers in Rio de Oro. By 1443 the European trade in slaves and gold had begun, challenging the monopoly held for centuries by North African trans-Saharan merchants.[52]

Slavery as an institution had been accepted or at least tolerated from ancient times by both state and church, although (as in the case of the Canaries) there was protest when Christians, or people in process of evangelization, were enslaved. Accordingly, Pope Pius II in 1462 instructed a bishop who was appointed for work in Portuguese Guinea to discipline "wicked Christians who were taking the recently baptized adult converts away into slavery".[53] In other cases, if the question was raised at all, Africans were presumed to have been "justly" enslaved.[54] Authorities in Europe were sometimes confused by the assumption that the Africans were "Saracens" or "Moors" and so "infidels", or else pagans who would be benefited eternally by having their souls saved even at the cost of enslavement to Christians.[55] For its first few decades this slavery was mainly in the form of domestic bondage in Portugal and Spain, before the settlement of the New World expanded the demand for estate labour in tropical America.

Religious motives were mingled with economic and political ones in the movement of maritime discovery in the fifteenth and sixteenth centuries.[56]

One cause of religious zeal was fostered in the Spanish Church by the Spanish Reformation. This movement is associated especially with the name of Cardinal Ximénes de Cisneros (1436–1517). It was well under way before the Protestant Reformation began with Luther in 1517. It was the fruit of a coming to power of ideals of complete dedication to Christ and the Church, held by Francis of Assisi and his more strict followers, such as the Observant wing of the Franciscan Order. Francisco Ximénes was an Observant who tried to bring the moral ideals of his order into the Church in Spain as a whole. He was supported by Queen Isabella who appointed him her confessor in 1492 and named him archbishop of Toledo (the highest ecclesiastical post in the land) in 1495. Under his leadership the monasteries were reformed and the low morality of monks and clergy disciplined and improved. Along with moral improvement went a zeal for education culminating in the founding of the University of Alcalá in 1508.[57] The Spanish Reformation was in touch with similar currents of reform in Italy, and the influence of Erasmus, the Dutch humanist and Christian reformer, was also felt in Spain.

This ecclesiastical reformation was in process while Columbus' discoveries were opening up previously unknown lands across the seas. Disciplined religious orders were now able to send large numbers of missionaries across the ocean. Zeal for study and learning would also be extended to the New World.[58]

But there was little sympathy for radical reform in Spain. After Martin Luther, the spread of Protestantism in northern Europe, and the birth of the Jesuit movement in Spain – a later expression of the reforming spirit within the Roman Catholic Church – the Spanish Church and nation became a bulwark of Catholicism. The Inquisition added Protestant heresy to its list of crimes and took care that it had no chance to spread in Spain or in the New World.

However in 1492 this belonged to the future. For the first quarter century of the Spanish Empire in America, Western Christendom was still in the era of the medieval Church, unshaken by what we call the Protestant Reformation.[59] And even for a century after that, the Caribbean knew little of Protestant ideas, except as they helped to inspire brief forays into the region by French, Dutch and English sailors who refused to recognize that the pope had assigned the Spanish crown to be in charge of the half-world west of his Demarcation Line.

3

The Spanish Catholic Monopoly
(1492–1655/1797)

Until colonies of other nations became planted in the seventeenth century, the Spanish Church, Roman Catholic in doctrine but Spanish by royal control, possessed a monopoly of the Christian religious life of the Caribbean. Some knowledge of the Spanish Empire and this Church throws light upon the later religious history in the English-speaking Caribbean, for two reasons:

(i) The Spanish were the first to deal with the problems of European colonization in the area, including the treatment of non-European peoples, both Amerindian and African. The pattern they set was not copied in all details by England and the other nations which followed, but there are resemblances as well as notable differences in religious as in other aspects of the colonial model.

(ii) The two largest English-speaking islands were under Spanish rule for lengthy periods. In Jamaica there was a complete break in ecclesiastical history at the English conquest, yet the Spanish Catholic era provides an interesting prologue. The Roman Catholic Church in Trinidad however has a continuous history from its settlement in 1592 to the present day.

The Early Days of the Spanish Church (1492–1510)

When Christopher Columbus first met the aboriginal occupants of the island of Guanahani in what we call the Bahamas, little did these Amerindians realize the enormous consequences of this seemingly happy event in their lives. They did not understand the significance of the prayers, the claiming of the land for a faraway king and queen, the naming of their island San Salvador ("Holy Saviour"), and the history behind the Crusade-like banners with their reminder of centuries of Christian military conquest. So far their encounter with these new and wonderful "men from the sky" was friendly.[1]

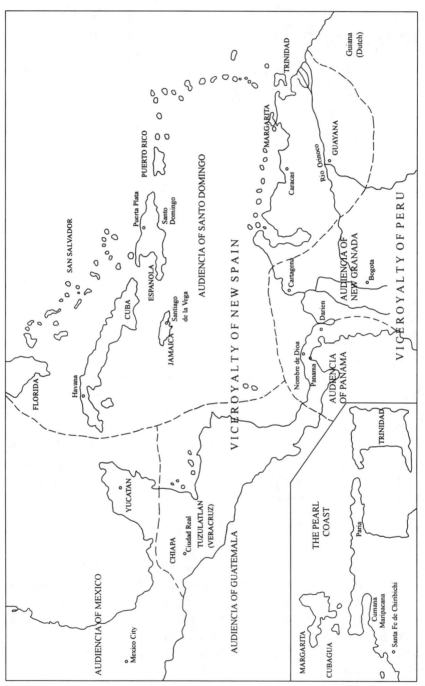

The Spanish Empire in the Caribbean

On the Spanish side, at least in the mind of the leader, the intention was avowedly peaceful. He soon concluded "that they were a people who could better be freed and converted to our Holy Faith by love than by force" and wanted his followers to treat them in a friendly way. Their Christianization was one of his chief concerns and that of the Spanish monarchs who had sponsored him.[2] But the cupidity of the Spaniards was soon aroused by the sight of gold ornaments, as was the temptation indicated by Columbus' own words: "They ought to be good servants and of good skill, for I see that they repeat very quickly whatever was said to them."[3] It may be said then that the Church had its first representative in the Caribbean in the person of a pious layman who reflected the strengths and weaknesses of medieval Christianity.[4] He had a continuous belief that he was under divine guidance.[5] His zeal for the Faith included some awareness of the importance of peace and love for that purpose, and at the same time approval of military action in the interest of religion.[6]

Many contemporaries in Europe, and some who later came to colonize, shared the admiral's religious zeal. But the Spaniards left at La Navidad after the shipwreck of the *Santa Maria* showed a more typical attitude: the selfish, cruel, lustful conquistador temper which cared little for the indigenous people. On Columbus' return to Española he found that these men had been wiped out by the Amerindians after wantonly mistreating them. This led to reprisals by the Spaniards. Initial friendliness was replaced by fear, anger, fitful co-operation and increasing oppression.

This change took place at the very time of the arrival of the first clergy, "the learned father, Fray Buil, together with the other *Religiosos* whom the said Admiral is to take with him". The instructions of Isabella and Ferdinand had told Columbus' to win over the inhabitants of the new lands to the Catholic faith, to compel those with him to treat the Indians well, and to punish any maltreatment of them in the name of their majesties.[7]

In spite of these orders, Columbus wavered in his intentions under pressure from his less scrupulous followers and from the fear that he would show a loss rather than a profit on his enterprise. He sent Amerindians as slaves for sale in Spain, arguing that they were "cannibals" and that by removing them from their environment and baptizing them their souls could be saved.[8] This action was one reason for Columbus' decline in favour with the queen, and she sent them back to the Caribbean.[9]

With the establishment of a settlement at Isabela, the saying of the first mass in January 1494, and the erection of a church building, formal Church life in the Caribbean may be said to have begun. It was not long until a blow fell: Father Buil, the vicar apostolic appointed by the crown with papal approval, was in open contention with Columbus as governor. He failed to adjust to pioneer life, and returned to Spain with another malcontent to lay complaints against the admiral at court.[10]

On Columbus' third voyage freed convicts were brought from Spain. This was the first but by no means the last instance of European governments endeavouring to populate their colonies by transferring their undesirables overseas. (It was a factor in English colonies in later times.) To assimilate these outcasts presented a further problem for society and the Church.[11]

In another respect however Spanish policy was strict. A royal letter to the newly appointed governor, Nicolás de Ovando, in 1501 forbade "the immigration of Moors, heretics, Jews, re-converts, or persons newly converted to our Holy Faith, unless they are Negro or other slaves who have been born in the power of Christians".[12] This was part of the national policy of religious conformity already pursued in Spain itself. The monarchs had no intention of allowing their overseas empire to become a haven for the unorthodox. The fact that this regulation was repeated frequently throughout the Spanish colonial period is evidence of its importance in the eyes of the crown, and also of its evasion from time to time. Certainly new converts of Jewish blood did reach America in considerable numbers, and slaves not "born in the power of Christians" began to arrive directly from Africa. The population did not remain as homogeneous as theory required.[13]

The first black slaves were in fact at least nominally Christians, being brought from Spain with Ovando in 1502, or possibly earlier. But they proved a disturbing element by escaping, joining with the Amerindians, and stirring up opposition to the Spaniards, so much so that the governor tried to stop their importation in 1503. Nevertheless some continued to arrive and in 1510 and 1513 the king authorized larger numbers to be shipped from Seville.[14]

In this pioneer period however the urgent question was how to reach with the Christian faith the indigenous population, which was rapidly declining. Among the islands which later became English colonies, the original Lucayans of the Bahamas were all carried off as slaves, raids on Trinidad had serious effects, and Jamaica lost its native people rapidly after settlement in 1510. Meanwhile in Española some efforts were made to convert them, especially by the already mentioned Hieronymite friar, Ramón Pane. The first Amerindian was baptized in 1496. In 1498 Columbus was begging the crown for priests to help Fray Pane who had only a few catechumens and one chapel for them.[15]

Twelve Franciscans came with Ovando in 1502, but according to Las Casas, almost nothing was done during the years Ovando governed the island (1502–9), either by him or by these friars, about Christianizing the Indians.[16]

The queen's instructions to Ovando had been to protect the Indians and to ensure that they were won to the Christian faith.[17] But he soon reported that unless compelled they refused to work for the Spaniards and that if left to their own free life they would not be converted. This plea brought the encomienda system to the Caribbean, establishing the pattern of forced labour, under European domination, in the tropical portions of the New World.[18]

Meanwhile Pope Alexander VI in 1493 issued four bulls which gave to Spain missionary responsibilities and territorial rights across the western ocean similar to those granted a generation earlier to Portugal in a southern and eastern direction.[19] These bulls are often studied in terms of their political consequences. But the expressly stated rationale of the documents is the assignment of missionary duties in new territories and only secondarily the matter of international arbitration. From the standpoint of the papacy, these bulls expressed the principle that the Faith could best be carried to new lands in an orderly and effective way under the aegis of the political powers which had pioneered their "discovery".

This decision was welcomed by Portugal, and the "Demarcation Line" was shifted westward by the Treaty of Tordesillas (1494), opening the way to Brazil. However to other rising nations, especially France, England and the Netherlands, the logic of these arrangements was unacceptable – the more so as the vast extent of the new lands gradually came to light. Little did anyone imagine, in 1493, that the "very remote islands and even mainlands, that hitherto had not been discovered by others" located "in the ocean sea, through western waters, as is said, toward the Indians" was in fact a new hemisphere.[20] By Spain, the pope's "donation" of these new lands was claimed as divine authority for its growing empire in America. The conditions of missionary responsibility were also taken seriously by the Spanish monarchs as well as by many churchmen, especially those in the monastic orders.

From the bulls of 1493 can be traced the beginning of the patronato real de Indias, the royal patronage of the Indies (as distinct from the real patronato Español in Spain itself). If the Spanish monarchs were to Christianize their newly acquired territories they would need considerable powers over the Church. They were given concessions and privileges, including the presentation of bishops and complete spiritual jurisdiction. Later the use of the ecclesiastical tithes in America was added, in return for paying the costs of the work of the Church and of missionary outreach.[21] In 1543 the power of fixing the boundaries of dioceses was added. Royal control of the Church in America was now more complete than in Spain itself.[22]

The Church Copes with its Situation (1510–1524)

In the period following 1510 the Church in the Caribbean became more active as colonization expanded to the mainland. The papal bull *Romanus pontifex* (August 1511) set up a Spanish colonial hierarchy with two bishops in Española and one at San Juan in Puerto Rico, subordinate to Archbishop Fonseca in Seville.[23] The first continental bishopric was established at Darien in 1513. Jamaica became an abbacy in 1515 and Cuba a diocese in 1518. In marked contrast to the later English colonies, where there were no bishops for two hundred years after the first settlement, it was Spanish policy to provide a bishop promptly in every new area.[24] The archiepiscopal see of Santo Domingo was set up in 1546, embracing the Greater Antilles (including Jamaica), and the north-eastern coast of South America (ultimately including Trinidad).[25]

In 1510 six members of the Dominican order under the leadership of their superior, Pedro de Córdoba, arrived in Santo Domingo. This is an important landmark because it was the beginning of a movement to reduce the exploitation of the indigenous people, and to develop new methods of evangelizing them. The first spokesman of this movement was Antonio Montesinos, who was chosen by Pedro de Córdoba and his fellow Dominicans to preach on the fourth Sunday in Advent in 1511 in the leading church in Santo Domingo. His sermon proved to be one of the epoch-making pulpit utterances of history. With the governor and many other officials and encomenderos in the congregation he declared himself to be "the voice of Christ in the desert of this island" and accused them of living in sin by enslaving innocent people and working them to death out of greed. "You are in no better state of salvation," he said, "than the Moors or the Turks." He exhorted them, remembering the Golden Rule, to care for the souls of these fellow human beings by winning them to the Christian faith.[26]

After the inevitable protest and opposition of the colonists the defiant friar returned to the offensive another Sunday, then betook himself to Spain to argue the case of the Amerindians before the king. As Henríquez-Ureña puts it, "a new type of crusade had begun". The result was the famous consultation of clergy and government officials in Spain which produced the Laws of Burgos in 1512, the first attempt to regulate by legislation the encomienda system in a somewhat more humane direction.[27]

The issue was now joined. For decades two viewpoints, which may be described as "Indianist" and "Colonialist", contended for control. The justice of wars and enslavement, reports of physical cruelty, the authority conferred by the bulls of 1493, the rights of Amerindian property and native government, the methods to be used for Christianization – these and related questions were debated by theologians and government officials. Appeal was made constantly to the king and his Council, and occasionally to the pope. Letters, petitions, delegations and individuals took concerns eastward over the ocean. Decrees, laws, emissaries and newly appointed officials carried the royal decisions back. But whatever these decisions were – and they oscillated from one view to the other – their implementation was in the hands of officials who were under strong pressure from the colonists whose fortunes depended upon forced labour.

This struggle took place, it is important to remember, within both state and Church, which were coterminous. The Indianist view was strong among the clergy, particularly the missionary friars, and among some consciously Christian laymen including Charles V and many of his advisers. The Colonialist position naturally was taken by most of the state officials in the Indies. But there were exceptions on

Bartolomé de Las Casas

both sides, and quite a few either vascillated or looked for a compromise. In the end, in the latter part of the century, it was a kind of compromise which prevailed.

One protagonist, Bartolomé de Las Casas, so dominated the struggle for almost half a century by his ubiquitous activity on both sides of the Atlantic, and by his voluminous writings, that the championship of aboriginal rights is described by some as the "Lascasian" movement. Yet he was "neither the first nor the only defender of the Indians". As Carro puts it, "Spain had many Las Casases", and large numbers in various ways supported the cause.[28]

Las Casas, after experience in Española as a youth, was ordained a priest in 1507, and became an encomendero in Cuba.[29] He was converted to the Indianist point of view in 1514 by the preparation of a sermon on Ecclesiasticus 34:18–22 (in the Apocrypha). He renounced his own encomienda. In this he was supported by his business partner, Pedro de la Rentería, a layman whose conscience had been awakened during a Lenten retreat he had made the same year in a Franciscan monastery in Jamaica.[30]

By 1515 Las Casas was on his way to Spain in company with Montesinos to make a further protest to the king, for the Laws of Burgos had not been enforced. On arrival they found that Ferdinand was near death. Cardinal Ximénes succeeded him as regent and it was to his sympathetic ear that they appealed.[31] He appointed Las Casas "Protector-General of the Indians", who after the death of Ximénes undertook to win the new King Charles I (later Emperor Charles V) to the Indianist cause.[32]

Meanwhile the Dominicans in the Caribbean had been pursuing their other objective: a programme of peaceful evangelization away from Spanish conquest and forced labour. They took note of the Pearl Coast, that is northern Venezuela near Cumaná and extending as far east as the island of Trinidad. The desire for labour for pearl fishing, as well as the decline in aboriginal population on the Greater Antilles, had made this region notorious for slave raiding. Pedro de Córdoba conceived the plan of protecting the Indians, and Christianizing them by persuasion, while this coast was still unsettled by Spaniards. He obtained a licence from King Ferdinand to send friars to the Pearl Coast for peaceful missionary work. About this time, two Dominicans, Francisco de Córdoba and Juan Garcés, went to Trinidad. They were killed by the inhabitants in 1513, after a Spanish slave raider treacherously took advantage of the trust they had built up and seized a local chief and seventeen others for sale in Española.[33]

In 1515 some Franciscans from Picardy and more Dominicans launched out again. For a time all went well, and friendly relations were established.[34] But slave raiding was still going on. A heinous massacre became known in connection with Juan Bono's seizure of 185 slaves in Trinidad. Since raids on this island were justified on the allegation that its people were Caribs (and so cannibals) Las Casas demanded an investigation of this charge. The inquiry by Rodrigo de Figueroa cleared the Indians.[35]

Meanwhile Pedro de Córdoba wrote to Las Casas in Spain urging him to obtain a grant of land on the Pearl Coast, for the exclusive occupation of Dominican and Franciscan friars. This was to be a place of safety for Amerindians, where they would be protected against enslavement and encomienda labour and led by kind treatment and careful instruction to the Christian faith. Here was the germ of the idea later developed as the Spanish reducción or mission.[36]

Accordingly in 1520 Las Casas obtained a grant of 260 leagues of coast stretching from the Gulf of Paria to the border of the province of Santa Marta – approximately the north coast of Venezuela – together with its hinterland. Against much opposition and ridicule he went ahead to recruit Spanish labourers to work with the friars, evolving a somewhat quixotic scheme of a colony manned by a new order called "Knights of the Golden Spur" which would work on a friendly basis with the Amerindians.[37] This utopian programme would probably have foundered on the weakness of human nature in any case. But it was cheated of a fair trial by continuing slave raids, and the project on the Pearl Coast had to be abandoned. The disillusioned "Protector of the Indians" embraced the monastic life and was welcomed into the Dominican Order at Santo Domingo in 1522. His enemies were happy to see him retire.[38]

Other developments brought the end of a chapter in the history of the Church in the Caribbean. The venerable Pedro de Córdoba had died in 1521. Colonization was rapidly shifting to the mainland following the conquest of Mexico, and the centre of missionary activity moved to that area.[39] Yet in the years 1510 to 1524 the major issue had at least been tackled: would the Church be only the passive adjunct of Spanish society in the New World, or would Christian principles be somehow asserted over against the system of conquest and exploitation?

Christian Humanism to Conservative Orthodoxy (1525–1574)

The second quarter of the sixteenth century is notable for a brief flowering of Spanish Christian humanism in the New World which deserves attention in spite of its ultimate eclipse. For its spirit lived on, in a modified and compromised form, in the later Catholic "missions" which were widespread in North and South America, including Trinidad.

To understand this movement the Reformation in the Spanish Catholic Church needs to be recalled. The emphasis on learning in the Spanish universities included enthusiasm for the ideas of Erasmus and Thomas More.[40] Erasmus stressed the ethical teachings of Jesus, criticized practices in the Church and European society that were out of harmony with them, and appealed for a simple loyalty to Christianity as a way of life. More's *Utopia* pictured an ideal society, governed by reason and love, set vaguely somewhere in the New World.[41]

In 1527 Juan de Zumárraga, much influenced by these ideals, became bishop of Mexico.[42] He gave much attention to the conversion of the Indians, and wrote catechetical material for their instruction. He also helped to establish a college (Santa Cruz de Tlaltelolco) for the education of an indigenous priesthood, and for the translation of the Scriptures into the native languages. He hoped to bring the people by religion and education to a status similar to that of the Europeans. This was not achieved, partly because the standard of training was entirely European and unsuited to the previous culture of the students, but even more because of the prejudice of the Spaniards, including most of the clergy.[43]

Another bishop of the humanistic school was Vasco de Quiroga. Drawing inspiration from More's *Utopia* and from contact with the Amerindians, he established two noted village communities known as hospital-pueblos. His experiment provided a model from which developed the later "missions" throughout the Spanish Empire.[44]

A third leader of this stamp was Bartolomé de Las Casas who had been devoting himself to study and writing at the monastery in Santo Domingo. He commenced his *History of the Indies*, which is an invaluable source for the public events, and especially the church history, of the times. A little later he began a lengthy Latin treatise, *De unico modo vocationis* ("The Only Method of Attracting All People to the True Faith") in which he stated his convictions on missionary method: that the way to spread Christianity is by kindness and persuasion, never by force. This is the first if not the only dissertation on missionary method produced in the Caribbean. Indeed considering its setting in the heart of the controversy over the Christian approach of European to non-European in colonial society, it is a pivotal document in the history of missions.[45]

Fray Bartolomé was of far too restless a disposition to remain a cloistered writer. When he emerged from monastic life, Las Casas was challenged in 1537 to try out the theories of *De unico modo* with a group of Maya Indians in central Guatemala, in a territory later called Verapaz, not far from the present Belize. For a time at least he was able to successfully put his methods into practice.[46]

During this period, news came of an important pronouncement by Pope Paul III, the bull *Sublimis Deus* of 1537. This ruling resulted from an appeal for a decision on the much debated question of the status of the Amerindians. Pope Paul said: "The Indians are truly men, . . . are by no means to be deprived of their liberty or the possession of their property . . . nor should they be in any way enslaved. . . . They should be converted to the faith of Jesus Christ by preaching the word of God and by the example of good and holy living."[47] This appeared to bring the highest authority of the Church to the side of the Indianists.

During these years the humanist movement reached its greatest success. In 1542 the "New Laws", drawn up by royal authority under the influence of Las Casas, enacted that the Indians were vassals of the crown and were not to be made slaves for any reason. Any that had been enslaved must be liberated. The encomienda system was to be abolished.[48] These changes encountered fierce opposition from the colonists, until the king issued modifications, particularly with regard to the encomienda institution which survived.

In the face of local hostility Las Casas, now appointed bishop of the diocese of Chiapa, which included the Verapaz region, tried to use his episcopal authority to enforce the provisions of the New Laws. He excommunicated many for disobedience, but finally had to accept failure of his attempt to enforce justice by ecclesiastical penalties. After returning to Spain in 1547 he resigned his bishopric.[49] In the continued fight for Amerindian rights, he debated in 1550–51 against the celebrated philosopher Sepúlveda the issues of the nature of the aboriginal people and the injustice of war against them.[50]

Efforts to Christianize the native people were at their height in the second quarter of the sixteenth century.[51] But what about the Africans who were captured and enslaved? As the indigenous population declined, the slave trade was expanded. Charles V sent an order in 1538 that owners of Negro slaves must send them to church.[52] But little concern was felt about their exploitation. Even humane Indianists drew a legalistic distinction between the Amerindians who had been free before the arrival of the Spanish, and Africans enslaved before leaving their own country.

In 1517 and in 1531 Las Casas had advocated this importation "in exchange for Indian freedom", believing that the Africans were more able to survive heavy labour. Some historians have incorrectly stated that the transatlantic slave trade was first introduced into the New World through his initiative. As we have seen, however, African slaves had been there by 1502 and various royal orders had been issued to regulate the trade before 1517.[53]

Nevertheless Las Casas's acceptance of African slavery for a time is a regrettable episode in a great man's life. He records in his *History of the Indies* his repentance, when he discovered "that the captivity of the Negroes was quite as unjust as that of the Indians".[54] Las Casas was in fact the first to recognize – though tardily – that the same human rights and the same divine justice were violated by African as by

Indian slavery, thus calling in question the entire slave trade. But he concentrated his efforts on one cause, to obtain relief for the Indians who could never be "justly" enslaved. Yet the implications of his arguments, and indeed of the whole Indianist movement, illuminate the subsequent history of colonialism and the perennial questions of forced labour and human rights.[55]

Other churchmen about the middle of the century began to examine critically the African slave trade. The Dominican theologian Domingo de Soto in his *De Justitia et Jure* (1556) attacked the notion that the enslavement of Africans was justified by making them Christians, applying the principle to them, as to the Amerindians, that Christianity must be accepted freely.[56] Alonso de Montúfar, Zumárraga's successor as archbishop, by a letter to the king in 1560 declared: "We do not know what reason there may be for Negroes to be captives any more than Indians . . . May it please Our Lord that this enslavement cease."[57] In 1569 Friar Tomás Mercado questioned the slave trade on the ground of humanity and theology, indicating that other Portuguese and Spanish theologians also disapproved it. Four years later Bartolomé de Albernoz, who had lived in New Spain, set forth similar views.[58] But these voices made little impression. Great numbers of enslaved Africans continued to be brought into Spanish and other colonies for almost three hundred years.[59]

Meanwhile a change of pace was observable in the efforts to Christianize the aboriginal people. By the middle of the century the first generation of missionary work was completed and a "second generation" situation had developed. The pioneers had died or in some cases grown disillusioned. High hopes of "utopia" had been frustrated by the failure of the native people to respond as expected, and by the non-cooperation of most of the Spanish colonists. Las Casas had been driven back to Spain. In spite of the new zeal of Jesuits and Capuchins, most missionary recruits lacked the hopefulness of the first generation.

Christian humanism had fallen out of favour in Spain. Although Erasmus and More had advocated reform within the Catholic Church, their ideas came to be associated in the minds of the Catholic leadership in Spain with the new heresy of Protestantism. Their books were put on the Index by the Spanish Inquisition. The Council of Trent (1545–63) produced the canons and the loyalties that would resist the revolution overtaking so much of the Church in northern Europe. The era of Spanish Christian humanism came to a premature end. Missionary endeavour was carried on in more conservative ways. No new social or educational experiments were begun after the mid century.

Equally tragic was a withdrawal from the development of indigenous leadership for the Church, in spite of Zumárraga's college. A provincial council in New Spain in 1555 ruled against the ordination of mestizos, Indians and Negroes, and a royal decree of 1578 made this a rule for the empire. Although this was modified in time and some notable non-white clergy were ordained in the colonies, the inhibiting policy became all too customary and local men hesitated to aspire to holy orders. The pattern of providing leadership for the Spanish Church from Europe became set in the sixteenth century – a precedent too often followed in the colonies of other nations in the New World.[60]

Even when criollos (American-born Spaniards) entered the priesthood they were rarely appointed to high office. In both state and Church European-born appointees were felt to be more reliable supporters of royal authority. The conflict between creoles and Spaniards became deeper as time went on, and it was one of the causes of the Spanish-American revolutions of the early nineteenth century.

The conservative reaction was strengthened by the accession to the throne of Philip II in 1556. He intensified the control of the crown over all aspects of colonial life including the Church. Little initiative was left to prelates on the spot even if they had been inclined like Quiroga to try idealistic experiments. The Spanish Inquisition was extended to the American colonies in 1569, replacing the less methodical Inquisition of monastic prelates and bishops. Philip restricted the freedom of the monastic orders, in principle at least subordinating them to the diocesan system.[61] However the orders were still badly needed, and they continued to play an important part, especially for mission work in frontier areas.

The more conservative role for the Church was defined in the New Laws of the Patronato Real of 1573–74. At the same time the state recognized at least in theory some of the principles for which the Indianists had fought: "conquest" was henceforth to be replaced by "pacification"; Indians were not to be enslaved; the encomienda became less oppressive.[62] Spanish-American colonial policy would henceforth rest upon this paternalistic compromise of Philip II, with churchmen playing the parts of priest and missionary but rarely the part of prophet.

The Mature Spanish Colonial Church (1575–1800)

This pattern of Church life was fixed by the last quarter of the sixteenth century and remained with modifications for over two centuries, to the end of the Spanish Empire. Only brief further comments are necessary.[63]

Much charitable work was done under Church auspices for the sick and indigent of all types: Spanish, Amerindian, mestizo, African, mulatto. The establishment and maintenance of hospitals, especially by the monastic orders, were often financed by bequests of the wealthy.[64]

Growing ecclesiastical wealth, although used in large measure to pay for its charitable and educational work, became a threat to the Church's spiritual influence. The monastic orders as well as other church bodies came to own vast tracts of land and large sums of money, often willed to them by pious colonists. These "trust" properties were shrewdly managed. Church bodies came to be major money lending agencies as well as managers of estate properties.[65] In Jamaica and Trinidad, however, poverty rather than wealth was the condition of the Church.

The picture of "a controlled, monolithic Spanish colonial church" needs to be qualified. Gibson states: "Church history in colonial Spanish America is a history of constant internal squabbles." These conflicts included jealousy and rivalry among secular priests and between European-born and creole clergy; between agents of the Inquisition and all other clergy including the bishops; between ecclesiastics and government officials. The friars, taking the side of the royal laws protective of the indigenous people, were frequently in conflict with colonists and government officials.[66] Illustrations of some of these "squabbles" can be found in the history of Spanish Jamaica and Trinidad, as will be seen.

Frontier missions to the Amerindians became very widespread in the seventeenth and eighteenth centuries, especially after a royal cédula in 1652 instituted the system in the Venezuela area. The "reduction" was a temporary stage between the "uncivilized" life of the aborigines in the forest and the more organized Indian parish or doctrina, which in turn was expected to give way ultimately to the full integration of the native people into Spanish colonial civilization. In other words it was an instrument of colonial policy and acculturation as well as a means of Christianization and of providing security and a settled life for the original inhabitants.[67]

Missionary activity was less organized among the African slaves who became numerous in the Caribbean through the asiento system of importation and also by smuggling and natural increase. In accordance with Catholic policy slaves were baptized and given at least a nominal Christian status, and the Church was prepared to enforce this upon the slave owner by the threat of discipline. Iberian Catholic tradition sought to protect slaves from the more extreme forms of cruelty, and encouraged manumission. Somewhat humane slave laws however, like the legislation protecting the Amerindians, were not always well enforced.[68]

Two outstanding churchmen who showed concern for the Africans in the early seventeenth century were Alonso de Sandoval and Pedro Claver. They served in a remarkable mission at Cartagena, one of the chief landing ports for African slave ships. For forty years Claver and his catechists visited these ships on arrival, taking food and other comforts to the prisoners, tried to bring a spiritual message to them, and subsequently visited mines and plantations where they laboured. He incurred enmity from slave traders and owners, but insisted that in the Church blacks and whites were to be treated equally.[69]

Sandoval not only ministered to individuals suffering from the slave trade but used his pen as well. A letter to a fellow Jesuit in Angola enquiring about the capture of slaves in Africa brought a reassuring reply in 1610. However this did not satisfy him, for his *De Instaurando Aethiopum Salute*, published later, is a ringing denunciation of the African slave trade, probably the first book to deal primarily with this subject.[70]

4

Jamaica and Trinidad
Under Spanish Rule

The two English-speaking islands which were long under Spanish control were ne-glected colonies in Spanish times, having been bypassed in the scramble for trea-sure on the mainland. Jamaica was a supplier of cattle and other products to the wealthier parts of the empire. Trinidad was settled in 1592 as a base for the search for "El Dorado".

Neither island had a large population. Jamaica was recorded to have 1,510 people in 1611 and about 2,500 including slaves when it was captured in 1655.[1] Trinidad's population was only a few hundred apart from the Amerindians until well into the eighteenth century. In 1777 an official report showed 3,432 people. A large influx of immigrants with their slaves more than quintupled the number in the following twenty years, making the figure 17,712 at the time of the British conquest.[2]

There is a record of concern to erect a simple church building from the time of the first settlement in each island. But the number of priests was less than half a dozen most of the time, sometimes no more than one or two. Franciscan and Dominican monasteries appear to have been tiny in both cases, often with only one or two friars and sometimes vacant.[3]

The story of the indigenous people differs in the two islands. In Jamaica the original population was decimated in the early sixteenth century. In Trinidad apart from slave raids they were left in possession of the island until Berrío's settlement in 1592. By that time Spanish treatment of the Amerindians was less severe, and they continued to be an important part of society until the nineteenth century.

The Jamaican Church and its Abbots (1509–1655)

Juan de Esquivel was appointed governor of Jamaica by Diego Colón in 1509 and sent to make a settlement, convert the Amerindians, and find gold. The colony was begun at Seville on the north coast. King Ferdinard wrote Diego in 1511 expressing satisfaction with the conversions reported by Esquivel and calling for "great care, and diligence so that the Indians may be Christians in fact as well as in name".[4] The following year however the king complained that Juan de Esquivel had served him "very negligently in the conversion of the Indians and pacification of the island as well as in the increase of our royal revenues".[5]

It is not clear exactly how the king expected the work of conversion to be carried out. Presumably Ferdinand had the matter in mind when he issued in 1512 a royal cédula to the Franciscan provincial instructing him to send a total of forty missionaries to Cuba, San Juan (that is, Puerto Rico), Jamaica and the mainland.[6] How many actually arrived in Jamaica is problematical, but the existence of a Franciscan monastery in 1514 is evidenced by Pedro de Rentería's Lenten retreat there, referred to previously. In fact, the first glimpse we have into the Church within Jamaica is that of Las Casas's partner meditating on his responsibility to the Indians. This must be imagined in a thatch-roofed hut or chapel in the new Seville, manned by a small number of friars.[7] In 1622 a royal instruction was sent to Jamaica that two Franciscan officials who were on their way to visit monks of their order should be given a proper welcome. There were also some Dominicans in the island at least after Santiago de la Vega was founded.[8]

The usual method of the allotment of Amerindians in encomiendas – theoretically for their religious instruction as well as for forced labour – was used, as the king refers to the new Governor Francisco de Garay (who replaced Esquivel in 1514) and his treasurer as "our repartidores for the island" and Diego Colón himself received the first allotment of three hundred.[9]

In 1515 the king took the initiative in appointing an ecclesiastical authority for the island. He requested the pope "to create and establish an Abbacy for the church in the Island of Santiago, which is situated in the Indies of the Ocean Sea and which before it was settled by Christians was called Jamaica", and nominated his chaplain and canon of Seville (Spain), Sancho de Matienzo, to the post. In an accompanying letter to the king's ambassador at Rome the reason is given: "Whereas the revenues and yearly profits will not suffice at present to establish a cathedral and bishopric in the said Island; we have decided that there be created and established an Abbacy or Administration *in spiritualibus et temporalibus* with proper jurisdiction and right of correction, visitation and decree; and further that for revenue it shall enjoy the tithes, as is customary where there is no bishopric established."[10]

While Jamaica remained under Spanish rule some uncertainty existed about the relationship of its abbacy to the episcopal hierarchy. Abbot Santiago in a report to the crown (1574), referred to his office as *nullius diocesis*, but in the same year the Council of the Indies ruled that Jamaica was subject to the see of Santiago de Cuba. Abbot Villalobos (1581) complained of interference in Jamaican affairs by the bishop of Cuba, but after his death (1606) the then bishop of Cuba was invited by Jamaican authorities to visit and direct church affairs. Abbot Balbuena later (1611) declared that he had "episcopal jurisdiction suffragan to the Archbishop of Santo Domingo, in whose district the Abbacy is situated".[11] In spite of difficulties, the abbacy lasted until the English capture of the island, and our knowledge of the Church in Spanish Jamaica depends to a great extent on the reports and letters of some of these abbots.

Matienzo, the first incumbent (1515–22), never reached Jamaica and indeed there is little of importance to record about any of these prelates until the 1570s. Repeatedly when one abbot died there was uncertainty, delay and sometimes rivalry before a successor was officially appointed. The most famous name among them is that of Peter Martyr d'Anghiera, author of the *Decades* and other writings about the New World, but he was already seventy years old when appointed, never visited Jamaica, and died about a year later (1526). He initiated a project to build a good stone church at Seville, but not much came of it before this settlement was abandoned as unhealthy, and the main town transferred in 1534 to Santiago de la Vega (or Villa de la Vega), the present Spanish Town.[12]

The successor to Peter Martyr was Fray Miguel Ramirez, a Dominican, who was concurrently Bishop of Cuba. He made a brief visit to Jamaica, the first abbot to do so. After him came a secular priest Amador de Samano who set out to live on the island. He received a rude welcome from Lieutenant-Governor Pedro Cano, which earned the latter a royal discipline.[13]

Unfortunately there is a sparcity of records of about forty years from this time (1535), not only for ecclesiastical but also political affairs. This seems to be the consequence of the transfer of Jamaica to the rule of Columbus' family in 1536. It appears that ecclesiastical business including appointment of abbots was left to the "Admiral" and that documents have not come down to us. As a result we know little of the building of the churches and monasteries in Villa de la Vega, which was now the centre of government and of the Church, and indeed the only important town in the island during the Spanish period.[14]

Documents prior to this generation of silence, however, give strong indications of the decline of the indigenous population. In 1519 the king warned Governor Garay to take care that these people were not ill treated or overworked. Alarming reports from Jamaica reached the court in 1521 of the high death rate from pestilence among Indians and also slaves. In 1533, during the period when Indianist agitation was growing strong at court, a residencia was instructed to enquire into "the treatment meted out to the native Indians".[15]

At the end of the century Governor Melgarejo proposed that steps be taken to establish a settlement for the small number of the native people that survived, and in the following year he raised the subject again.[16] A later governor's report on the island three years before the English conquest says flatly: "now none are to be found though they were an immense number at the discovery".[17]

A report of Abbot Mateo Santiago, who came for a brief time to Jamaica about 1574, states that confirmation had never been administered in the island and that he had invited the bishop of Cuba to come and hold this sacrament. He suggested that the pope authorize the abbot to perform the rite in the special situation there. This suggestion does not seem to have been approved since we hear that for a long period prior to 1608 no confirmation had taken place, and during the visit of the bishop of Cuba in that year more than 600 were confirmed. Another problem mentioned in the report was that of slave marriages, to which the owners objected, apparently fearing that this would diminish their control of the slaves.[18] In this they anticipated the resistance in later times by English (Protestant) slave masters to slave marriage, both in Jamaica and elsewhere.

Probably the most notable abbot of Jamaica was Francisco Marques de Villalobos, appointed in 1581 and active for a quarter century till his death in 1606. His first report (1582) describes the sad and poverty-stricken condition of the Church at the time.[19] Records had been neglected, tithes were insufficient, the church building in la Vega was poor, a Dominican monastery had only one or two monks in great poverty, and two hermitages (Saint Lucy and Saint Barbara) were unoccupied. A recent visit of the bishop of Cuba had sown confusion. Villalobos felt that two curates and the abbot were a sufficient burden on the budget: indeed two priests were all there had been in recent years. The town had only one hundred vecinos.[20] He complains of the injustices of rule by the Columbus family, but spoke highly of the importance of Jamaica as a producer of cattle and field crops, and expressed anxiety about the possibility of conquest by the enemies of Spain.

This abbot met with trials in the latter part of his tenure. His fears of foreign attack were realized during the raid by Sir Anthony Shirley in 1597 and he himself was robbed of money, jewels, furniture and other equipment. Later the same year a hurricane destroyed church and monastery. The king sent 2,000 ducats in 1599 to aid in repairs. The old abbot did his best to rebuild but died before completion of the work. He was buried in the church.[21]

Villalobos' "vicar-general" was a Jamaican, Juan de Cueto, "the first man born in the island to be ordained a priest" and a grandson of one of the first settlers. After the abbot's death he was left in charge of the work and was confirmed in this temporary position by the bishop of Cuba who visited the island for four months in 1608.[22]

In spite of poverty, enemy raids and neglect by higher authorities in the empire, the early years of the seventeenth century appear as a high point in the overall low of Spanish Jamaica's church life. Eight very qualified candidates aspired to the vacant abbacy.[23] The one finally appointed, Bernardo de Balbuena, was a man of parts, a poet of note, and after about ten years in Jamaica became bishop of Puerto Rico.[24] In his initial report he calculated, from confessions made, the following:

Spaniards (men and women)	558
Children	173
Free Negroes	107
Slaves	558
Native Indians	74
Foreigners	75
Total	1,510

There were two monasteries, Dominican and Franciscan, each with three monks. The church building however was still "poor and ruined and roofless" after the depredations of "the heretics" who had "sacked it three times", and the new abbot was much exercised about its repairs.[25]

His successor, Mateo de Medina Moreno, was the last abbot of Jamaica, ruling from about 1622 to 1650. There are few records of this period except for the final years when civil strife rent the community. However a Provincial Synod for the Archdiocese of Santo Domingo, which included Española, Puerto Rico, Cuba, Jamaica and the Venezuela area, was held from September 1622 to January 1623. The rulings of this Synod throw much light upon the life and the problems of the Church in the Antilles at this period, including Jamaica and Trinidad.[26]

We have an outsider's view of Villa de la Vega from Captain William Jackson, an English privateer who attacked the capital in 1640. In his "Briefe Journall" he describes it as "a faire Town, consisting of foure or five hundred houses . . . beautified with 5 or 6 stately churches and Chapples, and one monastery of Franciscan Fryers".[27] This glowing account contrasts with the report of a certain Licentiate Juan de Retuerta, dated 1644. "The principal Church is in very bad repair and little used," he says, adding that there is "a monastery of the order of St. Dominic with four monks and another of St. Francis with three who live very poorly on alms so that they cannot comply as they should with the duties of the community and the religious life". He is mainly concerned with the serious state of political affairs in Jamaica, but adds that the ecclesiastical situation was also disorderly, partly due to the age (over eighty) and ineptitude of the abbot.[28]

Finally, during a quarrel between rival political groups in the islands, Abbot Moreno became innocently involved. A young governor, Pedro Caballero, had antagonized the ecclesiastical personnel over a series of incidents, including the sermon of a Franciscan who preached against "the sin of card playing in high places", the baptism of a child of the governor, and an assault by the governor on the vicar general leading to his excommunication by the abbot. A new governor was then appointed and arrived in the island. At this critical juncture Caballero visited the

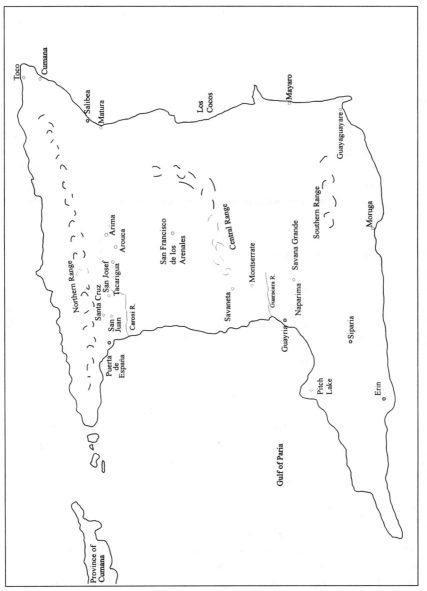

Spanish Trinidad, 1592-1797

abbot's house on New Year's Day 1650 and there, in an altercation with the new governor, Jacinto Sedeño y Albornoz, he met his death reportedly by his own sword. Sedeño was arrested and carried to Cartagena by agents of the Inquisition, of which Caballero had been an officer. The old abbot was imprisoned with him, commenting: "Blessed be God that at the end of twenty-eight years' pastorate Jamaica has given me this reward."[29] It was a sad end to the abbacy. No successor was appointed before the island fell to Cromwell's expedition in 1655.

Spanish Trinidad (1592–1797)

At the beginning of the sixteenth century, as mentioned in the previous chapter, Trinidad and the Pearl Coast in general were subject to slave raids from the pearl fisheries of Margarita and Cubagua and also from the more distant Española. The Church arrived in this area with the efforts of the Dominicans, the Picard Franciscans and Las Casas to cultivate a settlement for peaceful evangelization. These attempts came to an end in 1521.

Accordingly, the story of the Trinidad Church begins with the martyrdom in 1513 of the Dominican missionaries Francisco de Córdoba and Juan Garcés, as a consequence of Spanish slave raiding to the island. No immediate follow-up of mission work was possible.[30]

There is record however of an unsuccessful attempt by Dominicans from Cartagena to do mission work in Trinidad along Lascasian lines about 1540, when there was still no Spanish settlement there. This is of particular interest, being at the height of the Christian humanist movement and concurrent with Las Casas's enterprise in Guatemala.[31]

On five occasions during the sixteenth century governors were appointed to settle the island of Trinidad. In each contract there was the usual stipulation that priests were to accompany the colonizing expedition.[32] But two of these governors never reached Trinidad, and two others – Antonio Sedeño (1530–34) and Juan Troche Ponce de León (1569–70) – remained only a short time. Sedeño, in spite of his offer "to encourage the Indians to accept the knowledge of our Holy Catholic Faith", found that his main contact with them was in the form of bloody battle.[33] The work of the slave raiders had not been forgotten by the inhabitants. Ponce de León's attempt was even more short lived, being abandoned after nine months.[34]

Meanwhile the lure of something more exciting than pearls was attracting Spaniards and others to the Orinoco valley: the illusion that somewhere in the interior of the continent was to be found the city of Manoa and the famed "gilded man" who ruled it. And so in 1592 Domingo de Vera, agent of the fifth governor appointed, Antonio de Berrío, landed in Trinidad, the gateway to this fabled region. With the help of a Franciscan friar, Domingo de Santa Agueda, he planted a forty-foot cross taking possession in the name of the king of Spain. He then went up the Caroni River and founded San Josef de Oruña (St Joseph), selecting first a site for a church and having Fray Domingo say Mass on the spot. When Governor Berrío later arrived a mud church was already erected.[35] In the same year Berrío founded Santo Tomás (San Thomé) on the Orinoco River in "Guayana" in connection with his plans to find Manoa. A Franciscan friar was with him, and some Dominicans came soon afterward to found a monastery.[36] For Antonio de Berrío, and for Sir Walter Raleigh who turned up in 1595 to rival him in his search for El Dorado, Trinidad and Santo Tomás were seen as the portals of a new and wealthier Peru.[37]

But the dream of El Dorado did not come true, and Trinidad settled down to being a small agricultural colony raising tobacco and later cocoa for export, producing food for itself as best it could, and trading illegally with foreign ships since Spain sent no regular supply vessels.

Trinidad church life, along with the community generally, centred on the capital of San Josef in the seventeenth century and well into the eighteenth. The pastoral care of the Spaniards, and of the slowly increasing number of mestizos and later of black slaves and mulattos, was the responsibility of the priest or priests. In addition there were encomiendas of Amerindians, mostly in four villages in the nearby valleys of the Aricagua, the Tacarigua and the Arouca Rivers. The encomenderos had the duty to provide *curas doctrineros* for the religious instruction of the people in these villages. But this was not satisfactorily done, partly through shortage of clergy and partly because of lack of funds to pay them. In 1629 they were reported by the priest at San Josef to be still "living like barbarians using their false idolatries and their shamans speaking with the devils". However a lay brotherhood, the Cofradía del Glorioso San Pablo, undertook missionary work among them, claiming 250 conversions by 1645. It would be interesting to know more about this lay initiative.[38] Nothing was done until late in the century about the free aboriginals in the rest of the island.

The Trinidad Church was left at first almost entirely on its own. Nominally under the archbishop of Santa Fe de Bogotá, it had never received a visitor from this episcopal centre, and presumably the same was true of the province of Guayana.[39] In 1624 Santo Tomás and the following year the whole province of Guayana, together with Trinidad, was made a part of the diocese of Puerto Rico, as Cumaná and Margarita had been since 1558.[40] There Trinidad remained until at least 1662 when a proposal was made to return it to the archdiocese of Santa Fe. Presumably no action was taken as the request was repeated in 1707 and it is not clear when (or whether) the transfer took place.[41] Documents of the king and the Council of the Indies in 1722 and 1733 show that the crown was still dealing with the bishop of Puerto Rico concerning a Trinidad shortage of clergy, and that in May 1721 the bishop had made a two-day pastoral visit to the island. But in 1737 the Council recommended that the Viceroyalty of New Granada (which was about to be constituted in 1739) should support the church at San Josef and pay the clergy's salaries. It may be queried whether this was acted upon and whether the connection with Puerto Rico was broken, since in some matters such as judicial appeals the Venezuela provinces remained under the audiencia of Santo Domingo.[42] Finally in 1790 the diocese of Guayana was erected, including the provinces of Guayana and Cumaná and the islands of Margarita and Trinidad, suffragan to the archbishop of Santo Domingo. It was reputed to be the most impecunious diocese in America.[43]

In the confined and isolated community of San Josef serious strains developed at times, on occasion involving the ecclesiastical personnel. As early as 1617 the priest was complaining that the governor thought himself "Pope and King, and archbishop, bishop and vicar general".[44] A generation later the governor sent on to Guayana a French Jesuit who had come to set up the Inquisition in the island. This was done partly because Inquisitors and governors were known to become rivals for power, and also because there seemed to be little need for the Inquisition in Trinidad.[45] For more than two decades after 1735 successive governors and the cabildo (town council) were continually at loggerheads. The cabildo also quarreled with the vicar general and so tense did the situation become that church services in San Josef were suspended.[46]

The Capuchin Missions (1686–1713)

The year 1652 had brought a major change of policy with regard to the indigenous residents of the northern part of South America. The king ordered armed conquest to cease and established a system of pacification through Indian missions. The result was a long-term development of missionary work in the llanos of Venezuela, the vast basin of the Orinoco and its tributaries, and the island of Trinidad. In this the Capuchin, Franciscan, Dominican, Jesuit, Augustinian, Candelarian and Mercedarian orders all had a part.[47]

The Capuchins – a reform movement within the Observant Franciscan order and like the Jesuits born in the Counter Reformation – had become the missionary order assigned to the eastern Cumaná region and in 1686 they began work in Trinidad. In the following year a new division of the order for "Trinidad y Guayana" was formed, separate from the Cumaná mission.[48] A letter from the king to the governor prepared the way for the friars and at first the colonists and the cabildo welcomed the missionaries, believing that they would bring civilization to the wild Indians of the forests and that in a few years these would become available to them as labourers. The Amerindians also had reason to welcome them since the life of the mission offered a peaceful existence, protected from other native people yet free of the heavier labour required in the encomiendas.[49]

The first prefect of the Capuchin company in Trinidad was Father Tomás de Barcelona, and as his name suggests these friars were from Catalonia.[50] In October 1686 he travelled to the mouth of the Guaracara River, met with a large group of caciques and selected sites for the missions. One site was chosen at Savanna Grande (the present Princes Town), one at Guayria, ("the mount which they call Naparima", that is, San Fernando), and one at Savaneta (near Couva). Later another was established at Montserrate (Mayo). These four centres in the mid south-west of the island became the principal missions of Trinidad. Others were started later or had a short life: San Francisco de los Arenales (south of San Raphael), Mayaro, "Careiro" (probably at Guayaguayare), Los Cocos and Moruga. The village at Santa Cruz, which was made up of freed Amerindian slaves from San Josef after 1688, never became fully established as a mission.[51]

Eight priests and four lay brothers came in 1687 to man these stations and altogether in the twenty-one years of their heyday some twenty-four missionaries came to Trinidad.[52] As in other parts of the empire the missions were erected on the plan of a Spanish town, with the church, presbytery and other public buildings at the east side of a central square, while Amerindian houses were built on the other three sides. Elected representatives of the Indians formed a cabildo but had very little power, which was in the hands of the friars.[53] When this authority was resented by the inhabitants they could return to the forest, or in two cases they rebelled more directly.

The best known of the missions because of the "Arena massacre" is San Francisco de los Arenales, located in a remote area near the geographical centre of the island. There in December 1699 the native residents murdered three Capuchin friars and a Spanish carpenter and subsequently ambushed the governor and his party who were enroute for a visit to the mission, killing all but one man who escaped.[54] Other missions suffered attacks by Amerindians from outside the island, or in one other less serious incident, by revolt of those within the mission.[55]

The local planters had watched the growing prosperity of the missions with envious eyes and asked to hire their Indians in return for food, wages and Christian instruction. The friars allowed some to go out in this way, but after a few months they were found to be so worn out, underfed and neglected that the missionaries refused to permit this to continue. Then in 1701 the Spaniards petitioned that the missions be ordered to provide workers for the cocoa estates, arguing that the Christianizing work of the good Capuchins was now completed.

This reasoning was accepted by the officials, for a ten-year period was in theory the time the "reductions" were to continue. After this the native people were supposed to be entrusted to secular priests and incorporated into Spanish civilization. The Capuchins objected, but in 1708 a royal order instructed the missionaries to leave the island and turn over the missions to the corregidores de indios who would make labour available to the Spaniards. By 1713 this was put into effect. However, many returned to the forest rather than work for the planters.[56]

By the year 1724 Capuchin missions on the mainland of Guayana were permanently founded, and these absorbed the chief labours of the order for many decades.[57] From time to time however some of their number were brought back to Trinidad to revive the mission villages which tended to disintegrate without their leadership, although corregidores were appointed to take charge of them. As early as 1719 two friars were allowed to return to work in the missions because of the lack of secular priests who knew the language, and at times there are reports of Capuchins reuniting disintegrated missions or even starting a new one.[58]

In the latter part of the eighteenth century Capuchin missionaries in Cumaná province encouraged Chaima and Carib Indians to migrate to Trinidad with a view to mission work there. These centres were in the north-east corner of the island, at Toco, Punta de Cumaná and "Arrecifes". Salibia and Matura are also mentioned. It was in this period also that Arawaks settled at Siparia and Erin.[59]

Finally the government relocated the encomienda villages of Tacarigua, Cuara, and Arouca at Arima about 1785, to make land available to new immigrant planters. As it turned out Arima, which was established as a mission but not a strictly segregated one, became the third largest town of the island and maintained a diminishing Amerindian population into the twentieth century. Savanna Grande (and Montserrate), Siparia, and Toco (together with Cumaná and Salibia) were the other mission centres for which a native population was reported in 1797.[60]

It might seem that the Spanish missions of Trinidad have made no permanent mark on the shaping of the Church, since few Amerindians survived except as an element in the racial intermixture of the island and so of the Church's membership. Yet the work of the Capuchin friars is perhaps the most serious and prolonged Spanish missionary enterprise to be carried out in the Caribbean islands, the more successful for having started after the first age of conquest and acute exploitation. With the wisdom of hindsight it is easy to see that the methods were far from ideal by Christian or modern anthropological standards, but the devotion of the friars cannot be questioned, nor their positive achievements in terms of fostering a better livelihood for their people as well as knowledge of the faith. This tradition enriches the life of the Church even today.

The Eighteenth Century

After the dissolution of the missions, prosperity based on cocoa production continued for a few years until the cocoa blight in 1725 brought poverty and strain to the community. During this period, as has been noted, the Church was short of clergy and was so poor that New Granada was asked to come to its rescue. A further disaster was the smallpox epidemic of 1739.[61] Governor and cabildo were quarrelling, and this was aggravated by a growing rivalry between San Josef and Puerto de España

(Port-of-Spain). In 1757 the governor took up residence permanently in the port town. Although the cabildo and the tiny church establishment remained in St Joseph, its population was declining and its buildings deteriorating. Meanwhile Port-of-Spain grew in importance. It had asked for a priest of its own as early as 1716, but only in 1776 did it obtain a sacristan, and the following year a priest.[62]

The next quarter-century was to bring greater challenges to the Church. The first Cédula de Población (Decree of Population) of Charles III in 1776, which offered citizenship and land inducements to foreign Catholics, had the immediate effect of bringing to Trinidad a French-speaking population which soon equalled and then surpassed the number of Spanish-speaking people.[63]

The second Decree of Population (1783), resulting from the efforts of the Grenada planter Roume de St Laurent, stimulated this movement. One condition of entrance to Trinidad, stated in Article 1 of the cédula, was ability to prove Roman Catholic allegiance. Spain still wanted no heretics in her colonies. Article 24 further promises the appointment of two secular or regular priests "skilled and versed in foreign languages" to be parish priests to the new settlers, suitable stipends being provided without cost to their parishioners.[64]

Some Irish Catholics took advantage of the generous inducements of the new immigration policy, but the great majority were French planters with their African slaves. They came from the French islands which had been ceded to Great Britain in 1763, from St Domingue (Haiti) which was in the throes of revolution, and from the French Antilles torn between royalists and republicans. The situation in Trinidad was complicated by the antagonism between royalist and republican refugees among the French themselves.

The immigrants settled in Port-of-Spain and in new rural areas in the foothills of the Northern Range, in Naparima and on the east coast. The Church was still centred in St Joseph, where 80 percent of the population was Spanish. However two new parishes were founded in 1791, at San Juan and San Fernando. There was difficulty finding linguistically qualified priests, but two French-speaking Capuchins from Andalusia were finally appointed.[65]

Along with the ascendancy of French colonists, an equally important change in the social structure was the new predominance of African slaves and also the large number of free people of colour who came to the island. The first black slaves to enter Trinidad offically under the asiento had come in 1701. Before this however some had been smuggled in, with the connivance of local authorities – in one case as early as 1606 when some 470 were delivered by Dutch merchants.[66] Often slaves were resold to the continent for a quick profit. A population estimate in 1637 put the numbers of African slaves at 100. Yet in 1777 there were only 222 slaves out of a total of 3,432 people, that is, 7 percent. Labour was still largely Amerindian and technically free. But by 1797 the percentage of slaves had risen to 56 percent.[67]

The Spanish authorities responded to this changed situation with the relatively humane Trinidad Slave Code of 1789.[68] The Church had no new problem concerning the religion of these large numbers of blacks, for the French in the other islands had followed the Catholic tradition of baptizing and instructing their slaves. The many people of colour and free blacks, who were sometimes themselves slave owners, were likewise Christians. But the development of the sugar industry and the introduction for the first time of a majority of slaves altered the character of Trinidad society significantly.

Such was the position for society and the Church when in 1797 the British military conquest by Abercromby brought an unexpected turn to the drama. Not only did this put a new imperial power in control, but it brought to an end the unquestioned Catholic monopoly which had been maintained through two centuries of Spanish rule in Trinidad.

5

The Monopoly Breached
(1552–1670)

So strict was the control of the Spanish church and state that any challenge to their monopoly could only come from outside, in one of three possible ways:

(i) Infiltration might come through personal contacts in peaceful trade. Against this were the policy of mercantilism and the oversight of the Inquisition.
(ii) Challenge might come by attacks upon Spanish shipping and settlements. Often these had Protestant as well as nationalist motives.
(iii) The monopoly might also be broken by the settlement of territories not occupied by the Spaniards. With Dutch and English colonies, Protestants and also Irish Catholics came to the West Indies. French colonies introduced another form of Roman Catholicism, and French Protestants were found in them as well.

These techniques of peaceful trade, hostile attack and colonization were interconnected. The activities of French, English, Irish and Dutch were also at times neighbourly, and this introduced a new variety of colour into the Caribbean religious tapestry: mutual toleration of diverse traditions.

This chapter deals with the struggle against the Spanish Catholic monopoly and also the advent of toleration. The following chapter turns attention to the internal religious development of the successful non-Spanish colonies.

French Corsairs and Colonists (1552–1567)

Not until the outbreak of war between France and Spain in 1552 were there any noticeable effects in the Caribbean of the Protestant Reformation. Prior to this the new doctrines had spread through France, the Netherlands, Scotland, England and other parts of Europe. That continent became polarized between Catholics and Protestants, and national rivalries complicated the tensions.[1]

European wars between France and Spain during the four decades from 1519 to 1559 were inspired by nationalist rather than religious motives. The French monarchs were hardly less eager to stamp out Protestant heresy at home than were their opponents, Charles V and Philip II, on the Spanish side. However, they were quite willing to have Protestant subjects challenge Spain's position, which was strengthened by wealth flowing from America. France began to encourage corsairs to raid the fleets carrying gold and silver through the Caribbean, and to attack ports in the Greater Antilles and Central America.[2]

By 1552 it was obvious that the corsairs were in fact not merely French but largely Protestant. The Reformed faith had grown rapidly in France and notably so in the seafaring ports of the Atlantic and Normandy. King Henry II with one hand tried to stamp out this movement, but with the other hand encouraged these Protestant sailors to harass Spain. Moreover the French Admiral was Gaspard de Coligny, who later declared himself a Protestant. So it was that these *corsarios luteranos*, as the Spaniards called them, descended upon the helpless settlements in the Spanish Main with the fury of patriotism intensified by religious animosity. In 1554 François de Sorès captured Santiago in Cuba and the next year he sacked Havana. During the latter incident Spanish religious sensibilities were deeply shocked by destruction of images and other sacrileges in the church and by cruelty to the priests.[3]

So began an ugly chapter of attack and counter-attack between Huguenots (as the French Protestants came to be called about 1559) and Spanish in the New World. Under Coligny predominantly Protestant expeditions started settlements in America. One of these was at Fort Caroline on the St John's River in Florida under René de Laudonnière and Jean Ribault. Spain was acutely aware of this threat to the sea route from the Caribbean, which passed along the Florida coast on the return journey to Europe. Admiral Pedro Menéndez de Avilés was sent to destroy the upstart colony in 1565. In doing so he massacred the Huguenot prisoners, while sparing a few Catholics. The story arose that he advertised that he did this to them "not as Frenchmen but as heretics". Perhaps this was considered just retaliation for the religious atrocities at the sack of Havana ten years earlier. After two years Chevalier Dominique de Gourgues, himself a French Catholic, led a party of revenge upon the Spanish fort on the same river, killing its defenders "not as Spaniards but as murderers". The act of Menéndez did much to persuade England that Catholic Spain was a treacherous enemy.[4]

In the following years France was torn by civil wars between Catholics and Huguenots and ceased to be an active challenger of Spain. This mantle fell on the English and the Dutch, but the depradations of French corsairs continued, sometimes in co-operation with them.

Peaceful Trade to Hostile Attack: English and Dutch (1562–1628)

The alliance of England and Spain was shaken when Henry VIII sought annulment of his marriage with Queen Catherine, who was the aunt of Charles V, and when he broke with the pope by the Act of Supremacy, Philip II indeed tried another method of overcoming the heretical tendency of the English nation. In 1554 he married Queen Mary, who reigned from 1553 to 1558 and who was determined to restore the Roman Catholic faith in her country. For a few years it seemed that through this matrimonial alliance the English might be brought into a position similar to that in which the Netherlanders already found themselves – a part of Spain's European empire yet without rights in her American domain, and subject to a Roman Catholic autocracy while there was a strong Protestant movement among the people. Mary's death and the accession of Elizabeth I ended that prospect and reaffirmed the Protestant settlement in England. The kingdom of Scotland on its northern border became Protestant also in 1560.

Meanwhile a considerable number of English merchants were resident in Spain, maintaining a careful Catholic orthodoxy in the land of the Inquisition. A smaller number found their way to New Spain. The experience of one of these, Robert Tomson, in 1559 showed how little chance there was for Protestant ideas to spread to the Indies through such individual contacts. Tomson, in a household conversation in Mexico City, incautiously expressed some thoughts on the futility of saints' images, and the availability of direct access to God. He was promptly accused of Lutheran heresy before the episcopal Inquisition, and was condemned to wear the "Sanbenyto" for two years and to be deported for imprisonment in Castile for a year.[5]

Queen Elizabeth was willing to turn a blind eye to the activities of certain of her subjects who were ready to probe the exclusiveness of the Spanish American empire. As in France, a strong Protestant faith was commonly found among the sailors of England in the later sixteenth century and, as we shall see, in the Netherlands as well. This faith stimulated them to test the trading possibilities of the Spanish Caribbean, and afterward to move from peaceful to warlike challenges of the Spanish monopoly. The well-known exploits of John Hawkins and Francis Drake began in the name of trade, but contrary to Spain's prohibition of commercial dealings with foreigners. The interlopers were welcomed, however, by the Spanish colonists. Unhappily Hawkins's religion raised no more questions in his mind about the justice of African slavery than that of the Spaniards did with them, and so he became the first Englishman to engage in the transatlantic slave trade.[6]

A Spanish attack on the fleet of Hawkins at San Juan de Ulúa in 1568 changed the attitude towards Spain of many in England. English prisoners suffered various fates. Thirty-three were tried as Lutheran heretics. Three were burnt in *autos-de-fé*. Eighteen were sent to the galleys. Ten were assigned for religious instruction in monasteries. One was absolved and one freed after proving himself a good Catholic. A few escaped and returned to England.[7] Together with the execution of Huguenot prisoners by Menéndez three years earlier, this story provided the motive for a Protestant crusade against Spain.

English strategy changed from trade to privateering. Drake in 1573 captured the mule train which was transporting treasure from Peru across the Isthmus of Panama. He was helped by local Maroons and by the crew of a Huguenot corsair under one Captain Têtu, who also reported the massacre of Protestants on St Bartholemew's Day in France.[8]

By 1585 England was directly supporting the Dutch struggle for independence from Spain. This conflict, begun in 1568, was for national freedom from foreign rule combined with religious freedom. Philip II was trying to keep the Netherlands in the Catholic camp. Foremost in the fight were the Dutch seamen, many of whom were Calvinistic Protestants with a sense of divine destiny and of hostility to Spain and Catholicism. English defiance of Spain and sympathy with the Dutch cause culminated in the "Spanish Armada" of 1588. Its defeat helped to prepare the way for Protestant colonization in the next century. For the Dutch also it became the pivot from a defensive to an offensive period in their independence struggle.[9] Their boats appeared in large numbers at the saltbeds of Punta de Araya near Cumaná. Dutch trading posts, precursors of later settlements, appeared in the Guiana area and there is a report that as early as 1596 one of these, Fort Ter Hooge on the Essequibo, was destroyed by the Spaniards.[10] Sometimes the smugglers had contact in the Spanish settlements with residents from the Netherlands who were naturalized citizens but who were secretly Protestants and distributed heretical literature. Because of this, Spain expelled all Hollanders and Flemings from the Indies in 1606.[11]

English as well as Dutch adventurers continued to appear in the Caribbean in the 1590s.[12] One of them, Sir Walter Raleigh, focused his interest on the Orinoco valley, the site of "El Dorado", and the adjacent island of Trinidad. Raleigh raided Trinidad, made friends with the Amerindians, and carried away Governor Antonio de Berrío while he explored the Orinoco. He conceived the idea of seizing power in this part of South America in co-operation with the Indians and replacing Spain's empire with an English one. Sir Walter's *Discoverie*, published in 1596, stimulated many including the Dutch to think in terms of establishing permanent colonies in the Guiana area.[13]

With the accession of the cautious James I to the throne (1603) the initiative passed to the Netherlands. The Dutch West India Company was formed, challenging Spain's monopoly with a new one sanctified (as Goslinga puts it) "not by papal authority but the doctrines of John Calvin".[14] The climax of Dutch prowess was the seizing of the Silver Fleet by Piet Heyn at Matanzas in 1628. As church bells in Holland rang to celebrate this victory, many saw the feat as divine blessing and a judgment upon Spain.[15]

Writings that Stimulated Protestant Colonization

Raleigh was not the only Englishman to put on paper his hopes for an overseas empire. The pen was also wielded influentially by the clergyman and geographer

Richard Hakluyt in support of all anti-Spanish enterprises, and of Protestant colo-nization in the New World. Hakluyt had contact with Huguenots in France. In the 1580s he published some accounts of travel, discovery and colonization, including reports by Laudonnière and Ribault of the ill-fated French settlements in Florida.[16]

In 1584 Raleigh persuaded him to write a statement for Queen Elizabeth on the desirability of establishing English settlements in America. This argument is known as the *Discourse of Western Planting*. Although not published at the time it doubtless influenced many at court and its ideas were widely circulated.[17]

The document set forth religious reasons for Western enterprise. Hakluyt urged that it was "neccessarie for the salvation of those poore people which have sitten so longe in darkenes and in the shadowe of deathe, that preachers should be sent unto them" and concluded that the monarchs of England as "Defenders of the Faithe" could advance the cause of Christianity by planting colonies with this in view.[18] The idea of missions to the Amerindians was fostered by a sense of emulation of Catholic accomplishments – not without a touch of jealousy.[19]

The concern for missionary activity did not last very long when English settlers actually reached the American shores. On the whole Protestant colonies were less active in such work than those of Spain and France at least until the time of the Evangelical Movement.

Another religious motive, hostility to Roman Catholicism and to Spain, is emphasized in the *Discourse*. Hakluyt recalls how English traders living in Spain are "either inforced with wounded consciences to playe the dissemblinge hipocrites, or be drawen to mislike with the state of relligion mainteyned at home, or cruelly made away in the Inquisition".[20] He attacks Spain's claim to monopoly based on the papal bulls, her economic and military power from her empire, and her cruelty to the aborigines.[21]

On this last subject the enemies of Spain had come upon a handy weapon, the already mentioned *Brief Account of the Destruction of the Indies* written by Las Casas in 1542. This exposure of atrocities in America had been translated first into Dutch in support of the struggle against Spain. Hakluyt quotes from the first English edition some of the "moste outrageous and more than Turkishe cruelties in all the West Indies", making clear that they were written by "Bartholmewe de las Casas, a bisshoppe in Nova Spania". Other editions in Dutch and English appeared in later years. Las Casas fortunately did not live to see this use made of his tract on behalf of the Indians.[22]

Richard Hakluyt published records of overseas enterprise, culminating in his three-volume *Principal Navigations* in 1598–1600. He also left manuscripts that were posthumously published along with other material by Samuel Purchas, another clergyman with similar enthusiasm.[23] These compilers both stimulated and reflected English interest in the New World, and rivalry with Spain.

In Holland also William Usselinx, a Calvinist refugee, envisioned a plan for a company to colonize and Christianize the Guiana area, fight Spain in the New World and make a profit for Dutch merchants. This scheme, advocated in a series of tracts, was the seed idea out of which the Dutch West India Company emerged in 1621. By this time, however, Usselinx's missionary ideals were left aside. The Company was little more than an organization for trade, and war against Spain.[24]

Colonies and Toleration in the Eastern Caribbean (1604–1650)

Dutch, English and French colonies in Guiana and the Lesser Antilles challenged Spanish Catholic monopoly. They also introduced a *de facto* example of mutual toleration into the Caribbean scene.

The earliest efforts by Dutch and English to settle in the Guianas and on the Amazon were unsuccessful, defeated by famine, sickness, aboriginal opposition, lack of financial support, or by Spanish or Portuguese resistance.[25]

The Dutch were first to establish two lasting settlements. From the post at Kijkoveral on the Essequibo in 1616 is dated the first permanent non-Spanish colony in the West Indies. A few years later a similar start was made in Berbice.[26] Settlers were however few in number, as the Dutch emphasized trade rather than agricultural development. Little is recorded about church activity in these first trading posts.

The Pilgrim Fathers, prior to their settlement of 1620 in New England, seriously considered planting their colony in Guiana. One main reason they chose the North Atlantic coast was that it was less likely to be attacked by "the jealous Spaniards . . . as they did ye french in florida". One could speculate what might have been the history of Guiana and of the northern part of the Virginia patent, both religiously and politically, if these Puritans had decided to choose the tropics.[27] Indeed, it has been suggested that this decision was pivotal in the development of the South American coast, not only because the group from Scrooby did not come here, but because the Puritan migration which followed drew off financial and moral support to North America, leaving Guiana a poor third to this and the Lesser Antilles in the attention of England.[28]

In the Antilles the first colonies to be permanently established were St Christopher (by the English and French), Barbados and Nevis in the 1620s. Spain did nothing about Barbados, but in 1629 the Spanish fleet under Admiral Fadrique de Toledo made a devastating attack on Nevis and St Christopher. Ships were captured, houses and crops destroyed, but escapees returned and rebuilt.[29] As it turned out they were left alone afterward by the Spaniards. Spain found it wiser to concentrate her resistance upon the Dutch and upon English settlements in the western Caribbean which were a more serious threat to her treasure fleets.

In the 1630s Antigua and Montserrat were settled by the English and Irish; Martinique and Guadeloupe by the French; and St Martin, St Eustatius, Saba, Curaçao, Bonaire and Aruba by the Dutch. Unlike these lasting settlements, other attempted island colonies were unsuccessful, partly due to Spanish hostility. This was particularly true of the islands of Trinidad and Tobago where repeatedly small beginnings were destroyed, if not by the Spaniards then by illness or the Caribs. Weak as was her colony of Trinidad in itself, Spain was determined to defend the approach to the Orinoco from hostile and heretical occupation.

The Dutch West India Company considered Tobago its colony and before 1636 it had set up trading posts at "New Walcheren" (Plymouth) and also at Moruga in Trinidad. The governor of Trinidad, Don Diego Lopez de Escobar, made an expedition to liquidate these settlements and sent 72 prisoners to Margarita promising that they would be sent to St Christopher or Holland. The governor of Margarita however put the men to death, sparing the boys on the plea of some Franciscan friars. The following year the Dutch retaliated by sacking San Thomé and San Josef, and returned to the attack in 1640.[30] During this period a Baltic Protestant ruler, the duke of Courland, with some encouragement from the Dutch and also from the kings of England, planted colonies repeatedly in Tobago. English attempts were made on both Tobago and Trinidad under the "Pembroke Patent" acquired by the Puritan colonizer, the earl of Warwick. Scanty and conflicting records make it difficult to establish the complete story.[31]

At the other end of the island chain of the Lesser Antilles the Dutch and English had jointly settled the island of Santa Cruz (St Croix) in 1625. This was an independent enterprise, separate from the English proprietary colonies farther south. After a time the two groups quarrelled and the English drove out the Dutch. But the island was uncomfortably close to Puerto Rico and in 1650 the Spanish bestirred themselves to eliminate this unwelcome neighbour. It was their last success against the intruders in the Lesser Antilles, and a temporary one.[32]

In spite of the weakness of organized religion in the successful settlements, this first half century of non-Spanish colonization is an important era in the shaping of the Caribbean Church. New forms of the Christian faith were introduced and established de facto within the area of Spain's papal grant. Moreover two significant actions indicated that the monopoly could no longer be maintained.

The first was that of the Roman curia. In 1635 the French colonization of Martinique and Guadeloupe was undertaken by Cardinal Richelieu's Companie des îles d'Amérique. Approval was given by Pope Urban VIII for a mission by French friars to the indigenous inhabitants. Although not widely noticed at the time, by allowing France missionary privileges in the Indies, Rome had breached the monopoly set up by the bulls of Alexander VI.[33] As a matter of fact this was the expression of a policy which had been in formation at Rome at least from the time of Pius V (1566–72) who had endeavoured unsuccessfully to obtain from Philip II some papal influence over missionary work in Spanish domains. This purpose along with other reasons led ultimately to the establishment of the Congregation for the Propagation of the Faith in 1622 and the gradual assertion of worldwide papal authority over missionary affairs. French presence in the Antilles was an opportunity for the pope to become involved in the Caribbean from which he had been debarred by the Patronato.[34]

Documents show that in the same generation the participation of Irishmen in the colonizing movement brought to the attention of Rome the need of priests for them. One attempt was made through Spain to obtain clergy for the Irish for an abortive English settlement on the Amazon River (1610–45), but Spain had no intention of countenancing any colonies but her own. We next hear of representations in the 1630s and 1640s to the Congregation for the Propagation of the Faith for Irish priests to be sent to the New World to convert heretics and heathen, and to minister to Irish Catholics living among the Protestants there. By 1650 an Irish Jesuit priest was in the Leeward Islands.[35]

The second significant action was that of Spain itself. By the Treaty of Münster (1648) she conceded independence to the Netherlands, and the rights to trade and to hold territories already occupied in the West Indies.[36] Although not named in the treaty, these included Essequibo, Berbice and the Netherlands Antilles. By this historic step Spain implicitly acknowledged the right of non-Catholic religion to exist in the Caribbean.

Apart from these breaks in the Spanish Catholic monopoly, the actual experience of different nationalities working together against Spain, and against the perils of nature and the indigenous people, initiated a tradition of cosmopolitanism and religious toleration within the Caribbean. English, Dutch, Flemings, French, Irish and Courlanders lived side by side or in neighbouring communities, often with Amerindians and latterly African slaves. Only rarely did they quarrel on national lines and still more rarely over religion. English users of the Prayer Book, Dutch Calvinists or French Catholics might predominate in a given colony, but there were Puritans, and English, Irish and Dutch Catholics as well, and Huguenots and Jews in some places.[37] Leadership came sometimes from minority groups as with Robert Harcourt and Sir Henry Colt who were English Catholics; Le Vasseur, a Huguenot who was for a time the French governor of Tortuga; and the Dutch Catholic Captain Groenewegen of Kijkoveral (serving the predominantly Protestant West India Company) who "was a great freind of all new Colonies of Christians of what nacion soever".[38]

Unlike Spain with its Inquisition, all four of the major nations involved, England, Ireland, France and the Netherlands, were themselves religiously divided. In England Puritan Separatism on the one hand and surviving Roman Catholicism on the other differed from the established Church. The Church of England itself was divided between its Puritan wing and that which cherished vestments, bishops and Prayer Book. In Ireland ruling Protestants and majority Catholics had perforce to tolerate one another. France after its religious wars found relative peace under a king who was a Huguenot turned Catholic, and his Edict of Nantes. Most tolerant of all were the United Provinces of the Netherlands. There Protestants and Catholics had fought together against Spanish oppression. Both had been influenced by Erasmus' humanism, and both were ahead of their times in allowing freedom to those who differed from them. Calvinists, Lutherans, Anabaptists, Roman Catholics and Jews lived together and welcomed religious refugees from abroad.[39] From such backgrounds of at least incipient religious toleration it was not altogether novel for Dutch, English, Irish and French Protestants and Catholics to work together, for the most part in practical amity, in their isolated settlements in Guiana and the Caribbee Islands.

Toleration was reinforced by local geography and politics. Shortage of labour was a constant problem. Persecution in any form would have driven away needed population. It was almost impossible to prevent refugees from escaping to neighbouring islands (or river settlements in Guiana) or just across the border in the partitioned islands of St Christopher and St Martin.[40] As time went on, slaves were imported from Africa, but white employees were wanted, whatever their religion, to control them.

Trade also favoured tolerance. This was a major reason for the broad policy of the Dutch. Other colonies depended upon Dutch merchants for necessary and cheap supplies. The benefits of trade also favoured acceptance of the Jews. Religious freedom, in fact, was the partner of economic freedom. Resistance to the trade restrictions of the mercantilist system went hand in hand with resistance to European regulations to impose religious uniformity.[41]

Weakness of church organization also aided toleration. In the English and Dutch colonies the clergy were few and isolated and the laity not markedly zealous. In the French, the priests were divided among the different religious orders and there were frequent quarrels with the autocratic political leaders.

Some exceptions to the usual mood of religious toleration had their origins in events in Europe, such as the English Civil War, rivalry between France and England, and the royal reversal of the Edict of Nantes. Intolerance in the West Indies was reluctant and short lived. For the seventeenth century, religious freedom was relatively advanced in the non-Spanish Caribbean.

Puritans and Buccaneers in the Western Caribbean (1629–1641)

While non-Spanish colonization was spreading in the east, a romantic episode was taking place in the western Caribbean under the initiative of a group of Puritan aristocrats in England operating as the "Providence Company". They included Robert Rich, earl of Warwick, and others who subsequently became leaders of the parliamentary party during the Civil War and the Commonwealth. Their colonization project began as a wing of great Puritan migration during the time of Archbishop Laud's ascendancy in England. It ended as a sorry disaster, wiped out by Spanish attacks after deteriorating into a front for buccaneering. Because of its demise this effort was long forgotten, but twentieth century research showed its significant place in movements of the time, including English trade on the coast of Central America which in turn encouraged the settlement of Belize, the capture of Jamaica, and the heyday of the buccaneers in the later seventeenth century.[42]

Negatively, the failure of the Providence enterprise has an important significance for the religious history of the Caribbean in that the radical Protestantism of the Puritans did *not* take root in the West Indies as it did in the North American colonies.

"Providence" was the name given by the Puritans to the island called by the Spaniards Santa Catalina, off the coast of Nicaragua. (It is distinguished as "Old Providence"from "New Providence" in the Bahamas.) To the south was another island, San Andreas, which they renamed "Henrietta" in honour of their Queen.[43] Later they took under their wing the island of Tortuga (off the north coast of Haiti), calling it "Association". Trade began with the Moskitos, associating these inhabitants of the shore of Central America with Englishmen for centuries. Farther north there was about to develop a log cutting industry among adventurers at Campeche and at the Belize River.[44]

The Providence Company had its start through the privateering activities (1628–29) of Daniel Elfrith.[45] This man had observed the strategic position of the unoccupied islands of Santa Catalina and San Andreas in relation to the treasure routes from Panama through the western Caribbean. He communicated this observation to his son-in-law Philip Bell, the governor of Bermuda, who being a Puritan sympathizer reported it to the Warwick connection in England.[46] Elfrith was sent out to Providence with Puritan settlers who, like those bound for Massachusetts, were anxious to get away from the religious policies of Archbishop Laud. He also picked up in Bermuda some Puritans who had previously migrated there. The colonists built a town called New Westminster on the new island home.[47]

Since the Puritan island settlements failed to survive, they will not be examined along with the successful colonies in the next chapter. However their religious life is interesting for comparative purposes, and has a sort of negative significance in relation to the shaping of the Church in the other colonies.

The Company did its best to set a high standard of Puritan religion in its territories. Five clergymen were sent out to Providence and two to Association. Only one pastor, Hope Sherrard (or Sherwood), a conscientious man, stayed with his flock, until he was sent home by the deputy governor for criticizing a massacre of Spanish prisoners taken during an attack on the island.[48]

There also arrived in Providence an interesting minister, Nicholas Leverton, who during the course of his life served in no less than six different English colonies. Having worked in Barbados he went as chaplain with the unsuccessful expedition to settle Tobago. The survivors, unable to return to Barbados, made their escape with the wind all the way to Providence. Here he was invited to minister to those settlers who wanted the Prayer Book service, but he became converted by Sherrard to the Puritan position. He was sent home at the same time as Sherrard but the Company returned him by another ship, only to find the island captured by the Spaniards. After an unsuccessful battle to retake it "they continued in those seas for two years", perhaps as privateers. Leverton ministered in St Christopher and Bermuda before returning to England. After being ejected for nonconformity in 1662, he ended his days as a minister in Willoughby's colony in Surinam.[49] Leverton's peregrinations throw light on conditions in this period when colonization was a dangerous enterprise in which some clergy took part as freelance adventurers.[50]

From its distant position the Company heard that some in the island had sent for "cards, dice, and tables". Concerned for Puritan morality, they instructed the governor to "have them burnt, or at least sent back", and strictly prohibited their use under severe penalties. "Lawful recreations, such as chess, shooting, &c." were permitted. On another occasion they approved the governor's "proclamation for preventing mixed dancing and other vanity".[51]

Even if it had not been destroyed by the Spaniards, this tropical Puritan commonwealth was unlikely ground for the planting of a vigorous Christian church. The religious purpose of the colony became compromised, due in part to internal quarrels. Other adventurers appeared on the scene, more interested in plunder than in settled agriculture.[52] Perhaps the enervating climate had an effect on Puritan zeal. Certainly the introduction of African slaves for manual labour demoralized the slave owners.

It is interesting that one of the points of contention was slavery. Elfrith had been involved in the first sale of African slaves in Virginia and Bermuda in 1619. Although the Providence settlement started with indentured English labourers, Africans were imported in 1633. Some of them escaped to the woods. Samuel Rishworth, a Puritan religious leader though not a clergyman, questioned the slave system, even helping the runaways to escape. For this he came in conflict with the planters and the Company, which condemned him for his "groundless opinion that Christians may not lawfully keep such persons in a state of servitude during their strangeness from Christianity".[53] Rishworth, far ahead of his time, seems to be the first prophet to actively oppose slavery in an English colony.

Although the Company felt no compunction about African slaves in its domains and did not seem to contemplate Christianizing them, it was concerned for the aborigines of the Moskito coast. The spreading of the gospel to them, it declared, was "the greatest work both for itself and in our aim". They mentioned specially the "Christian education" of the children. Captain Axe, whose men had killed a number of Amerindians in a fight, was severely reprimanded, reminded that "the Lord is the avenger of blood", and advised "to humble himself before the Lord, and give public testimonies of the truth of his humiliation".[54] Not much if anything seems to have been done on the spot to implement the evangelizing zeal of the Puritans in England. If it had, it would have been in rivalry with Spanish friars who had tried repeatedly to convert the Moskitos.[55] English contacts with these people did however lead to mission work in the following century.

Providence, Henrietta and "Association" by their location were like daggers close to the jugular vein of Spain's empire. Tortuga was the first to feel her wrath. The English and French who were captured in a raid in 1635 were massacred and the buildings were destroyed. But it was reoccupied.[56] Providence managed to repel a Spanish assault a little later. From then on it became more and more a centre for privateering.

The whole enterprise deteriorated. The plan to develop Henrietta was abandoned and the more defensible Providence strengthened. Tortuga became a haven for buccaneers of various nationalities. In 1640 it was seized by the French under the Huguenot adventurer Le Vasseur.[57]

Providence itself was finally captured in 1641 by the Spaniards. This ended the Puritan effort to colonize the western Caribbean. The attention of the Company's leaders in England was diverted to the Civil War. English contacts continued however with the Moskito Coast and the Belize River area, and after the conquest of Jamaica the western Caribbean became a sphere of interest for it.[58]

A Protestant Conquest in Mid Caribbean (1655)

The culmination of the struggle against Spanish power was Cromwell's expedition under Admiral Penn and General Venables. For the Puritan Protector his "Grand Design" was a kind of seventeenth century crusade. Like its medieval predecessors this crusade was badly managed, unpredictable in its course, in achievement less than what was planned, and it drew participants who had no high religious motives.

Its basic idea – to seize control from Spain at a weak point and to replace her political and religious power with an English Protestant one – was not new. Raleigh and the Providence Company had both planned in such terms, and there were influential leaders on both sides of the Atlantic who encouraged Cromwell to undertake such an enterprise.[59] One was a renegade English Catholic priest, Thomas Gage, who had studied in Spain and served as a Dominican in Central America. Returning to England he converted to Protestantism and wrote an account of his life in the Spanish Caribbean. This was a defence of his change of religion and an incitement to Englishmen to see Spain as a decaying power that could be easily overthrown.[60] Gage wrote a brief to Oliver Cromwell in 1654 summarizing his book and urging him to take action against the Spanish Empire.[61]

Cromwell made a demand of the Spanish ambassador for trade privileges in the West Indies and also for freedom of English merchants from the Inquisition and "to have and use in Spayne English bibles and other religious books". He was told that "to ask a liberty from the inquisition, and free sayling in the West Indies, was to ask his master's two eyes".[62] Justification for an invasion was supplied after the event by Cromwell's *Manifesto*, written in Latin possibly by John Milton, in which the various wrongs of Catholic Spain were listed, especially the attacks on the islands of the Providence Company.[63] Cromwell further undertook in a speech before Parliament to explain his anti-Spanish policy with its religious overtones.[64]

The force accompanying Penn and Venables from England was insufficient, and they were instructed to recruit men in Barbados and the Leeward Islands. The ones thus obtained were for the most part undisciplined and undedicated to Cromwell's crusade. The leaders bungled an attack on Hispaniola, and seized Jamaica as a compensation prize not daring to report back to Cromwell empty-handed. The Protector resolved to keep the island, defend and populate it. The restored royal government of Charles II confirmed this policy. Jamaica was only under Puritan rule for five difficult years before it became a royal colony.

The capture and retention of Jamaica, in the very heart of the Caribbean, demonstrated that Spain not only could not occupy all the areas in America which she claimed but could not even be sure of keeping what she had. To the buccaneer haven at Tortuga was now added another centre, Port Royal, located in this new English possession. Spain had to become reconciled to the coexistence of rival empires in the Caribbean. By the Treaties of Madrid (1667 and 1670) she agreed to England's possession of the territories already held, as she had previously recognized Dutch colonies by the Treaty of Münster.[65] On the other hand England, now having a stake in the area, decided to call a halt to the anarchy of buccaneering and the threat of piracy.

By this time Europe was weary of religious wars. The Peace of Westphalia (1648) had acknowledged the coexistence of Protestant and Catholic powers on that continent. England, having passed through civil war and alternations of religious dominance, was less inclined for crusading, although the Restoration government took strong measures in the home country against nonconformity and continued the disabilities of the Roman Catholics there and overseas. Plurality was replacing uniformity; however, within each nation and its colonies, the idea still prevailed that there must be an officially recognized Church in some form.

The Heritage of the Buccaneers

It remains to be asked whether the colourful adventurers of the seventeenth century known as the buccaneers – and indeed the earlier privateers and the later pirates – have any religious significance. It has already been stressed that the French corsairs, the English trader-fighters of the sixteenth century and the Dutch and English raiders of the seventeenth were frequently inspired by Protestant hatred of Catholic Spain. The buccaneering movement however was, in a sense, native to the Caribbean. Although most of the "brethren" came from Europe, they had made the Caribbean their home. Others, at least in later years, were born in the English, Dutch and French West Indian colonies.[66]

For the buccaneers plunder was a way of life, but not (like pirates) without discrimination. They were united in common hostility to Spain, her wealth, her pretensions and her religious intolerance. Consequently they attracted mainly Protestants, even among the French, in the early days. Later, as the number of French Catholics among them increased, nationalistic differences grew and the international character of the movement weakened. English buccaneers in Port Royal left the French in Tortuga and western Hispaniola. England and later France began to suppress the buccaneers. With the Treaty of Ryswyck (1697) the age of buccaneering gave place to that of the pirates.[67]

The Providence episode exposed the corrupting influence of privateering upon the religious objectives of the Puritans there. What of the buccaneers in their heyday, the third quarter of the century?

The "brethren of the coast" were a strange mixture. There were former indentured servants (English and French) who had finished their term of service but had received, or wanted, no land to work for themselves, or who lacked capital to operate as planters. There were unruly characters escaping punishment for crime, the discipline of their ship, or debt. Some were religious or political refugees. Others were simply restless and ambitious spirits who saw scope for gain and fame in this way of life.[68]

Among such a motley collection one does not find the kind of religion which would be thought worthy in most churches. But the seventeenth century was a religious age. Irreligion, "secularism" and atheism were still quite exceptional. Père Labat's stories (from the end of the century) of sailors who celebrated Mass with the accompaniment of a salute of cannon, and of Captain Daniel shooting dead a seaman who failed to give proper "respect to the Holy Sacrifice" are indicative of the rough and superstitious piety to be found among buccaneers and pirates. We hear of clergymen who followed this life, sometimes as chaplains of the ships. And from time to time churches were presented with valuable gifts, especially when ecclesiastical wares were found in the cargo of captured ships.[69]

Clearly such religion as was found among these cut throats contributed little to the growth of the Church. Port Royal, for example, although it had its church, was notorious for riotous living and after the terrible earthquake of 1692 the local clergyman readily attributed it to the discriminate judgment of God upon the accumulated sins of the place.[70]

The way of life of the buccaneers and other raiders had negative effects upon society and upon the Church in the Caribbean, since it prolonged and encouraged the tradition of ruthlessness, violence and greed only too characteristic of the region from the days of the conquistadors. This was compounded by the slave trade and slavery. Yet this tradition went along with a formal allegiance to the Christian faith. The slow death of piracy in the eighteenth century, and abolition and emancipation in the nineteenth, removed its more spectacular expressions, but the spirit of the buccaneers was not thereby fully expunged from Caribbean life. The story of the shaping of the Church is in part the account of a struggle both within and outside the Church against that spirit.

6

Seventeenth Century Colonization and the Churches

The Church's life in the early non-Spanish colonies in many ways reflected contemporary ecclesiastical conditions in European countries from which settlers came, especially England and also Ireland and France. Yet conditions in the New World were very different. Transplantation to the Caribbean environment was part of a larger interrelated colonizing movement including Guiana, Virginia and Bermuda,

This chapter is concerned mainly with the Church among European settlers. The coming of African slaves and their relation to the Church will appear in the next chapter.

Puritans, Anglicans, and Roman Catholics in England and Abroad

The Reformation during the reigns of Henry VIII and Edward VI, the failure of the reaction under Mary I, and the Elizabethan settlement had made England a predominantly Protestant nation and the Church of England independent of the pope. But along with the struggle between Roman Catholicism and the national church, another polarization began to take place between "Puritans" and "Anglicans" in the established Church itself.[1]

The origin of the Puritan movement can be dated from the return to England of refugees who had fled to Europe during the persecution of Protestants in the time of Queen Mary (1553–58). These exiles had lived in such places as Geneva (where Calvin was located), Frankfurt and Zurich. They now intensified the Calvinist tendency in the Church of England. Their desires were for a strictly Bible-centred as against a traditional worship and doctrine, an emphasis on preaching, and the abolition of such "popish" practices as priestly vestments, kneeling at the Lord's Supper, the sign of the cross at baptism and of the ring in marriage.

For a time this movement was treated with sympathy, although the desired changes were not achieved. The more extreme Puritans began to think of

Separatism, the leaving of the national Church and establishing small "reformed" groups "without tarying for anie". These groups were organized on a congregational basis, independent of any higher ecclesiastical organization. By the 1590s some of these Independent congregations went into exile. One such group, the Pilgrim Fathers, found refuge in the Netherlands until they moved on to America.

Meanwhile a contrasting Anglican position had been developed as a counterblast to Puritanism. Richard Hooker gave a moderate and classic statement of it in his *Laws of Ecclesiastical Polity* (1594–97). Soon many of this persuasion adopted "Arminian" doctrine over against Calvinist teaching on predestination. The Anglican viewpoint was also associated with episcopacy as its bulwark. Monarchs and bishops saw themselves as allied against Puritanism. With the death of Elizabeth, James of Scotland became king and soon sided with the Anglicans. In 1618 he angered the Puritans by issuing his "Book of Sports" supporting what they regarded as sinful merrymaking on the Lord's Day.[2]

Such was the situation during the earliest phase of English colonization in the New World, from 1604 to the 1620s. At this time many Puritans found their way to Virginia and Bermuda. Then, when Bishop (later Archbishop) William Laud began to enforce Anglican orthodoxy, and Charles I decided to rule without Parliament, the tension exploded into open conflict in England. A large migration of Puritans seeking religious freedom went to New England, and some (as noted before) to Providence. Others mingled with settlers in other continental and island colonies.[3]

Among the migrants were also Roman Catholics, mostly from Ireland. In that country the Reformation had been welcomed by only a small number, and under English rule Catholicism had become identified with national feeling.[4] In the Caribbean a large proportion of the labour force was Irish. Both in England and the New World, Catholics found it necessary to keep a low profile in the observance of their rites, and in any case there was a scarcity of clergy. Their political loyalty was suspect in the eyes of the Protestants. In contrast to the Puritans they had doubts about seeking religious freedom as a group overseas: only in Maryland did this motive play a part.[5]

During the Civil War and the Commonwealth in England the Anglicans in turn were persecuted. A considerable emigration of leading Cavaliers took place to Barbados and Bermuda, as well as to Virginia and Maryland. Defeated English, Scottish and Irish royalist soldiers also were expelled by the victorious Cromwell, adding to the ranks of indentured servants in the West Indies.[6]

With the Restoration of Charles II and the "ejections" of 1662, Puritan nonconformists as well as Roman Catholics found themselves isolated as dissenting bodies outside the national Church. It is important to remember that until then the Puritans – with the exception of the Independents, Baptists, later Quakers and a few other small groups – had remained *within* the established Church of England

and aspired to reform that Church in line with their ideals. In the West Indies such Puritan clergy and lay people as there were lacked any independent organization, as they had in New England. Only a few Separatists and Baptists found their way to the Caribbean. A significant minority of Quakers however played a distinctive and interesting part in seventeenth century colonial society.

In the reign of James II favour was shown briefly to Catholics and general toleration was proposed by the king. Then after the Revolution of 1688 an Act of Toleration was passed removing some disabilities of the nonconformists but leaving Roman Catholics much as before.[7]

In the West Indies the difficulties of pioneer life, the scramble for wealth and growing dependence upon African slavery tended to distract attention from the doctrinal and liturgical disputes which throve in England and in the continental colonies. Neutrality, indifference and ambiguity on the points at issue, common enough in England itself, were still more common here.

The Early Years: Guiana, Virginia, Bermuda (1604–1624)

One notable characteristic of the pioneer phase of English colonization was the attention given to the hope of winning the indigenous people to Christianity, notably in certain abortive beginnings in Guiana, and in Virginia.[8]

Captain Charles Leigh, the founder of the 1604 Wiapoco colony, reported to the Privy Council on his contacts with the inhabitants of the region and their request for religious teaching, asking that "able preachers" be sent out for this purpose.[9] In writing to his brother he tells how the chiefs had asked "that I would bring them men to teach them to pray, which motion of theirs, proceeding from themselves and in that humble manner, strooke me I assure you with an admiration of joy", and in his closing words begged him to "forget not to send Preachers, sober and discreete men, and such as are well persuaded of the Church government in England".[10] This led to the recruitment of a Mr Tederington, the first clergyman to come to any English colony in the Caribbean area. He sailed in the autumn of 1604 on the relief ship which was sent to the struggling settlement. Of this man we know little more than his name. What he did in the few months he lived there, and whether he had any contact with the Arawaks, we do not know. He returned to England by the same ship in April 1605. The colony ended soon afterward, and the survivors left by Dutch and French ships during the following months.[11]

Three years after Leigh's settlement Robert Harcourt made another attempt on the same river. He had with him two Guianese Amerindians who had spent some years in England, and found two others there who had returned before. Of these four, who had been befriended by Raleigh or by Leigh or their men, three are referred to as Christians.[12] Harcourt in his *Relation* repeatedly speaks of the conversion of the Indian people as one of the primary purposes of his enterprise.[13] As a Catholic he did not share the hostility of most of his English contemporaries to Spain's religion as such, and he admired her missionary work in the New World, although regretting her "bloudy battles, and much cruelty". At the same time he supported Raleigh's view that the English nation could win the aboriginal people to Christianity more effectively, and that they would benefit from English rule.[14]

Harcourt's unsuccessful efforts in Guiana were contemporary with the enterprise of the Virginia Company, which produced the permanent colonies of Virginia and Bermuda. Here also the religious and missionary aspect of the undertaking was expressed, in the royal patent and "Instructions" of 1606.[15]

It is interesting to compare the Virginia Company's "Declaration of Purpose" of 1609 with the "Three principall ends to be observed in every foraine action" set forth by Harcourt in his *Relation* four years later. The threefold structure of these manifestos – "to the glory of God; the honour of our Soveraigne, and the benefit of our Countrey". as Harcourt puts it – suggests that this was a common formula in colonizing circles. In each case the missionary purpose was placed first, although the difference between the Company's Calvinistic concern for the "accomplishment of the number of the elect" and Harcourt's Trinitarian language is intriguing.[16]

Anglican, Puritan and English Catholic were thus at one in their expressed desire to Christianize the aboriginal people. How this was to be done was the question since none of them could turn, like the Spanish and French, to the ever-ready religious orders to do the work. Thought was given to the question, however, and also to the proper relationship with the native inhabitants. William Crashaw, for example, in a sermon published in 1610 spoke of their rights: "A Christian may take nothing from a Heathen against his will, but in faire and lawful bargain." He supports this by recalling the example of Abraham who insisted on paying for land to bury Sarah.[17] This high principle was not very much followed on the other side of the Atlantic.

In Virginia there were at first genuine efforts, by some at least, to live with the native people as neighbours and to share with them the Christian faith and the benefits of education. Alexander Whitaker, one of the ministers, stimulated missionary concern in England by a sermon published in 1613. In it he argued for the common humanity and rationality of the Indians and their need of the gospel, in a way that reminds us of passages from Las Casas.[18]

In England much interest and money raising activity, with the support of James I and the bishop of London, was centred upon the provision of churches and schools to educate both native people and the children of the settlers.[19] All this met with sudden and unexpected catastrophe in March 1622, when 347 settlers, men, women and children, were massacred in Virginia. The result was that the early optimism and good will of the settlers gave way to distrust and cynicism, especially as George

Thorpe, a missionary who had particularly befriended the native people, was among those slain. The plans for education were abandoned.[20]

This tragedy virtually brought to an end the early period of active missionary interest although the ideal of Christianization was not entirely forgotten.[21] But even among the clergy the view became prevalent which had been expressed by one of them in Virginia, Jonas Stockam: that there was little hope of bringing the Indians to conversion by means of kind persuasion.[22] If Whitaker and Thorpe remind us of Las Casas, Stockam is their Sepúlveda, and the conflict of opinion within the Church of the sixteenth century is echoed in the seventeenth.

In the old empire of the seventeenth century, tidewater Virginia is the North American settlement most nearly resembling the West Indies through its plantation economy, its mixed racial composition, and also the established position of the Church of England. Bermuda, an island colony having frequent contacts with the Caribbean islands, may also be compared with them. Common to all these territories was a church structure closely linked with the government and dependent on local politics, and a parish and vestry system remote from episcopal or royal supervision. Virginia and Bermuda provide a useful prelude to the history of the Church in the West Indies, notably regarding the life of the early clergy, the vestries, and efforts to legislate morality.

At first the work of the Church centred around the labours of individual ministers sent out by the Virginia Company, and the later Somers Island Company. Most of them were Puritan clergy. Yet Whitaker complained in a letter dated 1614 "that so few of our English Ministers that were so hot against Surplis and subscription come hither where neither are spoken of. Do they not either wilfully hide their tallents, or keepe themselves at home for feare of loosing a few pleasures?"[23] This comment reflects both the preference – no doubt for practical as well as theological reasons – for simpler and less formal worship in pioneer days, and also the continual shortage of clergy in the English colonies while they were dependent upon the "home" country for trained leadership. It was never easy to find suitable ministers, whether Puritan or Anglican, for the colonial Church.

After Virginia became a royal colony in 1624, the Puritan influence gave way to that of the established Church with its Prayer Book. The Church in Bermuda, on the other hand, through the long tenure of the Somers Island Company (1615–85), was led by a variety of rather individualistic clergymen and lay leaders, mostly of a strong Calvinistic outlook.[24] In the Caribbean however the Puritan influence either among clergy or laity was never strong.

In Virginia and Bermuda, as later in Barbados, the Leeward Islands and Jamaica, the unit of church life, and also of some purposes of government, was the parish. The administrative body was the vestry and executive officers the churchwardens. This was a natural transference of the system in England itself, although in the various localities west of the Atlantic there developed differences from England and from one another.[25] It is difficult to trace the earliest beginnings of church organization, but in Virginia the duties of churchwardens and vestries, and the term "parish" are found in early documents.[26]

It has been said that "Anglicans in other colonies copied the Virginia type of vestry".[27] This may be true of the mainland colonies but for Bermuda and the West Indies the records suggest rather a parallel development from English antecedents. The Bermuda parish was mentioned in legislation of 1618 (earlier in fact than Virginia). Four parishes were then formed by the grouping of the eight "Tribes", earlier divisions in some ways unique to this colony.[28] The duties of churchwardens were defined about 1621.[29] Even before this, one Puritan minister, Lewis Hughes, had appointed elders according to the Presbyterian system, but Governor Butler apparently did not countenance this departure from the canons of the church of England.[30] Vestries were set up about 1626 but were quickly suspended again after some quarrelling. Governor Bell in 1628 had an altercation with a minister who tried to hold vestry elections. The minister lost this mini-contest between church and state. In this small colony church affairs seem to have been vigorously administered up to 1685 by the Company, and by governors, Councils and Assemblies, churchwardens and ministers. Perhaps vestries were considered an unnecessary addition.[31]

In the West Indies we shall find that parishes were established in Barbados only two years after the settlement, that the vestry was clearly in existence in the 1630s, but that in the Leeward Islands parochial organization developed more slowly.

During the years 1610 and 1611 in Virginia a series of regulations often called "Dale's Laws", for the "care of true Religion" and "military discipline", was approved by the governors in charge, apparently with the intent of ruling the colony like an army. They were directed, by the threat of harsh punishments, to make people go to church, observe the Sabbath, refrain from impious talk and respect the constituted authorities. The clergy were similarly obliged to carry out their duties faithfully.[32] These rules are not an isolated curiosity conceived by a soldier-governor. A copy of them was carried to Bermuda by Governor Tucker in 1616 and influenced his erratic rule there.[33] In later years orders and laws were issued from time to time such as Governor Butler's "Proclamacon for the observacon of the Sabaoth day" (1620) and his instructions to the churchwardens and sidesmen "for the suppressing of prophanenesse and vngodliness".[34] That there was public support for religious and moral legislation (though not in the extreme form of "Dale's Laws") can be seen from the fact that after Virginia was given its own Assembly it proceeded to re-enact some of the same regulations, with less severe punishments for offenders, and there is evidence that these milder laws were enforced.[35]

The attempt to legislate people into religious living was a common one in the seventeenth century, whether the ethos of the place was Puritan or Anglican, and

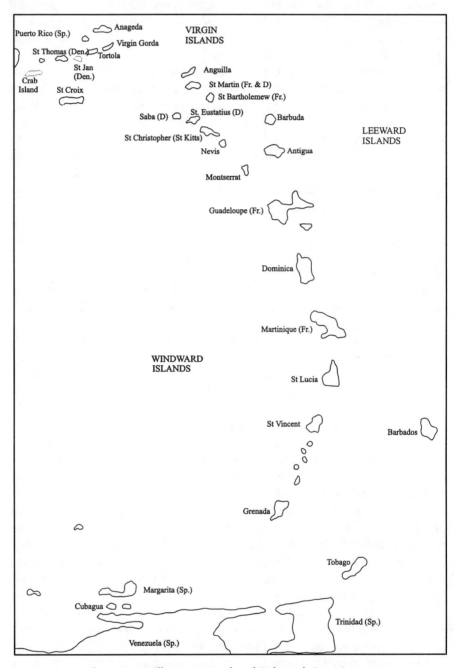

The Lesser Antilles: Seventeenth and Eighteenth Centuries

whether power lay with a Company in England or with the local Governor or Assembly. It was natural for Englishmen to regard their Church and society as one, and therefore to legislate the proper conduct of the citizen-church members. (Even Separatists and Presbyterians in New England had their own established Churches.) As will be seen, such legislation was common in the West Indies also.

Pioneers in St Kitts, Barbados and Nevis (1624–1629)

The first permanent English settlements in the Caribbean were made by private adventurers who established a foothold before seeking authority under a proprietor from the crown, beginning with the landing party of Thomas Warner on St Christopher in January 1624. In the first two years little can be said about the Church.[36]

Captain Warner returned to England to obtain royal recognition of his plantation. This was achieved in the form of an authority from Charles I in 1625, by which he was "incouraged . . . to proceed in a worke soe likely to tend to the propogation of Christian Religion the honor of us and good of our people".[37] When Warner returned he carried with him the first Protestant clergyman to work in any of the permanent West Indian colonies, Master John Featley.

Warner had cultivated good relations with the Carib Indians and their "King Tegreman". Yet he heard of the Virginia massacre of 1622 and he did not trust his allies very far. Then he received a warning of impending attack. And so took place that incident which blots the early days of St Kitts, the "preventive" massacre of the Caribs in which even Tegreman was killed.[38]

Featley was concerned that the colonists should show an attitude of Christian sincerity to the native people. But this history of distrust and violence made the possibility of missionary activity very remote. In the Caribbean, then, English colonization had no initial period of idealism and Christianizing zeal like that of Virginia. Such efforts as were made in the seventeenth century to convert the island Caribs were made by French monks of the Dominican, Capuchin and Jesuit orders, and later by secular priests. They were almost completely unsuccessful. However these missionary endeavours dating from the 1640s may be said to have begun the history of the Church in Dominica and St Vincent, later ceded to Great Britain.[39]

Presumably John Featley carried on the pastoral and liturgical duties that would be expected of him in St Christopher, and we know that he took his preaching duties seriously since some later sermons of his were published. He had a close relationship with the Warner family, and when Thomas Warner returned once again to England we find Featley there too. At this time Warner had to negotiate for a commission as governor of St Christopher from the earl of Carlisle who was now proprietor under the crown for the Caribbee Islands. This was obtained in September 1629. In the same month Warner was knighted and Featley preached a famous sermon in London in preparation for the return journey to the West Indies.[40] After word reached England of the Spanish raid on Nevis and St Christopher, which had also taken place in that eventful September, Warner gathered new recruits and returned with his minister to rebuild the shattered colony. Featley appears as a witness to a will at St Christopher dated 20 January 1629 (that is, 1630 N.S.) and is listed as a member of the Council of St Christopher in May. However his second published sermon appeared in London in 1632, which probably shows that he had gone back to England by that time.[41]

Featley's final stay in St Kitts was during the Civil War. Although a strong Calvinist, he was episcopalian and had become chaplain to Charles I in 1639. In 1643 he went back to St Christopher with his family, but three years later was living in Holland. His later publications include one after the Restoration, dedicated to Charles II.[42] John Featley's life story reflects the stormy vicissitudes of the Church of England in the period during which the early English colonies were being planted in the Caribbean.

Insight into the thinking of this pioneer clergyman is found in his sermon of 1629. In the absence of other records of this time it is of interest to outline its message, providing as it does a small window into the minds of the earliest English settlers through that of their spiritual adviser. Unlike most of the printed sermons and pious tracts supporting colonization in the early seventeenth century – which were important as mass media in that day – this was preached by one who had actually shared in the pioneer enterprise overseas.[43] It seems also that this was the only published sermon directed to the circumstances of the West Indies.

The text is Joshua 1:9. Featley applies it to "some of us most particularly, whose occasions command us to take leave of our Native Soile, that we may possesse the Land of the Hittites and Amorites, the Habitations of Salvage-Heathens, whose understandings where never yet illuminated with the knowledge of their Maker". With a strong Calvinist emphasis upon the sovereignty, providence, guidance and judgment of God he goes on to exhort:

> Let us the more especially assure our selves that we are dispatched with Joshuas Commission, that the Sea may be but a Jordan unto us, and the Land we goe to inhabit, a Canaan. Our examples must as much teach the Salvages *what* we obey, as our Precepts, *whom* we obey. Or Religion must be as well clad in Sinceritie, as our Strength in courage; that so those ignorant Infidels observing our religious Conversation, may joyne with us in a happy Resolution.[44]

For Featley at least, the recent massacres had not destroyed a sense of responsibility for Christian witness to the Caribs, and a hope of winning them by example.

The sermon continues by citing the dangers of the enterprise: "surging waves of a swelling sea"; "tempestuous winds" (the St Kitts settlers had already experienced

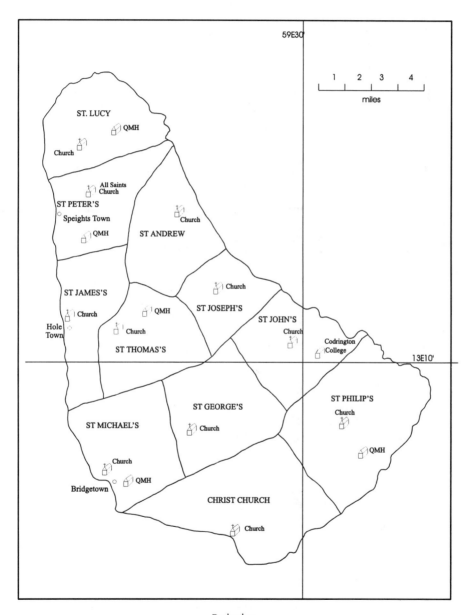

Barbados

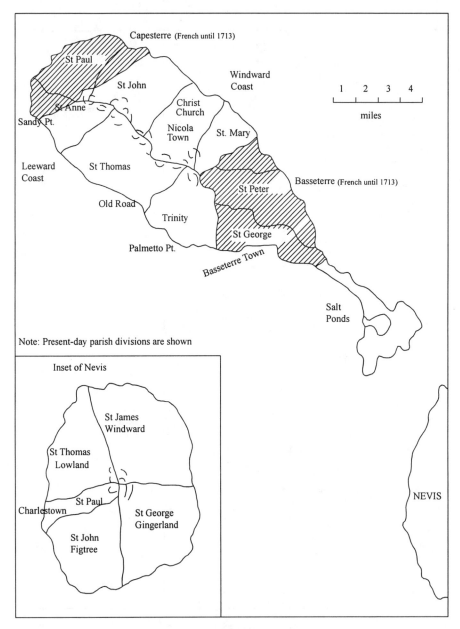

Capesterre (French until 1713)

St Paul

St John

Windward Coast

1 2 3 4

miles

St Anne

Christ Church

Sandy Pt.

Nicola Town

St. Mary

Leeward Coast

St Thomas

St Peter

Basseterre (French until 1713)

Old Road

Trinity

St George

Palmetto Pt.

Basseterre Town

Salt Ponds

Note: Present-day parish divisions are shown

Inset of Nevis

St James Windward

St Thomas Lowland

St Paul

Charlestown

St George Gingerland

St John Figtree

NEVIS

St.Christopher (St Kitts) and Nevis

a hurricane which destroyed their first tobacco crop); the "blustring noise of Guns" (Featley had seen action with the Spaniards), and "the companie of Indian archers". He concludes with the divine assurance of the text: "Be not afraid, neither be dismaid; for I will be with you whithersoever ye goe."[45]

Barbados was unoccupied when settled. The first plantation was made by an Anglo-Dutch Company, the Courteen Brothers, in February 1627 on the site of the present Hole Town, under Captain Henry Powell, backed by the earl of Pembroke. In June 1628 another body of settlers sent by a rival patentee, the earl of Carlisle, landed at Bridgetown. These opposing parties almost came to a contest of arms later in the year, and the first evidence we have of a clergyman in Barbados is in the record of the *Memoirs*:

> and both Partys being ready to engage in Fight, they were prevented by the Pains and Intercession of a pious Clergyman, one KENTLANE, who running in between the Partys, persuaded them to a Parly, and afterwards to a Reconciliation, and that disputes should be referred to the two Earls [Pembroke and Carlisle] . . .[46]

Whether Mr "Kentlane" came out with the Courteen or Carlisle expedition, is not clear. We do not hear of him again, unless he is the same as Thomas Lane, a minister who will be found writing to Archbishop Laud in 1637.

The only other clergyman mentioned in the records before proprietary government brought a measure of stability to the Caribbee Islands is one who appears as a passenger on a ship bound for Nevis from Barbados in 1629. The boat was directed by Carlisle's unscrupulous agent, Henry Hawley, who had just seized control of Barbados by a treacherous arrest of the leader of the Courteen party. He was now planning to use similar tactics to install an appointee of Carlisle as governor of Nevis. At this juncture the minister managed to send a secret warning of the plot to his brother Captain Jacob Lake ashore, thus enabling the people of Nevis to frustrate it. We are left to wonder whether this clergyman was on his way to serve as a minister at Nevis. In any case the entire operation came to disaster when "ye Spanish Armado" sailed in and made its unexpected attack on Nevis and St Christopher. We may presume that Mr Lake the minister found himself among the prisoners sent back to England by "Don Frederigoe".[47] These are examples of the adventures that might overtake colonizers, whether lay people or clergy, in the pioneer days.

Proprietary Rule in the Caribbee Islands (1627–1643)

Although in theory, Barbados and the Leeward Islands were under the government of a proprietor from 1627 to 1663, this was effective only from 1629, when the earl of

Carlisle made good his claim, to the outbreak of the Civil War leading to the appointment of Warwick's Parliamentary Commission for Plantations in 1643. From that time until the acquiring of proprietary rights by the crown after the Restoration, the proprietor had little power.[48]

The religious needs of the colony were supposed to be the responsiblity of the proprietor. It is ironical that Carlisle's patent defined his rights and jurisdiction in terms of those of a bishop of Durham.[49] The earls, father and son, had rather less than episcopal interest in ecclesiastical matters. The appointment of clergy, along with governors, tax-collectors and other officials was a privilege of the king's patentee. The earl of Carlisle's commission to Warner as governor of St Christopher contains a number of pious phrases, and instructs him "to take most especiall regard that the divine service according to the formes and present Customes of the Church of England be duely observed".[50] In fact Carlisle cared for little except money from the colonies to pay debts. On occasion he used his privilege of appointment, but the evidence indicates that most clergy were secured by subordinates or by the local vestries.[51]

Carlisle's first governor of Barbados, William Tufton, did make a serious effort to put the Church as well as the government on an organized basis. Under his short rule of a few months in 1629 and 1630 six parishes were defined, ranging along the leeward side of the island.[52] Then or soon afterward churches were built and vestries established. Tufton appears to have been a concerned Christian gentleman. Not only did he take the initial steps on behalf of the Church, but he tried to mitigate the cruelty of the system of indentured labour. It was this which brought his downfall, for he criticized the planters for misusing their "apprentices" and even threatened to take servants away from masters who oppressed them. The planters appealed to Carlisle, who sent Henry Hawley to replace him as governor. Tufton then became a planter himself but was later executed by Hawley on a charge of "sedition". What he had done was to petition against Hawley's arbitrary rule during the "starving time" of 1631. He is an instance of that rare breed of colonial official who tried to put into practice his Christian sympathy with the oppressed against local vested interests.[53] Thus, hardly three years from the founding of the colony, was signalized the injustice of the forced labour system before African slaves had even appeared on the scene at least in any numbers.[54]

During most of the decade of the 1630s, the heyday of proprietary rule, Hawley was the ruthless governor of Barbados. Planters here and also in St Christopher complained of heavy taxation. "Men women & Chilldren paid 20 lbs |tobacco| per annum for pol |tax| to the Lord Carlile's use, or 7d per pound and 2d there, 20 lbs to the Governour, 10 lbs to the Captain, 10 lbs to the minister, and for three years a hen a head and 20 lbs for every hen not paid."[55] Indentured servants were treated so harshly that in 1634 in Barbados they conspired to revolt, kill their masters and take to sea, foreshadowing the many slave revolts of later years.[56] To an outside observer such as Sir Henry Colt with upper class sympathies the white servants appeared as "lazy". Descriptions of the time speak of widespread drunkenness, quarelling and indifference to human suffering.[57]

The condition of the Church is glimpsed in a letter of Thomas Lane from Barbados to Archbishop Laud in 1637. Lane speaks as "a brother minister" and addresses Laud as "a principal of the learned Commissioners appointed by the King to examine and rectify all complaints from the plantations".[58] He reports that "within the past five or six years" six churches (that is, one for each parish) have been built by the people "besides some chapels" (which probably became the nucleus of the new parishes soon to be formed). "The care of the parishes is committed to some of the principal men in each parish, who are called the vestry, and have power to place and displace their ministers, and to allow them yearly stipends". The governor also takes part in this lay control of the clergy "and agrees with them as he pleases, whereby we are made and esteemed no better than mercenaries". Ministers and their families have to pay the poll tax and also maintain the parish clerks.[59] This is the first specific account we have of church life in the West Indies, but it is by no means the last complaint about domination of the clergy by vestries and governors.

Although Laud and his Commission no doubt would have tried to improve the position of the Church overseas, the affairs of church and state in England itself were deteriorating. Laud was imprisoned in the Tower. Parliament transferred the oversight of colonies to his enemy, the earl of Warwick. In fact very little was done from the mother country about church affairs until the Restoration. The Revd Mr Lane's complaints remained unsatisfied, and the pattern of church life characteristic of the West Indies for almost two hundred years became established. This pattern, in the absence of a bishop, was almost congregational. The vestries and churchwardens, chosen by the parishioners from among the leading planters for the most part, had the duty of caring for the church building and other property, of choosing and paying the minister (except in some colonies where the island government took a more active part in this), of overseeing the morals of the community, of providing for indigent persons, and usually of maintaining roads and carrying out other functions of local government.[60]

In the smaller islands of the Leewards we have little detail concerning the establishment of the churches in the proprietary period. Because of the threat of the Caribs, military divisions played a more important part in the civil organization of the islands in the early days and this slowed the development of the parish as the religio-political unit of local self-government. Gradually in all four islands however the military divisions either became parishes or were combined in some way to do so. This process took place first in St Christopher by about 1655, in Nevis and Montserrat in the 1670s and in Antigua by 1681.[61] But of course some of the features of parish organization for church purposes may have begun earlier than this.

The congregational tendency of the parochial system was offset to some extent by the power of the governor when he chose to exert it. Where church and state were offically assumed to be coterminous this was taken for granted. In 1641 the governor and Council in Barbados acted as an ecclesiastical court to consider complaints concerning the conduct and attitude of the rector of St Thomas parish and deprived him of his position.[62] In St Christopher charges brought against Governor Everard in 1659 included one that "John Price, a godly minister, has been unjustly turned out of his living" by the said governor.[63]

In 1641 a new lieutenant governor, Philip Bell, came to Barbados and remained as head of administration throughout this decade. He had had experience as governor of Bermuda and of Providence. In line with the rapidly increasing population and its spread throughout the island on the wave of prosperity from sugar culture, the six parishes set up by Tufton were increased to eleven. The new parishes on the windward side were probably carved out of the hinterland of the original ones.[64] The Assembly, begun by Hawley, was advanced to the status of a legislative body. The parishes became the constituencies from which the Assembly members were elected.

The Assembly began to play a part in religious affairs. Three Acts affecting the Church were passed during Bell's governorship. The only one that carried a date (13 March 1648, that is, 1649 N.S.) empowered vestries and churchwardens to make sale of lands in lieu of parish taxes.[65]

One undated law formally made the Church of England the established Church in Barbados. It required conformity by all "to the Government and Discipline of the Church of England as the same hath been established by several Acts of Parliament". Its wording suggests that it must have been passed *before* Barbados had learned of Parliament's outlawing of the Book of Common Prayer in 1644. However it was mainly directed against Separatist preaching and the holding of "conventicles", which had become rife in Barbados as in Bermuda at this period.[66]

Another Act, also undated, set out to enforce religious observance along lines reminiscent of the laws of Virginia and Bermuda. Family prayers were to be said in every home morning and evening. Church attendance was required twice a Sunday of those within two miles of a church, twice a month if farther away. Fines were to be exacted of delinquents. If a "Servant" was absent from church he might be punished, or his master if the latter were at fault. The clergy were ordered to provide regular church services and catechizing of the youth. Punishment was prescribed for swearing and cursing. It was directed that constables, churchwardens and sidesmen shall in some time of Divine Service every Sunday, walk and search Taverns, Alehouses, Victualling-houses or other Houses, where they do suspect lewd and debauched Company to frequent. And if they shall find any Drinking, Swearing, Gaming, or otherwise demeaning themselves, that forthwith they apprehend such persons and bring them to the Stocks, there to be by them imprisoned for the space of four hours, unless every such Offender pay five shillings to the Church-wardens of the said parish for the use of the Poor.[67]

One may wonder how effective this method was in promoting piety among the unwilling portion of the inhabitants.

In Montserrat the governor and Council issued an order in 1638 requiring Sabbath observance on pain of a fine of 1,000 lbs. of tobacco. This was confirmed by an Act of Assembly in the 1660s with specific prohibition of "unlawful Gaming, immoderate and incivil Drinking, irreverent and illegal association, tumultuous Hubbubs, or any other prophane and illicious Labours of the week-days, as digging, houghing, baking, crabbing, shooting and such-like indecent Actions".[68] In Nevis also an Act was passed requiring attendance at the established Church, but this seems to have been occasioned by a struggle against the Quakers.[69] Antigua, apparently alone among Caribbean colonies, legislated in 1644 and 1672 against miscegenation.[70]

Legislation of this sort is evidence, not only of the assumption that the ruling authorities should oversee the religious and moral life of the community, but also of the particular zeal of these authorities at a given time, and indeed of the existence of the offences prohibited.[71] Enforcement is another matter. It tended to be discriminative and sporadic, and took place notably when some crisis occurred such as the struggle for power between royalists and parliamentarians in Barbados, or the growth of troublesome Independent or Quaker preaching.

Repercussions from the Civil War in England

When king and Parliament came to open conflict, the control of the colonies was important to both sides. Parliament asserted its claims by the appointing of a committee under the earl of Warwick "for the better governing, strengthening and preservation of the said Plantations, chiefly for the advancement of the true Protestant Religion, and farther spreading of the Gospell of Christ".[72] Since the proprietor was a Royalist he was deprived of his colonies for a time. The colonists for their part tried to maintain a neutral stance towards the quarrel between Roundheads and Cavaliers. They did however benefit from the committee's cancellation of the powers and the taxes of the proprietor. The earl of Warwick tried by correspondence to win the governors of Barbados and St Christopher, whom he knew personally, to the parliamentary cause, and his committee offered an increased measure of self-government and "Liberty of Conscience in Matters of Religion", as a counterblast to the recent plans of the Laudian regime to ensure conformity to the Anglican establishment in the British Isles and overseas. The governor and Council in Barbados replied that they already had freedom of worship and that "if any man here have suffered (Minister or Lay) either by Deprivation, Banishment, or Imprisonment, it hath been for preaching Blasphemies or Heresies, or for maintaining or promulgating known Errors in the Fundamentals of Faith". They also persisted in requiring attendance at public preaching to counteract such false teaching.[73] Clearly the colonists intended to make their own decisions regarding religious affairs rather than accepting dictation from England, whether one way or the other. That the claim to tolerance of diverse viewpoints was not an idle boast is shown by Richard Ligon's account of the "loving, friendly, and hospitable" gentlemen planters who at this time

> though they are of several Perswasions . . . made a Law among themselves, that whosoever nam'd the word *Roundhead* or *Cavalier*, should give to all those that heard him, a Shot and a Turky, to be eaten at his house that made the forfeiture; which sometimes was done purposely, that they might enjoy the company of one another.[74]

In the later 1640s an influx of Royalists, following reverses suffered by the king's armies in the war, greatly affected society and the Church in Barbados and Bermuda. In the case of Barbados the wealthier Royalists bought land and set up as planters. This coincided with the sudden prosperity of the sugar revolution. In both islands, and even in Antigua, the Royalists became influential in political life. At the same time many common soldiers from the king's armies were "barbadosed", to use Cromwell's term. Politically attached to the royal cause, religiously dedicated to the established Church and opposed to Puritanism, these newcomers had a permanent influence particularly on Barbados, contributing to its long-standing Anglican majority.

In Bermuda the religious conflicts of the time in a curious way inspired the beginning of colonization in the Bahama Islands. Preachers of Separatist convictions had been causing disunity in Bermuda, and some of their flock under the leadership of William Sayle organized an expedition in 1648 to settle one of these islands which they renamed "Eleutheria", land of liberty. (The name was later shortened to Eleuthera.) After the execution of King Charles in 1649 many Puritan Independents were forced to leave for Eleuthera by the Royalist regime in Bermuda which had temporarily come to power. Two years later, after Parliament had brought this regime into line, they were allowed to return. Meanwhile the pioneer Bahamian colony had fallen on difficult days partly owing to internal factions, and at a critical time it was aided with food by the Puritans of New England.[75] Although this first settlement dwindled away through the years, it was from Bermuda again that New Providence was colonized about 1666.

The execution of the king provoked waves of anger especially among Royalists in the island colonies, which brought some of them into collision with the victorious Parliamentary government in London. During the following months there was a struggle for power in Barbados between the Cavalier party led by Humphrey and Edward Walrond and the Roundhead sympathizers including James Drax. A group of moderates with Thomas Modyford, not fully committed to either cause, complicated the picture. Local rivalries of course were as important as the politico-religious issue being fought out in England and Scotland. Pressure on Governor Bell and on the moderates, the accusation of a Roundhead plot, a propaganda war and the threat of armed force were all employed.[76] Support of Prayer Book worship, as against attendance at "conventicles", was taken as the acid test of political loyalty.[77] This movement climaxed in May 1650 in a proclamation:

> Charles Stuart, Son to the late King, was with great solemnity proclaimed King of England, Scotland, France, and Ireland, &c. Immediately thereupon the Booke of Common Prayer was declared, to be the only Pattern of true worship, and commanded to be distinctly, and duly read in every Parish Church, every Lords Day &c.[78]

At this juncture Carlisle's lessee, Lord Willoughby, carrying a commission from Charles II, arrived at Barbados, taking the wind from the sails of the Walrond party. Although he favoured moderation the Royalist party managed to send him off to the Leeward Islands to declare his Commission there, while they proceeded with their plans to disarm, fine and banish the "Independents" as they called their opponents.[79] After Willoughby's return the Assembly acknowledged him as governor and Charles as king and declared for "the unanimous profession of the true religion in this Island, and imposing condign punishment upon the opposers thereof".[80]

An expedition sent out by Parliament in 1651 under Sir George Ayscue led ultimately to a negotiated capitulation by the Royalist government of Barbados in January 1652. In this settlement a number of rights of Englishmen in the colonies were agreed to by Ayscue and later by Parliament. Of these rights the first mentioned is:

> 1. That a liberty of conscience in matters of religion be allowed to all, excepting such tenents as are inconsistent to a civil government; and that laws be put in execution against blasphemy, atheism, and open scandalous living, seditious preaching, or unsound doctrine sufficiently proved against him.[81]

While this obviously falls short of true toleration, it is one of the earlier documents in the slow process by which freedom of religion came to be recognized in the English-speaking world.

What "liberty of conscience" would mean in practice was another matter. Who for instance would decide what form of worship was to be used in the parish churches?

Such Puritans as had not been exiled, or who returned to the island from England where the Book of Common Prayer was now illegal, would expect that public worship would follow English practice, this was ten years before the Act of Uniformity made Puritans into "nonconformists". The governor appointed under the Commonwealth, Daniel Searle, was a diligent Puritan. Soon after taking office he requested the government to send "four or more faithful ministers" to Barbados.[82] Considering it his duty to enforce the policy of his home government, in October 1652 he directed that the Book of Common Prayer, "whose Efects to make up a dumb and lasie Ministry hath been answerable to what could be expected from their idolatrous original", was no longer to be used. Copies of the forbidden book were to be given up at the next Privy Sessions. One clergyman Charles Robson refused to do this and was about to be arrested when a certain Major Bailey led the crowd present to rescue him. A riot almost ensued.[83] Barbados was asserting its determination to decide for itself, rather than simply following the policy of the mother country.

The details of Church affairs in the West Indies in the 1650s are somewhat obscure because of lack of records, although documents from the expedition of Penn and Venables supply a glimpse of Barbados and the Leewards and the new colony of Jamaica in 1655.[84] Settlers began to migrate to Jamaica. Cromwell sent defeated Royalists, Scots and Irish as labourers. Population movements, especially from Barbados due to the squeezing out of small proprietors by large sugar magnates, were continual during this period.[85] Independents, Baptists and Quaker missionaries were free to preach.[86] The Church of England, with or without its Prayer Book, was left to its own local resources.

In any case by this time religious disputes were losing interest for colonists in the West Indies. Other concerns were more urgent. By 1661 for example Sir James Drax, the former Commonwealth supporter, wrote from London to his old enemy Humphrey Walrond, now governor of Barbados, on matters concerning the political future of the colony.[87] Roundhead and Cavalier were ready to sink their differences and the West India interest was born. If the gentlemen of the plantocracy were not quite back to the camaraderie of "the Shot and the Turky", they were at least ready to join hands against proprietor, Parliament or king to protect their own welfare. The short period of politico-religious rivalry gave place to the more usual attitude of religious toleration – except when the Quakers challenged the *status quo* – and the planter class accepted the established Church as a formal institution of its life.

Catholics and Huguenots in the Antilles (1624–1700)

There were no major group migrations for religious reasons to the Caribbean – except for the unsuccessful ones to Old Providence and Eleuthera – as there were in some of the North American colonies. However non-religious factors threw together people of different ecclesiastical allegiances, with curious results.

The first diversity came with D'Esnambuc's French settlers on St Christopher in 1625. The association of French and English began through common fear of the Caribs and the Spaniards, but it survived for almost ninety years until the Treaty of Utrecht gave the whole island to the British. A Treaty in 1627 between D'Esnambuc and Warner was renewed several times in the following decades.[88] The island was divided into a central portion for the English and two end portions for the French, Basseterre and Capesterre. The English part was itself divided by mountains into leeward and windward sections which had to communicate with one another either by sea or through French territory. The saltponds at the tip of Basseterre were common property.

This extraordinary arrangement brought the English and French settlers into close contiguity and as the century progressed it produced interesting situations. The English colony had a number of Roman Catholics, notably Irish indentured servants. The French colony had a number of Protestants. These minorities found themselves drawn to churches of their own faith across the border. The respective governing authorities did not look with favour upon this kind of fraternization but only spasmodically did they try to prevent it. There was at one time a Catholic chapel in the French sector for the Irish, and at another a French church in the English part of the island for Huguenots. The French government recognized that repressive orders against Protestants could not be enforced as strictly in St Christopher as elsewhere "par les facilités que les religionnaires y ont d'aller au prêche chez les Anglais".[89] So close was the mingling of the two nations that at one point the Council of (English) St Christopher asked that the bishop of London should send out clergy

> of riper years and better read in divinity than those last young graduates that came hither, lest, if any dispute should arise between them and the clergymen of the Church of Rome they should be foiled in argument. There are many Roman priests on the French part of the Island who are questionless men of great learning and parts.[90]

The feelings of Irish servants had been spectacularly revealed at the time of the Spanish attack of 1629. On Nevis the island militia, made up mostly of these labourers, deserted. Hilton's "Relation" tells how "our Servants proved treacherous, runn away from us & swimed aboard & told them where we hid our provissions, & in what case our Islands stood in . . . Ye most of them being Servants cryed out, 'liberty, joyfull Liberty'".[91] Two years later Sir Henry Colt after a visit to St Christopher described Sir Thomas Warner's precautions against an expected further attack by the Spaniards. He points out that the "men servants" are more numerous than the planters:

> Butt these servants of ye planters rather desyer ye Spaniards might come, yt by itt they might be freed, then any willingnesse they shew to defend ther masters. Ther was two of these men yt ridd uppon a wooden horse wth weights of ther feet by ye command of ye Governour for words to ye like effect.[92]

The fact that the Irish servants were of the same religion as the Spaniards no doubt increased their readiness to desert. Protestants, if they knew of the fate of Hawkins's men in the previous century under the Inquisition, would think twice about taking refuge with them. But the desire to escape from forced labour was primary, religion only secondary. When war broke out between English and French in 1666 and again in 1689 the French also were able to benefit by the support of many Irish who co-operated with them against the English.[93]

The island of Montserrat was settled mostly by Irish Catholics from the mother colony of St Christopher. By 1632 many servants who had completed their indenture welcomed the opportunity to take up land there. This does not mean that in the new colony the Roman Catholics enjoyed self-government. Anthony Brisket, the governor, was from Ireland but held his post under the earl of Carlisle. He set about erecting an Anglican church of stone and brick, but reports indicate that the Irish Catholics greatly outnumbered the ruling Protestant group.[94]

Shortly after the settlement of Montserrat Father Andrew White, a Jesuit priest with Lord Baltimore's expedition to found the colony of Maryland, wrote an account of their voyage which gives a glimpse of Barbados and the Leeward Islands in 1634. In the former, he reports, "some few Catholiques there be both English and Irish".[95] After a three-week stay in Barbados they proceeded on, and on 26 January: "By noone we came before Monserat, where is a noble plantation of Irish Catholiques whome the virginians would not suffer to live with them because of their religion". At St Christopher, "we staied 10 dayes, nobly entertained by Sr. Thomas Waroner, governour, Captaine Jefferson, Lieuetenant Coronell, by 2 Catholiques Capt. Caverley and Capt. Pellam, and my selfe in particular by the governour of the ffrench Colonie in the same Iland".[96]

This "Relation" seems to be the only evidence of Irish Catholics from Virginia in Montserrat as early as this. It is surprising that Father White gives no details of a circumstance that would be expected to hold great interest for him. Probably in their brief stop at Montserrat they had little or no contact with the settlers ashore.[97] In any case if this information is correct Montserrat is one exception to the general statement that the Caribbean colonies were not settled for the sake of religious refuge.

A French Jesuit, Pierre Pelleprat, throws light on the situation in the Leewards sixteen years after Father White. He tells of an Irish priest, "Jean Destriche," whom Gwynn identifies as Father John Stritch of Limerick, coming to the French part of St Christopher in 1650 and building a chapel there. He invited Irish Catholics from the English sector to come and be served by a priest of their own nationality, to their great delight.[98] After three months there he went to Montserrat where he could not operate openly as a priest but disguised himself as a wood merchant, working in the forest. There the good father gathered his Irish flock in the mornings for mass and confession, and employed some of them in his lumber business.[99]

After spending some time in Montserrat, Father Stritch returned to St Christopher. By this time the English authorities, distrusting the Irish Catholics, decided to put a stop to their crossing the border to the Jesuit's chapel. This was the time of Puritan ascendency in England and something of the ruthless policy of Cromwell found its way to St Kitts. Some 125 Catholics were deported to Crab Island (near Puerto Rico). Others went to Guadeloupe in 1653.[100] This instance of persecution doubtless aggravated relationships and contributed to the war of 1666 when the French, in an attack led by the governor and urged against the "heretics" by the priests, took over the English part of St Christopher, burned down two churches and reconsecrated four others for Roman Catholic use.[101] Just after this a second Irish priest, Father John Grace, spent about two years working among his compatriots in the Antilles and reported to Rome on the need of thousands of Irish Catholics who were scattered among the French and the heretical English in these islands.[102] Although the Treaty of Breda had restored the partition of St Christopher, French-English relations remained strained. For more than a century religious differences aggravated imperial rivalry, and Roman Catholics (especially Irish) in the English colonies were distrusted and closely watched.

After the Restoration a policy of religious toleration for the West Indian colonies was laid down through royal instructions to the governors. "Persons of different judgments and opinions in matters of religion" were encouraged to settle, and the oaths of allegiance and supremacy were required only of higher government officials.[103] This toleration seemed at first to be intended for Roman Catholics as well as nonconformists, who at this time were also being restricted in England, but in 1680 the instructions excluded "papists" from it. Then during the short reign of James II the king's Catholic correligionists in Jamaica were given "protection, countenance, and encouragement". James sent a priest, Father Churchill, as "chief pastor" over "our Roman Catholic subjects" in that island, with orders to the governor to give him assistance.[104] Sir Nathaniel Johnson, governor of the Leeward Islands, granted freedom of religion for Catholics and exemption from church rates. Congregations in Montserrat and St Christopher were active in building chapels at this time.[105] But after the Revolution of 1688 the standard royal instructions were restored to read "liberty of conscience to all except papists", and so they continued for many decades.[106]

Meanwhile the Huguenots in the French colonies had been under increasing pressure from the government in France. In the home country the religious peace of 1598 began to deteriorate after the assassination of Henry of Navarre in 1610, but in the Antilles tolerance was maintained in practice pretty well until the Revocation of the Edict of Nantes in 1685. The Charter to D'Enambuc of 1626, like the Commission of Sieur de Monts for Acadia earlier in the century, had said nothing about the religion of the colonists and a significant minority of the first settlers were Protestants. Only a few secular priests were at Saint Christophe until the formation under Cardinal Richelieu's guidance of the Compagnie des îles d'Amérique in 1635. Under the new constitution only French Roman Catholics were to be allowed in the Antilles. There is ample evidence that this was not enforced, including a new and stronger edict of 1642 and the protests of priests of the religious orders who were now numerous in the islands, such as the historian J B Dutertre. Huguenot congregations met privately for worship, served at times by Walloon pastors. After the failure of the Compagnie in 1648 the islands came under proprietary rule by their governors. In 1654 even some Dutch Protestants and Jews were allowed to settle in Guadeloupe and Martinique.[107]

In 1664 the government of Louis XIV began to assert its control over the colonies through the Compagnie des Indes Occidentales, and ten years later direct royal government was instituted. New restrictions on Protestants and Jews were proclaimed. Those of "la religion prétendue reformée" were forbidden to meet even privately for worship. Yet persecution was not enforced with the vigour that was used in France itself. The frequency of the repetition of the royal orders is evidence of the reluctance with which they were applied. In spite of occasional instances of punishment the comparative tolerance in the West Indies increased the number of Huguenot refugees seeking freedom overseas though still within the French community.[108]

Early in 1685, seven months before the Revocation of the Edict of Nantes, the Code Noir ordered Jews to leave the colonies, banned all but Roman Catholic religious practices, and forbade marriage and thus legitimate birth to non-Catholics.[109] With the Revocation itself there came an influx of Huguenot prisoners transported for forced labour in the Antilles. However in the West Indies this persecution could not be maintained. Many escaped to English or Dutch islands or across the border in St Christopher. They received sympathy from French Catholic neighbours. By 1688 the worst was over. Instructions were received to relax the pressure.[110]

The Caribbean was a vital sector in the larger movement of Huguenot migration to the New World, before and after the Revocation. Following the return to France by the Treaty of Breda of parts of St Christopher overrun by the English, a number of French Protestants who had bought land there were allowed to remain. They were permitted to build a French Protestant church and to send for a minister.[111] Similarly, when the French part of the island was finally ceded to Great Britain by the Treaty of Utrecht, some French declared themselves Protestant landowners and requested to stay on under English rule.[112] Many Huguenots found their way to the more tolerant parishes in the French islands themselves, to other Caribbean islands, to Bermuda and to North America. One of them, Lewis Galdy in Jamaica, became well known through his marvellous escape at the time of the Port Royal earthquake, as later recorded on his tombstone. Father Labat, the tolerant priest-historian, at the turn of the century visited Huguenot refugees in Barbados, St Thomas and Saba.[113]

Puritans and Quakers (1655–1700)

Five years after the capture of Cromwell's colony of Jamaica, he himself was dead, as were many leaders who had shared in the "Western Design". New England had failed to respond with much enthusiasm to the Protector's invitation to send settlers, although 300 came from there. Most of those who did arrive, from various places, were ready to accept the Church favoured by the restored monarchy.

In the eastern Caribbean as well as Jamaica such nonconformists as there were lost influence after the Restoration. Some moved elsewhere, particularly to North American colonies where people of their own faith were active and where new colonies such as Carolina, New Jersey and Pennsylvania were offering inducements to settlers, including freedom of religion.[114] Puritanism seemed to lack the will to maintain an independent witness in the tropical master and slave society. A contemporary writer in Jamaica said in 1682: "We have very few papists or sectaries, for neither Jesuits nor nonconforming parsons do or can live amongst us: some few have attempted, but never could gain proselytes enough to afford them sustenance."[115] The position was not much different in the other islands.

There were however exceptions during the later seventeenth century to this general trend. Some Puritan ministers either continued to serve in parishes after the Restoration, came to the colonies after being ejected in England, or were invited from New England.[116] One episode is recorded of a dissenting congregation in Jamaica, started among some prisoners of war from the Monmouth rebellion who had been transported and sold as servants to work on estates near the east end of the island. This is a pioneer instance of Congregationalism in the West Indies but it lasted only a few years.[117]

Another Puritan, Thomas Bridges, played an interesting part in the development of the Bahama Islands. Beginning as "a conventicle preacher" in Jamaica he was discouraged there. After the Spanish capture and sack of New Providence in 1684 had caused it to be deserted, Bridges took a group of his followers from Jamaica two years later and succeeded in re-establishing the colony. The proprietors gave him a commission as governor of the Bahamas, but his stay was hardly long enough to place any Puritan stamp upon the islands.[118]

A decade later Barbados was visited by Francis Makemie, a minister of Scotch-Irish origin who afterward became famous as a successful pioneer of Presbyterianism in the North American colonies. His coming seems to have been a response to an application in 1678 to the Presbytery of Laggan (Northern Ireland) by one Captain Archibald Johnson for a Presbyterian minister for Barbados. During a lengthy stay in the island Makemie endeavoured to establish a common Protestant front with the Church of England, on serious theological grounds, by pointing to the Calvinist content of the Thirty-nine Articles. He published a book which was subtitled "a Pastoral letter to the Reformed Protestants, in Barbados" and dated "Barbados, December 28, 1697". It is a rare instance of a theological treatise written in the West Indies in colonial times.[119] Makemie's failure to gain a response on the basis of such arguments is a measure of the weakness of Calvinist tradition, whether Puritan, Scottish or Scotch-Irish, in the Caribbean at the end of the century.

In addition to conservative Puritans of Independent and Presbyterian persuasion, some from among the radical sects which arose in England in the Commonwealth period had found their way to the islands. "Anabaptists", "fanaticks". Quakers and "other dissenters" are mentioned occasionally in official correspondence. In Barbados, one "Captain Joseph Salmon, cobbler and anabaptist" – actually a Ranter, who was in controversy with the Quakers in the 1650s – seems to have maintained a cause until he was silenced by the despotic Governor Dutton in 1682.[120]

The radical group which made the most significant mark upon the history of the West Indies sprang from the preaching of George Fox. Nicknamed the Quakers, these revolutionary Christians were later known as the Society of Friends. In some ways, such as their rejection not only of Prayer Book worship and episcopacy but of the sacraments and of any paid clergy at all, Fox's followers seemed to be simply a more extreme form of Puritanism. But they also had a peace witness which would not bear arms under any circumstances, a strict refusal to take oaths or to pay tithes to the established Church, a radical equalitarianism, and a doctrine of "the Light of Christ in every man" (the Inner Light) associated with silent worship. In these respects Quakerism stood apart from the usual Puritan pattern as a distinct interpretation of Christianity.[121]

One asset that this group had in the New World was its independence of ordained clergy and reliance on the witness and preaching of ordinary members, both men and women. In 1655 two woman Quakers, Ann Austin and Mary Fisher, arrived in Barbados to proclaim the new faith. Other missionaries followed, such as Henry Fell in the following year.[122] The response was remarkable. Many people were "convinced" including some leading citizens, notably Lieutenant Colonel Rous, a former Roundhead leader, his son John, and Ralph Fretwell, a judge who consequently was removed from his position for refusing to take again the oath of office.[123] Barbados, partly because of its strategic location in the age of sail, became a "nursery of the truth". Within three years it sent missionaries to Nevis and to New England. One of them, William Leddra, was executed in Boston for his faith. Jamaica and later Antigua and Bermuda also had active Friends' meetings, but St Christopher and Montserrat do not seem to have been penetrated. Their numbers were increased by the arrival in 1665 of over a hundred Quakers who had been imprisoned for boldly maintaining their witness in Restoration England and then transported to Jamaica, Barbados and Nevis.[124]

At first, during the time of the Commonwealth, the new sect was treated with tolerance, although Governor Searle in Barbados disliked their judgmental attitudes and D'Oyley in Jamaica wrote to England for advice as to whether they could be trusted.[125] During the following three decades however they were subjected to imprisonment, fines and other ill-treatment, particularly in Barbados, Nevis and Antigua, and during the 1680s in Jamaica. The common reasons for this were: "Their refusal to bear Arms or Fight; . . . Their constant Observance of the Precept of Christ, *Swear not at all*; . . . Their refusing to contribute to the Maintenance of the Priests by Law established, and towards the Charges of repairing the publick Worship-houses."[126] The prosecutions brought against Quakers from time to time, the special acts passed by some Assemblies, the punishments meted out, and the extra-legal actions taken by officers in some cases against them, are meticulously documented by their chroniclers.[127] These accounts not only depict the conflicts of Friends with the society around them but throw much light on conditions generally in the latter half of the seventeenth century.

The unpopularity of the early Quakers with other colonists was natural enough. Unwillingness to take oaths caused them to refuse the oath of allegiance to King Charles II, which was demanded in Barbados (before the king's own policy of releasing any but top officials from this oath became known). As a result thirty-six Friends were imprisoned in 1661.[128] In all the islands, in a time when able-bodied men were expected to drill in the militia to prepare against foreign attack, a group refusing to take part for religious reasons seemed disloyal and dangerous. In 1671 there were said to be as many as seven hundred of the militia in the Caribbee Islands who had turned Quakers and were refusing to fight.[129] Their attitude to the established Church also caused exasperation. On the one hand they tried to speak "prophetically" in the church services, only to be forcibly removed, or they posted "Warnings" in or on the building for the congregation to read.[130] On the other hand they refused to pay taxes either towards the stipends of the clergy or the upkeep of the church buildings, although willing to pay toward a fund for the poor, road building and customs, as well as erecting and maintaining their own Quaker meeting houses and looking after their own poor.[131] The "testimony" of refusing hat-honour, intended as a rebuke to human pride, also was an irritant. The authorities in Nevis responded by passing a law that "Whosoever for the future should come into any Court with his Hat on, should pay a Fine of 500 lb. of Sugar, or suffer a Month's Imprisonment".[132] All these peculiarities suggested that Quakers were enemies of an ordered society, and when they also invited blacks to their meetings and concerned themselves with the moral and spiritual welfare of the slaves, the suspicion was confirmed.

In spite of its unpopularity with most people the Quaker movement grew rapidly. Crowds gathered to hear visiting preachers, including George Fox himself in 1671, William Edmundson, and others. Five meeting houses were built in Barbados. Visitors mention Port Royal, Kingston and Spanish Town as Quaker centres in Jamaica, with small groups in Nevis, Antigua and Bermuda. Altogether there were several hundred converts and a good many sympathizers, enough to cause alarm to the authorities. Governor Kendall and the Assembly of Barbados in 1693, for example, considered them a serious threat to political power in the island.[133] Yet by the end of the century the growth of the Society of Friends had turned to decline. Some time in the eighteenth century it ceased to exist in the Caribbean.[134] Close links with Friends in Pennsylvania and other North American colonies led many to migrate there from the West Indies. Cooling of religious zeal, and social pressure from the militia law, the slave holding culture and the general moral laxity, completed the decline of the movement. Yet these early Friends by their very presence in the Caribbean, temporary though it was, bore a prophetic witness to new ideas which were ultimately to prove revolutionary in both Church and society, and this in three ways:

(i)   Conscientious refusal to pay taxes for the clergy and maintenance of the established Church (while paying their own religious expenses) was an early testimony for religious freedom and voluntary Church support as against the time honoured institution of a state favoured and tax supported Church.

(ii) Their insistence on inviting slaves to their religious meetings and "instructing" them in the Christian way of life challenged the refusal of the planters generally to share Christianity with the Africans.

(iii) The advice of George Fox to treat slaves well and after a time to emancipate them, and William Edmundson's doubts about slavery itself, although not immediately effective in causing Quakers to break with slavery, were the first whispers of that leadership later given by Friends in the anti-slavery movement.

These three themes, religious voluntaryism, evangelization, and emancipation, will play an important part in the following chapters. Here it is enough to note that the issues were raised as early as the seventeenth century. The Society of Friends thus has a significance out of proportion to its numbers in the history of the West Indian Church.

7

Sugar, Slavery and the Planters' Church (1655–1824)

The colonies of the earlier seventeenth century, as seen in the preceding chapter, were marked by ecclesiastical disorganization and considerable religious diversity. This diversity continued during the rest of the century but on a diminishing scale, as Puritan influence declined.

By the third quarter of the century three developments presaged a new period in the life of the Church, in an era which coincided with the long heyday of slavery and planter dominance in the West Indies. These were:

(i) the revolution brought about by sugar cultivation and a social structure which virtually excluded slaves from the Christian community;

(ii) the enlargement of the English-speaking colonial area to include Jamaica, and the establishment throughout this area of the Church of England as the predominant ecclesiastsical body; and

(iii) the institution of direct royal government in 1660, under which the monarch as nominal head of the Church, together with the bishop of London and later also the Society for the Propagation of the Gospel (SPG), maintained some shadowy authority in ecclesiastical and social affairs – an authority however which was resisted in a number of ways by the colonial plantocracy.

Planters, Slaves and the Church

The colonization of the Caribbee Islands had begun with tobacco culture and a labour force of indentured white servants. Plantations were small and both masters and servants were at least nominally Christian English, Welsh, Scottish and Irish.[1]

The shift to a master and slave society took place first in Barbados in the 1640s. When Richard Ligon lived in the island (1647–50) the transition was well advanced and he described the lot of servants, slaves and masters with vivid contemporary detail.[2] Oppression of the white servants was severe enough to provoke at least two attempts at bloody rebellion.[3] Governor Bell's laws endeavoured to enforce church attendance by servants as well as masters, but it may be suspected that Christian fellowship in the Church in those days left much to be desired. Of course after their indenture, ex-servants could slowly identify themselves with the master class by owning slaves or at least by working as artisans on large estates. Others managed to exist by subsistence farming, took up buccaneering, returned to the British Isles or migrated to North America.[4] With the scarcity of Roman Catholic priests, many of the Irish gradually conformed to the Church of England, or (in the Leeward Islands) moved to French territory and became identified with the French.[5] As slaves were introduced, the lot of "Christian servants" improved since they were wanted as security guards and soldiers for the militia. The chronic need for more such "deficiency men" against the French military threat and slave revolt, is reflected in the many attempts to secure their immigration and the passing of "Deficiency Laws".[6] Many of these men and many of the planters themselves, found mistresses among the slaves, producing an increasing number of mulatto slaves and a new class of "free people of colour". These took their place in the class and colour hierarchy of island society.[7]

In Barbados the African population probably exceeded the European late in the 1650s.[8] By 1673 there were more blacks than whites in Jamaica, and a few years later the balance tipped in the Leeward Islands.[9] In the coastland frontier of the time, Antigua and Jamaica (and also South Carolina) were populated in part by migration from Barbados and Nevis, the colonies where land was scarce and large estate owners were buying out smaller operators.[10] As planters migrated they took with them the pattern of Church life which they had known.

The darkest blot upon the established Church in the West Indies in this era is its failure to do anything effective about the physical or spiritual welfare of the slaves. Today this seems incredible. For the seventeenth century however, the ancient institution of slavery remained unchallenged by churches or governments. Only rare individuals dared to question it in principle, although the enslavement of fellow Christians was condemned.[11]

Portugal, Spain and France, still in contact with the slavery of the Mediterranean world and following the official Roman Catholic teaching with reference to it, had no difficulty about bringing African slaves into their colonies, took steps to ensure their baptism and some Christian teaching, and (less consistently) legislated certain principles of humane care for them.

The approach to the problem in English, Dutch and Danish colonies was different. In northern Europe slavery and also serfdom had withered away, due mainly to socioeconomic developments, even before the rise of Protestantism cut off these nations from strict conformity to Roman Catholic traditions. In the predominantly Protestant colonies, while the exploitation of slaves went on as elsewhere, there seemed to be more difficulty in harmonizing it with prevailing social and religious conceptions.[12] Instead of the rationalization that slavery was justified as a means of saving the souls of these Africans, the idea that it was not lawful to hold fellow Christians as chattels was used as an excuse for barring slaves from baptism.

The earliest record of this attitude is the often-quoted story which Richard Ligon tells of his attempt in Barbados to help a slave become a Christian. In the course of a friendly conversation with an African known as Sambo about the wonders of the compass, Ligon found that he wanted to be a Christian "for, he thought to be a Christian, was to be endued with all those knowledges he wanted". Ligon carried the request to "the Master of the Plantation":

> But his answer was, That the people of that Iland were governed by the Lawes of England, and by those Lawes we could not make a Christian a slave. I told him, my request was . . . to make a slave a Christian. His answer was, That . . . being once a Christian, he could no more account him a Slave, and so lose the hold they had of them as Slaves, by making them Christians; and . . . all the Planters in the Iland would curse him. So I was struck mute, and poor *Sambo* kept out of the Church; as ingenious as honest, and as good a natur'd poor soul, as ever wore black, or eat green.[13]

A few years later one of the leaders of the West India Expedition wrote from Barbados that the masters "strive to keep their slaves in ignorance, thereby thinking to make them hopelesse of freedom". He adds:

> It would grieve your heart to talke with the nigor slaves in the island, and especially with thos that are most ingenious, with whom I have had some discourse; and asking them, whether they know God, they sayd noe. I asked them, whither they went when they died; they said to the ground, and noe whither else . . . I asked them, why they would not be Christians? They sayd, they could get nobody to teach them. I asked them, whether they were willing to learne? They said, with all their hearts, which I must confess strucke me to the heart.[14]

The status under English law of slaves who became Christians was a problem which remained unsettled for some decades.[15] Churchmen concerned for their Christianizing, as well as slave owners and legislators anxious to safeguard "rights of property", undertook to make it clear that conversion and baptism did not mean emancipation.

Some enquiries by the Lords of Trade and Plantations about the baptizing of slaves were gingerly dropped, after an unfavourable reception from Barbados. Thereupon the bishop of London, Henry Compton, prepared in 1680 a "memorandum concerning the Church" which included the reassurance that the "apprehensions of planters that the conversion of slaves may deprive the owners of their present power and disposal of them" are to be "dispelled as groundless".[16]

The most definitive pronouncement on the point by a Protestant churchman was in the letters of the bishop of London in 1727 "To the masters and mistresses of families in the English plantations abroad" and "To the missionaries there", which among other things replied to the widespread objection of planters to the baptizing of slaves:

> Christianity, and the embracing of the Gospel, does not make the least Alteration in Civil Property, or in any of the Duties which belong to Civil Relations; but in all these Respects, it continues Persons just in the same State as it found them. The Freedom which Christianity gives, is a Freedom from the Bondage of Sin and Satan, and from the Dominion of Mens Lusts and Passions and inordinate Desires; but as to their *outward* Condition, whatever that was before, whether bond or free, their being baptized, and becoming Christians, makes no manner of Change in it.[17]

The apprehension of the planters was allayed somewhat by positive laws passed by several colonial legislatures including the Jamaica Act for the Better Ordering of Slaves (1696), specifying that the status of slaves was unchanged by baptism, and in 1729 by a legal opinion to the same effect by Yorke and Talbot, attorney general and solicitor general in Great Britain.[18]

The legal question was not the only argument of the planters for opposing the Christianizing of their slaves. A deputation of "gentlemen of Barbadoes" in 1680 declared to the Lords of Trade and Plantations in London

> that the conversion of their slaves to Christianity would not only destroy their property but endanger the island, inasmuch as converted negroes grow more perverse and intractable than others, and hence of less value for labour or sale. The disproportion of blacks to white being great, the whites have no greater security than the diversity of the negroes' languages, which would be destroyed by conversion, in that it would be necessary to teach them all English.[19]

The following year the Barbados Assembly, refusing to take any action towards the conversion of slaves, said simply that they were "incapable" of becoming Christian due to "their savage brutishness", adding (not very seriously) that "if a good expedient could be found, the Assembly and people would be ready to promote it".[20]

Much detailed evidence concerning the attitudes of planters at this date may be gathered from the writings of Morgan Godwyn, an Anglican clergyman who spent some time in Barbados and Virginia in the 1670s. In his *Negro's and Indians Advocate*, written in Barbados, he undertook to expose and refute the arguments of those who either declared the conversion of the blacks impracticable, castigated it as

"Popish Supererrogation", or (more commonly) simply resisted on the ground that it would diminish their profit or threaten their safety. The refusal of Christianity to the slaves is shown to be a well recognized custom, supported by some at least with the rationalization that the Negro was not fully human.[21] Godwyn's efforts to combat these views will appear in the next chapter.

The Bermuda Assembly as well as "the gentlemen of Barbadoes" voiced the belief that Christian slaves were less docile than others: "We have long endeavoured the conversion of negroes to Christianity, but find that the greater their instruction in religion, the greater their insolence, obstinacy and incorrigibleness."[22] This belief was so widespread that Bishop Gibson, in his *Letters* already referred to, undertook to argue that on the contrary Christianity made better slaves.[23]

Candidly, Governor Russell of Barbados wrote home that "the keeping of Christian holy days will be the great obstacle, most of the planters thinking Sundays too much to be spared from work".[24] Bishop Gibson's Letter also dealt with the objection "that no Time can be spared from the daily Labour and Employment of the Negroes, to instruct them in the Christian Religion", and expostulated against requiring them to work on the Lord's Day.[25]

Again and again throughout the eighteenth and early nineteenth centuries, reports and letters from concerned clergy and others witness to the persistence of the planters' objection to Christianizing of their slaves. Dr Francis Le Jau, for example, with experience in Montserrat and St Kitts, reported from the latter island in 1705:

> The negroes, of whom there were 2,000 in his three parishes, were 'sensible and well disposed to learn'; but were made stubborn by 'the barbarity of their masters'. . . . If a minister proposed the negroes should be 'instructed in the Christian faith, have necessarys' &c the planters became angry and answered 'it would consume their profit'. They also objected 'that baptism makes negroes free'; but Dr Le Jau believed the true ground of their objection was that they would be 'obliged to look upon them as Christian brethren and use 'em with humanity'.[26]

As late as 1808 Colin Donaldson, a clergyman in Jamaica, when commending a tract of Bishop Porteous on the religious instruction of slaves "was told that the bishop had no business interfering with the rights of private property".[27]

Most of the clergy simply made no attempt to reach the slaves, either because they shared the planters' attitude or because they did not dare to defy it. It must be added that some claimed to have attempted religious teaching without success, concluding that this was due to the incapacity of the Africans. This included certain of those appointed by the SPG to instruct the slaves on the Codrington estates.[28] On the other hand persons like Ligon, Berkenhead and Le Jau who approached the slaves as human beings worthy of becoming Christian comment upon their rational and moral qualities as well as their readiness to respond to teaching.[29] Even in the 1780s this belief was still having to be argued by advocates of conversion and better treatment of slaves, some of whom by this time were looking forward to an end of the slavery system itself.[30]

In 1723 a questionnaire from Bishop Gibson to the clergy of the colonies asked among other things what means were used for the conversion of "any Infidels, bond or free, within your parish". The replies from the West Indies were not encouraging. In only three of twenty-eight parishes responding was the claim made that any slaves had been converted.[31]

By common consent historians, both religious and secular, have written off the established Church in the West Indies in the slavery period as a mere travesty of what a Church should be.[32] This verdict must stand. It was a Church in which the values and lifestyle of a vested interest, that of the planters, held control. As such, it was without a sense of mission and with little concern for the standards of Christian morality. Although part of the cultural link of Englishmen with the traditions of the past, in its transplantation the spiritual roots had been broken.

Yet this is not the whole truth. There were a few significant exceptions to the general trend even in the West Indies. Contact with the Church in the mother country kept alive some awareness of the deeper meaning of the Christian religion, although it too was at a low ebb spiritually in the late seventeenth and early eighteenth century.[33] Three components of the Anglican tradition – the monarch as supreme governor of the Church with his advisors, the episcopate, and (after 1701) the royally chartered SPG – exerted some influence in spite of geographical distance. They will be considered after an outline of the shaping of the planters' church.

The Established Church in the Islands

The captured colony of Jamaica had a difficult beginning. Sickness and indiscipline among the occupying troops slowed the commencement of ordered life. For some years the island was under martial law because Spanish resistance continued in the mountains and on the north coast. During this period escaped slaves of the Spaniards formed the core of the Maroon settlements in the centre of the island.[34] Cromwell offered inducements to settlers, specifying that they were to be Protestants only, and some began to come.[35] Several clergymen who had come to Jamaica, including Thomas Gage, died or departed to England and a group of army officers wrote the Protector begging for at least one replacement to be sent out.[36]

After 1660 the Spanish threat was withdrawn and Governor D'Oyley was confirmed in his position by the restored Charles II, with instructions "to discountenance and punish drunkenness and debauchery, and give the best encouragement to ministers that Christianity and the Protestant Religion, according to the profession of the Church of England, may have due reverence and exercise".[37] Because of its buccaneering base at Port Royal, Jamaica's early years had a style more colourful than that of the Leewards and Barbados, and until the 1692 earthquake the church in the port-city looked around with some dismay upon the prevalent "debauchery".[38] At the same time planters from the Leeward Islands and elsewhere were acquiring new land in large tracts for sugar cultivation in other parts of the island. As already noted, they also transplanted the attitudes and the parochial church patterns familiar to the older plantation colonies.

For several years (1664–70) of this formative period the governor was Sir Thomas Modyford who had been a leading figure in Barbadian affairs and for a short time had been governor there. While very much an opportunist and not a deeply religious man himself, Modyford nevertheless was instrumental in taking some early steps in the establishment of the Church. The first elected Assembly in 1664 passed an Act for the maintenance of the ministry. Another set up seven parishes. They occupied about a third of the island in the south-eastern region. A little later other parishes were defined, farther west along the south shore and on the north coast, leaving two unnamed areas near the centre and at the extreme north-west.[39]

According to a report by Modyford in 1671 there were then only four ministers on the island, in St Katherine's, Port Royal, St John's and St Andrew's, although St Thomas and St David's in the eastern end had shared a minister until he died. He adds that

> the plantations are at such a distance that it is impossible to make up congregations; but they meet at each others houses, as the primitive Christians did, and there pray, read a chapter, sing a psalm, and home again; so that did not the accessors to this island come so well instructed in the articles of our faith, it might well be feared the Christian religion would be quite forgot.[40]

How widespread or how long-lasting was this kind of religious vitality among the laity cannot be known, for such informal gatherings for worship leave little permanent record. It is interesting that Governor Stapleton of the Leeward Islands in the following year informed the home government that only Nevis had "some few ministers and schoolmasters" but that in the other islands "parents and housekeepers endeavour the instruction of their own families".[41] Doubtless the seventeenth century Church owed much in its remoter parishes to the spontaneous expression of religious faithfulness by lay people, both in maintaining some kind of worship and teaching when no clergy were available and in supporting the latter

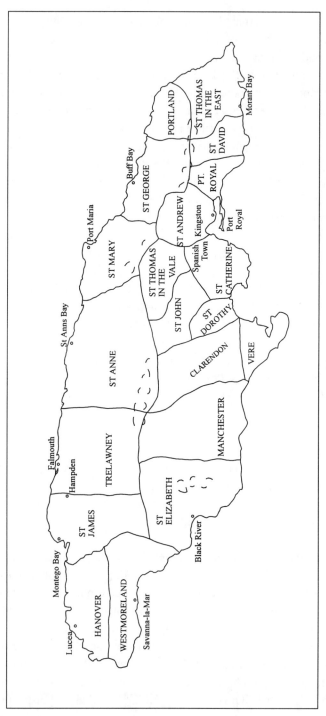

Jamaica before 1870

when they arrived. Yet the significance of Modyford's remarks lies also in the closing hint that the survival of Christianity in the plantation economy was dependent upon new accessions of both laity and clergy from outside. The master and slave society in itself did not nourish the Christian faith.

In 1675 the next governor Sir Thomas Lynch indicated that, out of fourteen parishes in the island, only four were supplied with ministers and two years later two of these were petitioning the king in Council for action to receive their salaries.[42] After another four years however considerable improvement had taken place. Deputy Governor Sir Henry Morgan (the ex-buccaneer) wrote:

> In St Thomas there is a church and minister; in St David's the like; both at Port Royal, and so in St Andrews's; a church and minister in St Katherine's the like in St John's; a church building in St Dorothy's but yet no minister; a minister in Clarendon and the church building; in St Elizabeth's a minister but no church; for all the parishes on the north side neither church nor minister. The settlements there are not much above five years' standing, but they improve much and will provide for their religion as soon as their condition will stand the charge. The burial and christenings are difficult to return where there is no registry. Being at a distance the people bury in their plantations and forbear christening some years till the accidental arrival of a minister.[43]

This catalogue of eight ministers and the same number of church buildings reflects both the development of the Church in Jamaica itself and also no doubt the support of the Lords of Trade and Plantations and the bishop of London who (as will shortly be seen) showed active concern during this period for the state of the Church in the colonies.[44]

During the 1680s a comprehensive Church Act and a Supplemental Act were passed to require the election of vestries and churchwardens, provide taxation for the Church and the poor, set minimum stipends, ensure the registration of "Births, Christenings, Marriages and Burials," and direct other parochial affairs. Later it was found necessary to add "An Act for the Encouragement of good and able Ministers to come to this island" (1707), raising clergy stipends (except at Port Royal where earthquake and fire had reduced the importance of the parish), and permitting vestries to pay substantial bonuses at their discretion.[45]

While in Jamaica the Church was thus slowly finding its feet, in Barbados and the Leewards it was struggling to emerge after the Restoration from the somewhat disorganized state of the proprietary and interregnum periods.

Wealthy Barbados, where the parishes were strongest, took the lead. In May 1661 the Council reported that ten of the eleven parishes had ministers but some were unordained. It asked the archbishop of Canterbury to send "some able religious ministers", offering each 12,000 lb. of sugar yearly "besides other conveniences". Later in the year an Act was passed by the Assembly "for the Encouragement of all faithful Ministers" providing a stipend of one pound of sugar per acre annually to be paid without fail to the minister of each parish and allowing vestries to supplement this, "due Respects being to be shown to the Merits of each".[46] Thus the Assembly asserted some oversight of the vestries, perhaps because of dissatisfaction with their power over the individual clergymen, and prescribed a minimum standard of ministerial support. In 1705 a new Clergy Act set a minimum stipend of 150 pounds plus "Mansion House and glebe" where existing, together with fees and "farther Additions" by the vestry "as any Ministers may merit", thereby giving some at least of the Barbados clergy a very adequate income.[47]

Conditions were not so prosperous for the Church in the Leeward Islands. Here sugar cultivation was not as far advanced and here also the French attacks on English St Christopher, Antigua and Montserrat in 1666–67 destroyed property including some churches, led to displacement of population, and crippled agriculture. Ten years later Christopher Jeaffreson wrote of the situation in St Kitts: "twenty yeares' peace will hardly resettle the devastation of one yeares' warre".[48] It is not surprising that Sir Charles Wheler, arriving in 1671 as first governor of the separate jurisdiction of the Leeward Islands, found an unsatisfactory ecclesiastical situation: according to his famous quip, he found "one drunken orthodox priest, one drunken sectary priest, and one drunken parson who had no orders".[49] Five years later his successor was to report a total of ten churches, five ministers and need of six more who could be supported, although if all parishes were supplied fifteen or more would be required.[50]

Wheler had had a genuine concern for the Church and evolved a plan which might have made a vast difference to the West Indian Church if it had been seriously considered by authorities at home. He advocated the sending out to the colonies of young ministers in rotation, along with a master from Cambridge University as bishop who would also found a college to produce locally trained clergy. They could then be ordained on the spot without taking the long journey to England for this purpose. Thus early was the need of local theological training and also of episcopal leadership in the Caribbean identified. But Wheler was recalled on another matter and his vision lost.[51] In Jamaica another thoughtful layman, Sir Thomas Lynch who was twice governor there, had a less elaborate suggestion resembling the later commissary system:

> if the King would affix to that island two considerable prebendaries, as of Eton, Westminster, Lincoln, &c, such persons by the Bishop of London's directions might have a superintendance of Church affairs, keep people in their duty, convert sectaries, and suppress atheism and irreligion, which people there much incline to.[52]

Due to inertia on both sides of the Atlantic these early proposals to found a disciplined organization for the colonial Church came to nothing at the time.

Instead of Wheler's plans for long-term reform, the Leewards were supplied with the pragmatic leadership of Governor William Stapleton who (although accused of being a secret Roman Catholic) succeeded, in co-operation with the Lords of Trade and Plantations, in bringing in several new clergymen.[53] While still deputy governor of Montserrat he had seen to the passing of "An Act for the raising of maintenance for a preaching Minister, &c" (1668). In 1681 Nevis made similar provision for clergy, and Antigua defined its parishes. The Church was now established in the current style.[54] Under subsequent governors more elaborate legislation was passed such as Antigua's Church Act of 1692 and the Leeward Islands "Act to secure the Payment of Ministers Dues" of 1705.[55]

By this last-mentioned Act – unlike those of Barbados and Jamaica where the clergy were paid in local currency – the standard stipend was still "Sixteen Thousand Pounds of good Merchantable Muscovadoe Sugar" and there was no mention of supplemental payments. Payment in kind was unreliable, and even the local currency was subject to fluctuation.

On the other hand in the Caribbean we do not hear of vestry presentation of ministers or of the policy for which Virginia was notorious, the hiring of ministers on a year to year basis without presenting them to the governor for induction and thereby for security of tenure. The colonial governors normally made the appointments of clergy to the parishes. Indeed some governors were accused of selling presentations. Occasionally, however, vestries objected to particular appointments, and of course their discretion to give or withhold the "Supplement" was a powerful tool for keeping clergymen in line.[56]

The replies to Bishop Gibson's seventeen "Queries" of 1723 are among the Fulham Papers. Unhappily those from the West Indies are incomplete: 10 of 11 Barbados parishes reported, 12 of 19 in Jamaica, but only 5 of 24 in the Leewards, none of these from St Christopher. Nevertheless they provide a fairly representative sampling of the established Church after its pattern had been formed in the slave society, and before the breezes of eighteenth century humanitarianism had begun to produce mild waves on the surface of its complacency. On the basis of 28 returns out of 54 parishes a few observations may be made.[57]

Twenty-five parishes offering figures on the number of families report a total of 4,163 (excluding 88 Jewish in Jamaica, and 69 Roman Catholic in two Montserrat parishes). This is an average of 166 Protestant families to a parish. If this average holds for the remaining parishes – which is doubtful – the total number of families would be a little under 9,000. The total white population at this time for the West Indies was estimated at 36,695.[58] While the average figure of four persons per "family" would not appear excessive, such data as we have for the free population of the West Indies in the eighteenth century show that the number of children falls markedly below the number of adults.[59] This fact implies a difference between population figures calculated from these clergy returns and those from government sources, which may be attributed to the usual shortfall in ecclesiastical statistics compared with census figures, and perhaps in part to omission of single white adults such as servants or inclusion of them in their master's "family". In any case the potential church constituency was in those days considered to be the same as the white population, and this was less than 40,000. Nor was there a normal increase as time went by. Only in Jamaica did the number of whites increase notably during the eighteenth century – to about 25,000 in 1786 – and even there it fell off afterward.[60] Clearly as long as the African slaves were given no place in the church, its numbers would be small and virtually static.

Not only so but the proportion of whites who were interested in religion was small. Only ten parish clergy attempted to estimate their Sunday church attendance and their congregations averaged 39. These do not include, however, the large centres of Kingston, Spanish Town and Bridgetown which must have had considerably larger numbers. Ministers in four other parishes describe their congregations' attendance as "good". Others use the terms "most", "fair", "not good", "less than one fifth", "one third", "few of the richer sort", or "most Protestants" (in Montserrat where Catholics were numerous). One minister, who had no church building, said that often only his own family attended the service held in the parsonage. Another, whose service varied from 10 to 40 people, added that at Christmas and Easter 100 to 150 turned up. The number of communicants at the Lord's Supper varied from a dozen or less in most rural parishes to 50 in Kingston and Bridgetown.[61]

The almost complete lack of response to Bishop Gibson's "Queries" about schools and libraries draws attention to the want of intellectual content in the culture of the planter community.[62] The paucity of educational facilities, the absence of any university, the callousness ingrained by slave ownership, low moral standards, heavy drinking, display of wealth and love of pleasure, early mortality and absenteeism were characteristics of the society which militated against a healthy cultural and religious life.[63]

This cultural and ecclesiastical pattern, together with the social stratification which went with it, continued with remarkably little change through a century and three quarters.[64] Over ninety years after Gibson's Queries a British House of Commons publication reported ecclesiastical data (among other things) on the West Indies. The established Church had changed little in almost a hundred years. Even the stipend of clergymen in St Christopher is reported still as "16,000 pounds weight of Sugar . . . exclusive of all Surplice Fees", an ironic symbol of the conservatism of the planters' Church.[65] By this time there were a few new but isolated benefices of the Church of England in the Windward Islands (taken from the French), the Bahamas (which became a royal colony in 1718), Guiana and elsewhere. Of these new territories only Grenada had more than one Anglican clergyman.

The activity of nonconformist missions and the establishment of episcopates in Barbados and Jamaica in 1824 emphatically changed the Church of England at last. But at the very time of the arrival of the bishops a churchman-observer, Richard Bickell, was still deploring the religious indifference, want of missionary zeal, moral laxity and lack of dedicated leadership within the Church, and of inhumanity within the social structure, as had been denounced by prophetic voices a century and a half before.[66]

The Royal Instructions and West Indian Society

The planters' church was a prime example of the so-called Erastian principle of the subordination of ecclesiastical to secular power. But in the colonial situation it was far from clear where this power lay. King and Parliament were both far across the ocean. They might assert their authority in matters political and there was little question that the British navy had the final word in the island-world of the West Indies. Yet seventeenth century political events in England had opened the way for a measure of self-government through the colonial assemblies, and when it came to religious affairs there was not the will to govern them strictly from afar.

The real control of the established Church was in the hands of the governor, the island assemblies and the parochial vestries. These laymen – occasionally one or more of the clergy also played a part in the game of local politics – might quarrel among themselves, but they were united in managing church matters with a view to upholding the existing order of society. This included the defence of "property rights" in slaves and their virtual exclusion from the Church. It will be shown that it also included resistance to any form of ecclesiastical discipline, at least over the laity.[67] These two prejudices led in turn to a deep suspicion of episcopal authority, and to a firm rejection of unwelcome initiatives from England, royal or otherwise, whenever they appeared to threaten the existing social structure.

These conditions accepted, the planters and their allies (including attorneys for absentee owners, merchants and professional men, military officers and government officials) were loyal to the religious tradition of their nation. They took pride that their Church was modelled on the Church of England with its vestries, church wardens and church taxes, and with clergy drawn mostly from the mother country. The parishes in the Caribbean were recognized as in principle under the hierarchical structure of that Church, of which the monarch was "supreme governor" and the episcopate a vital part. Ultimately it was the tie to the home country that transformed the established Church in the era of emancipation, with the extension of the episcopacy to the West Indies as the focal point of this change.

The governor in each colony was "the Ordinary", a sort of lay bishop. Not only did he have specific jurisdiction in the three matters of probate of wills, granting of licences for marriage and collating benefices, but he often exerted other authority over the Church, either on the basis of royal instructions in specified matters or simply by personal initiative as the king's representative.[68] The personality and churchmanship of the incumbent governors were therefore of considerable importance for the Church, and they were by no means always helpful.

When at the Restoration royal government replaced Cromwellian rule in Jamaica and proprietary authority in the Caribbee islands, the colonies came directly under the king's prerogative. The king in Council, not Parliament, was the authority. Moreover the monarch was nominally head of the Church of England. The later Stuarts took a personal interest in colonial affairs but after the Revolution control passed into the hands of political party (usually Whig) leaders.[69] In practice business was transacted by the Privy Council operating through committees under various names; the Council for Foreign Plantations (1660–72), the Council of Trade and Foreign Plantations (1672–74), the Lords Committee of Trade and Plantations (1675–96), the Board of Trade (1696 to mid eighteenth century). These bodies drafted commissions and royal instructions for the governors, including directions on religious and moral affairs.[70]

The royal instructions to the governors provide the outlines of official policy with regard to the Church in the colonies, and these orders, although not always successfully implemented, underlie many developments in ecclesiastical as well as political affairs in the Old Empire.[71] These and related documents show that the main outlines of metropolitan intention with regard to ecclesiastical and moral affairs were drawn up in the first three decades after the Restoration. The most fertile period was the decade 1675–85, the time of greatest activity of the Lords of Trade and Plantations, and of Bishop Henry Compton's involvement in their affairs.[72] The basic principles laid down in this early generation were repeated, usually in identical words, for a century and longer.

In 1660 Charles II had set up his Council for Foreign Plantations with instructions

most especially to take an effectuall care of the propogacôn of the Gospell in the severall Forraine Plantacôns, by provideing that there be good encouragement settled for the invitacôn and maintenance of lerned and orthodox ministers, and by sending strict orders and injunccôns for the regulating and reforming the debaucheries of planters and servants, whose ill example doth bring scandall upon Christianitie, and deterr such as yet are not admitted thereunto, from affecting or esteeming it. And you are to consider how such of the Natives or such as are purchased by you from other parts to be servants or slaves may be best invited to the Christian Faith, and be made capable of being baptized thereunto; it being to the honoʳ of our Crowne and of the Protestant Religion that all persons in any of our Dominions should be taught the knowledge of God, andbe made acquainted with the misteries of Salvation.[73]

Here we find three objectives of major concern to the royal administration of the colonies:

(i) The encouragement of religion in accordance with the faith and practice of the Church of England;
(ii) The prevention of vice and regulation of morals;
(iii) the conversion of Africans and Amerindians to the Christian faith.
Two other themes emerged shortly afterward:
(iv) The declaration of "liberty of conscience" and of a somewhat qualified religious toleration; and
(v) The humane treatment of servants and slaves.

The first of these objectives was mentioned, as has been seen, in instructions to Governor D'Oyley of Jamaica early in 1661. His successor, Lord Windsor, received similar orders the following year.[74] When proprietary government in the Caribbee Islands was ended in 1663 and Francis Lord Willoughby designated as first royal governor there, he was likewise charged:

> to take especial care that the Gospel be preached and propagated according to the doctrine of the Church of England, that Divine service be decently and reverently celebrated, and the Sacraments duly administered; that there be a settled provision for encouragement and invitation of learned and orthodox ministers, and bounds set out for parishes and churches erected in the several islands to which he shall present clerks well known for loyalty, learning and piety.[75]

Although the first "standard" instructions for the West Indies on this subject, beginning in 1680, spoke only of providing "good and sufficient stipends and allowances" for ministers, they were amplified in 1689 along the lines of the above directions (of 1663) but specifying also – what was certainly implied earlier – the use of the Book of Common Prayer.[76]

More specific ecclesiastical measures were laid down. Beginning in 1678 governors were forbidden to prefer any minister to a benefice unless certified by the bishop of London. Shortly afterward they were directed to make enquiry concerning the ordination or otherwise of the clergy already in office and to report on this to the bishop. Schoolmasters were also required to have the bishop's licence.[77] The special authority of the bishop of London implied in these injunctions was made explicit in 1685, when governors began to be instructed to encourage the exercise of the ecclesiastical jurisdiction of the bishop of London "so far as conveniently may be", with the exception of "the collating of benefices, granting licences for marriages, and probate of wills", long reserved for the governor himself.[78] The clause "so far as conveniently may be" and the division of episcopal powers between bishop and governor left sufficient ambiguity for dispute through the years, especially when bishops began to delegate "commissaries" to exercise some of their "jurisdiction" in the colonies.

As a result of Compton's discovery of the treatment some clergy were receiving from their vestries, which tended to regard them simply as employees, it was enjoined that each minister should be made a member of the vestry.[79] Orders were also given to provide every church with copies of the Church of England table of marriages, the Thirty-nine Articles and the Book of Homilies, and to see that they were duly used.[80] Some of the Homilies, for example those dealing with the use of Sunday, and with sexual morality, must have sounded challenging when (and if) they were read in these churches of the plantation society.

This brings us to the second objective of official policy, the regulation of morals. Royal authority was invoked to reinforce the tradition of strict legislation in matters of personal conduct which was observed (in Virginia, Bermuda, Barbados and the Leewards) in the preceding chapter.[81] There was one difference, however: in line with the policy of "liberty of conscience" no mention was made in these royal instructions of the enforcement of church attendance. The list of proscribed vices began with "drunkenness and debauchery". Modyford in 1664 found "swearing and blasphemy" added, and he as well as Lord Windsor before him were charged to give public trust or employment to no one "whose ill-fame may bring scandal thereupon".[82] The standard instructions for about sixty years followed this wording, with the later addition of a positive side, "the encouragement of virtue and good living", and the purpose that by good example "the infidels may be invited and desire to partake of the Christian religion".[83] Whether there were any results by way of reform from these injunctions would be difficult to show, but they were not spectacularly successful.

In 1727 Bishop Gibson submitted to the king a petition that he should "send instructions to the governors of all the several plantations in America that they cause all laws already made against blasphemy, profaneness, adultery, fornication, polygamy, incest, profanation of the Lord's Day, swearing and drunkenness in their respective governments to be executed". In addition more effective laws were recommended for the purpose of punishing the aforesaid vices, and it was proposed to use the churchwardens as accusers "in the temporal courts of the several parishes at proper times of the year to be appointed for that purpose", and to establish schools for the teaching of reading and the principles of religion.[84] This enlarged definition of the moral problems of the colonies was no doubt inspired by reports which the bishop had received from the various territories.[85] The authorities in England were becoming more aware of the nature of the master and slave society with its sexual exploitation and its disregard of the day of rest and worship, and they hoped by a royal fiat to remedy it. Yet they failed to grasp how deeply ingrained in the life of the dominant class were these lax standards – so far that it was ironical to appeal to their church officers to enforce the virtues that had been widely abandoned.[86]

The third objective of royal policy, the conversion of non-Christians, has been (and will be) discussed in other contexts. Both Charles II and James II personally were convinced of the importance of it, partly at least through their close contact with the Spanish and French courts where this aspect of colonial policy was emphasized. Soon after his accession James, expressing the desire "that the negroes in the Plantations should all be baptized", inveighed against "that impiety of their masters prohibiting it, out of a mistaken opinion that they would be *ipso facto* free".[87] His reign was too short and troubled for the matter to be pursued but if he had, characteristically, tried to force action on it he would certainly have come into conflict with the slave owners in the colonies.

As colonial affairs came increasingly under Whig government after 1688 the ideal of Christianization was maintained, but discreetly. The royal instructions begun in 1680 were repeated decade after decade requiring each governor "with the assistance of the council and assembly to find out the best means to facilitate and encourage the conversion of Negroes and other slaves to the Christian religion". Sometimes the stipulation was added: "wherein you are to have a due caution and regard to the property of the inhabitants and the safety of the colony".[88] This was an easy escape clause which, combined with the attitude of the plantocracy, made the official policy a dead letter.

The fourth objective of royal policy, liberty of conscience and a somewhat qualified toleration of non-Anglican religion, has been seen as already characteristic of attitudes in the non-Spanish Caribbean. Perhaps the first indication of its becoming a royal policy for the colonies is in the Minutes of the Committee of Plantations in June 1662 where it was resolved "that liberty of conscience be granted to all that shall plant in Surinam". In October the same year Lord Windsor, doubtless with official approval, made a proclamation of religious freedom in Jamaica.[89] In 1664 it was included in Sir Thomas Modyford's instructions for the same island, and the first governors appointed in the following decade to the Leewards and Barbados likewise were told to protect those with "scruples in conscience" from "any discouragement there". In all these colonies in this initial stage the oaths of allegiance and supremacy were to be dispensed with, except for the Council. After 1680, however (barring the reign of James) "papists" were excluded from religious liberty.[90]

From time to time in the West Indies the fear of Roman Catholicism appears in legislation resembling that of England itself. This fear was more political than strictly religious. It was excited by such circumstances as the proximity of the Irish, an upsurge of Catholic activity in James II's time in Barbados and Jamaica and in the 1740s in the Leewards, and the recurring wars between Great Britain and France (and sometimes Spain also).[91] At the time of the Treaty of Utrecht (1713) a mutual agreement between France and Britain marked an advance in toleration, as French who wished to remain in territories ceded to the British were promised freedom to practice their Roman Catholic religion "entant que le permettent les loix de la Grand Bretagne". In return Louis XIV undertook to release Protestants condemned to the galleys on account of their faith.[92] In spite of this agreement the French in St Christopher were substantially evacuated as was perhaps inevitable after a half century of strife within this tiny island.[93] The problem of dealing with conquered Roman Catholic colonies in a more tolerant fashion was faced first therefore in the case of the Acadians left by the same treaty in Nova Scotia, rather than in the Antilles.[94]

By the Treaty of Paris (1763) Grenada and the Grenadines, Dominica, St Vincent and Tobago (which were placed by the British under a joint government known as "Grenada") were added to the British Empire, along with Quebec and the Floridas. The anti-"papist" bias of colonial policy was further relaxed in these territories, or at least changed to a more subtle plan of proselytizing through Protestant schools and land grants to converts, together with some restriction of Roman Catholic ecclesiastical privileges.[95]

From 1690 the established Church of Scotland had been reconstituted on a presbyterian rather than an episcopal basis. A Scottish attempt in 1701 to plant a colony in Darien failed. A few years later the union of England and Scotland took place, and gradually the number of Scots taking up sugar estates or otherwise migrating to the West Indies increased. For the most part they conformed to the Church of England, and a number of Scottish episcopalian clergymen also served in the established Church, including at least two who became commissaries.[96] However in Jamaica in 1813 a "meeting of wellwishers of the Presbyterian form of religion for the purpose of establishing a Presbyterian Place of Worship in Kingston" led to the founding of Scots Kirk in that city, and two years later the Church of Scotland in Demerara (later British Guiana) began its history with the organization of St Andrew's Kirk. Since the Church of Scotland was the established Church in northern Great Britain, both these congregations were supported financially by the local assemblies.[97]

When nonconformist evangelical missionaries began to win converts among the slaves late in the eighteenth century, intolerance and persecution of this movement by the planters were inspired by social rather than religious prejudice. This episode will be seen more fully in the next two chapters. The point to be noted now is that official policy in London consistently supported the missionaries and the principle of religious freedom for them, as against the hostility of the West Indian plantocracy.

As for the fifth objective of policy under royal government – humane treatment of servants and slaves – instructions to the governor of Barbados began to appear in 1673 asking for legislation "for the restraining of any inhumane severity which by ill masters or overseers may be used towards their Christian servants". "Slaves" were added for Jamaica in 1681.[98] Particular concern was expressed that no sufficient punishment was provided by law for the "willful killing of Indians and Negroes". This concern was repeated for decades without result until it was dropped from the instructions in 1756 in consequence of a letter from Governor Henry Grenville of Barbados stating that the legislature was unwilling to pass such a law "from the apprehension of the dangerous effects it might have on the spirits of the negroes, by lessening that awe in which they ought to stand to their Masters, and perhaps inciting them to Insurrections".[99]

In short, the royal instructions were fairly effective with regard to the two objectives which were in accord with the attitudes of the plantocracy: the encouragement of the Church of England and a qualified freedom of religion. They failed almost completely on the other three subjects which ran counter to the prejudices of the colonists: the regulation of morals, slave conversion, and the humane treatment of slaves.

The Bishop of London, Commissaries and a Colonial Episcopate

As a part of the Church of England overseas, the established Church in the West Indies until 1824 was under the care of the bishop of London, although strictly speaking not within his diocese. The intricate story of this relationship is too long to give here.[100] It is sufficient to say that the precedent of the bishop of London's jurisdiction originated in "the Stuart policy, instigated by Laud [who had been bishop of London before becoming archbishop] of seeking to extend the Church of England establishment to every part of the known world where the English government had a foothold".[101] After the Restoration the bishop of London began to participate in consultations on colonial affairs, but it was not until the accession of Henry Compton to the see in 1675 that measures were taken to affirm his ecclesiastical authority overseas.[102] Compton doubtless knew of reports such as those of Governors Lynch and Wheler asking for better ecclesiastical supervision, and the pamphlet *Virginia's Cure* (1662) addressed to his predecessor, Bishop Sheldon, concerning the needs of that colony.[103]

Immediately after taking office in 1676 Bishop Compton took several steps to improve ecclesiastical conditions. He instituted an inquiry by the Lords of Trade and Plantations into "the authority of the Bishop of London over foreign plantations" with a view to its clearer definition.[104] He studied the available evidence as to conditions in the colonies, and submitted to the same body in July 1677 a "Memorial of Abuses which are crept into the Churches of the Plantations".[105] This was followed by episcopal memoranda on the problems of the Church in Jamaica (1677) and Barbados (1680).[106]

From this energetic concern of Henry Compton came the developments of royal policy already described. The most specific power of the bishop himself, under this, was the authority to certify new clergy going to the colonies.[107] As time went on, this initial control over the selection of ministers going overseas proved to be the only episcopal authority which was exerted consistently. Even this was not always acknowledged by colonial governors and local law.[108] Once certified a clergyman was no longer under his control, and once inducted by the local governor only the most scandalous conduct could lead to dislodgement of an unsatisfactory incumbent of a parish.

For a little more than half a century the attempt was made to extend episcopal influence in America and the West Indies by the appointment of "commissaries", and this too was initiated in Compton's time. Although James Blair of Virginia is rightly regarded as the first firm appointment to this office in 1689, the bishop of London's memorandum concerning the Church in Barbados nine years earlier had proposed as its first item "That a Commissary be appointed under the Governor to exercise the ecclesiastical jurisdiction". Unfortunately about the same time Governor Dutton began an aggressive campaign to regulate the Church there, proposing in 1682 to establish an ecclesiastical court "to let the people know that there are religious as well as civil duties to be required of them". He appointed John Kenney, rector of Christchurch, his "surrogate" in ecclesiastical matters and asked that he be "vested with full authority to inflict ecclesiastical censures as provided by law in the English ecclesiastical courts", perhaps with the title of "Chancellor".[109] Dutton became very unpopular in Barbados, and apparently nothing was done about this suggestion to the Lords of Trade and Plantations, but in the year of his recall it seems that Bishop Compton appointed Kenny as "commissary". According to a later holder of this office, William Gordon, this proved abortive only because Compton himself was suspended by James II soon afterward.[110] The episode of Governor Dutton started the name "ecclesiastical court", and possibly "commissary" as well, towards disrepute in Barbados.

In most cases little more than the names of the commissaries of the West Indies are now known. William May held the post in Jamaica from 1720 to 1748 discreetly but conscientiously. Francis Byam of Antigua, from a well-known West Indian family, fulfilled a similar role in the Leewards (1739-48).[111] In Barbados however the office became a storm centre in the time of William Gordon and Governor Lowther, with long-lasting consequences for church discipline, popular attitudes towards the episcopate, and the work of the SPG among the slaves.

Two or three clergymen had served as commissaries in Barbados before Gordon was appointed in 1716.[112] He had given active leadership before this time in promoting the Clergy Act of 1705 and became embroiled in local politics.[113] A struggle for power had followed between Gordon, most of the clergy and several leading laymen on the one side, and Governor Lowther and his friends on the other. Ultimately it came to involve the bishop of London, John Robinson, and those other churchmen in England who governed the SPG and (as will be seen shortly) its new estates in Barbados. One objective of the Society was to obtain the appointment of four bishops for the American colonies, two for the continent and two for the islands, one of whom was to reside in Barbados, combining his episcopal functions with the presidency of the new college to be established in accordance with Christopher Codrington's bequest.[114] Robinson was appointed to the see of London at this time and after an appeal to him for support from Gordon and his colleagues in their up and down contest with Lowther, Gordon was made commissary. By this time the drive for American bishops had been frustrated by the death of Queen Anne, the fall of the Tories and the return of the Whig party to power in Great Britain.[115] At this critical point Gordon, whose Commission the governor refused to recognize, held an ecclesiastical court which tried to overrule Lowther's granting of a certain marriage licence on the ground that it was bigamous.[116] The governor promptly challenged this court and also the bishop of London's jurisdiction in general, demanding to know the grounds of his authority, and the Barbadian agents appealed to the king. This led to an enquiry by the Board of Trade into the bishop's powers overseas. They were found to be weak, resting only on the royal instructions to the governor to honour his jurisdiction "so far as conveniently may be". The board advised Robinson to replace Gordon as commissary and confine commissarial jurisdiction to the clergy only. The Barbadian Council and Assembly in 1719 proceeded to pass "An Act to quiet the minds of the inhabitants against the terrors of an ecclesiastical court", providing that "no ecclesiastical Law or Jurisdiction, shall have power to enforce, confirm or establish any penal Mulct or Punishment".[117]

Although Lowther was recalled soon afterward, and Gordon was cleared by the Barbados Assembly of charges that had been made against him, this law against any spiritual court remained on the statute book. Moreover it was not only Barbadian colonists who had resisted ecclesiastical interference in their established form of society. Jamaica in 1681 and 1748, and Antigua in 1692 passed legislation limiting the powers of Church jurisdiction to those over the clergy.[118] Planter controlled assemblies at times took steps to exercise their own discipline over the clergy.[119] The attitude of the ruling class is reflected in the comments of the planter-historians Long and Edwards later in the century:

> The bishop of London is said to claim this island as part of his diocese, but his jurisdiction is renounced and barred by the laws of the country; and the governor or commander in chief, as supreme head of the provincial church, not only inducts into the several rectories, on the requisite testimonials being produced that the candidate has been admitted into priest's orders according to the canons of the Church of England, but he is likewise

vested with the power of suspending a clergyman of lewd and disorderly life *ab officio*, upon application from his parishioners.[120]

Robinson's successor as bishop of London, Edmund Gibson, made a careful enquiry into the historical background of his authority in the colonies, in the course of which he obtained information from William Gordon, who recently had had to make similar enquiries in connection with his own legal contest with Governor Lowther.[121] He decided to remedy the doubt raised by Lowther and the Board of Trade enquiry by seeking a specific commission from the king. It was a restricted jurisdiction which he obtained, particularly with reference to the laity.[122]

Bishop Thomas Sherlock (1748–61), Gibson's successor, declined to seek a similar commission. Instead he tried to persuade the Whig government to appoint colonial bishops.[123] How this aim was frustrated by the resistance of Puritans and other nonconformists in the New England and Middle Colonies from this time to the American Revolution is a familiar story.[124] Less attention has been given to the fact that there was considerable resistance also in the Southern mainland colonies which were supposedly "Anglican", with the Church established there.[125] Still less well known is the strength of suspicion in the West Indies, where nonconformist opposition was negligible. Moreover, because American historians have usually concluded their research at the point when American bishops were consecrated for the Protestant Episcopal Church in the newly formed United States, the question why it took another generation before bishops were sent to the West Indies has not received adequate attention. One hint is found in the response of Francis Byam, commissary in the Leeward Islands, to Sherlock's enquiry concerning the willingness of the people of his area to receive a bishop. He wrote in 1753 that he thought they would be willing, if they did not have to foot the expense of his support and that no ecclesiastical courts were set up with authority over the laity.[126]

It is instructive to compare Byam's view with the "Observations regarding a Suffragan for America" written by Bishop Compton in 1707. These show that this experienced cleric, before either the controversies in the mainland colonies or those in Barbados, was aware of the long standing tendency to "alarm" in "the several colonies" at the idea of an "absolute Bishop". It went back, he says, to "K. Charles ye 2ds time", and "the grounds of that great opposition are generally still ye same". His suggested remedy was to give the new bishop much the same powers as the now-familiar commissary, and thus to try out the new ecclesiastical order "insensibly" and "gradually".[127] Robinson however, coming in new to the London see in the time of Queen Anne's Tory government, backed a commissary (William Gordon) who was facing the widespread opposition to ecclesiastical discipline head on, thus bringing even that office into disfavour in Barbados at least.[128] The collapse of this enterprise, and also of the attempt to establish American bishops in the same period, warned Gibson (and doubtless the "good and wise men" of the SPG also) *"quieta non movere"* like the Whig government on all such matters. Subsequently Sherlock's more aggressive policy likewise failed, and he discontinued the appointment of commissaries. Later bishops of London followed this precedent. Even Beilby Porteous (1787–1808), keenly interested in the evangelization of the slaves in the West Indies, was cautious about asserting his episcopal authority to advance that cause or to discipline the overseas clergy.[129]

In the end it was the continuing importunity of the SPG , and the response of the British government to the pressure of the anti-slavery movement by its programme of "Amelioration", which finally instituted an episcopate for the West Indies, as will be seen in chapter 10.

The Codrington Bequest and the SPG Estates (1703–1824)

REPRODUCED COURTESY OF UNITED SOCIETY FOR THE PROPOGATION OF THE GOSPEL

Christopher Codrington

The long possession by the SPG of two Codrington estates in Barbados in slavery days has been viewed in various ways. It was seen by the leaders of the Society itself as a God-given opportunity to pioneer the Christianization not only of its own slaves but of all those of the British West Indies. It was regarded in the eighteenth century by most Barbadian planters as a quixotic and dangerous experiment by impractical churchmen who believed that African slaves could be converted and instructed in religion.[130] It was condemned as hypocrisy by many abolitionists during the anti-slavery campaigns and by critics since emancipation.[131] Later it has been sympathetically studied as "an experiment in altruism" which in spite of mistakes and failures helped to prepare the way for the change to a free society, and as a prime example of Anglican humanitarianism reaching across the Atlantic to mellow the materialism of colonial life.[132] Without doubt it was in the context of the management of these estates, and the college located there, that the definitive conflict took place between the typical attitudes of West Indian planters and the forces within Anglicanism which, although accepting the existing social order, affirmed the slaves as human beings and desired their Christianization. Codrington College also holds an honourable pioneer place in the emergence of higher education and of theological education in the Caribbean.

This enterprise was conceived in the mind of a remarkable planter-governor, Christopher Codrington. Belonging to the third generation of a family of Barbados and Leeward Island residents, whose father had risen to be governor of the Leewards, he himself, after a scholarly and social career at Oxford and military service in Europe was appointed to the same gubernatorial post after his father's death in 1698. Before he came out to the West Indies in 1700 to take up this position he spent time in England pressing for the payment of his deceased parent's salary.[133] During this time the Society for Promoting Christian Knowledge (SPCK) was founded and soon afterward (in 1701) the king granted a charter to the new Society for the Propagation of the Gospel in Foreign Parts. These pioneer organizations of missionary outreach reflected the early stirring of religious zeal in an age of indifference and rationalism, and the serious side of the youthful Christopher was open to it.[134] For in 1703, when about to enter upon a military campaign against the French at Guadeloupe, he made his will, including the famous "Item":

> I give and bequeath my two plantations in the Island of Barbadoes to the Society for the Propagation of the Christian Religion in Foreign Parts erected and established by my late good Master King William the third, and my desire is to have the plantations continued intire and 300 negroes at least always kept thereon, and a convenient number of Professors and scholars maintained there all of them to be under the vows of poverty and chastity and obedience who shall be obliged to study and practise Phisick and Chirurgery as well as Divinity, that by the apparent usefulness of the former to all mankind they may both endear themselves to the people and have the better opportunitys of doing good to men's souls whilst they are taking care of their bodys, but the particulars of the constitutions I leave to the Society composed of wise and good men.[135]

Codrington came safely if not too successfully through the campaign but as a result of illness retired to a scholarly life in Barbados. In April 1710 he died and after a period of litigation over the terms of the will, the SPG became owner of the two Barbadian estates.[136]

The Society had already begun supporting a mission to African slaves in New York. The work was started by a Frenchman, Elie Neau, who had had an earlier sojourn in the Caribbean. A little later Francis Le Jau, another Huguenot (already mentioned), after working in St Kitts began a similar mission in South Carolina.[137] This was not, therefore, an entirely new enterprise for the Society. But to have thrust upon it the trusteeship of two sugar estates with three hundred slaves was certainly new. The bishops and other churchmen in England found themselves in the position of absentee planters, difficult enough for West Indians in England who had lived in the Antilles already. The only possible way to cope with this was through agents on the spot, but these were accustomed to entirely different objectives from that of a missionary society. For them it was axiomatic that the *raison d'être* of a sugar plantation was to produce a profit. Indeed from the standpoint of the Society it was essential to keep the business solvent, and the establishment of the missionary college depended upon the earnings of the estates.

In spite of the problems the SPG undertook the challenge, and promptly declared that the slaves on their estates should be Christianized. Bishop Fleetwood put it in the first Annual Sermon after the bequest, in February 1711:

> That if all the Slaves throughout America, and every Island in those Seas, were to continue infidels forever, *yet ours alone must needs be Christians*: We must instruct them in the Faith of Christ, bring them to Baptism, and put them in the way that leads to everlasting Life. This will be preaching *by Example*, the most effectual way of recommending Doctrines, to a hard and unbelieving World, blinded by Interest, and other Prepossessions.[138]

This sermon, which incidentally criticized the slave owners overseas for their failure hitherto to provide religious instruction and baptism for their slaves, was widely distributed in the West Indies as a declaration of purpose by the SPG. It provoked some angry backlash.[139]

The following year the Society carefully set about appointing the first missionary to the slaves, the Revd Joseph Holt, who seemed to be qualified medically as well as theologically in accordance with Codrington's plan. Unfortunately he did not prove satisfactory, and three successors (two of whom soon died) also accomplished very little.[140] From 1717 to 1726 no catechist was appointed, while political strife in Barbados left the future of the whole enterprise uncertain. Commissary Gordon and his allies had appealed to the SPG for support as well as to the bishop of London, and this deepened the distrust of most of the planters toward the Society and its activities in Barbados.[141] Apart from this interval however a steady succession of catechists and chaplains was appointed to bring the slaves on the Codrington estates to a knowledge of Christianity. With varying degrees of zeal they tried a series of experiments in instructing them, but for most of the century only slight success was achieved. Some of these teachers were sent from England, others recruited in Barbados. Some had little grasp of what was likely to be comprehensible to the children and the few adults who were allowed to be away from work, and who showed any interest in the classes. Some had to share their time with duties in the college or regular parish work.

The estate managers were reluctant to disturb the prevailing pattern of estate labour, especially with reference to Saturdays which the Society asked to be made free so that Sunday could be used for adult teaching. Other Barbadian planters ridiculed any effort to educate and baptize the slaves. In the 1750s and even more in the 1760s the chaplains were mostly sceptical of the value or possibility of teaching Christianity to the Africans, and from 1760 to 1768 nothing was done, not through failure of the SPG to appoint chaplains but through those appointed failing to do this work.[142]

While these depressing results were obtained in Barbados, the SPG in England had been hopefully pursuing the theory that, as Humphreys expressed it in 1730, "the most effectual Way to convert the Negroes, was by engaging their Masters, to countenance and promote their Conversion". It was trying to devise means for this not only on their own estates but in South Carolina, Jamaica, the Leewards and elsewhere as well.[143] By 1768 it was becoming clear that the means used on the Society's own estates were not working. How could they be an example to others?[144]

At the same time the very existence of the Codrington estates seemed in the balance. There was financial trouble, the number of slaves had declined by excess of deaths over births and purchases, and soon afterward the American Revolutionary War brought economic dislocation. The first indications of anti-slavery opinion in Great Britain and America had begun to challenge the holding of slaves by a Christian missionary society. The SPG and its Barbadian agents were spurred on to avoid buying new slaves from Africa and to improve the care of those they had. Finally after a ten-year lease of the estates to a friendly and competent planter, John Brathwaite, they were restored to a sound financial basis in 1793.[145]

Another slow transformation took place in the Society's method of evangelization. The chaplain of 1758–60, John Hodgson, had hopelessly concluded that only "a general Change of their Condition, by introducing among them the Regulations, and Advantages of civil Life" could make possible the slaves' Christianization. In 1783 Bishop Porteous in the Annual Sermon had optimistically put forward the same view. Such ideas were still anathema to the planters and the SPG itself only gradually accepted them. It continued however to experiment with increasing success, as education, civilization and religious teaching went hand in hand.[146] Schools for the children on the Codrington estates were established in 1797, under female teachers, well before education for slave children was established anywhere else. In 1819 the Revd J.H.Pinder began his notable career as chaplain and director of Negro schools.[147]

If the work of Christianization at Codrington proved disappointing for most of this period, the plan for a College to train medical evangelists for the purpose was even more a failure. The SPG on the whole accepted the view of Christopher Codrington himself that missionary work was a task for special personnel apart from the parish clergy, although his idea of a teaching staff and students with quasimonastic vows was quietly ignored.[148] Also ignored after the abortive attempt with Joseph Holt was the design of providing medically qualified religious workers. Still more subversive of the original scheme was the determination of Barbadian authorities that the school should be devoted to the education of white children at the grammar school level. In spite of the donor's will this is what the college was for the greater part of a century after its opening in 1745.[149]

Thus the vision of Christopher Codrington and the good intentions of the SPG, like the proddings of royal instructions and episcopal attempts at discipline, failed to make any deep impression on the planters' church before the coming of bishops to the West Indies in 1824.

Other SPG Outreach

In certain parts of the Caribbean which were not typical sugar islands the work of the SPG was important for the shaping of the West Indian Church. These were the Bahamas, the Moskito Shore and Belize.

The Bahamas had emerged from being shelters for pirates with the appointment of Woodes Rogers, the ex-privateer, as royal governor in 1718. Under his successor Governor Phenney some effort was made in communication with the bishop of London (and Commissary Garden of South Carolina) to provide clergy in New Providence and also in Harbour Island.[150] Under royal instructions to Woodes Rogers in his second term of office the Church of England was established in the islands.

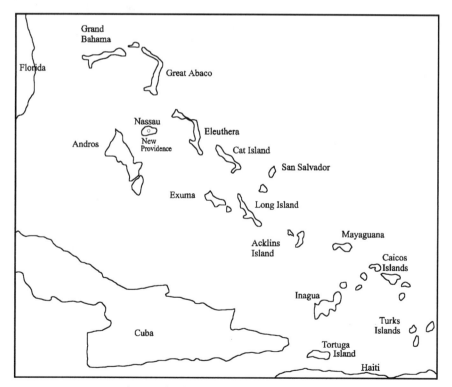

Bahama Islands, and Turks and Caicos Islands

The governor took steps in 1731 to obtain the aid of the SPG in supplying and supporting clergy, the colony itself (925 whites and 453 slaves) scarcely being able to finance this.[151]

In 1733 the SPG responded with the appointment of the Revd William Smith, the first of a series of the Society's servants over several decades in the Bahamas. Until Loyalist settlers came to the archipelago after the American Revolution the chief centre of population was New Providence, with small numbers in Eleuthera and Harbour Island. In 1772 one SPG clergyman supplied New Providence and another the latter two islands.[152] Following the Loyalist influx the Society began to work in Long Island, Exuma and the Caicos Islands. However in 1807 it had to discontinue sending missionaries to the Bahamas, for financial reasons, until after emancipation. Meanwhile with the new immigrants greater support for the Church was obtained locally, the population having risen to about ten thousand. Of this total a much higher proportion (at least two-thirds) now consisted of African Americans, the new settlers having brought their slaves with them from Georgia and South Carolina.[153] This meant that the Bahamas towards the end of the eighteenth century presented a challenge to missionary activity along with the similar call of the sugar islands farther south. This challenge, as will be seen in the next chapter, was taken up by the evangelicals.

In the western Caribbean also, contacts between the British and the Amerindians of the Moskito Shore, going back to the years of Old Providence, had issued in 1739 in an appeal by "Edward, King elect" of the Moskitos to Governor Trelawney of Jamaica for educational and religious aid. This was passed on to the SPG Efforts to obtain a suitable missionary led in 1765 to the appointment of Christian Frederick Post, a Moravian with twenty-two years' experience with Amerindians in North America. For another twenty years this devoted man lived among the people of the Moskito Shore, but other missionaries who went to help were able to stay only for short periods. After Post's death in 1785 the mission was not maintained.[154]

In 1776 Robert Shaw, an SPG missionary who had been briefly in the Moskito mission, moved to Belize and became chaplain to the settlement, the first clergyman in that area. Others followed and the Anglican Church became well situated in 1812, when the population was less than 4,000 people, with the erection of a church building.[155]

8

The Evangelical Movement
and the Slaves (to 1823)

If the gospel was to reach the masses of the people in the days of slavery, it had to come through some other channel than the planters' church. As the eighteenth century progressed it began to reach increasing numbers through lay preachers and missionaries from the evangelical movement. Evangelization in the Caribbean therefore was largely a nonconformist enterprise.[1] During the period from 1732 to 1823 this brought into existence Moravian, Methodist, Baptist and Congregational Churches, most of whose membership came from the slave population.

A New Conception of Christianity

What characteristics of the evangelical movement made it effective in winning many slaves to Christianity while the established Church failed? Outstanding among them may be identified its experiential emphasis, its evangelistic and missionary zeal, its equalitarian tendency, its practical ethics, and its lack of commitment to older ecclesiastical and social traditions.[2]

Beginning with pietism, the evangelical movement laid emphasis upon personal experience, upon feeling rather than dogma or the appeal to reason. Conversion, faith and salvation – biblical words used in common with Christians generally – were no longer a matter of intellectual assent or institutional affiliation or sacramental practice, but primarily a transforming experience of the individual. This individual experience, however, took place in a context of fellowship with other like-minded persons and found expression in an urge to share this experience with others.

Consequently evangelicalism early began evangelistic and missionary enterprise, at home and abroad. Among the places which appeared to be in need of such outreach were the slave plantations of the nominally "Christian" colonies of Denmark, the Netherlands and Great Britain.[3]

The evangelicals were convinced that every person, regardless of status, race or culture, was capable of the experience of salvation – whether rich or poor, clergy or lay, free or slave. Indeed within this equalitarian outlook there was a special urgency to carry the Good News to the common people, the most despised sinners, and the "heathen". This urgency reflected the Bible's special concern for the unprivileged. Lay men and women became deeply involved in church activities. Schools and popular education were encouraged. Lay preaching and teaching were common.

Evangelicals saw the Christian life as the simple, practical expression of biblical ideals of purity of life, personal saintliness, and deeds of mercy to the needy. Although their ethic was apparently individualistic in the first instance, they tended to move into organized social service and at times into radical social criticism. Being less bound by traditions of a hierarchical social order and canon law standards of morality, they were open to new humanitarian ideals. These came gradually to include the abolition of slavery, which emerged in sectarian (mainly Quaker) and radical secular thought during the same period.

Church life was supremely a matter of Christian fellowship, biblical nurture and common diligence in the aforesaid activities. It tended towards the pattern of a "church within the Church" or alternately of a "gathered Church" or sect. This pattern was balanced by a strong ecumenical tendency, since converted Christians were recognizable within other churches as well as one's own. The evangelical movement reinforced the trend to religious tolerance as far as institutional expressions of religion were concerned, and sat lightly towards older allegiances to a state church and clergy controlled sacraments. The kind of ecclesiastical disputes which had agitated the seventeenth century were eschewed, although some new controversies emerged. Within the evangelical groups themselves there was a strong moral discipline, but this was an educational process sanctioned by loss of church membership rather than (as under earlier laws) by civil penalties.

In the setting of the Caribbean, for the planter class such religion had little appeal. For them Christianity was a traditional form and they were not ready for a change of life. They had no missionary interest. The idea of equality, either spiritual or social, was unthinkable. The Church was an Erastian institution which they could control. They scarcely sought for spiritual fellowship and they resisted moral discipline of any kind.

During the period of this chapter, with some notable exceptions, evangelical concern was directed toward the conversion of the slaves, not their emancipation. In the following two chapters the impact of the anti-slavery movement upon missionary outreach will appear.

Antecedents of the Evangelicals

After beginnings in the Danish colonies the evangelical movement reached the English-speaking Caribbean in the 1750s in Jamaica and Antigua. But certain earlier voices, not normally regarded as part of this movement, at least in some ways anticipate the missionary and humanitarian message that later found expression among the evangelicals. In the West Indies these voices were mainly Quaker and Anglican.

The evangelical movement was, of course, a Protestant development, not only by historical circumstance but because theologically it shared the Reformed emphasis on the doctrine of salvation by faith. Yet one important aspect of it was the recovery of missionary purpose that had been largely ignored by Protestant churches for two centuries. Thus it had a kinship with this element of Roman Catholic tradition. It is not, therefore, entirely fanciful to recognize some of the Spanish and French missionaries who have been mentioned in previous chapters as antecedents of the evangelical spirit in the Caribbean – not least the author of *De Unico Modo* among the Amerindians, Sandoval and Claver among the African slaves, and Breton with the Caribs.[4]

The first Protestant missionary body, the Society for Propagation of the Gospel in New-England, founded in 1649, received a royal charter after the Restoration through such men as the Puritan Richard Baxter and the Anglican Robert Boyle. This enterprise was directed towards the Amerindians.[5] In more southern colonies, the early experiment in Virginia, ending in the massacre of 1622, had discouraged further missionary enterprise. Willoughby's temporary English colony of Surinam (1650–67) however, with its Arawak people, inspired two Puritans with zeal for a new initiative: John Oxenbridge, who published a "Proposition" on the subject, and John Wesley (grandfather of the founder of Methodism) who for a time planned to be a missionary there.[6] Two pioneers did go to Surinam: the Quaker John Bowron, and Baron Justinian Von Weltz, a Lutheran, who met his death there in the 1660s.[7]

Concern for the African slaves was expressed by Richard Baxter, who wrote for "those Masters in foraign Plantations who have Negro's and other Slaves". In his *Christian Directory*, written about 1665, he addressed them on their duty to care for both the spiritual and temporal welfare of their bondsmen. This is done under the title of "The Duties of Masters to their Servants" which is part of "The Family Directory". Religious writers in the seventeenth century, using the biblical analogy of domestic bondage, tended to subsume the servant-slave relationship under that of family life.[8] On the ground of the common humanity of master and slave, and the redemption of Christ, Baxter urged that the Africans be evangelized:

> Those therefore that keep their *Negro's* and slaves from hearing Gods word, and from becoming Christians, . . . do openly profess Rebellion against God, and contempt for Christ the Redeemer of souls, and a contempt for the souls of men, and indeed they declare that their worldly profit is their treasure and their God.
>
> If this come to the hands of any our Natives in *Barbado's* or other Islands or Plantations, who are said to be commonly guilty of this most heinous sin, yea and to live upon it, I entreat them further to consider . . . How cursed a crime is it to equal *Men* and *Beasts*?

He goes on to accuse the slave owners of worse villainies than the slaves ever committed, and attributes some West Indian disasters of fire and shipwreck to God's judgment upon them: "Will not your money and you perish together?" He concludes: "Let their salvation be far more valued by you than their service."[9]

Because of the eclipse of Puritanism in the Caribbean, Baxter's advice had little if any influence there, although it had some effect in England and the New England colonies. During the time of the growth of the Society of Friends, however, the West Indies was directly challenged by an appeal on the subject of evangelization of the slaves by George Fox himself. In 1657, only two years after Quaker missionaries reached Barbados, he wrote a letter "To Friends beyond Sea, that have Blacks and Indian Slaves," reminding his followers that "God is no respecter of persons", and "that the gospel is preached to every creature under heaven; which is the power that giveth liberty and freedom, and is the glad tidings to every captivated creature under the whole heavens".[10] On a 1671 visit to Barbados Fox followed up this advice. In the home of Thomas Rous he spoke "touching the Government of Families according to the Law of Jesus", urging that slaves be treated in the manner of the Old Testament patriarchs as part of the household, sharing in the spiritual blessings of God. He told them, as Christians, to "preach the everlasting Covenant, Christ Jesus, to the Ethyopians, the Blacks and Tawny-moors, as Philip did . . . in your Families". This address was printed, with a final exhortation to give slaves time off work "to wait upon the Lord", and thus provide "an Example to all other Masters, to bring their Servants from under Oppression to know the Lord".[11] In 1679 he returned to the subject in another epistle.[12]

Not only did George Fox urge his own flock to Christianize their slaves but he exhorted the civil authorities and the clergy of the established Church to do so also. While in Barbados in 1671, he and his companions were so concerned to befriend the slaves that they were accused of "teaching the Negroes to Rebell". Fox's letter of defence against this accusation explained the moral principles they did in fact try to teach the blacks, and went on to say that all masters were responsible to God to do the same.[13] He further published in 1672 a challenge to the clergy:

And if you be Ministers of Christ, are you not Teachers of Blacks and Taunies (to wit, Indians) as well as the Whites? For, is not the Gospel to be preached to all Creatures? And are they not Creatures? And did not Christ taste Death for every man? And are they not Men? . . . Are they not part of your Parishioners if not the greatest part? And why do you find fault with the Quakers (so called) for teaching of their Families, and instructing them (to wit) the Blacks and Taunies, and Whites?[14]

This tract more than justified itself through its effect upon an Anglican clergyman and grandson of a well-known bishop, who visited Barbados, the already-mentioned

Morgan Godwyn. In *The Negro's and Indians Advocate*, published in 1680, Godwyn acknowledged the truth of Fox's charge that his fellow clergy had neglected their duty. He wrote extensively to stir up concern in the colonies and in England.[15] He told how Fox's pamphlet had stung his conscience:

> Now upon this I began to question with my self, If the Gospel be good tidings, why should it be concealed, or hid? And since designed so to all People, why should not these partake of it as well as others? If we are bound to pray for their Conversion, why are we not also to endeavour it?[16]

At great length and with almost scholastic meticulousness he undertook to prove "the Negro's (both Slaves and others) . . . equal Right with other men to the Exercise and Privileges of Religion", and the inexcusableness of neglect to promote Christianity among them. The "Pretences" put forward by slave owners to deny this right were refuted at length, including arguments based on "Complexion, Bondage, Pretended Stupidity, and Barbarousness of Manners". Showing the capabilities of the Africans he pointed out that "Africa was once famous for both Arts and Arms", and cited Ethiopia and Nubia as Christian nations.[17]

Godwyn does not attack slavery as such, but insists that the slave has rights "both for his Soul and Body". "Slavery," he says, "is but a lower degree of Poverty and Misery; but not the lowest."[18] He replies to the charge that Christianity instigates men to mutiny and rebellion, repudiating the "dangerous" idea of equality. At the same time he indicts the masters' cruelty to the bodies as well as the souls of slaves, and also of white servants.[19]

His proposal is that the clergy should preach at least monthly the duty of owners to prepare their slaves for baptism, and set the example themselves. The clergy also must be protected from discrimination because of such zeal by being freed from dependence on their vestries.[20] He pleads for the colonists "to make the Negro's case our own", citing the golden rule. Then in a closing exhortation to the Negro himself, Godwyn assures him of God's mercy. The "Evangelical Promises" are for him: "Then art thou, as to thy Soul, and all the ends and purpose of the Gospel, no longer a Slave but a Son. . . . For we are all one in Christ Jesus."[21] While this clergyman is clearly a man of the seventeenth century, there is more than a hint of the humanitarianism and evangelicalism of the future in his words. In his sermon published five years later he shows a perceptivity of the exploitation of the colonial system and the slave trade remarkable for his time. The neglect of evangelical duty is attributed to greed for money and the consequent irreligious attitudes of the planters. However the only remedy he offers is to see that the blessings of the Gospel are given in return for the material benefits Englishmen have received from the plantations:

> We have as it were conspired with Satan, and entred into a confederacy with Hell itself.
> ... That we have exceeded the worst of Infidels, by our first enslaving, and then murthering
> of Mens Souls. For how can it be endured that a Nation once so famous for Zeal and
> Piety ... should prostrate her self to that foul Idol Mammon, and worship Trade?[22]

The stridency of Morgan Godwyn's polemic against the planters, and against their
control of the colonial church, made him many enemies. His message at the time
was largely ineffective. Yet his challenge, though delayed, awakened attention in
important places. Bishop Compton, probably Christopher Codrington, and
members of the SPG must have been aware of his publications.[23]

George Fox's visit to the West Indies had been a short one, but it was followed
up by the Quaker missionary William Edmundson. In 1675–76 he was in Barbados,
preaching for five months. He had an altercation with an Anglican clergyman named
Ramsey, and wrote a letter to the governor in which he boldly declared:

> God at the beginning made Whites and Blacks of one Mould, and Christ Jesus died for
> Blacks as well as Whites. . . The Lord took away the Land of Canaan from those that did
> corrupt it, and gave it to the Jews, and when they tolerated Wickedness, and oppressed
> the Poor and Strangers, then the Lord, after many Visitations and faithful Warnings,
> took his Land from them and gave it to others, and the Lord is the same to Day as then,
> and his Ear is open to the Cries of the Oppressed, and to the crying Sins which cry for
> Vengeance, and no doubt he will visit for both.[24]

It is not surprising that this prophecy of judgment led to the passing of the notorious
Act "to prevent the People called Quakers from bringing Negroes to their Meeting".[25]
There were three provisions in this law: first, to put a stop to the Quakers converting
the blacks; second, to require schoolmasters to take the Oath of Allegiance and
Supremacy (which no Quaker could do); and third, to prohibit travelling preachers
(like Edmundson) from speaking in Quaker meetings unless they had resided in
the island for twelve months. When the Act was renewed two years later the
prohibition of preaching was extended to residents as well, making all preaching
at Friends' meetings illegal.[26] It is difficult to judge the effect of this law. On the
one hand, there is little evidence of indictments under it. Three which are recorded
led to acquittal, to the disgust of the informer and the prosecuting officials.[27] Among
the 473 cases of Quaker prosecution in Barbados, listed by their chronicler which
were mainly for refusal to take oaths, bear arms or pay church dues there seem to
be no other instances of suffering for disobeying the 1676 Act, whether by
evangelizing Negroes, teaching school or preaching.[28] Did Quakers lose zeal in
defying this particular law? Or did the three acquittals result in discontinuance of
prosecutions under it? There seems to be little evidence of black membership in
the Society of Friends in the island.[29] In any case, by the end of the century Quakerism

generally had entered a quietistic and seclusive phase of its history, abandoning its original evangelizing zeal among whites as well as blacks.[30]

Other developments were preparing the way for the evangelical movement in Europe. Quietly, what were known as the Religious Societies cultivated a new earnestness among some Anglicans in the pleasure-loving milieu of Restoration England. Societies for the Reformation of Manners, including Dissenters as well as Church of England people, set out to enforce the disciplinary laws which were falling into abeyance.[31] On the continent the pietist movement was shaking the dry bones of Lutheran orthodoxy with a more dedicated approach to Christianity.[32] Persecuted Huguenots found their way to England and America, and identified themselves with the Church of England and other churches, bringing new zeal with them. The challenge of rationalism, culminating in deism, provoked a reaction among Christian thinkers. The SPCK and the SPG, brought into being by the skill and persistence of Thomas Bray, gave focus to concern for missionary outreach in the established Church. This concern was weighted towards the Erastian pattern of Church life, yet co-operated with pietist leaders in Germany, and welcomed the contribution of Huguenot workers such as Le Jau and Neau in America, pietist missionaries such as Ziegenbalg and Plütschau in India, and the Moravian Christian Frederick Post on the Moskito Shore.[33]

Early in this period Christopher Codrington was appointed governor of the Leeward Islands. He had received royal instructions "to facilitate and encourage the conversion of Negroes", and to "endeavour to get a law passed . . . for the restraining of any inhumane severity" towards Christian servants and slaves.[34] Codrington replied:

> I have alwaies thought it very barbarous that so little care should be taken of the bodys and so much less of the souls of our poor slaves . . . I shall certainly be opposed by all the Planters in generall if I should go about to secure their limbs and lives by a law, (tho' I will certainly recommend something of that kind) but much more if I should promote the baptising of all our slaves.

It may seem whimsical to think of Codrington as a prophet or an antecedent of evangelicalism. Nevertheless he had the independence of mind and the religious concern to question some of the ingrained prejudices of the society of which he was a part, and to propose a radically new approach to the Christianizing of the slaves. He saw this as "a design that may be pleasing to God and truly beneficial to my fellow-creatures", and recognized the necessity of procuring specialized and dedicated personnel for the task:

> Indeed a work of this nature is only fit for a regular clergy who are under vows of poverty and obedience . . . I would humbly propose this might be recommended to the

consideration of the Archbishop and Bishop of London. If they can find such a number of apostolical men who are willing to take much pains for little reward my protection and countenance shall not be wanting.[35]

This was written before the foundation of the SPG (but after that of the SPCK) and at the time there were almost no examples of Protestant missionary work in existence.

Codrington's sincerity was confirmed when he wrote his will. Before doing so he had had contact with a Jesuit priest in St Christopher (the island was still shared by English and French) and their conversation confirmed his conclusion that the only way to bring Christianity to the Africans was through committed missionaries like the Roman Catholic regulars.[36] In this he showed remarkable independence of mind in a generation when everything "papist" was scorned. His own Protestant loyalty, of course, was never in question.[37] One may well believe that had he lived some decades later he would have welcomed the work of the Methodist preachers Nathaniel Gilbert and John Baxter, and the Moravian Peter Braun, in his own Antigua.

Perhaps the most astonishing fact about Codrington (and it would seem of his father also) is that in spite of profiting by the slavery system he was able to admire some of the slaves as "born Heroes", going so far as to declare, with reference to an incident in which some "Corromante" slaves had killed their master, that the latter must have been in the wrong. Codrington's verdict that it was necessary to treat such men "like a Friend rather than a Slave" may seem ironic, but at the beginning of the eighteenth century it was a radical recognition of African humanity and capabilities, akin to the attitudes of the later evangelicals which the planters found so threatening to their sense of superiority.[38]

During the 1720s – while the SPG's Codrington estates were haltingly beginning Christian teaching under the catechist system and Bishop Gibson was exhorting masters and mistresses to give Christian instruction to their slaves – George Berkeley, the philosopher-churchman and later bishop of Cloyne, was pursuing a scheme of establishing a college in Bermuda with a view to training missionaries for work among Negroes and Indians in the British colonies of the New World. In line with the contemporary Anglican point of view this was to be supported by the home government and Berkeley had been led to believe that Walpole would procure financial support for it. After some years' delay Bishop Gibson had to advise Berkeley that this support would never be forthcoming and the project was abandoned in 1731.[39]

In the following year a very different initiative originated not in the British Isles but in central Europe.

Evangelical Pioneers (1732–1783)

The first Protestant effort at evangelization of slaves in the West Indies came from the fusion, at Herrnhut in Saxony, of two historic streams of Protestant faith, one from the migration of refugees of the Moravian Brethren, the other from German Lutheranism and its pietist reformation under Spener and Francke. This apparently obscure event in 1727, known as the reconstitution of the Moravian Church, led to a worldwide missionary upsurge that firmly planted evangelical Christianity in the Caribbean, and the Moravian Church as an important element in West Indian life. It also influenced the growth in Great Britain of Methodism and of evangelicalism within Anglican and other churches, and the subsequent birth of several Protestant missionary societies in the last decade of the century, which in turn came to work in the Caribbean.[40]

The Moravians who escaped from persecution in their native country in 1722 had had a long history of suffering for their faith.[41] They were allowed by a sympathetic nobleman, Count Nicolaus Ludwig von Zinzendorf, to settle on his land. Zinzendorf had been nurtured in the pietist movement, having known Francke personally. Accordingly the Moravian colony became a haven also for some German pietists who desired a place of freedom for the service of God. Zinzendorf became deeply involved in this community of faith and gave it his own leadership and social prestige.[42]

At the coronation of King Christian VI of Denmark, who was a friend of his, the count met a veritable "man from Macedonia" in the person of Anthony Ulrich, a

slave from the Danish West Indies, who told of the desire of blacks there for an opportunity to hear the Christian gospel. He was later brought to Herrnhut where he repeated his plea. The result was a sense of call by two brethren, Leonard Dober and Tobias Leupold, and its careful sifting by the Herrnhut community. Dober, a pietist from Württemberg, and David Nitschmann, a Moravian refugee from Zauchtenthal, were the ones finally chosen to take the gospel to St Thomas in the Danish West Indies. They left Herrnhut on 21 August 1732, and arrived at St Thomas on 13 December.[43]

REPRODUCED BY COURTESY OF THE MORAVIAN ARCHIVES, BETHLEHEM, PENNSYLVANIA

Leonard Dober

It is important to understand that the early Moravian evangelists of the eighteenth century were not missionaries in the usual modern sense of persons financially maintained by a Church or missionary society abroad. Nitschmann, who was a carpenter, supported himself and Dober by his own hands. After the carpenter's return to Herrnhut, Dober, a potter, having found his trade useless in St Thomas because of the lack of suitable clay, tried to become a fisherman, took employment for a time as a house steward, then as a night-watchman and an overseer. Like the apostle Paul, these missionaries had to finance themselves. This necessity led, in the Danish islands, in Surinam and in Jamaica later, to the unfortunate decision to earn a living, like other Europeans in the West Indies, as planters and slave owners. Thus the Moravians, like the SPG on their Codrington estates but for different reasons, were entangled by seeming necessity in the system of slavery.[44]

In spite of the handicap this placed upon their relation with the slaves, the personal sincerity of these Moravians was able to reach a good many of them. Particularly effective was Frederick Martin, who succeeded Dober in St Thomas. Originally a refugee from Upper Silesia to Herrnhut, he was an ordained Moravian minister, unlike the two pioneers who had been laymen. During the fourteen years between 1736 and 1750 he built up the work of evangelization, education in the faith, and church organization including the encouragement of leadership from among the blacks themselves. This became a pattern for Moravian missionary labour which was followed for decades in several other islands.[45]

After Brother Martin began to baptize significant numbers of slaves, opposition arose from planters and from the pastor of the Dutch Reformed Church in St Thomas. The latter challenged the regularity of Martin's ordination. Martin and his colleague Freundlich and even the latter's wife were imprisoned because they refused to take oaths in court. At this juncture, in January 1739, Count Zinzendorf himself arrived unexpectedly in St Thomas to see how his workers were faring. Discovering that they were in jail he protested to the governor, obtained release of the prisoners, and on his return to Denmark secured an order to give religious freedom to the missionary Brethren and to punish infringements of the same.[46] This is the first instance of persecution, which reappeared later in several West Indian territories, either when missionaries began to preach or when the ruling class decided to try to curb their success. Appeals then had to be made to the metropolitan government in Europe to obtain religious freedom.[47]

After this, Moravian evangelization in the Danish islands gradually spread. Centres were established in St Thomas at Posaunenberg (1737), later renamed New Herrnhut, and at Niesky (1771); in St Croix at Friedensthal (1755) and Friedensberg (1771) and in St John at Bethany (1754) and Emmaus (1782).[48] The local "Negro-English" dialect was used and Scripture portions, a doctrinal summary and a hymn-book were printed in this medium. During the first fifty years of Moravian work in the Danish West Indies a total of 11,807 persons were baptized, 8,833 adults and 2,974 children.[49] This was a remarkable accomplishment in the eighteenth century, considering the obstacles of opposition, food shortages, hurricane, war, fire, sickness and the mortality of missionaries.[50] Remarkable also was the Christian witness rendered by local converts.[51]

These Virgin Islands, then Danish but now American, were the cradle of black West Indian Protestantism. Although the major part of this enterprise was that of the Moravians, in 1755 the Danish Lutheran Church, influenced by pietism, also undertook a mission to the slaves. Later in the century this mission had a membership of about a thousand blacks, and at times the Fredericksted Lutheran Creole congregation was led by a slave named Michael Samuelsen. Schools for black children were also established by the Danish government.[52]

Meanwhile on the South American continent pioneer work was undertaken by the Moravians in Berbice, at that time under Dutch rule but later to become part of British Guiana. After consultations in the Netherlands an exploratory visit was made to Paramaribo in Surinam in 1735. Two missionaries were sent to Berbice in 1738. Deflected by planter opposition from their original plan to preach to the African slaves, they decided to establish in 1740 a centre for Amerindian work about a hundred miles inland on the west side of the Berbice River. It was named Pilgerhut. This mission station, successful for a time, was scattered and burned to the ground in 1765 at the time of the slave revolt in Berbice, and left no permanent results. It is notable for the pioneer work of the linguist Solomon Schumann, "the Apostle to the Arawaks", who translated parts of the New Testament into Arawak and also wrote a dictionary and grammar of the language.[53]

Moravians began work in British Caribbean territory first in Jamaica. Two absentee English planters, William Foster and Joseph Foster-Barham, inspired by a Moravian evangelist in Yorkshire, asked for missionaries to take the gospel to the people on their estates.[54] In December 1754 three Brethren, Zecharias George Caries, Thomas Shallcross and Gottlieb Haberecht started work among five Foster and Barham estates in St Elizabeth. This parish was the major centre of Moravian activity for many decades. In 1755 Haberecht died, and in the same year the Moravians acquired a 700-acre sugar estate (New Carmel, later known as Old Carmel) to support themselves and to serve as their headquarters.[55] Despite this compromise with slave ownership the earliest missionaries made a strong impression upon some of the blacks. New stations were opened, including Mesopotamia in the neighbouring parish of Westmoreland. A later arrival, Brother Frederick Schlegel who was in Jamaica from 1765 to 1770, obtained a considerable response.[56]

On the other hand, dissension among the missionaries themselves, over the requirements for baptism in terms of scriptural knowledge and evidence of a change of life, limited the growth of the work. In the first fifty years only 936 Negroes were baptized.[57] From 1770 to 1809, the missionary-historian Buchner sadly concludes, "not much was, or could be, reported of the labours of the missionaries".[58]

The work of the Moravians in the British colonies received approval on the whole among government authorities. Parliament had recognized the Church of the United Brethren as sober, quiet and industrious people, and had endorsed their missionary work. It also exempted them on grounds of conscience from oath taking and military service.[59] There was some argument however as to whether this Act of 1749 applied in the Caribbean colonies where militia service by all white men was regarded as mandatory. When Moravians in Jamaica appealed to it in justifying their refusal to prepare to fight, the freeholders of St Elizabeth parish in 1763 petitioned the Assembly against them, but without success.[60] This annoyance about military duty was added to the usual suspicion of most planters about evangelization of the slaves and reluctance to allow them time to attend church meetings. Persecution on a small scale broke out at times.[61] Gradually however some of the planters came to recognize that Moravian slaves were reliable and valuable workers and looked favourably on the missions. Their preachers received less opposition than did Methodists and Baptists in later years.[62]

Two years after the commencement of work in Jamaica, the Moravians undertook a mission in Antigua, which proved to be more effective during the eighteenth century. The initiative came from the nearby Danish islands. Samuel Isles, after eight years' service in St Thomas, was sent to Antigua in 1756 and began preaching on some estates where this was permitted to him. In 1761 he obtained land for the first missionary station in St John's.[63] Progress was slow until the arrival in 1769 from the Moravian settlement in North America of Brother Peter Braun, a native of the Palatinate. Under his leadership, winsome personality and evangelical ardour the slaves began to flock to his preaching, and in their free time they enlarged the place of worship in St John's. Following a hurricane in 1772 the spiritual awakening became so great that a new chapel had to be built. In the same year the first black "Helper" was appointed to assist in pastoral care, and within three years there were ten of these, four men and six women, all but one being slaves. In 1774 a second mission station, Bailey Hill, was opened near Falmouth on the opposite side of the island, then eight years later was moved to a new site named Gracehill. By this time there were 2,069 baptized blacks connected with the Moravians, and almost as many more regular hearers and catechumens. Soon afterward some seven hundred were added within one year to the membership, and in 1785 Brother Braun writes of three thousand baptized to date. It became necessary to divide the congregations, both at St John's and Gracehill, into two sittings for the Lord's Supper. Preaching took place also on several plantations. One black leader on his

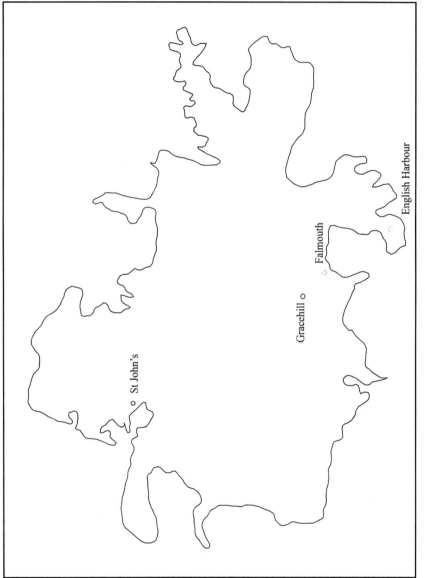

St John's

Gracehill

Falmouth

English Harbour

Antigua

own initiative erected a chapel on one of them large enough to hold four hundred people.[64]

Thus, after the Danish Virgin Islands, Antigua became the prime place of growth for the Moravian Church. One reason for this was that the Antigua missionaries were unencumbered with the burden of estate management and of slave ownership. While this created hardship for the workers themselves it relieved them of duties that were incompatible with their purpose, and it made for better relations with the slaves. It was possible because in addition to whatever they might earn in other ways locally the missionaries received support from abroad.[65]

During this closing period of the Old Empire, small Moravian missions were commenced in Barbados and St Kitts. The effort in Barbados, begun in 1765, was not rewarded with large numbers in the eighteenth century. In 1767 a period of some success began with the arrival of the English Moravian Brother Benjamin Brookshaw. He had the good fortune to find a Quaker planter, Mr Jackman, whose son had had contact with Moravians in Pennsylvania. These two were friendly and allowed Brookshaw to preach to their slaves.[66] The pioneer mission station of Bunker's Hill ("Old Sharon") was purchased in the same year. Although in a poor location this was the centre of work for almost thirty years, during which time frequent deaths of missionaries, a hurricane in 1780, and some opposition inhibited its growth. In 1784 there were only fourteen communicants.[67]

In St Kitts also the mission only began to flourish after the period now under review. It was started as knowledge spread of the work in Antigua.[68] A lawyer and plantation owner, John Gardiner, approached the Moravian missionary leaders Benjamin La Trobe and John Wallin when he was in England, and this led to the sending of Brothers John Gottwald and James Birkby (a German and an Englishman) and their wives to St Kitts. However the beginning was slow, and the French occupation of the island in 1782–84 unsettled the community, although the invaders did not interfere with the Moravians and actually encouraged them. By 1784 the number of converts was about forty.[69]

One circumstance which encouraged Moravian work in Antigua was the presence of another evangelical group, the first Methodist Society of the West Indies. As early as 1760, four years after the arrival of Samuel Isles from St Thomas, the Hon. Nathaniel Gilbert, a lawyer and member of the Antigua Assembly, began lay preaching among his family, friends and slaves, and later on a wider scale. He had been converted by the reading of some of the writings of John Wesley sent to him from England by his younger brother Francis Gilbert, especially the *Earnest Appeal to Men of Reason and Religion*. In 1757 he had gone on a visit to England with the purpose of hearing Wesley himself. Two of his slaves were the first blacks ever to be baptized by Wesley, during this visit.[70]

The Great House, Gilbert Estate, Antigua

Nathaniel Gilbert, supported by his wife and his children's governess, Mary Leadbetter, built up a Methodist Society of some two hundred persons, mostly slaves. In spite of the disapproval of his religous zeal by many in white society, Gilbert's prestige was great enough that he was elected speaker of the House of Assembly in 1763. He retained the post until he resigned voluntarily six years later to concentrate his attention on his religious work. By 1773 the combined efforts of Methodists and Moravians in Antigua was so great that Francis Gilbert reported to Wesley that "almost the whole island seems stirred up to seek the Lord" as he begged for a missionary from England to aid in the work.[71]

After the death of Nathaniel Gilbert in 1774, and Francis's return to England for health reasons two years afterward, the Methodist Society was led by two women, Sophia Campbell, a black, and Mary Alley, a woman of colour, until in 1778 a Methodist local preacher from England, John Baxter, came to the island as a shipwright at Nelson's Dockyard. Under the unpaid leadership of "Daddy Baxter", as the slaves called him, the cause began to grow again, with six hundred blacks reported by Baxter in the Society the following year. By 1783 he and his supporters built a chapel in St John's capable of seating two thousand people.[72] Help was given by Mary Leadbetter Gilbert (who had first married Francis Gilbert, then returned to Antigua after his death in England in 1779) and by an elderly Irish Methodist who was driven by a storm (like Dr Coke three years later) to Antigua and settled there.[73]

In summary it may be said that by the early 1780s pioneer preaching by Moravians had established small, mainly black, evangelical communities in Jamaica, Barbados, and St Kitts, and flourishing ones in the Danish Virgin Islands and, alongside the Methodists, in Antigua.

New Initiatives (1783–1800)

The end of the Old Empire, resulting from the American Revolution, had two consequences that initiated a new era of evangelical activity in the Caribbean:

(i) Loyalist migration brought hundreds of new residents from the mainland to the West Indies. Some who were influenced by the "Great Awakening" (the American branch of the Evangelical Movement) founded Baptist congregations here.

(ii) The separation of the United States from the empire meant that churches in Great Britain, including the growing Methodist movement, increased their concern for the West Indies.[74] Attention also was drawn towards the state of slavery in the remaining colonies and in 1787 the Society for the Abolition of the Slave Trade was formed.

The origins of the Baptist movement in Jamaica and the Bahamas (and later in Trinidad) are found in the American religious revival prior to the Revolution. The Great Awakening, having begun among Dutch Reformed and Presbyterian churches in the middle colonies, spread to the Congregational churches of New England in the 1730s in the era of Jonathan Edwards.[75] Tours by George Whitefield along the coastal regions stirred the fires of the revival and extended them in the South. His preaching kindled zeal among scattered Baptist churches, including some in South Carolina and Georgia.[76]

Meanwhile in Connecticut the "New Light" movement produced a group known as the Strict Congregational Churches, which stressed the freedom of all gifted members to preach, the giving of communion only to the converted, and the separation of religion from civil power and hierarchical control. Persecution by the Congregational civil authorities pushed many of these people to the more radical position of the Baptists who rejected infant baptism.[77] From among these "Separate Baptists" of Congregational and Baptist origins emerged a small group led by Shubal Stearns, Daniel Marshall and others, who in the 1750s moved southward, preaching from Virginia to Georgia.[78]

As the Great Awakening came to the South, the message was proclaimed to the slaves as well as the whites. This had been pioneered by Presbyterian evangelists, but the Baptists in the course of their wide itinerating reached a much larger number of blacks.[79] They were accepted on the same basis as whites – a credible witness to their personal religious experience – and some Baptist churches held a majority of blacks. Preachers arose among them, and on both sides of the Savannah River in South Carolina and Georgia some entirely black congregations were formed under these leaders in the 1770s and later. One of these was the Silver Bluff Church in

George Liele

South Carolina some 12 miles east of Augusta, Georgia, "the first Negro Baptist Church in the western hemisphere", founded between 1773 and 1775. With this congregation was associated a slave who had shown ministerial gifts, George Liele.[80]

After the British occupation of Savannah, Georgia (1778) a church was formed at Yamacraw, a suburb of that city, among slaves (many of them from Silver Bluff) who in response to the offer of freedom given by the military government had gone to live in British-controlled territory. George Liele, who had been licensed as a probationer and ordained in 1775, had been given his freedom by his master because of his religious work. He became pastor of this church. When Savannah was recaptured by the Americans at the end of 1782, he went to Kingston, Jamaica, with a British officer, Col. Kirkland, who had befriended him. The same postwar movement took many other people to Jamaica, the Bahamas and elsewhere, including soldiers, free blacks, white planters and their slaves.[81]

Another black preacher and friend of George Liele, "Brother Amos", went to New Providence in the Bahamas. Both these men became evangelists in their new homes. We are informed that in 1791 Brother Amos had "about three hundred members", and that by 1812 this had increased to 850.[82]

George Liele, however, is better known to history. After two years during which he became established as a free Negro in Jamaica he undertook Christian work. "I began," he says, "about September 1784, to preach in Kingston, in a small private house, to a good smart congregation, and I formed the church with four brethren from America besides myself, and the preaching took very good effect with the poorer sort, especially the slaves." In the seven years following he endured some persecution, baptized four hundred people, enrolled "nigh three hundred and fifty members", recruited an assistant, Thomas Swigle, as deacon, promoted "a free school for the instruction of the children, both free and slaves" of which Swigle was schoolmaster, purchased land for a "meeting-house" in the east end of Kingston, and began construction on this chapel. The Church was organized with deacons, elders and trustees; there were also "teachers of small congregations in the town and country". Liele received no pay for his religious work, supporting himself by farming and conveying goods by horse and wagon.[83] An elaborate but effective discipline was maintained by the use of a church Covenant "Begun in America, December 1777, and in Jamaica, December 1783". This covenant prescribed both ritual and moral standards for the congregation, supported by scriptural quotations, and ensured against opposition by requiring that slaves have their masters' approval before joining the church. By 1793 Liele reported the completion of the church building (at Windward Road) and the commencement of work in Spanish Town, where government officers were favourable.[84]

Others were active in the movement. Liele's deacon Thomas Swigle in turn had "a principal helper and fellow labourer" James Pascall. Swigle established a second church in Kingston, and speaks of a chapel and 254 brethren at Clinton Mount, a coffee plantation in St Andrew, 16 miles from Kingston. Like Liele he was not paid for his religious work.[85] In the north-west Moses Baker, a free man of colour from New York who was baptized by Liele in Kingston, was invited by the Quaker planter, Isaac Lascelles Winn, to come and instruct his slaves in the Christian religion. Winn and another planter, Samuel Vaughan, gave him "compensation" for this work. By 1802 he was said to have "fourteen hundred justified believers, and three thousand followers", and he was asking for an assistant to take up similar work on two estates in neighbouring Westmoreland. Swigle sent him "one of our exhorters, . . . a native of America", George Vineyard, with the promise of "a House, and maintenance, a salary, and land for him to cultivate" by a Mr Hilton in that parish.[86] Another man of colour from one of the Southern States, George Gibbs, began a congregation sixteen miles from Spanish Town in St Thomas-in-the-Vale. Still another, John Gilbert, a free black, pioneered in St George parish in the north.[87]

Thus was built up a tradition of great freedom of evangelizing and of personal initiative by individual preachers, mostly uneducated, to collect their own flock – a practice that had precedent in pioneer conditions in the mainland colonies during the Great Awakening. Baptist principles of congregational independence encouraged it. By the end of the century congregations were recorded in Westmoreland and St James in the west, in Kingston, St Andrew, St Catherine, and St Thomas-in-the-Vale in the south-central area, and St George in the north-east. Various scattered groups – many of them, called "Native Baptists", incorporating elements of African religion into their life – were widely criticized. The planters became alarmed at the rapid spread of the movement, and early in the new century persecution broke out against Baptists, and also against Methodists, who by this time were active in Jamaica.

We now turn back in time to recount the events that launched Methodist missionaries into the Caribbean during the last decade and a half of the eighteenth century.

Dr Thomas Coke

In January 1784 the Revd Thomas Coke opened his career as a missionary statesman with the issuance of his "Plan for the Society for the Establishment of Missions among the Heathens".[88] Later in the year he began a series of trans-Atlantic voyages during which the Methodist Episcopal Church in the United States was first instituted. In September 1786 he sailed from England for Nova Scotia on his second voyage, accompanied by three fellow ministers. Frequent storms and a mid Atlantic leak in their vessel carried the little party to the West Indies instead. Their safe arrival at St John's, Antigua, just in time to meet John Baxter on the street before his Christmas morning Methodist chapel service, was seen as a spectacular manifestation of divine overruling.[89] It should be noted however that one of Coke's fellow passengers, William Warrener, was already appointed to work with Baxter in Antigua, and was expecting to arrive there by a more indirect route. What the providential storms accomplished was to bring Coke himself to the West Indies sooner than would otherwise have been the case, to divert the other two missionaries, John Clarke and William Hammett, from their destination in Newfoundland, and to begin the rapid spread of Methodism throughout the Caribbean.

Some days were spent in the congenial surroundings of Antigua with its two thousand members in the Methodist Society. Then, after an "Infant Conference", Coke, Baxter, Clarke and Hammett sailed southward, leaving Warrener to his work in Antigua. They had an urgent invitation to visit St Vincent. On their way, both going and returning, their boat stopped at Dominica and they found opportunities to preach there. Even greater openings appeared in St Vincent, and Clarke was left to commence that mission.[90] This was the first evangelical approach to any of the islands ceded by France (in 1763), to which many British planters had moved from the older British colonies.

When Coke returned to the Leewards, a welcome was received for Methodist work in St Christopher both at the Basseterre end and at the opposite tip of Sandy Point. Although at first disappointed in the prospects at Nevis, later indications convinced him of possibilities there also.[91] Then took place the first of a series of episodes in the Dutch island of St Eustatius, a few miles north-west of Sandy Point.

In this trading station English was widely spoken, and Coke made his first venture beyond British territory. Here a black lay preacher from North America – like George Liele but with a Methodist rather than a Baptist background, and a slave rather than a freeman – had aroused his hearers. The initial favourable attitude of the government authorities to "Black Harry", as he was called, had just changed when Coke arrived and he had been forbidden to preach. Coke was able before leaving the island to form six "classes" to care for the converts, three of them under Harry's care. Brother Hammett was left in St Kitts to develop the work there and in St Eustatius.[92]

In seven busy weeks, before leaving for South Carolina in February 1787, Coke with his companions had instituted a pattern of missionary expansion. In the older British islands of Antigua and St Kitts, and in Barbados and Jamaica, approached two years later, Methodist enterprise operated alongside the quieter labours of the Moravians who had preceded them. The two evangelical bodies operated on friendly relations with one another. In the ceded territories of St Vincent, Dominica and Grenada however, the Methodists were the first to establish work.[93] St Vincent came to be the centre of the second Methodist District.[94] They also pioneered evangelical work in Nevis, Tortola, Montserrat and Swedish St Bartholemew (1796), and in a later period in Anguilla (1813) and St Martin (1817).[95]

Thomas Coke made altogether four Caribbean tours – curiously reminiscent of the apostle Paul's journeys and perhaps also of Columbus' voyages – returning in 1788–89, 1790–91, and 1792–93. On the second of these tours, a missionary, Benjamin Pearce, was left in Barbados, where he encountered stiff resistance.[96] In St Vincent an enthusiastic attempt was launched to reach the "Black Carib" Indians, in addition to the work centred in Kingstown. Already a couple, Mr and Mrs Joice, had been sent to start a school for Carib children, and John Baxter and his wife now volunteered to live and labour among them. This mission however almost immediately became frustrated by the activities of the French at the time of the Revolutionary War in the Antilles, and the outbreak of the "Carib war" in St Vincent in particular, culminating in the confiscation of the lands of the Caribs and their expulsion to Roatan.[97] William McCornock was assigned to begin work in Dominica, but he died after a short time and for a decade little success was achieved in this island.[98]

Moving north to the Leewards, Coke found the work in Antigua and St Kitts flourishing, and also in St Eustatius in spite of government opposition. Missionaries were left in Nevis and for a short time in Dutch-ruled Saba. Farther north, a beginning was made under William Hammett in Tortola, hitherto neglected by any organized church. An approach to the Danish island of Santa Cruz (St Croix) however met with an unsympathetic government and the Moravians were already well established.[99] At the close of the journey Coke reached Kingston, Jamaica, and prepared the way for the first Methodist missionary later in 1789 – the ubiquitous Hammett, by that time replaced in Tortola.[100]

During the remaining two journeys, in addition to revisiting the work already begun, Coke extended the Wesleyan cause southward to Grenada, and his journeys across Jamaica from Montego Bay through Spanish Town to Kingston and Port Royal prepared the way for gradual extension of missionary activity throughout that island.[101] By the time he held his final Caribbean Conference in Antigua in February 1793, membership in Methodist Societies in the area was reported as 6,570, more than three times what it had been in Antigua alone when he first arrived in 1786.[102] This included a Society of twelve persons in Montserrat, led by a "pious coloured person".[103] By 1804 Coke published statistics showing 14,376 members in the West Indies, of whom 112 were whites, the rest coloured and blacks. There were 160 in the Bahamas, where during the 1790s some black Methodists began religious work at Nassau.[104]

Apart from numbers the achievement of these years was remarkable. Evangelical activity was now commenced in almost every British colony.[105] The Wesleyan itinerant system was well adapted to the island society, with frequent change of personnel and the consequent building up of a strong loyalty to the Methodist societies (and later churches) in each place, rather than to the particular missionary. The "class-meeting" structure of the Methodist societies not only strengthened the Christian fellowship while a missionary was present but enabled it to carry on during the not infrequent vacancies when he was sick or died. In some cases (as in St Eustatius, Grenada and Montserrat, and later in Demerara, Anguilla and St Martin) such groups built up the cause before any missionary was appointed. Active lay participation was encouraged, with "exhorters" and local preachers. Others offered their property for religious meetings, collected money for building purposes and offered their talents and labour in such enterprise. The religious zeal and leadership abilities of blacks as well as whites and people of colour were encouraged and utilized.

The example of Coke's journeys laid the foundation also for a growing regional (Caribbean) consciousness at least within the Methodist connexion. The holding of district conferences, begun in this period, was continued and expanded as soon as the number of leaders and other circumstances permitted. This consciousness was promoted also by printed publications, notably Coke's own Journals and Reports and his *History of the West Indies*.[106] It is to be remembered that in these early years the financing and control of the missions was largely in the hands of Coke himself, working in co-operation with the British Conference. He imparted his wide vision to his missionaries and through them to the Church in formation in the West Indies.[107] This large outreach and the favourable religious climate were strengthened by a miniature evangelical diaspora in the Caribbean from Antigua,

North America, England and Ireland. This included Methodist and Moravian slaves moved or sold away to various islands, people formerly in contact with the Gilberts and Baxters, soldiers from England or Ireland, British people influenced by Methodist preaching at home or in the continental colonies.[108] In a few cases, notably in Grenada, the local Church of England clergyman was personally encouraging to the evangelical cause.[109]

While these new initiatives were being developed by Baptists and Wesleyans during the closing years of the eighteenth century, Moravian missionaries continued their long-established work. It was not a time of notable advance in Jamaica, but in Antigua growth was rapid and by 1799 their figures showed approximately 11,000 members. A marked increase took place also in the Danish islands.[110] The St Kitts mission began to thrive under the leadership of Brother and Sister George Schneller who arrived in 1788. In Barbados the mission station was transferred to Sharon, a more favourable site, in 1795.[111] Brother John Montgomery and his wife, missionaries from Barbados (and parents of the poet and hymn-writer James Montgomery), pioneered work in Tobago in 1790 when the island was occupied by the French. Their illness and death terminated the effort the following year. From 1799, with the island back in British hands, another start was made by Charles Schirmer, later joined by John Church. After four years, illness and other difficulties again forced the closure of the mission. Moravian occupation of Tobago did not become permanent until 1827.[112]

While it is difficult to obtain reliable figures of membership in the three evangelical denominations at the end of the century, it seems clear that about this time Moravian converts still outnumbered the Methodists if those in the Danish islands are included in the totals, but that numbers were not far from equal if only the British West Indies are considered.[113] Even more clear is that by this time active nonconformist evangelicals in the British colonies, almost all blacks and people of colour, greatly outnumbered practising members of the established Church, who were by all accounts a small fraction of the total white population, together with some of the free coloured.[114] It is not surprising that, realizing this fact, an increasing number of clergy and other church people and also of colonial governments, and ultimately the imperial government itself, became concerned to provide "religious instruction" for the slaves under the auspices of the state church. At the same time, as will be seen in the following chapter, there were sporadic attempts in the Caribbean to prevent by persecution this alarming spread of a new form of Christianity which was not under the control of the plantocracy.

New Missions and Growth in the New Century (1800–1823)

Evangelical expansion received reinforcement just before the turn of the century with the creation in Great Britain of several new missionary societies. The first was the Baptist Missionary Society (1792). The next, launched in 1794, is less well known than others, but was specially formed for the Caribbean. It was named "The Incorporated Society for the Conversion and Religious Instruction and Education of the Negroe Slaves in the British West India Islands" and was known as the Slave Conversion Society (later as the Christian Faith Society). There followed the London Missionary Society (LMS) (1795), the Edinburgh (later Scottish) Missionary Society (1796), the Church Missionary Society (1799) and the British and Foreign Bible Society (1804). The Wesleyan Methodist Missionary Society, initiated in 1813, was fully organized in 1817–18, although Dr Coke with his workers, under appointment by the Methodist Conference, had been effectively engaged in mission work long before that.[115] These societies were all active in the Caribbean in the early years of the new century.

The first of the new missions to appear was the Slave Conversion Society. Two clergymen arrived in Jamaica and Barbados in 1794, one in St Kitts the following year and another in Antigua in 1798. They were sent by Dr Bielby Porteous, bishop of London, to work among the slaves in fulfilment of his long-cherished plans for their Christianization and education. Others followed to Nevis (1805) and St Vincent (1810). In the latter year a schoolmaster was appointed to Antigua. In other cases clergy on the spot were paid for part-time service.[116]

This Society was hardly an evangelical missionary agency in the usual sense, intending as it did to work with and stimulate the established Church and the planters to provide "religious instruction" for the slaves.[117] The bishop complained of the same apathy and lack of co-operation that had been faced by Bishop Gibson and by the SPG in previous decades.[118] No doubt Porteous' support of slave trade abolition helped make his agency suspect to the proprietors.[119] However, after his death, as nonconformist missionaries continued to win followers, planters and churchmen looked more favourably on the religious instruction offered by these more conservative emissaries of the Bishop of London's Society. By 1823 the "West India Planters and Merchants of London" and at least two branch societies in the West Indies were contributing support to the work of the fifteen agents in six colonies.[120]

Three missionaries of the Scottish Missionary Society landed in Jamaica in 1800. Within a short time two of them died. The survivor, Mr Reid, a catechist, became a teacher but was silenced from religious work in 1802 by the Assembly's "Act to prevent preaching by persons not duly qualified by law". Permanent work by this Society was not secured until Revd George Blyth arrived in 1824.[121]

British occupation of the Dutch colonies of Essequibo-Demerara and Berbice during the Napoleonic wars (permanently from 1803), and the capture of Trinidad in 1797, paved the way for the opening of evangelical work in the Southern Caribbean, apart from the Moravian work in Surinam and Berbice already

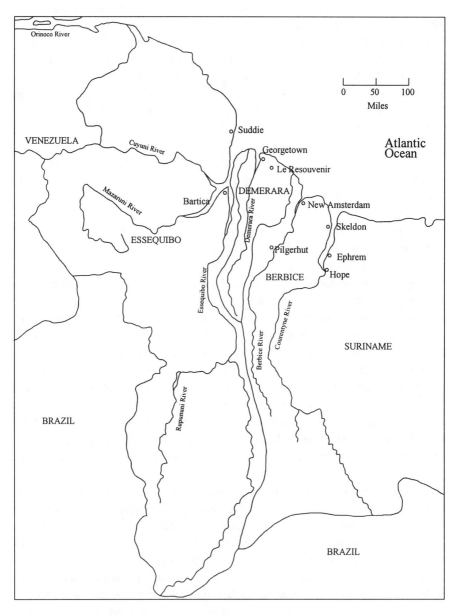

Guyana

mentioned. Here Methodists and the LMS were the pioneers. In Guiana there had been many British estate owners. Although the Dutch Reformed Church had been officially recognized, that body had done very little apart from the intermittent ministrations of Dutch predicants appointed from time to time to serve as preachers and pastors to the white population. Lutheranism had been represented by a single congregation in Berbice, founded in 1743, which maintained a continuous existence by lay initiative but had pastors for less than ten years up to 1779, and then none until 1818. Nothing was done by either church for the slaves. At the beginning of the nineteenth century there were but two church buildings in Guyana: the Lutheran in New Amsterdam, and a Dutch Reformed church on Fort Island on the Essequibo.[122]

Two free blacks from Nevis, named Claxton and Powell, having gone to Demerara in search of employment, formed a Methodist Society and appealed to Coke for a missionary. In 1805 John Hawkshaw was sent from Barbados, landing in Stabroek (later named Georgetown) in September. He was ordered by Governor Beaujon to leave by the same boat that had brought him. Nine years later a Methodist mission in Demerara was actually commenced by Thomas Talboys, who had already pioneered in Trinidad in 1809.[123]

Meanwhile just after the abolition of the slave trade, the LMS sent workers to Demerara and also to Tobago (1808), and the following year one of them, Thomas Adam, moved from Demerara to Trinidad. The missions in Tobago and in Trinidad lasted only a few years.[124] In the former Dutch colonies however LMS agents began a work which, although not in the long run outstanding in numbers, made an indelible mark upon the subsequent history of the British Caribbean. The unplanned involvement of missionaries Wray and Smith in the anti-slavery struggle will be recounted in the next chapter.

It was not any of the British settlers but a Dutch planter, Hermanus H. Post, who first invited the LMS to send someone to preach to his slaves at his Le Resouvenir estate in Demerara, seven miles from Georgetown. With Post's strong support John Wray, the pioneer, made rapid progress. A chapel was built on the estate before Post's death in 1809. In that year work was begun in Georgetown, and in spite of hostility from certain governors and slave owners, in a few years' time there were four mission stations including Berbice (to which Wray had moved in 1813) and West Coast Demerara.[125] At Le Resouvenir, served by John Smith from 1817 to 1823, some two thousand people were reported in catechism classes. His fellow worker comments: "I greatly lament that the missionaries in Demerara are not permitted to teach the slaves to read. Mr Smith would willingly devote part of the day to this work; and yet, after all, many do acquire the art of reading".[126] During these years the Methodist Society in Demerara founded by Claxton and Powell was augmented by Talboys and other missionaries to over twelve hundred people, and two circuits were formed at Georgetown and Mahaica.[127]

In Trinidad on the other hand, because of Roman Catholic opposition and the policy of Governor Woodford to favour and protect the Anglican and Catholic churches, both Methodists and LMS missionaries encountered difficulties. In 1818 the governor demanded of them a bond to abstain from argument about the doctrines of the recognized Churches. This requirement was disputed as contrary to the Toleration Act. Nonconformist chapels were closed for a time. Ultimately the LMS withdrew completely from the colony. Prior to emancipation only a small Methodist congregation in Port-of-Spain survived.[128]

However in this period evangelical Christianity was extended in rural Trinidad, especially in the south, apart from the action of any missionary body. After the War of 1812–14 some African-American ex-soldiers who had served in the war on the British side were given the opportunity of settlement in Trinidad. The first fifty of these arrived in 1815.[129] Together with others who followed later, these free blacks, who were mostly of a Baptist background, formed the "Company Villages" in the Savanna Grande area, near the present Princes Town. They carried on religious activities among themselves, and the name of William Hamilton, lay preacher in the Fifth Company Baptist Church, is to be added to those of George Liele, Moses Baker and Brother Amos as pioneer leaders of that denomination in the West Indies.[130] The LMS missionary Thomas Adam contacted them and offered to serve among them but was refused permission by Governor Woodford on the ground that it was had "in contemplation . . . to send a Clergyman of the Church of England for their service".[131] Nothing in fact was done by that Church and ultimately in the 1840s the Baptist Missionary Society made connection with these communities.

It was in Jamaica that the BMS first began work in the Caribbean. In the early years of the nineteenth century the Baptist congregations successfully established by George Liele, Moses Baker, Thomas Swigle and others suffered under repressive laws aimed at nonconformist religious activity of any kind. These pioneers continued to communicate with Baptist leaders in England.[132] Their concern led to the sending of John Rowe to the island in 1814 as the first BMS missionary. He visited the aging Baker at Crooked Spring (Flamstead) in St James, and in nearby Falmouth tried to establish a mission station as teacher and preacher. Two years later he died. Other missionaries, notably James Coultart, followed, developing school and church work in Kingston, Spanish Town and elsewhere. Further ill-health and mortality of missionaries kept progress slow at first, and not until the early 1820s did the spectacular spread of the Baptist mission get under way.[133]

The (Evangelical Anglican) Church Missionary Society (CMS) was founded as a "Society for missions in Africa and the East". Its policy was to leave the New World to the SPG. Hence it did not become involved in the Caribbean except in a small way and for a limited period before and after emancipation. In 1813 a former governor of Sierra Leone and member of the CMS Committee, William Dawes, went to live in Antigua. He offered to serve as an unpaid lay catechist, working among the blacks. The Society willingly agreed, and afterward granted money for the support of teachers for day schools and Sunday schools which Dawes sponsored.[134] Some of these schools were later taken over by agreement, together with their teachers, by the Methodists and Moravians.[135] Certain members of the Gilbert family in Antigua were associated with the work of the CMS.[136]

In Barbados the CMS was involved in 1818 through a personal contact with a zealous evangelical, a lieutenant of the Royal Artillery posted to that island, by the name of R. Lugger. At this time, following the recent slave revolt in Barbados, there was a surge of interest in education supported by the governor, Lord Combermere. This resulted in the formation of the "Barbados Society for Promoting Christian Knowledge" and the founding of schools for the coloured and black population. Similar activity was later undertaken in St Vincent and Dominica.[137]

The British and Foreign Bible Society, founded on an interdenominational basis by evangelical leaders in Great Britain, became concerned with the West Indies as early as 1808, when 900 Bibles and New Testaments were sent to a Quaker in Antigua who had offered to distribute them in places not reached by missionaries.[138] The following year the Revd C.I. Latrobe, secretary to the Missions of the United Brethren, wrote asking for 12,000 Bibles for distribution by Moravians in the British colonies as well as 500 for Surinam. These scriptures were received with thanks in Barbados, Antigua and St Kitts.[139] The annual reports record a stream of Bibles and New Testaments shipped to the Caribbean colonies, at least some of them intended "for literate negroes". The consignees include clergy of the established Church as well as persons connected with the evangelical groups: Moravian, Baptist, Wesleyan, CMS and LMS.[140] More than half of these scriptures went to Antigua and St Kitts where evangelical activity was long established, and mention of "schools" (in Antigua) is a further indication that education – with reading of the Bible as an important subject – was already a growing expression of Christian activity among the churches and missions, including Sunday schools and day schools.[141]

Alongside the coming of these new missionary societies, Moravians and Methodists continued their established work, usually successfully but with occasional setbacks. They proceeded for the most part quietly in the smaller islands and in the rural districts in St Elizabeth and neighbouring parishes which were the base of Moravian work in Jamaica.[142] On the other hand, in the Lesser Antilles and the Bahamas, the Barbados slave rebellion of 1816 precipitated temporary difficulties.[143] During most of this period Methodist activity in Jamaica was dominated by the struggle against persecuting efforts by island authorities. In spite of this, or perhaps in part because of it, membership grew from a few hundred to over nine thousand.[144]

It was not only in the Southern Caribbean that Methodism found new locations for work. William Turton, a Barbadian, was sent by the British Conference to the Bahamas in 1800. From New Providence evangelization spread to Eleuthera, Harbour Island, Abaco, Long Island and finally the Turks Islands.[145] John Hodge, a free coloured lay preacher (later ordained after nine years' service), pioneered in Anguilla and St Martin, and a missionary was finally sent to aid the Methodist Society long sustained by lay initiative in Montserrat.[146]

After almost sixty years of discouraging activity the Moravians in Jamaica began a notable growth. Around the year 1812 an upsurge of interest took place among the slaves in their vicinity. This was stimulated by the labours of George Lewis, a black slave first converted by Baptists in Virginia, who had begun to preach in Manchester and St Elizabeth. His freedom was purchased by the Moravian congregation at Old Carmel. Although Lewis did not become a Moravian himself he co-operated with them for a time as an evangelist, and this joint effort produced lasting effects.[147] In the Mile Gully region a similar awakening, likewise initiated by lay workers, built up the Moravian congregation at the Bogue, some twenty miles away. In 1820 the first chapel specifically for worship was erected at New Eden.[148] In all the islands the practice of "Speakings" – regular interviews of Moravian members with the missionaries on spiritual things, especially in preparation for the Communion services – helped to deepen the quality of religious life among the converts.[149]

Thus evangelicalism was widely diffused in the pre-amelioration era.[150] Essential to that spread was the fact that many converts – black, coloured and a few whites – became active propagators of the gospel message, by individual contact with their neighbours and also (to the dismay of the authorities) as preachers, class-leaders, "helpers" and congregational officers. Many slaves suffered punishment from hostile masters for their religious activity. Persecution of these converts, and of the missionaries themselves, had the unintended result of intensifying their zeal and attracting attention of others to their cause. It also stirred public opinion in Great Britain to support the missions, and ultimately to back the demand for emancipation of the slaves. These developments will be considered in the next two chapters.

9

Other Pre-Emancipation Developments (to 1823)

During the later decades of the slavery era, while evangelical missions were expanding, other forces also were affecting the life of the Church:

(i) The Roman Catholic Church, discountenanced in the older colonies, gained a place in the English Caribbean community, due to the accession of the former French colonies and Trinidad, and also to new migrations of Catholics from Latin America and Europe. Denominational pluralism, which had been largely lost early in the eighteenth century, was now decisively restored.

(ii) Parallel to this religious diversification, the antislavery movement, in part religious but also economic and political, was gathering strength in Great Britain, and threatening the whole structure of West Indian society.

(iii) Another force undermining the old order, within the Caribbean itself, was conflict over the presence of the missionaries who befriended the slaves. As planters sensed that their preaching was subversive of the mores and the existing social order, sporadic persecution broke out against them, and also against converted slaves.

The Rehabilitation of Roman Catholicism (1763–1824)

In the non-Spanish Caribbean, as seen in previous chapters, considerable freedom of religion prevailed in pioneer times, and also "Royal Instructions" from London confirmed a policy of toleration, but usually with an exception for "papists".[1]

Prior to the Seven Years' War an official account of the Roman Catholic Church in the American colonies mentioned some Catholics "almost all of Irish birth or descent" in Jamaica, Barbados, Antigua, St Kitts and Montserrat. Only in the last-mentioned island was there a considerable number (three or four hundred) and a settled leadership – "two Irish missionaries".[2] After the Treaty of Paris (1763) a similar document noted the importance of the French Catholic inhabitants of the ceded islands of Grenada, Dominica, St Vincent and Tobago, and hoped "that they will not be disturbed in the practice of their religion".[3] Although these people were distrusted by their English neighbours as long as wars between France and Britain continued (that is, until the Congress of Vienna in 1815), these "ceded islands" through the Treaty of Paris became in fact the base of Roman Catholic revival in the British Caribbean.[4]

By 1768 London's policy of toleration went as far as to grant to some Catholics "participation in the executive as well as the legislative offices of government" of the ceded islands, an innovation which caused strenuous opposition from new British settlers who had flocked there, expecting to have monopolistic rights.[5]

Resistance came to a head in the island of Grenada. In 1774 by "the Campbell case" the royal power to impose taxation over the elected Assembly was ruled illegal. The same principle was applied to the toleration measures of the British government when in 1790 the crown lawyers in London declared that only the colonial legislature could initiate exemption from the Test (the declaration against transubstantiation required of assembly and council members). At the same time the churches and glebes of the Roman Church were ruled to be at the king's disposal by right of conquest.[6] Meanwhile the Roman Church had enjoyed official freedom in spite of opposition from the British planters. The reimposition of the Test by the Assembly after twenty-one years, as the culmination of other anti-Catholic measures, was one of the causes of Fédon's rebellion (1795–96) in which forty-eight British prisoners including the governor were massacred.[7]

Other formerly French islands, notably Dominica and later St Lucia, adapted themselves quietly to the age of toleration.[8] At first the Roman Church in the ceded islands had retained ecclesiastical association with nearby Martinique.[9] However the French Revolution and the subsequent Napoleonic Empire created turmoil in the Church in the French Antilles.[10] Then in 1797 the capture of Trinidad, with its Spanish and French Church, substantially increased the number of Roman Catholics under British rule. The French and Spanish in these islands, together with their slaves, maintained their Catholic tradition.[11]

The cession of Santo Domingo to the French in 1795 by the Treaty of Basel had begun a series of changes in the ecclesiastical associations of Trinidad. This island was a part of the (Spanish) diocese of Guayana, with its seat at Angostura on the Orinoco River, which in turn belonged to the archdiocese of Santo Domingo.[12] The Trinidad Church suddenly found itself under British rule and with its archbishop in Hispaniola already in French territory. Then in 1803 the diocese of Guayana was made part of the new archdiocese of Caracas, which was more or less coterminous with the later boundaries of Venezuela. Eight years later Venezuela declared its independence from Spain. However, royalist armies, supported by the Capuchin missionaries, held out in the Orinoco region until 1817, at which time the bishop-elect of Guayana left the diocese with the withdrawal of royalist troops.[13]

With these sweeping changes in the Spanish Empire, the post-revolutionary disturbance in the French Church, and the new political allegiance of Trinidad, the time had come to stabilize the position of the Roman Catholic Church in the Protestant-ruled colonies of the Caribbean.

The British government's policy of toleration was extended in the case of Trinidad. It gave official recognition to the Roman Catholic Church, and by an irony attributable to the Spanish *patronato real*, its first bishop was confirmed (1820) by the British monarch. The curious anomaly of a British king, and head of the Church of England, authorizing the appointment of the first resident episcopal authority of the Roman Catholic Church in the British Caribbean was the logical result of his having become, by right of conquest, successor to the Spanish monarch in Trinidad, with his right of veto over ecclesiastical appointments. After nomination by the Holy See, the Rt Revd James Buckley, Bishop of Gerren *in partes infidelium*, was confirmed by George III as vicar apostolic. Bishop Buckley's jurisdiction included the British, and also the Dutch and Danish West Indies. This episcopal arrangement was five years earlier than the institution of bishoprics for the established Church of England in the West Indies, nine years before Catholic emancipation in Great Britain, and thirty years before bishops were appointed in the French Antilles. The Protestant governor inherited a sort of patronage over the Roman Catholic Church in Port-of-Spain.[14] This was especially notable in the time of Governor Woodford (1813–28).[15]

With reference to the Christianizing of the slaves, the French and Spanish Catholics had the advantage of having long emphasized the importance of baptism, a measure of religious instruction, and plantation prayers with the masters. Their priests moved actively among the people, and the continued use of the French and Spanish languages helped them keep the loyalty of both whites and blacks.[16] Clergy of the established Church of England in Dominica and Grenada pointed out such difficulties when Bishop Porteous, newly translated to the see of London, circularized the clergy of the West Indies in 1788 urging them to undertake the religious instruction of the slaves.[17] Evangelical missionaries encountered the same problems and their progress was slow in the former French territories and Trinidad, at least until the influx of people from other colonies increased the number open to their message.[18]

As already noted, Montserrat with its Irish Catholic background was believed to be difficult for similar reasons, but it is by no means clear that Irish Catholicism in that island was comparable to that on the nearby French islands in its dealing with the slaves.[19] On the whole the Roman Catholic example in the ceded islands, and in Trinidad and St Lucia, like that of the evangelicals throughout the West Indies, stimulated at least some of the English plantocracy, the clergy of the established Church, and government authorities to try to Christianize the slaves.

The legal traditions of the Catholic French and Spanish colonies also indirectly strengthened the move towards more humane treatment of the slaves, though not the demand for full emancipation. The French islands had been governed since 1685 under the Code Noir, however incompletely its somewhat humane requirements had been enforced.[20] Trinidad, like other Spanish colonies, had a cédula (1789) for the protection of slaves which was more enlightened than the French *Code*. The British government thought it wise to use the Trinidad edict in some ways as a model for its own programme of amelioration. Since Trinidad and St Lucia, and also Demerara-Essequibo and Berbice, were crown colonies, it was able to impose this new policy by Order-in-Council.[21] In the older colonies which had their own legislatures, however, there was stubborn resistance to such reforms emanating from London.

Before the amelioration period, Roman Catholicism had begun to win a foothold in traditionally Protestant colonies as well. In 1792 the vicar apostolic in London sent Father Anthony Quigley, an Irish Franciscan, to Jamaica to care for Spanish and other scattered Catholics who had found their way there. This restored the Church to recorded activity after an interval of 137 years since the English conquest.[22] In the following year French refugees from St Domingue entered Jamaica and one of them, a Dominican, succeeded Quigley as pastor in 1799. Another refugee, from revolutionary New Granada, Benito Fernández, took charge in 1824.

The Anti-Slavery Movement (to 1823)

In the 1670s two Quaker preachers, the already mentioned George Fox and William Edmundson, were the first to raise questions about slavery in the West Indies. Fox's counsel in Barbados, being based upon the Old Testament idea of slaves being part of the "family", was of course irrelevant to the plantation society. But it included the radical advice to let their slaves "go free after a considerable term of years, if they have served them faithfully; and when they go, and are made free, let them not go away empty-handed". Fox's *Journal* indicates that thirty years was the approximate time of service he had in mind, not indeed the six years (for fellow Hebrew slaves) of the text to which he referred.[23] Later Edmundson wrote a "Letter to the Governour and Council and all in Authority in this Island of Barbadoes" which contained several references to divine punishment of "Oppression", indicating the trend of his thinking. Seven months later, after the Barbados Law had been passed prohibiting Quaker evangelization of the slaves, he was ready to go a step further. Now in the slave trading city of Newport, Rhode Island, Edmundson wrote in an epistle to Friends in America:

> It would be acceptable with God, and answer the witness in all, if you did consider their condition of perpetual slavery, and make their conditions your own, and so fulfil the law of Christ. For perpetual slavery is an aggravation, and an oppression upon the mind,

and hath a ground; and Truth is that which works the remedy, and breaks the yoke, and removes the ground. So it would do well to consider that they may feel, see, and partake of your liberty in the gospel of Christ.

So far it might seem that Edmundson, like Fox and the Old Testament, was opposed only to the permanent condition of slavery, and was appealing simply for manumission after a temporary servitude. But the implications are more far-reaching. Edmundson finally asked bluntly: "And many of you count it unlawful to make slaves of the Indians: and if so, then why the Negroes?"[24] This Quaker evangelist, having experienced, like other missionaries after him, the disposition of West Indian planter society to put obstacles in the way of preaching the gospel, had come to see that slavery *as such* was wrong. Christianity and slavery were incompatible. In the century and a half which followed, many others were to come to this conclusion.

His contemporaries, Baxter the Puritan and Godwyn the Anglican, came near to saying this, but fell short of the final insight. Even Edmundson does not seem to have pursued the matter further, but he lived long enough (1712) to see others take it up. As is well known, the movement to eliminate slavery within the Society of Friends first expressed itself corporately in 1688 in the formal remonstrance against slavery by a Friends' Meeting at Germantown (near Philadelphia).[25] The story has often been told of how, in America and England through the following decades, Quaker participation in the slave trade, and then in slave ownership, was whittled down to zero.[26] That story need not be related here, for Quakers of the West Indies were hardly involved directly in this movement.

Yet indirectly they were involved. The profitable trade in slaves from Quaker merchants in the Caribbean colonies to their coreligionists in North America was one ugly reality which began to cause American Friends to search their consciences. In 1698 the Philadelphia Meeting sent an official letter to the Barbados Meeting asking Friends there to stop shipping slaves to Pennsylvania.[27] This advice against trade in slaves was reiterated in 1711, and by the Rhode Island Yearly Meeting in 1717.[28] West Indian Quakers were feeling their means of livelihood questioned by Friends abroad. Travelling Quakers kept them aware of the issue. Thomas Chalkley tells how on a visit to Barbados in 1735 he rebuked the "tyranny and cruelty" of slave owners, thereby provoking a disturbance at the meeting, and suffered wounds afterward when an exasperated hearer "meeting me on the King's High-way, shot off his Fowling Piece at me, being loaded with Small-shot".[29] One problem was that, while the mainland colonies had other varieties of trade or business, in the islands almost every occupation involved slavery. It is more than coincidence that as the anti-slavery movement grew, Quaker meetings in the West Indies dwindled and their overseas correspondence ceased.[30] Friends left for less iniquitous occupations elsewhere, or cooled their zeal and identified with the rest of the planters.

Another link between the Caribbean and the anti-slavery movement was the residence there of Ralph Sandiford and of Benjamin and Sarah Lay, three English Quakers. Sandiford had spent time in Barbados, the Bahamas and South Carolina, and in 1729 published in Philadelphia an angry attack on slave ownership.[31] Lay and his wife, some time prior to 1731, moved from England to Barbados where they lived by keeping a store. Horrified by the cruelty they observed, they migrated to Philadelphia, hoping to find there a more congenial Quaker community. Instead they found that Sandiford had been ostracized by the Yearly Meeting over his battle for the slaves. Benjamin and Sarah Lay were both hunchbacks, and he at least was very eccentric. From a home in a cave outside the "city of Brotherly Love" he carried on a provocative anti-slavery campaign like an Old Testament prophet until and after the Friends disowned him in 1738. Thus Barbados had a share in the making of the most colourful of Quaker abolitionists.[32] Later the saintly John Woolman, a still more important figure in the Friends' wrestle with slavery, considered visiting Barbados, but he would probably have been disappointed in the response from the few Quakers who were left there in 1769.[33]

While this crusade within the Society of Friends was going on, several intellectual influences in Britain were slowly converging on the question of slavery. One of these was the liberalizing theological and ecclesiastical movement within the Church of England known as latitudinarianism. This school of thought praised the feeling of benevolence and was relatively open to new ideas. Many were involved in the SPG and in other humanitarian projects. Against the deists they developed a theology of progressive revelation which allowed for the hope of social change and improvement.[34] Because this "broadness" of view was combined with an innate conservatism, however, its influence on the anti-slavery movement was largely an indirect one.

A second aspect of the intellectual ferment was philosophical, moving from the "moral sense" doctrine of Shaftesbury to the teaching of Francis Hutcheson. This Glasgow professor, the son and grandson of dissenting ministers, expounded "a benevolent theory of morals" as an empirical rather than a religious system, although acknowledging the divine wisdom and goodness as a parallel principle. His advocacy of a "calm, stable, universal goodwill" towards the "greatest happiness" of all, and his stress on "the sympathetick sense, Compassion" appealed to many.[35] He took the important step of directly controverting the "classical" Aristotelian assumptions that some men are slaves "by nature" and others by right of conquest, affirming "the natural Equality of Men" and their rights. Adam Smith, Hutcheson's successor in the chair of Moral Philosophy at Glasgow, reaffirmed and extended his ideas in his own first work, the *Theory of Moral Sentiments*.[36]

From another philosophical perspective Baron de Montesquieu had begun to challenge the traditional arguments in favour of slavery about the same time as

Hutcheson (in the 1730s). Other leaders of the French Enlightenment, notably Voltaire, Rousseau, the Encyclopedists, Raynal and some of the Physiocrats, joined the attack. Liberty and natural law were seen as incompatible with human bondage. However the rationalism of the Enlightenment (even of Montesquieu and Voltaire) was by no means univocal on the subject of slavery.[37] The *philosophes* were widely read in Scotland, England and North America and there was reciprocal influence as well. In the English-speaking world however religious thought played a greater part.[38]

In the field of literature also a growing interest in Africa and Africans, marked by admiration and sentiment about "the noble savage", contributed to the swing of public attitudes on slavery.[39]

These diverse winds of thought were brought into focus by Anthony Benezet, a Philadelphia Quaker. Himself an incisive writer he was also a publicizer of other men's anti-slavery arguments, and of knowledge about Africa and the slave trade. He became an agitator with wide international connections and indefatigable energy in the cause he had made his own. In 1762 his *Short Account of that part of Africa Inhabited by the Negroes* quoted the criticisms of slavery of Hutcheson and others.[40] He corresponded on the subject with notable persons including John Wesley, Benjamin Franklin, Abbé Raynal and Nathaniel Gilbert of Antigua. Gilbert sent him a courteous and sympathetic reply, indicating that this Methodist pioneer and slave owner was troubled about the slave system.[41]

Benezet became involved in a debate that was going on across the Atlantic in the forum provided by the annual sermons of the SPG.[42] Although as early as 1750 one preacher, Bishop Richard Trevor, had spoken of the slave trade as "a sort of Traffick not easy to be vindicated", fifteen years later the SPG pulpit was used by Bishop Philip Yonge to air some very conservative views on the relations between Europeans and Africans. He tried to justify the slave trade.[43] The following year (1766), probably with this in mind, Bishop William Warburton, a controversial writer and churchman, used the occasion to make a bold attack on the whole institution of slavery, including the following:

Gracious God! to talk (as in herds of Cattle) of Property in rational creatures! Creatures endowed with all our Faculties, possessing all our qualities but that of colour; our BRETHREN both by Nature and Grace, shocks all the feelings of humanity, and the dictates of common sense . . . Yet nothing is more certain in itself, and apparent to all, than that the infamous traffic for Slaves, directly infringes both divine and human law. *Nature* created Man, free: and Grace invites him to assert his freedom . . .

Be so gracious then, ye petty tyrants over human freedom, to let your Slaves judge for themselves, what it is which makes their own *happiness*. And then see whether they do not place it in the Return to their own country, rather than in contemplation of your grandeur, of which, their misery makes so large a part.[44]

In 1767 Benezet published A *Caution and a Warning to Great Britain and her Colonies*, appending to it an extract of Warburton's sermon. He wrote the SPG, sending copies of this booklet and pleading with it to "seriously consider whether the necessity of at least endeavouring to put a stop to this infamous Traffick is not an Object peculiarly worthy the attention & labour of a Society appointed for the Propagation of the Gospel". Dr Daniel Burton, Secretary of the Society, replied in February 1768 in a much-quoted letter that set forth its position at the time. Expressing concern for the good treatment of slaves and pointing to their own policy in this regard on their estates in Barbados, "hoping that the good effects of their Example will have a proper, & by degrees, a general influence on other owners of Slaves in America", he continues:

> But they cannot condemn the Practice of keeping Slaves as unlawful, finding the contrary very plainly implied in the precepts given by the Apostles, both to Masters & Servants, which last were for the most part Slaves; And if the doctrine of the unlawfulness of Slavery should be taught in our Colonies, the Society apprehend that Masters, instead of being convinced of it, will grow more suspicious & cruel, & much more unwilling to let their Slaves learn Christianity; & that the poor Creatures themselves, if they come to look on this doctrine, will be so strongly tempted by it to rebel against their Masters, that the most dreadful consequences to both will be likely to follow.[45]

In the same month Bishop John Green's SPG sermon took a similar stand, refusing to oppose slavery as such but asking for its amelioration.[46] Here the matter rested until 1783 when Bishop Porteous's sermon again challenged the Society's complacency about West Indian slavery.[47] Thus, as in the sixteenth century thinkers of the religious orders had disputed in Spain about the enslavement of the Amerindians, so in the eighteenth episcopal preachers debated the rights of African slaves in the colonies. Because of its ownership of the Codrington estates the SPG was particularly vulnerable to criticism.[48]

By the 1770s other religious leaders emerged within the anti-slavery movement. The celebrated "Mansfield Judgment", ensuring that a slave could not unwillingly be moved abroad from England, was the result of the work of Granville Sharp, a layman who was the son and grandson of prominent churchmen and who became one of the "Clapham sect" in later years. Although not legally emancipating slaves on English soil (as has often been said) this landmark decision was an initial victory in the drive against the slavery system. Together with a similar Scottish decision in 1778, it threw colonial slave owners on the defensive and brought the issue graphically before the British public.[49] Sharp became a correspondent and collaborator of Benezet, and tried to stir English churchmen to awareness of the cruelties of slavery.[50]

The publication of John Wesley's *Thoughts upon Slavery* in 1774 signalled the beginning of Methodist involvement in the movement. It contained such forthright statements as: "All Slavery is as irreconcileable to Justice as to Mercy . . . I deny that villany is ever necessary . . . *Men-buyers* are exactly on a level with *Men-stealers*".[51] This book had been inspired by a recent writing of Benezet, and was reprinted by him in turn in Philadelphia.[52] Wesley's stand, which was reaffirmed in his *Serious Address to the People of England* (1778) and was made official Methodist policy by the Conference of 1780, became an important factor in the West Indian situation. Methodism was now identified with the anti-slavery cause in the eyes of the planters, in spite of efforts to de-emphasize the policy in the colonies.[53]

Thomas Coke, who originally shared Wesley's animosity to slavery and made a bold effort in Virginia on his first trip to America to persuade slave owners to free their bondsmen, met with such violent opposition that he concluded that to air these views where slave owners were in power was futile. It would make it impossible to bring the gospel to the slaves, "our work being in too infantile a state to push things to extremity". This was in 1785, before he reached the West Indies.[54] By 1787 (after his visit here) he wrote in his journal, "I now acknowledge that however just my sentiments may be concerning slavery, it was ill-judged of me to deliver them from the pulpit." His *Journal*, however, was published with this remark in it, showing his real attitude, and in 1807 he had successfully advocated in conference the policy of forbidding Methodist preachers in the West Indies to marry women who owned slaves.[55]

Another significant dimension of the anti-slavery movement was brought into the open in 1776 by Adam Smith. Linking (as he believed) the principles of benevolence and happiness with economic utility, he advocated in his *Wealth of Nations* the policy of free enterprise and free trade, providing a rallying cry for many of the new entrepreneurs of Britain in the coming decades. He attacked the system of mercantilism within which the West Indian sugar industry operated.[56] He also observed that slave labour was more expensive than free labour and therefore less profitable, attributing its popularity to the pride of slave owners rather than to economic value.[57] The financial and political influence of the new industrial and commercial middle class was growing in the same period as the moral crusade against slavery.[58]

Thus by the mid 1770s a variety of influences, religious, philosophical, literary and economic, had combined to challenge the traditional acceptance of the institution of slavery. Educated opinion in Britain was largely won over to this view.[59]

How much response was there in the Caribbean to these winds of change? We have seen in earlier chapters that neither Quakerism nor evangelical religion nor even the limited humanitarianism of the SPG gained much recognition in the circle of the plantocracy. As for the philosophical, literary and economic thinking of the age, there was lacking in the West Indies not only a university but any other agency for serious intellectual study and discussion.[60] Schools were few, and children of the well-to-do were sent to the United Kingdom for an education. Many remained there. Absenteeism left control of plantations and culture in the hands of a remnant with limited outlook.[61] Where the press existed it reflected local interests, not larger issues. Writers (who had to publish in England except for brief pamphlets) were few, and shared the viewpoint of the privileged class.[62] Clergy of local origin, sent to England for ordination, usually had little educational training. Ministers born and educated in England or Scotland were starved of intellectual companionship among their parishioners or with each other in their scattered locations. They frequently complained of indifference toward religion in their communities, but only occasionally was there mention of secular or unorthodox philosophies.[63] The question now was: how would the new anti-slavery conviction reach from Great Britain to the West Indies, where the slave system prevailed?

REPRODUCED BY COURTESY OF THE NATIONAL PORTRAIT GALLERY, LONDON

James Ramsay

At the time of Warburton's and Wesley's outbursts against slavery there was in St Kitts a clergyman who was in direct contact with slave conditions and who ultimately, in Lascasian fashion, recrossed the Atlantic to attack them in the imperial homeland. He was James Ramsay, a Scotsman educated in Aberdeen under the philosopher Thomas Reid. Unable at first to enter his preferred profession, the ministry of the Church, Ramsay became a surgeon in the Royal Navy.[64] In 1759 he was called to a slaveship which was travelling near his vessel among the Antilles, to treat the victims of an epidemic, thus gaining firsthand knowledge of conditions on the middle passage. Becoming lame shortly afterward by an accident aboard his own ship, he turned his thoughts again to the service of the Church and was recommended for a vacancy on St Kitts. He was ordained by the bishop of London in 1762 and took up the livings of Christchurch, Nicolatown and St John's Capesterre on the windward side of the island.[65] Here he began to befriend the slaves, tried to teach them Christianity, and added medical work among them to his pastoral duties for his white parishioners.[66]

Ramsay soon found himself in conflict with the slaveholding interests, although he had married into a planter family. After fourteen years of contention he returned to Great Britain and then, during the American Revolutionary War, to the West Indies squadron of the navy.[67] Finally he resigned his Kittitian livings and became rector of Teston and Nettlestead in Kent, England. During the remaining eight years of his life he published several critiques of Caribbean social conditions, conferred with anti-slavery leaders, and became a storm centre of the movement against the slave trade. Hounded ruthlessly by the gentlemen of the West India interest, he died in July 1789.[68] By this time the anti-slavery movement had become organized with the formation in 1787 of the Society for Effecting the Abolition of the Slave Trade.

Two other Scotsmen, like Ramsay, were stirred to action by residence in the West Indies. James Stephen, on his way to St Kitts as a lawyer, observed in Barbados in 1783 a grossly unfair trial of a slave who was condemned to death. Becoming increasingly restive in slave society, he supplied facts and information to Wilberforce in England, then after his return there openly joined the anti-slavery movement. He and his sons became leading strategists in the campaign.[69] A little after him Zachary Macaulay went to Jamaica where he spent four years as an overseer.[70] These men became active members of the fellowship of Anglican Evangelicals known as the Clapham sect, along with William Wilberforce, Granville Sharp and others, who contributed actively to the fight against slavery.[71]

We are here concerned only indirectly with the details of the struggle for abolition of the slave trade and (later) for emancipation. This story has been told from various points of view.[72] The debate about causes – the relative importance of social idealism, Christian zeal, economic forces and the slaves' own struggle for liberty – will doubtless continue. Scholarship reveals how complicated was this unprecedented campaign. In its complexity the importance of religious and philosophical factors has been restated and even enlarged, while slave resistance and economic and political influences have been more broadly recognized and analysed. Without the combination of socioeconomic and "idealistic" motives the overthrow of slavery would have been far more protracted, and the shaping of the Church in the West Indies, as well as the fate of the institution of slavery, would have been quite different. Moreover the implications of this line of study extend beyond the point of the abolition of slavery itself. The tensions seen most clearly in that struggle were not magically dissolved by making slaves into freed people. They recur in some measure in the system of indentured labour which replaced it, and in "the ordeal of free labour" which broke out into such disturbances as those of 1865, 1919, 1937 and 1970.[73]

Our chief concern with the anti-slavery movement is its effects on the environment in which the Church was operating. The campaign for abolition of the slave trade alerted the planters to the possibility of imperial interference with their labour supply. The French Revolution, with its slogans of "liberty, equality and fraternity", launched uprisings in the Antilles. The one in St Domingue sent shockwaves throughout neighbouring English-speaking islands.[74] The Maroon war in Jamaica, Fédon's rebellion in Grenada and the Carib war in St Vincent brought civil strife to these islands themselves. Although the conservative reaction in Great Britain following the French Revolution delayed abolition for several years, legislation to stop the foreign slave trade was passed in 1807.

To enforce this policy, the registration of slaves in the colonies was demanded. Revolts of slaves, common enough before this time, now came to be related to the expectations raised by news of the advocacy of their cause in Britain. Such a revolt in Barbados in 1816 led to a proclamation by the Prince Regent denying that emancipation had been ordered, but recommending "to the Local Authorities in the respective colonies to . . . promote the moral and religious improvement, as well as the comfort and happiness of the Negroes".[75] This recommendation gained little response, but legislatures finally passed slave registration bills. There the matter rested until the formation of "the Society for the Mitigation and Gradual Abolition of Slavery throughout the British Dominions" in January 1823. During the following decade the evangelical missions and the established Church in the West Indies were entangled in events which led up to emancipation, as seen in the next chapter.

Persecution of Religious Work (1787–1823)

Opposition to evangelical preaching, as already noted, appeared as early as 1739 in St Thomas. Yet in the earlier decades, while tactful Moravians, the planter Gilbert family and the shipwright Baxter carried it on, there was little persecution. George Liele and the other Baptist pioneers, after initial difficulties, disarmed the suspicions of slave owners that religion would make their bondsmen rebellious. The "Native Baptists" however, and the aggressive missionary strategy of the Wesleyans, their itinerant system and zealous cultivation of lay leadership, aroused the anxiety of the plantation interests. If not the missionaries themselves, at least many of their friends in England were supporting the drive against the slave trade. The arrival in the new century of other nonconformist missions, and the eager response of the slaves to preaching addressed primarily to them, compounded the situation. From time to time the planters tried to stop the activities of people whom they could not control and whom they suspected of disturbing the security of the established social order.

What were the real reasons for this suspicion? In fact missionaries exhorted converts in New Testament language to "obey their masters" and give respect to them, "even to the froward". They had been instructed by their Societies to avoid political and social questions and concern themselves solely with their religious work.[76]

In spite of this prudent policy the "religious" work of evangelizing inevitably created conflict with the prevailing pattern of life in slave society. Let us consider some important sources of friction between preachers and masters.

The root of the matter was the call of the evangelists to a primary allegiance to God. The system laid a total claim by the owner upon the life and obedience of the slave who was his "property". Christianity introduced this counter-claim which ultimately challenged such absolute power, even though loyalty to God was clearly taught as including obedience to the master. A "lawyer under the Crown" wrote to Lord Bathurst in 1816:

> On my arrival at Demerary I found it to be the general sentiment that the doctrines of the missionaries in rapidly loosening, if not destroying, all the common bonds of authority and obedience, were already in themselves great evils, and might ultimately prove fatal to the prosperity of the colony.[77]

The Jamaica Assembly sixteen years later blamed "the sects called Baptist, Wesleyan Methodist, and Moravians" for

> producing in the minds of the Slaves a belief that they could not serve both a Spiritual and a Temporal master; thereby occasioning them to resist the lawful authority of their Temporal, under the delusion of rendering themselves more acceptable to a Spiritual Master.[78]

This religious claim required attendance at corporate worship, evangelistic meetings, class meetings and the like. It meant regular, even if small, contributions to church expenses. It might involve volunteer labour in erecting chapels, appointment to office in the congregation, or other assistance in the church's work. All this was seen by the profitminded planter as a threat to his right to the time and labour of his slaves and as "idleness on pretence of having time for religious duties".[79] He feared also that gatherings of slaves out of his control, particularly if held at night, would give opportunity for conspiracy. Hence repeated attempts by colonial legislatures to forbid such meetings between sunset and sunrise, which of course was the only time apart from Sunday that most of the slaves were free of estate work.[80]

Sunday observance was another religious duty. This day of the week, although usually left free of plantation work except in crop time, was the interval for slaves to cultivate their gardens, and Sunday was also their marketday. Missionaries, some clergy and their converts wanted another day free from work so that the Lord's Day could become a day of rest and worship.[81]

Yet another religious duty was Bible reading, which called for church members to learn to read. Apart from the time away from work that this would involve, masters feared that literacy would diminish subserviency and facilitate conspiracy. In spite of scattered earlier efforts to start educational programmes for adults and children, the founding of Sunday schools, day schools and evening schools was not very successful until the amelioration period, and only came into its own after emancipation.[82]

The very idea of allowing slaves to marry went against the absolute power of owners over the lives of their chattels. In particular it would cause difficulty when a married slave was to be sold off the estate. The breaking up of families through such sale already was criticized by missionaries, the slaves themselves, and abolitionists abroad. How much more if the union had been blessed by Christian marriage. In spite of efforts by missionaries and the British government to encourage slave marriage, few such ceremonies took place prior to emancipation.[83]

Moreover it was part of the slave system that female slaves were available for concubinage not only to their owners but to white overseers, bookkeepers and other officers on the estates. This of course in the eyes of missionaries was contrary to Christian principles. The teaching of moral purity in this sense was one of the most vexatious things that the missionaries did.[84]

Another source of tension was that the evangelicals, in line with their conviction that all are equal before God, undermined the sense of inferiority which slavery sought to impose upon the slaves in order to make them docile. Lay leadership by blacks and people of colour (as well as whites) was encouraged, and an increasing number of preachers, "exhorters", and other officers in the churches began to blur the race-class distinctions of slave society. Governor Woodford complained to Bathurst: "My present principal objection to the Methodist preacher is that he teaches and allows the slaves to preach."[85] Moreover in a racist social order these white missionaries refused to identify themselves with white society. "From the intimacies which they contract with the negroes, their presence is always a source of uneasiness."[86] Any equalitarian tendency was anathema to the plantocracy. As one of its spokesmen wrote: "The religious doctrine that all men are equal in the sight of God is very liable with the ignorant to a political misinterpretation."[87] It is true that for some of the missionaries themselves the social implications of this theological message were still obscured by traditional social attitudes and even predestinarian doctrine.[88] In historical perspective it is necessary in later times to remember that the egalitarian or democratic ideal was struggling for acceptance also in Great Britain at this time. Distinctions between slave and free, and between black, coloured and white in the Caribbean were compounded with traditional distinctions of class still widely accepted in metropolitan society. The missionaries for the most part came from working class or lower middle class backgrounds. They transferred to the West Indies the empathy and human contact with the common people, combined with a cautious political conservatism, which was characteristic of the British evangelicals at home. This enabled them to gain a wide response to their message while minimizing conflict with the political authorities.[89]

The missionaries, and societies that sent them, were suspected of being in sympathy with the abolitionists in Great Britain. Here again the policy of silence endeavoured to conceal the truth in this suspicion. Many of them cautiously sympathized with the aims of the anti-slavery campaign, and some kept in touch with its leaders in Great Britain. As time went on those became fewer who, although looking forward to "ultimate" emancipation, believed the slaves were "not yet ready" for freedom. The policy of silence was broken more frequently by events on both sides of the ocean. Each partial success – abolition of the slave trade, the drive for slave registration, Canning's resolutions for "amelioration" – intensified the suspicion of collaboration.[90]

The missions were also suspected of encouraging slave rebellion. This supposition was turned into legal charges in 1823 in Demerara and in 1831–32 in Jamaica. Such mistrust was of course groundless as far as the missionaries themselves were concerned. When they came to hear of the possibility of resistance they counselled energetically against it, not only because they believed such violence to be wrong but also because they knew that it would result in ruthless punishment or death for any converts and other slaves who were, or seemed to be, insurgent.[91]

What of the church members themselves? Here the answer is not so simple. No doubt many accepted the teaching that it was their duty to be loyal to their masters, that it was wrong to resort to violence or take life, and that to take part in rebellion would be foolish and dangerous. At the same time they knew that they had friends in Britain who were working for their freedom.[92] Clearly many others were not convinced, because they were thinking and feeling for themselves about some of the biblical passages they had heard or (in the case of those who could do so) had read for themselves.[93] When Governor Murray of Demerara "expostulated for at least half an hour" with rebellious slaves near John Smith's Le Resouvenir in 1823, they told him that "God had made them of the same flesh and blood as the whites, that they were tired of being slaves to them, that they should be free and they would not work any more".[94] With this theological premise, it is not surprising that Murray in the same despatch concluded (however inaccurately): "It is evident that this mischief was plotted at the Bethel Chapel, that the leaders are the chief men of the chapel, that the parson could not have been ignorant of some such project under the circumstances".[95] Somewhat similar theological ideas are found in the statements recorded of Samuel Sharpe, active in the Baptist church in Montego Bay, who admitted starting the Christmas rebellion eight years later in Jamaica.[96]

All in all, the words of the *Royal Gazette* in Demerara in 1808 proved to be prophetic:

> It is dangerous to make slaves Christians without giving them their liberty. . . What will be the consequences when to that class of men is given the title of *beloved brethren*, as is actually done? Will not the negro conceive that by baptism, being made a Christian, he is as credible as his Christian white brethren?[97]

Just how explosive and how contrary to the temper of slave society was the evangelical teaching may be seen in two sermons preached in Barbados by the Revd William Shewsbury, who soon became widely known when his Methodist chapel was torn down by a white mob.[98] His sermon of 10 October 1821 (a government appointed Fast-Day commemorating the 1780 hurricane) took Amos 4:11–12 ("Prepare to meet thy God, O Israel") as a text. Pointing to a series of hurricanes, earthquakes, floods, fevers, the Souffriere volcanic eruption of 1812 and the slave revolt of 1816, he warned:

> These Islands . . . seem to have been selected as the theatre on which to exhibit public displays of the just and holy government of God . . . In all these visitations, the *chief* sufferers have been the civilized, European, Christian inhabitants . . . Whether in this respect we have been like the Jews, impenitent and unyielding, it now becomes us on this day of fasting and public humiliation most seriously to set our hearts to know.

Going on "to substantiate the charge:– (It is God's charge and not mine)", he quoted Isaiah 58:1–7, which includes: "Is not this the fast that I have chosen? to loose the bands of wickedness, to undo the heavy burdens, and to let the oppressed go free, and that ye break every yoke?" Then he dealt in turn with swearing and blasphemy, drunkenness, adultery, fornication, Sabbathbreaking, and "tolerance in society for these things" as prevailing sins.[99] In another sermon, "Methodism Explained", Shrewsbury quoted the Methodist "standing instructions" to missionaries, and commented: "while we are the servants of you all for our Master's sake, we do ingenuously acknowledge that we are *especially*, the servants of those who are slaves. Of the appellation 'Negro Parsons', which has often been contemptuously given, we are not ashamed." Regarding Methodist discipline, he lays the blame for failure in "Sabbath-keeping" on the masters:

> Conceiving that the fourth commandment is specially directed to those who hold 'men-servants and maid-servants' we conclude, that if established customs necessitate the

servants to labour, they, not being in their own power, may be graciously forgiven; while the accumulated guilt must lie upon those who require it at their hands.

The Methodist system is then explained, with its lay church officers, class meetings, and love feasts – where the whole Society takes bread and water together "to remind us that we are all of one family".[100]

Such equalizing ideas were resented likewise if discovered among the clergy of the established Church. As early as 1739 Lewis de Bomeval, a clergyman in Jamaica was accused by Governor Trelawney of encouraging defiance of their masters by telling Negro converts to keep the Lord's Day holy. In the same island in 1808 Colin Donaldson was sued by a proprietor whom he had accused of cruelty to his slaves. The vestry asked to have him removed from the parish and disciplined.[101]

Apart from James Ramsay, the most outspoken Anglican critic of slave conditions was the Revd Charles Peters of Dominica, who startled his congregations on Good Friday and Easter Sunday 1800 with sermons calling for justice and equity to slaves. The *Dominica Journal* or *Weekly Intelligencer* told him to "exchange his gown for the party coloured trappings of the French Republicans". He returned to England to avoid prosecution and co-operated with Wilberforce in the anti-slavery cause.[102]

In short, religious intolerance, although directed mostly against the nonconformist "sectarists", was only to a small extent based on religious zeal or denominational prejudice. When clergy of the established Church, here or there, stepped out of line by reproving the *status quo*, they fared no better. Such earlier prophets, before the arrival of bishops in 1824, were solitary individuals lacking the help of co-religionists. Being directly under the control of government officials and parishioners, they were silenced or exiled.[103]

Some note must be taken of the methods of persecution that were used against the evangelical missions. The most common form initially was the disturbance of religious services. George Liele says: "The people at first persecuted us both at meetings and baptisms".[104] In addition the lives of preachers were occasionally in danger. Threats were made against persons offering their premises for meetings. Coke records various instances of harassment, often by "young Bucks and Bloods" or "gentlemen inflamed with liquor".[105] In both Barbados (1789–90) and Jamaica (1790–91) the opening of Wesleyan chapels stirred prolonged opposition by ridicule, threats and riots. The gates of Kingston Chapel were broken down. A bizarre variation was the invasion of the meeting house in St Vincent in 1791, when the crowd carried off the Bible and hung it from the public gallows. The missionary Brownell (already mentioned) was the object of riots in Nevis in 1797, "it being generally believed, that we were connected with Mr. Wilberforce in England, to support his application to Parliament to abolish the slave-trade".[106]

Since this kind of interference was a breach of the peace, the magistrates at times had to intervene. In other cases the authorities took no action and the preacher stood firm, or withdrew temporarily. Gradually it was realized that such sporadic opposition was not only unlawful but ineffective, and gained support for the victims.[107]

While riotous outbreaks reappeared periodically later, they were replaced for the most part by deliberate efforts of hostile officials or legislative bodies to stamp out or prevent evangelical work by arbitrary authority or by legislative tactics. The Methodists encountered these patterns of conflict first in Dutch St Eustatius in 1787. After the silencing of the slave preacher "Black Harry", a law was published against praying in public and Harry was flogged and banished from the island. In spite of Coke's efforts to get the government in Holland to ensure religious freedom, many years passed before local officials relaxed their hostility.[108] In 1792 a bill was passed in St Vincent forbidding any except rectors of a parish to preach without a licence, and requiring twelve months' residence in the island before the granting of such a permit. The missionary Matthew Lumb carried on in spite of the law, and was jailed. Coke visited him in prison, and after his return to Britain secured the disallowance of the legislation. Meanwhile on his release Lumb had to leave St Vincent.[109] In Dominica in 1796 a Methodist missionary was called to report for the militia and when he claimed exemption was ordered to leave the island on the suspicion that he taught doctrines of "equality" to the slaves.[110]

Early in the new century anti-nonconformist laws were passed in Bermuda, Jamaica, Demerara and other colonies.

The Bermuda "Act to prevent persons pretending, or having pretended to be ministers of the gospel, or missionaries from any religious society whatever, and not invested with holy orders according to the rites and ceremonies of the Church of England, or the Church of Scotland, from acting as preachers or schoolmasters" (1800) resulted in the imprisonment for six months of John Stephenson, pioneer Methodist worker, his departure from the islands, and the suspension of evangelical activity until Joshua Marsden's arrival eight years later. It took three years for the law to be disallowed in London and for this to be publicly announced in Bermuda.[111]

In Jamaica, in 1802 the first of a series of laws brought to a halt evangelical preaching everywhere except in Kingston. The Act provided punishment "in case any person not duly qualified and authorized or permitted, as is directed by the laws of this Island and of Great Britain, shall, under pretence of being a minister of religion, presume to preach or teach in any meeting or assembly of negroes or people of colour" and also for any person allowing such assembly on his property. Many preachers were silenced, including laymen John Williams of Morant Bay (the first to suffer imprisonment under the Act), Moses Baker in St James, Ebenezer Reid of the Scottish Missionary Society and Revd Daniel Campbell, a Methodist, who was prosecuted until he left the island. This law was in effect for two years before its disallowance by the crown became published. Meanwhile the precedent had been established of applying for licences to preach to the magistrates of each parish (who were mostly members of the plantocracy). Arbitrary refusals and unpredictable interpretations of the law were common.[112] The year of abolition of the slave trade, during which also the Methodist Conference forbade its ministers to own slaves or marry a woman who owned slaves, brought renewed measures of restriction. A Kingston ordinance (June 1807) repeated the 1802 hindrances and banned the holding of meetings between sunset and 6 a.m. The Jamaica Consolidated Slave Law (November) limited religious instruction to "the doctrines of the Established Church of this Island" and prohibited any "Methodist missionary, or other sectary, or preacher" from "presuming to instruct our slaves". An official committee Report objected to the missionaries on the grounds of Methodist disapproval of slavery. Kingston and Morant Bay chapels were closed. The Consolidated Slave Law was disallowed, but in 1810 a similar law to be in force for one year was re-enacted. Where law failed, officialdom still obstructed. This period of repression lasted until 1815.[113]

In Demerara John Wray faced similar frustration in 1811 when Governor Bentinck issued an order prohibiting meetings of slaves between sunset and sunrise. Wray promptly made a trip to England to appeal to the British government, and succeeded in getting the restriction modified with the help of Wilberforce and Stephen. This began a close association with the anti-slavery "Saints" which earned for Wray and the LMS much antagonism from the planters, and which helped to aggravate suspicion of the Methodists also. In 1812 Wray was asked by the Commissioners for Managing the Crown Properties in South America (among whom were Wilberforce, Stephen and Macaulay) to start a mission among the crown slaves in Berbice, with the opportunity to ameliorate slave conditions there. This he did the following year.[114] The Barbados slave rebellion of 1816 and the writings of Joseph Marryat who was a critic of Wray, the Wesleyan Talboys and "Methodistical" missionaries generally, stirred legislative restrictions in Trinidad, Grenada, St Vincent and the Bahamas.[115] From Berbice in 1817 Wray once again visited England to take up the case of a woman slave named "America". His denunciation of the slave system there aggravated planter hostility. In the same year John Smith arrived to take over the work at Le Resouvenir. Despite his "Instructions" Smith's antipathy to slavery was no better concealed than Wray's. In 1822 he wrote home a letter graphically describing the conditions of the slaves on the estates. The stage was being set for his "martyrdom".[116]

Another form of persecution, much greater in terms of physical suffering, was directed to the slaves. Threats, floggings and other forms of punishment were used by hostile masters, attorneys and overseers to keep them from attending religious meetings, and from taking part by prayer and preaching or reading Bibles, hymn-books or catechisms.

In this connection a proclamation by Governor Murray in Demerara in May 1823, a few weeks before the slave revolt, is of interest. He warned the slaves against the "misconception" that "the permission of their masters is unnecessary to authorize their quitting the estate on Sundays for the purpose of attending Divine Worship", urges planters to grant such passes, but recommends "a system of prevention, as preferable to that of punishment after transgression", by having slaves accompanied "to the place of meeting, by an overseer, or other white person which would be in other respects advantageous, by enabling the Planter to judge of the doctrine held forth to his slaves".[117]

The harassment of converts continued as long as slavery itself. It could be successful at times, but in other cases it failed as the blacks persisted, or found ways to hide their participation from the overseers. It deepened their interest and their determination to learn more of the gospel. Although in the nature of the case this kind of opposition is not so profusely documented as the abuse of missionaries, it played a vitally important part in the shaping of the Church. Moreover, as it became known in Great Britain through accounts relayed to the missionary societies and the Anti-Slavery Society, it helped to stimulate public opinion toward emancipation.[118]

It is also true that a minority among the planters or other local authorities supported, and sometimes initiated, the work of preachers and missionaries, for example, Foster, Barham and Winn in Jamaica, the Gilberts in Antigua, Jackman in Barbados, Gardiner in St Kitts, and Post in Demerara. Coke found co-operative planters in many of the islands, and Scottish missionaries began work in Jamaica in the 1820s on the invitation of the Sterling and Barrett families.[119] Besides those who provided a base for operation through their possession of estates, others encouraged or at least acquiesced in their slaves' attending religious meetings. Although this kind of "patronage" required of the missions a kind of dependency upon the favour of the prevailing powers, without such support or toleration evangelistic work would have been practically impossible in slave society.[120]

10

Emancipation
and After (1823–1870)

Although "Emancipation" dates from 1834 and 1838, in a broader sense emancipation was in process from the 1823 parliamentary announcement of "amelioration" which was to initiate the gradual abolition of slavery. Hereafter the West Indian churches operated under new tensions and new hope, as this purpose laboured to fulfilment.

Before and after 1834 a new social order was emerging. In this the Church was involved through the coming of two bishops for the Church of England, through the rapid growth of all the churches in the 1820s, 1830s and 1840s, and through their activity in education. Some churches also participated in the establishment of "free" settlements, and in Jamaica an abortive attempt was made to gain political influence for the liberated people through the vote. Missions to Africa and the beginnings of financial self-support were other initiatives of the time.

After the optimism of these early postemancipation efforts the churches experienced a period of declining membership, social unrest and other problems. Then after the Morant Bay rebellion of 1865 and the adoption of crown colony government, the pluralistic "shape" of religion was officially acknowledged by the disestablishment of the Church of England in most of the colonies.

The Climax of the Anti-Slavery Struggle

The kind of persecution described in the last chapter was somewhat relaxed from 1815 to 1823, but a series of events in the latter year introduced a new era. The Anti-Slavery Society was already bringing a new focus on the freeing of the slaves in the colonies. Buxton's motion in the British Parliament that "the state of Slavery is repugnant to the principles of the British constitution and of the Christian religion and that it ought to be gradually abolished", Canning's "Amelioration" Resolutions, and Bathurst's subsequent despatches to the colonies provoked stubborn opposition in the West Indies.

This offer by the British government of a policy of gradual mitigation of the evils of the system was not accepted. Leaders of the plantocracy chose to defend the existing economic and social order which seemed to them essential for survival. They struck out against the alien element within their society, the missionaries and the indigenous preachers and other leaders of mission churches. This anger led to two major incidents of violence during the year 1823, in British Guiana and in Barbados.

In Demerara, Governor Murray's delay in proclaiming the contents of one of the British government's despatches led to a slave revolt in August, in the neighbourhood of Le Resouvenir estate where John Smith was the agent of the London Missionary Society. Smith was arrested and tried in a prejudiced manner on a charge of aiding and assisting the rebellion. He was condemned to death, with a recommendation for mercy, but died in prison in February of the following year. An Anglican minister, W.S. Austin, who had investigated the circumstances of the revolt, concluded that Smith's teaching had in fact "prevented a dreadful effusion of blood". He testified at the trial as a witness for the defence, and was hounded from the colony by letter writers to the newspapers and by Governor D'Urban himself.[1]

Even while Smith's trial was in process in Georgetown in October, in Barbados a handbill boasted that

> a party of respectable gentlemen formed the resolution of closing the Methodist concern altogether; and with this in view they commenced their labours on Sunday evening, and they have the greatest satisfaction in announcing that by 12 o'clock last night they effected the Total Destruction Of That Chapel.

The minister William Shrewsbury (whose sermons we have sampled) fled to St Vincent "avoiding that expression of the public feeling towards him, personally, which he had so richly deserved". The handbill concluded with the "hope" that "true lovers of religion will follow the laudable example of the Barbadians, in putting an end to Methodism and Methodist chapels throughout the West Indies".[2] So electric was the atmosphere in the Caribbean, and so aroused was public opinion in Britain by reports of these two incidents, that some months later four Wesleyan missionaries in Jamaica tried to forestall a storm by preparing a statement for the press dissociating themselves from the anti-slavery movement and even from the belief that slavery was incompatible with the Christian religion. A storm of another sort developed when the Committee of the Missionary Society in England censured their action and recalled two of the offenders, including the District Chairman. Meanwhile their "Resolutions" were quoted by the West India interest in support of slavery. On the other hand the sympathy of the Missionary Committee with (at least gradual) emancipation, and of members of the staff in Jamaica who had refused to be associated with the statement, became known.[3]

It was clear that mission work would no longer be able to remain uninvolved in the dispute over slavery. The British public was becoming convinced that a choice was inevitable between this institution and religious freedom in the colonies. Planters eyed the missions, and even the new Anglican bishops and some of their clergy, with distrust.

The culmination of the anti-slavery struggle in the 1830s, which is a pivotal era in West Indian political and social history, is also a major turning point in the shaping of the Church. The series of dramatic events is too well known to require detailed recording here. The Anti-Slavery Society's decision in 1830 to campaign for immediate emancipation increased the excitement in the Caribbean colonies. A slave strike in north-west Jamaica, inspired by Sam Sharpe, a leader connected with the Baptist chapel in Montego Bay, turned into fiery rebellion in the Christmas season of 1831. This "Baptist war" (as it was nicknamed) was followed by martial law and ruthless reprisals, not only against the slaves but against the evangelical churches that were alleged to be in collusion with the liberation movement. Unsuccessful court charges were brought against Baptist missionaries Gardner and Knibb, and the Moravian Pfeiffer. Thomas Burchell had to escape to the United States and an attempt was made to tar the Methodist Henry Bleby. The formation of the "Colonial Church Union" by planters, abetted by their clerical friend George Wilson Bridges, led to the destruction of ten Baptist and four Methodist chapels plus damage in other locations.

When these violent events, and the determination of the slaves to obtain their freedom, were reported in Great Britain, the drive for emancipation was intensified. The Baptist Missionary Society was converted to open support of abolition. Knibb, Burchell, the Methodist Duncan and others went on speaking tours in the campaign. The January 1833 election under the new Reform Act franchise made possible the passing of the Emancipation Act later in the year.[4]

Meanwhile in Jamaica the threat of mob rule posed by the Colonial Church Union had finally stirred the local authorities to outlaw that organization. This brought to an end not only the persecution of nonconformist missionaries but the verbal threats against evangelically minded "missionaries and curates" and "the Episcopal government" of the Church of England itself.[5]

When the day of partial emancipation came for the slaves on 1 August 1834, the prognosticators of trouble were found to be mistaken. Services of thanksgiving were held in chapels and churches through most of the West Indies, and were thronged with peaceful worshippers. The period of "apprenticeship" which followed was shortened from six years to four years (for praedials), partly as a result of the criticisms and pressure of missionaries and their friends, and the exposure of abuses of this system of half slavery. When complete emancipation arrived on 1 August 1838, church services again celebrated the end of the old and the coming of a new era.[6]

During this period of struggle the religious faith of the missionaries and of many slaves, and of leaders such as Buxton and Wilberforce, became so identified with the achievement of emancipation that the Christian Church as a whole became the focus of gratitude and popularity.[7]

The Rebirth of the Church of England (1824–1842)

Without intending to do so, the planters' church in the West Indies had found itself participating in the changes which were in process. The initiative came from the government in London in the midst of the tension following the 1823 disturbances in Demerara and Barbados. Announcement was made in Parliament that two bishops were to be appointed for the West Indies and among other things would advance the cause of religious instruction for the slaves.[8] Why this action at this particular time? Why indeed did the established Church have to wait until now for an episcopate, especially in light of the fact that New World Anglican bishops had been consecrated for the United States and Nova Scotia as early as 1787 and for Quebec in 1793?

Two grounds for inaction, originating in the islands themselves, were identified in chapter 7: (i) the fear of episcopal discipline, especially over the laity; and (ii) the anticipated cost. Two further reasons were less articulated: (iii) complacency with regard to existing ecclesiastical arrangements, including lay control by vestries and colonial governors; and (iv) the suspicion that bishops might concern themselves with the spiritual and even the temporal welfare of the slaves. Even at the distance of England, had not Bishops Fleetwood and others of the SPG – Gibson, Warburton and Porteous – expressed views that challenged the religious and social order in the colonies?

The British government's decision in 1824 took into account the first two of the above reasons: (i) The new bishops would have power over the clergy only, and (ii) the cost would be borne by the imperial government, at least for a time. The third and fourth reasons for reluctance, as will be seen, created difficulties for the new bishops.

By the beginning of the nineteenth century the attitude of many within the established Church to religious instruction of the slaves had been changing, at least in theory. Because of the example of evangelicals and Roman Catholics, as well as some quickening of conscience and urgings from Britain on the matter, they had accepted the idea of religious teaching if done by their own clergy. During the campaign against the slave trade some West Indians in England had made a defensive flank attack with a resolution in Parliament to refer to colonial governors and assemblies the amelioration of slave conditions and provision of moral and religious instruction. This initiative of Sir William Young and Charles Ellis in 1796–97 (opposed by Wilberforce as a ruse) led to "Amelioration Acts" in Antigua (1797) and the Leeward Islands (1798), and the Jamaica Act of 1797 which required the rectors of parishes to give instruction to slaves on Sunday afternoons. There were disappointing results from this legislation, although in some places clergy or planters arranged for large numbers of slave baptisms.[9] Faced with the continuing growth of the evangelical movement, the Jamaica Assembly in 1815 had resolved to "investigate the means of diffusing the light of genuine Christianity, divested of the dark and dangerous fanaticism of the Methodists". The following year the Additional Curates Act provided for an extra clergyman in each parish and facilities for religious teaching, but "this expensive establishment became . . . little better than a provision for the assistance of the rectors in their own appropriate duties".[10] It was evident that the established Church was failing to reach the hearts and minds of the slave population. What was the remedy? Was it, at long last, time for the episcopal Church to have bishops in the Caribbean instead of London?

The SPG had been saying so for over a century. It renewed its appeal in 1823 on the ground that "the arguments which determined his Majesty's Government to place the Churches of America and India under the direction of Provincial bishops, apply with at least equal force to the case of the West Indies".[11] The crown had approved the establishment of a Roman Catholic episcopate for Port-of-Spain, and at the same time (1819) Governor Woodford begged the Colonial Office "to do what you can ab^t a Bishop for us".[12] Then Charles Ellis, as spokesman for the West India interest, asserted that there were good intentions in the islands to provide instruction for the slaves, but blamed the Church in England for holding on to an ineffective superintendence of West Indian church affairs.[13]

The decisive reason for action in 1824, however, was the British government's concern with the religious side of its policy of amelioration. It had offered to assist the colonies with the financial cost of religious instruction, on condition that the assemblies abolish the Sunday markets and give slaves another free day in the week. This proposal was rejected. Government leaders then consulted with Ellis and the bishop of London as to suitable men to be appointed as Caribbean bishops. William Hart Coleridge was named for a See of Barbados and the Leeward Islands (including the Windwards, Trinidad and ultimately "Guiana"), and Christopher Lipscomb for that of Jamaica (including the Bahamas and "Honduras"). They proved to be successful choices. Coleridge served until retirement for health reasons in 1842, Lipscomb until his death in 1843.[14]

The two bishops surmounted the difficulties of transition to a new ecclesiastical regime. They obtained new clergy and other personnel for outreach to the slaves,

REPRODUCED BY COURTESY OF THE DIOCESE OF NASSAU AND THE BAHAMAS

William Hart Coleridge

and they supervised a programme of establishing schools to provide education for the freed people and their children. This period was the vital turning point in the life of the established Church.[15] The "planters' church" became at last the Church of England, or as it later would be called the Church in the Province of the West Indies.

One problem Coleridge and Lipscomb faced was constitutional. How was the bishop to assume episcopal powers in a Church that had been virtually lay controlled for two centuries? Colonial governors had operated in the matter of parish appointments (as well as marriage licences and the probate of wills). Clergy, once appointed, had security of tenure. Laws were now passed in Barbados and Jamaica to define the new ecclesiastical position. The Barbados Act cautiously ensured that the only control the bishop had over the laity was to summon witnesses to ecclesiastical courts, and that "any power, jurisdiction, or authority, which the Ordinaries of this island have" should be "preserved in the manner as if this Act had never been passed". In the end a compromise was worked out: royal instructions from London gave the bishop the right to present clergy to the governor for him to induct to the parish. This system, which lasted until 1872, did at least give the bishop control over the selection of the clergy.[16] In Jamaica episcopal authority over the clergy (not the laity) was ensured by requiring the bishop's certificate before clergy stipends would be paid by the receiver-general. This was directed especially against absenteeism.[17] Criticism of the new episcopal power was voiced in Jamaica and Barbados, but the two bishops calmly continued their tasks.[18]

Clergy were recruited both in England and locally, and ordinations took place for the first time in the West Indies. Catechists were employed. The CMS and the Slave Conversion Society (renamed the Christian Faith Society after Emancipation) – as well as the SPG, sent out workers. Bishop Coleridge in 1830 succeeded in restoring Codrington College to the purpose of its donor as a theological college for the training of clergy in and for the West Indies. Archdeacons and rural deans were appointed to administer subregions of the large dioceses.

Since buildings were inadequate to accommodate the large number of slaves who were now to be invited for worship and instruction – although not yet, because of planter opposition, to learn to read and write – church, and later school building programmes were launched. Funds were obtained locally (from subscriptions, legislative grants and land taxes) and in England (from government grants and after emancipation from the SPG's Negro Education Fund). The building programme was the more demanding in Barbados after a hurricane in 1831 destroyed many churches, including fifteen newly erected ones.[19]

The new bishops led their dioceses through the social change of the amelioration and emancipation periods, while attitudes had to be altered within the Church to accord with the coming new society. One need was the abandonment of the social exclusiveness that went with slavery.

An incident in Barbados in 1827 gives some indication of the ferment of the times. In the parish of St Lucy the Revd W.M. Harte and his catechist H.J. Leacock were involved in serious trouble when they allowed black members to take their places at the communion rail along with whites in the parish church. Although Bishop Coleridge backed the rector on the issue, Harte was charged by his white parishioners with preaching an "offensive" sermon and

> disgraceful conduct while administering the most holy Sacrament of the Lord's Supper, thereby endeavouring to alienate their slaves from a sense of their duty, by inculcating doctrines of equality inconsistent with their obedience to their masters and the policy of the island.

The case came before the Court of Grand Sessions where Harte was fined one shilling. He appealed to the king and was granted a royal pardon. Controversy continued until 1829. During this the island Assembly suspiciously asked the Colonial Office for copies of all documents sent to London by the bishop respecting Mr Harte. Leacock (who later pioneered the West Indian mission to the Rio Pongas in Africa) was ordained by Coleridge and, in view of his unpopularity in Barbados over the incident, was appointed to St Vincent and later as Rural Dean in Nevis.[20]

Although the transformation of the Church of England owes much to episcopal leadership, the help of the missionary societies was also important. The SPG and the Christian Faith Society worked closely with the bishops, placing personnel and funds directly under them. The co-operation of the SPG was vital to the rejuvenation of Codrington College and to the raising of money for the £177,777 Negro Education Fund.[21] The CMS had workers in Jamaica, Trinidad, Antigua, some other islands, and Demerara. Beginning in 1829 at Bartica (Essequibo), John Armstrong pioneered a mission among the Amerindians of Guiana, work that was later extended under

St John's Cathedral, Belize

Thomas Youd and J.H. Bernau.[22] In the older colonies the CMS adapted with some difficulty to the episcopal and parochial system. During the 1830s, at the time of the Society's "lay-secretaryship" of Dandeson Coates, lengthy negotiations took place with both West Indian bishops over the relation of missionaries to ordination, support, episcopal appointment and discipline.[23] In the 1840s the Society encountered financial problems and – founded as it was primarily "for Africa and the East" – decided to withdraw from the Caribbean, in spite of pleas from Lipscomb's successor, Bishop Aubrey Spencer, to continue.[24]

Bishop Lipscomb made a visit to the Bahamas in 1826. He went to "Honduras", – not yet formally a colony – the same year. St John's Church in Belize (built in 1812) was consecrated during this episcopal visit.[25]

Coleridge gave attention to the newer colonies – the Windward Islands (at that time including Tobago), Trinidad, Demerara-Essequibo and Berbice (called British Guiana after 1831) – where isolated clergy had hitherto done little more than serve as chaplains to English planters, merchants and government officials.[26]

The Growth and Formation of the Churches (1823–1870)

For the evangelical missions as well as the Church of England, the "amelioration" and immediate postemancipation years were a time of great activity. They were bursting with zeal to evangelize and to provide education for the freed people. Even though until 1834 some local governments were still obstructive, the missionaries knew that the imperial power was friendly and officially committed to the gradual abolition of slavery. They continued to win over increasing numbers of the slaves as well as many of the people of colour and a few whites. This period of euphoria lasted well into the 1840s.[27]

Thereafter, cooling of postemancipation enthusiasm both in the Caribbean and in Britain affected the churches and missions. Parliamentary grants for West Indian education ceased in 1845 and the Negro Education Grant was used up by 1850. Colonial legislatures, still controlled by the plantocracy, did not cheerfully maintain the burden of school support. The Sugar Duties Act (1846) removed British favour to West Indian produce, causing financial stringency, A cholera epidemic in 1850-51, followed by smallpox, left tens of thousands dead. Economic, social and religious unrest continued during the 1850s and 1860s.[28]

In order to summarize the development of the churches in this era we will consider the communions ("denominations" as they came to be called) in the following order:

(i) those which were widely spread over the Caribbean under episcopal government: the Anglican and Roman Catholic;
(ii) those missions which were similarly widespread through a broad unified policy: Methodist and Moravian;
(iii) other church families which did not have an overall unified strategy of expansion in the Caribbean, but grew by a variety of initiatives, missionary and local: Presbyterian, Congregational, Disciples, and Baptist.

The Church of England in the West Indies had a sense of unity through its special connection with church and state in England. The pioneer bishops, in less than twenty years, had set the Church on a new course. They left to their successors the task of consolidation, and in some ways of retrenchment due to the difficulties of the times.

In terms of diocesan structure, when Bishop Coleridge retired in 1842, the Archdeaconry of Guiana was ready to become a separate diocese under William Piercy Austin.[29] At the same time Antigua (with the other Leewards and nearby Danish, Dutch and some other islands) became the bishopric of Daniel Gateward Davis, while Thomas Parry in Barbados retained the Windwards and Trinidad.[30] A year later, on the death of Bishop Lipscomb, he was succeeded (as already noted) by Aubrey Spencer. Part of this diocese, the Bahamas (together with the Turks and Caicos Islands), was to become the see of Nassau in 1861.[31]

In Guiana one of the consequences of the 1823 slave revolt had been the institution of a system of church establishment intended to exclude the nonconformists. Parishes were assigned, some to the Church of England and some to the Church of Scotland. (The Dutch Reformed Church was at first included, but was too weak to assume responsibility.) Along with this parallel establishment began the system of "concurrent endowment" which came to be adopted also in some other colonies, and to include some nonconformist churches. This system – of government grants in proportion to numbers for the various churches, as reported at the most recent census – survived in some territories after disestablishment, and even beyond Independence.[32]

In British Guiana the Revd William H. Brett began in 1840 his forty-year service in missionary work among the Amerindians under the SPG, taking over in 1845 from the CMS on its withdrawal from the Caribbean.[33]

In Jamaica the Diocesan Church Society for the Propagation of the Gospel (1844–53) under Bishop Spencer was active in the education of thousands of children of the former slaves. It was revived by Bishop Courtenay in 1861 as the Jamaica Home and Foreign Missionary Society, with a broadened agenda to provide church care for neglected parts of Jamaica, to support overseas work among Moskito Indians in Central America, and to assist the new mission in West Africa which had been initiated from Barbados.[34]

In Trinidad "anglicizing" political leaders and also CMS missionaries, who had come in 1837 to work in the southern part of the island, were challenging the predominance of the Roman Catholic Church. Bishop Parry was urging the government to have the Church of England established and better endowed. This was done in 1844 by the colonial government's "Ecclesiastical Ordinance" which officially recognized it as the established Church, divided the island into parishes and increased its financial support. Unfortunately acute tension, which had been building for some years, was aggravated over a series of issues between the Catholic majority and the Anglican minority, coming to an end only with disestablishment in 1870.[35]

The Roman Catholic Church, from its base in the former French colonies and Trinidad, meanwhile continued to grow, and to show its presence in other British colonies during the emancipation and postemancipation period.

With its first bishop, James Buckley (1820–28), resident in Port-of-Spain, the building of a cathedral was begun with Governor Woodford's active support. It was completed in 1832. While rivalry intensified with the Anglican church, sixteen new Irish and French Catholic priests were brought to the island (1837). The above-mentioned Ecclesiastical Ordinance initiated a quarter century of religious and political strife.[36]

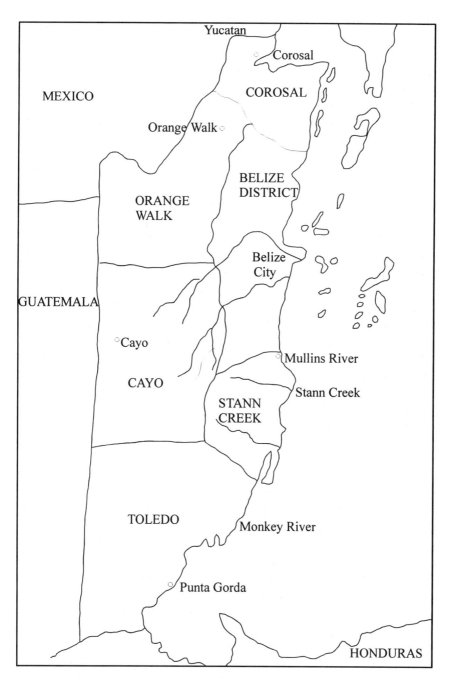

Belize

In Jamaica the pastor, Benito Fernandez, who had come there in 1824, was still at his post in 1837. In that year the island was separated from the Port-of-Spain district and became the Vicariate of Kingston. Fernandez was appointed the first vicar apostolic. (This new vicariate included British Honduras and, for a time, the Bahamas.) Later in the same year two Jesuit priests (one English and one French) were introduced to help with the Jamaican work, thus beginning a long association with Jesuit clergy from abroad. About the same time the opening of a High School in Kingston started Catholic education in Jamaica.[37]

In 1837 British Guiana also received its own vicar apostolic, pioneer work having been done by priests sent out from Port-of-Spain – four Irish and one French – after 1825. The outstanding missionary of this preliminary period was Father J.T. Hynes, a Dominican, who arrived in Demerara in 1826. He became vicar general in 1833, and returned as vicar apostolic ten years later.[38] The cosmopolitan population of this South American mainland colony included, according to an 1841 document by the earliest vicar apostolic, William Clancy, ten thousand parishioners made up of "a thousand Spanish Indians together with numerous emigrants from Westphalia in Germany, Madeira, Malta, Martinique, Guadeloupe, Cayenne, Ireland, and Italy professing the Roman Catholic faith", as well as two hundred "Protestant converts".[39] The Madeiran Portuguese especially, who began to arrive as indentured workers in 1835, became "the backbone of the Catholic Church in Guiana".[40]

Thus by the time of full emancipation there were three strategic centres in the English-speaking Caribbean, Trinidad, Jamaica and British Guiana. The Church was geared for further expansion in the decades that followed.

In the eastern islands of the West Indies, recorded Roman Catholic Church history began in Barbados (1839) and in the Bahamas (1845). These were added to the Vicariate of British Guiana and the Diocese of Charleston (South Carolina) respectively.[41]

On the west, in what later became the colony of British Honduras, by 1832 a Franciscan, Fray Antonio, was serving some refugees from Spanish Honduras at Mullins River. Then during the War of the Races in Yucatan (1848–76) the vicar apostolic of Jamaica sent a number of Jesuits to work among the thousands of refugees who crossed over into northern British Honduras. This began the marked growth of the Roman Catholic Church in the territory.[42]

The Methodist missions, under the Wesleyan Methodist Missionary Society in England, operated with a policy from the time of Thomas Coke of a Caribbean-wide outlook and of frequent interchange of ministerial personnel.

During the vacancy in Barbados following the dismantling of Shrewsbury's chapel in 1823, the work was held together by the courage of a lady of colour, Mrs Ann Gill, and other lay people until the crisis was over three years later.[43] The Wesleyans went methodically forward throughout the Caribbean. On the western side they commenced work in the Belize area in 1825, and extended it to other parts of

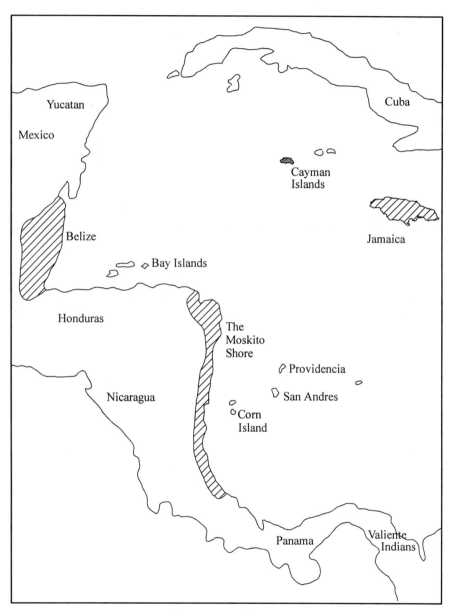

The Western Caribbean

"Honduras" including the Bay Islands (and to Stann Creek where some of the St Vincent Black Caribs had moved), and to Corozal and Toledo.[44]

Methodism encountered its chief troubles in Jamaica in the amelioration years, by the familiar pattern of restrictive legislation, "inquiries", court charges, imprisonments and occasional violence. Some flagrant cases, such as the shooting attack on William Ratcliffe's home in St Ann on Christmas night 1826, and the floggings of slave Henry Williams (and also the Baptist deacon Samuel Swiney) became *causes celèbres* in Great Britain. In 1832 six Methodist church buildings were destroyed or damaged by the Colonial Church Union.[45]

As with other missions and churches Wesleyan membership growth was rapid for a decade after emancipation, doubling in Jamaica from 1833 to 1840, and in the West Indies as a whole reaching over 54,000 in 1844. Then for two decades the numbers declined, by some 7,000 in Jamaica and a similar number in the other colonies, before beginning to climb again in the late 1860s.[46]

Note should be made of the work of the Wesleyan Methodist Missionary Society that was going on at the same time in Haiti, because later (in the 1880s) it became a part of the newly formed Western Conference of the Methodist Church in the Caribbean. This mission had begun as early as 1816 on an invitation of President Pétion to establish school work in Port au Prince. Although the missionaries had to withdraw for nine years on the death of Pétion (1818) local converts carried on, more than doubling their membership. A Haitian Methodist named St Denis Baudrey became an outstanding leader in the generation that followed, serving for a total of thirty-five years.[47]

Moravian missions had solidarity by their relation to the Unitas Fratrum centred in Herrnhut and governed by its General Synod and Unity Elders' Conference. Financial support and missionary personnel came from churches in England, the United States and Germany.

In Jamaica the Moravian missionaries were released from the necessity of earning their living by secular work, as their Church abroad in 1823 undertook their support from mission funds. They were strengthened by moving their chief station to Fairfield in the parish of Manchester, by the opening of other stations and by the starting of Sunday schools and day schools.[48]

A new mission was undertaken on the Moskito Coast of Central America in 1849. On the suggestion of some Germans who were planning a settlement in this area, the Revd Heinrich Pfeiffer of the Jamaican Moravian mission and two others went to Bluefields and formed a congregation among the residents, many of whom were of Jamaican origin. From there developed a mission to the Moskitos and to another tribe, the Sumus. Study of the native languages was undertaken and the first of several mission schooners, for travel along the coast, was built in 1858. During the following decades this work grew into a successful indigenous church.[49]

In the eastern Caribbean the Moravian mission in the Danish islands celebrated its hundreth anniversary in 1832. Although emancipation in these colonies was not achieved until 1848, the influence of events in the neighbouring British islands stimulated a notable expansion of Moravian schools for the slave population with government help.[50]

In nearby Antigua the Moravian mission, with other churches, recommended to the government in 1834 that no period of "apprenticeship" was necessary for the island's slaves. It was the only Caribbean colony to introduce immediate complete emancipation. Here also the mission schools had made notable progress. In Barbados and St Kitts also advance was made in this era, and in Tobago in 1827 the mission, which had twice been frustrated in earlier attempts, was secured with the founding of strong congregations at Montgomery, Moriah and elsewhere.[51]

Presbyterianism appeared in the Caribbean in a variety of ways. We have seen that congregations were founded by Scottish residents with government support in Jamaica (1813) and Guiana (1815). In the latter territory, after 1823, there came to be an established Church of Scotland in its specified parishes, parallel with the Church of England. Later other Scottish churches were founded in Grenada (1830) and Belize (1850).[52] Over the years the membership of all these churches became creolized.

In Jamaica a strong Presbyterian presence was established through the Scottish Missionary Society (which was nominally "undenominational" like the LMS) in cooperation with the United Secession Church, and after 1847 through the United Presbyterian Church.[53] After an abortive beginning in 1800, the SMS resumed activity on the invitation of some proprietors, with the arrival of George Blyth at Hampden in 1824. He and five other missionaries who followed in the northern part of the island formed an embryonic presbytery in 1832. Two years later the United Associate Synod of the Secession Church sent two workers, and a Jamaica Missionary Presbytery was constituted in 1836. The first Synod of the Presbyterian Church of Jamaica was held at Falmouth in 1849.[54] Evangelical and educational in approach, these Scottish brethren co-operated with other missions, but brought a Presbyterian style of church organization, less free than the Baptist, less itinerant than the Methodist, and more nearly resembling the Moravian by stressing pastoral care of converts by the minister, when possible with a closely associated group of lay leaders (the elders). This difference tended to limit the numbers in the Presbyterian Church to those who could well be served by available trained personnel.[55]

The Presbyterian mission in Grand Cayman had a dramatic beginning in a shipwreck there in 1845 of a boat on its way from Jamaica to Scotland, carrying the Revd Hope Waddell with the purpose of commencing a West Indian mission in Africa, as will be seen below. This apparently providential mishap led the following year to the posting of James Elmslie to commence work on the island. Another

Presbyterian venture in the western Caribbean was the sending of a minister to Belize by the Colonial Committee of the Free Church of Scotland in 1852 to serve the new church there.[56]

Presbyterian work in Trinidad began with the arrival in 1836 of the Revd Alexander Kennedy from the United Secession Church in Scotland, with support from Greyfriars Church, Glasgow, to found Greyfriars Church in Port-of-Spain. Outstations were added later at Arouca, Sangre Grande, San Fernando and elsewhere.[57]

One remarkable group of about 600 immigrants from Madeira came to Trinidad in 1845 to escape religious persecution. They had been converted to Protestantism by a Scottish medical doctor, Robert Kalley, in their native island. His introduction of Scripture reading and Protestant worship had brought persecution from Roman Catholics. After finding their way to Port-of-Spain these refugees held Portuguese services in Greyfriars Church, and later founded St Ann's Church, with a Portuguese minister. This congregation became associated with the Free Church of Scotland. However most of them moved on to the United States, and St Ann's gradually became a second English-speaking Presbyterian congregation in Port-of-Spain.[58]

A short-lived attempt begun in 1843 by the Associate Presbyterian Church in the United States, to start a mission at Iere Village among the ex-slaves, ended with illness and death among the missionaries. It is chiefly remembered as having provided a starting place for the "Canadian Mission" to East Indians in 1868, as seen in the next chapter.[59]

The Congregational churches in British Guiana and Jamaica grew from missions of the LMS. Its work in Guiana suffered a temporary setback after the death of John Smith, but it was resumed. By 1834 a pastor of African descent, the Revd George McFarlane, was serving the mission. Ultimately (1883) the LMS churches were formed into the Congregational Union in that colony.[60]

After emancipation, concern abroad for the newly freed people led to two new missions in Jamaica, both of them (although technically undenominational) having Congregational connections. These had lasting effects in spite of their late start. The LMS was the first, reaching the island in 1834. The second was that of some Americans from Oberlin College in Ohio who came in 1839, the first missionaries to be sent from the United States to the West Indies.[61] Originally a kind of "faith mission", a few years later they welcomed support from the American Missionary Association which was founded to aid slaves in the United States. At the time of the American Civil War, this association withdrew from Jamaica for financial reasons. Its congregations continued, some in connection with the LMS churches, some with the Presbyterian and some with the Methodist.[62]

The Disciples of Christ in Jamaica were founded in connection with the Christian Church (Disciples of Christ) in the United States.[63] The mission in Jamaica began in an unusual way. One of the Oberlin Congregational missionaries mentioned above, Julius Beardslee, returning to the United States, accepted the teaching of the Disciples on adult baptism by immersion, and joined with them. He then came back to Jamaica in 1858 under that church's American Christian Missionary Society (ACMS) to found the Disciples of Christ in Jamaica. His influence brought a number of Congregational churches over to the Disciples and he also founded new ones. At the time of the American Civil War (1866), however, the ACMS had to withdraw financial support and Beardslee returned to the United States. For several years lay people in the Jamaican congregations maintained the church's work on their own initiative, until American missionaries, under the Christian Woman's Board of Missions (CWBM), came back to resume the work of the mission.[64]

The Baptists in Jamaica in the 1820s found their work immensely reinforced by new Baptist Missionary Society (BMS) missionaries. Notable among these were James M. Phillippo, Thomas Burchell and William Knibb, a famous trio who became powerful figures in Spanish Town, Montego Bay and Falmouth respectively. Baptist membership multiplied phenomenally in the emancipation and postemancipation period, but, like other churches, declined in the difficult years after 1845.[65]

James Bourne from the BMS had begun work in the Belize area in 1822. By the time of emancipation school and church work there was growing, and contacts were made not only among English and Africans, but also among Spanish and Amerindians. Openings were made in San Andrés and Providencia by American Baptists in 1845, and about the same time in Haiti by the BMS. The mission in Haiti was turned over to the Jamaica Baptist Missionary Society (JBMS) in 1883.[66]

As it had done earlier in Jamaica, the BMS sent aid, to the Bahamas (1833) and to Trinidad (1846), to churches already founded by African American lay preachers. An English minister, the Revd George Cowen, originally with the Mico organization, had begun a small mission in Port-of-Spain in 1843, and in 1854 St John's Baptist Church was opened in that city. Meanwhile Cowen had actively assisted church and school work among the former American ex-soldiers who had been granted land as free Negroes in "Company Villages" in the south of the island. He worked alongside "Brother Will" Hamilton, who was the outstanding leader and preacher in the Fifth Company area from 1816 to 1860. The BMS (known locally as the "London Baptist" mission) became associated with these churches.[67]

In summary it may be said that during the postemancipation period, in spite of many obstacles – among them decline in membership and in zeal, poverty of the people, and loss of financial support – the expansion of the churches was sound enough to be confirmed over the following decades, through Christian education (by churches and schools) and also through renewed evangelization. The West Indian Church as a whole was immeasurably stronger in 1870 than in the days of slavery.[68]

New Initiatives in the Postemancipation Era

During the period of optimism which followed emancipation, new enterprises were vigorously undertaken. Some of them succeeded and played an important part in shaping the future of the Church. Others were ahead of their time, or became side-tracked through lack of finances or leadership, in the circumstances of colonial life.

The Churches and Education

The apprenticeship period brought an urgent demand for schools for the children. Full emancipation in 1838 accelerated the demand. Over a ten-year period churches and missions founded networks of elementary schools wherever their work existed. For example the Moravians, who had begun school work before emancipation, expanded this side of their service to their communities.[69] The Lady Mico Charity also, in co-operation with the British government and a number of church leaders, did pioneer work in setting up schools throughout the West Indies, especially during the years 1835 to 1842. This organization encouraged the idea of nondenominational Christian education using the Bible as a basis rather than a particular catechism or creedal statement. Later it played an important part in the training of school teachers.[70]

The British and Foreign Bible Society made a contribution to education as well as evangelization by raising over £16,000 to print some 100,000 "Emancipation New Testaments" (which included the Psalms) to be given to former slaves and children who had learned to read. These books reached the West Indies by August 1836. The Revd James Thomson was sent to Jamaica in 1834 as Society agent. West Indian Auxiliaries, several of which were already raising funds for the work of the Society, increased in number throughout the Caribbean and have remained active ever since.[71]

From the 1830s may be said to commence, with variations from colony to colony, the typical West Indian pattern of schools sponsored by churches and missions, usually with some form of government financial aid.[72] The primary schools were intended to provide "the three Rs", along with religious knowledge based on the scriptures and/or the doctrines of the denomination that organized and managed the school. This arrangement contributed both to education and to the strength of the churches.[73]

In time some secondary schools were founded, continuing the education of the primary schools. At first these were especially for pupils who might aspire to become school teachers or church pastors. In Jamaica, Calabar College was established in 1843 by the Baptists. The following year the Presbyterians founded the Montego Bay Academy. The Moravians opened a training college for male teachers at Fairfield in 1839 and one for women in 1861.[74] In a book published in 1843, the Baptist missionary, James M.Phillippo, with remarkable vision advocated the founding of "a College in Jamaica, after the model of the University College in London", on a nondenominational basis. This dream remained unfulfilled until the opening of the University College of the West Indies in 1948.[75]

Ministerial Training

As early as the seventeenth century Sir Charles Wheler, the Leeward Islands governor mentioned in chapter 6, had recognized the need for educating clergy in the West Indies rather than in England. But even the bequest of the Codrington will a generation later did not produce results until Bishop Coleridge succeeded in establishing the theological college in 1830. This institution has produced scores of clergy since then.[76]

Missionaries of the evangelical missions early undertook to train indigenous preachers and other leaders. Teaching on a work-and-study basis, within each mission, was the earliest method. In a more organized way, part-time training of catechists for the Jamaican Presbyterians commenced at Goshen in 1841 and a theological tutor was appointed in 1851 in connection with Montego Bay Academy.[77] Calabar College and the Moravian secondary school at Fairfield likewise were intended to provide teachers and preachers. Jamaica Methodists had to postpone for a generation plans for "a Theological Institution for young West Indian Preachers", but this was achieved in 1875.[78]

In the Lesser Antilles the Moravians were recruiting trained teachers into the ministry, adding private studies under missionary supervision leading up to ordination where possible.[79] One of the two Mico Teacher Training Colleges had been established in Antigua, and the Moravians from this and other islands were able to recommmend students for training there. They found it necessary in 1846 to open Cedar Hall, a training school for boys who lacked primary schooling, to qualify for entrance to the Mico college. A number of Mico graduates became leaders and some local preachers in the church. One of them, John Andrew Buckley, became the first West Indian of African descent to be ordained a Moravian minister in 1856. The first (white) West Indian minister, James Young Edghill, had been ordained in Barbados in 1853.[80]

The "Free" Settlements

When full emancipation came in 1838, missionaries such as William Knibb and George Blyth in Jamaica, who had the confidence of the freed slaves, were able to advise the workers, or mediate between estate owners and their new wage employ-

REPRODUCED BY COURTESY OF THE NATIONAL LIBRARY OF JAMAICA

William Knibb

ees in negotiating for a fair and realistic wage.[81] Agreement was possible where there was goodwill on the side of management, but in other cases workers were treated so unreasonably that they left the estates. What leverage did the freedmen have? Apart from the fact that if they withheld their labour the estate owner might lose his crop, in those colonies where there was available uncultivated land, as in Jamaica and Trinidad, there was, at least for some, the option of becoming settlers on such land, either by purchase, rental or squatting. These plots might be close enough to the estates to provide day labour for them, but many freed slaves had begun to move away from the plantations, preferring independence to any kind of wage labour. Uncultivated estates and even remote and mountainous regions were being occupied.[82]

Some of the missionaries in Jamaica decided to assist and to guide new settlements. They purchased land and resold it, thus building up "free" villages which had a church and school at the centre of the community.[83] Most active in this movement were the Jamaican Baptists, beginning with the organization of Sligoville near Spanish Town in 1835 by Phillippo. Knibb, Burchell and John Clark sponsored a number of other villages in the north of the island. Their neighbours, the Presbyterians Blyth and Waddell, were busy with similar enterprises. The Moravians established villages in Manchester and Westmoreland. Even the Methodists (whose usual policy was to stay out of social and political matters) bought some land for resale.[84]

For those in the smaller islands the only option was to migrate, for example from the Virgin Islands, Antigua and Tobago to Trinidad or British Guiana.[85]

In addition, of course, wherever settlements were initiated by freed people themselves or by government, churches and schools could be established in or near them. In Jamaica the new Congregational missions (the LMS and the Oberliners) recognized the need of settlements already forming and this led them, for example, to places in Clarendon and Portland where there were new communities not served by the older missions.[86] Occasionally settlements were begun by government action as in Trinidad in Governor Harris' time (the later 1840s). Here Roman Catholic and Presbyterian Churches followed the people in the Arima and Arouca region.[87] In 1869 Governor Gordon opened more widely the crown lands for purchase of small farms. Besides African former slaves and Spanish-speaking *peons*, many East Indian indentured labourers who had fulfilled their contract were able to set up for themselves. In such settlements schools and churches followed.[88]

A Bid for Democracy in Jamaica

The three decades after emancipation were a time of uncertainty during which the implications of freedom were being tested. Would education, eagerly espoused by the missions and the imperial government but only reluctantly supported by local legislatures, prepare the way for political rights? Or would it be a minimal concession to the freed people who were to remain the necessary source of labour for a plantation economy? When times were hard, would the masses of the people demand attention to their poverty, or suffer in silence? Would the traditional structures of power in society be shaken?

As early as 1834 and 1836 the Jamaica Assembly, fearing the possibility of freed slaves becoming property owners and claiming the vote, passed franchise acts to raise the property requirement for voting from £10 to £50. This was disallowed in London. They next raised the qualification for membership in the legislature to the point that only rich men could stand for election. Meanwhile the Baptist missionaries and leaders in their congregations agitated for political rights for the freed people. Issues were laws concerning vagrancy, tenancy, petty debts, peddling and fishing which were aimed at the ex-slaves. Petitions were sent to the local government and the imperial authorities to abolish these oppressive measures. When this failed they tried to broaden the electorate by persuading the small holders, once they could qualify as property owners (especially those in the free villages) to register as voters, in order to elect sympathetic friends to the Assembly in the election expected in 1845.[89]

A newspaper *The Baptist Herald and Friend of Africa*, edited by William Knibb in Falmouth, drew attention to specific injustices: taxation to pay for immigration of new labourers (allowing the planters to pay lower wages to the ex-slaves); poll taxes payable by all; the burden on the poor of import duties on foodstuffs; and the inequity of nonconformists having to pay taxes toward the Church of England while at the same time giving voluntary support to their own "chapel". A political party, the "Anti-State-Church Convention" was organized with a view to contesting the forthcoming election. (The name was inspired by the concurrent Anti-State-Church movement in England.) Not only Baptists but also some Congregationalists, Quakers, Presbyterians and Methodists supported the move. But suddenly the Governor, Lord Elgin, called the election early and aborted the plan.[90]

Within a few months William Knibb died (November 1845), and Burchell a little later. There were few others zealous enough to keep the vision alive. This idealistic effort to transplant democratic practices for the poorer classes – new enough in England itself – did not succeed. For a century missions and churches scarcely became involved in the struggle for democracy as they had in the conflict over slavery. The issue of Church establishment and endowment did however rise up again in a new context, in the 1860s.

Missionary Outreach to Africa

Another remarkable enterprise of the years following emancipation was the sending of missionaries from the Caribbean to Africa. The Moravians were the first to actually send such personnel, in 1841. After a visit to Jamaica by two missionaries of the Basel Mission, who had been working at Akrapong (near Coast Castle, Guinea), five Moravian families responded to their appeal to go from Jamaica to Africa to assist their work.[91] About the same time, men of vision such as Knibb and Presbyterians Blyth and Waddell, neighbours in the north-western part of the island, were inspired by a book by Thomas Buxton advocating such missions to take the gospel to Africa. In the same year that Calabar College was founded the Baptist mission ship *Chilmark* sailed from Jamaica for Fernando Po with forty-two persons aboard. Two years later (1845) the Waddells sailed for Scotland, and (after their unexpected shipwreck on Grand Cayman) the next year their company of Scots and Jamaicans reached Calabar in Nigeria. About the same time a Grenadian Methodist, Henry Wharton, started a twenty-eight-year missionary service in Ghana.[92]

Richard Rawle

Among Anglicans in Barbados an association was formed in 1851 for a West Indian mission to West Africa, which commenced in 1855 at the Rio Pongas. This was to a large extent the result of the vision of Richard Rawle, the principal of Codrington College. Of the two pioneers of the mission to the West African location (about 115 miles north-west of Sierra Leone), the Revd H.J. Leacock died within a few months. John Duport, who went out with him as a catechist was later ordained and for some years was superintendent of the mission. He worked under difficult conditions for eighteen years, much of this time alone at his station. Having mastered the language, he translated Bible portions and liturgies into Susu, and became the effective missionary founder of this West Indian enterprise.[93]

Financial Self-support

Optimistic aspirations to church self-support also resulted from the postemancipation sense of progress. A declaration to that effect was made by the Jamaica Baptist Union in 1842 (not without later misgivings on the part of some). This was the pioneer venture in local self-sufficiency. Plans for self-support were also mooted in Presbyterian and Methodist circles in the 1840s and for Moravians and Congregationalists in the 1860s. Missionary Societies in sending countries were asking for such moves but these were for the most part discouraged by the general poverty. In other cases, already mentioned, supporting missionary societies simply withdrew because of budgetary or personnel problems, as with the CMS and (at the time of the Civil War in the United States) the American Missionary Association and the Disciples.[94]

"Revival" (1860–1861) and the Presence of African Traditions

As postemancipation euphoria began to wane during the 1840s, life for the freed people settled down to the hard realities of wage labour, peasant agriculture or small business. Economic depression on the plantations, especially after the Sugar Duties Act, affected estate owners and wage earners alike, and put pressure on colonial treasuries and on the churches. Heavy taxation on necessities like clothing and building materials was a grievance. The association of the missionaries with the struggle for freedom was not forgotten, but loyalty cooled with time, as was to be expected. Insofar as this directed church members to more permanent reasons for faith, it was a desirable corrective. The fact that the majority remained in the churches is perhaps as worthy of note as the decline in numbers. Loss of membership through cholera (1850–51 and 1854) and smallpox (1852) was partly compensated by a renewal of seriousness encouraging church attendance.[95]

Signs of "revival" were recorded in Demerara in 1856, and in Nevis some years later. But the most notable religious awakening took place in Jamaica. Traceable to a "Home Missionary" movement within the Moravian Church following its centenary celebrations in 1854, it came to fruition in the years 1860 and 1861. Gatherings of people for prayer and evangelism brought new zeal into the Moravian churches; fourteen new congregations and a more than doubling of communicant membership are recorded in the four following decades.[96]

The surge of evangelistic activity spread to other churches. This revival quickened the zeal of church members and gained new converts. There emerged also signs of high emotionalism, comparable to some phenomena observed in England in Wesley's time and in North American mass evangelistic meetings. There were also evidences of the presence of African religious influences.[97] All through the years, outside the recognized churches especially in rural areas, religious activity had been going on, often "unorthodox" and continuing African traditional ideas and practices. In the mixture of African and European elements in creole society during and following the slavery era, it was assumed in ruling class circles that African religion had been largely erased, although "obeah" remained as a "dangerous superstition". In fact, many African religious customs and beliefs were still present, either in practices hidden from the upper classes and from the missionaries, or in the form of merry making such as the "John Canoe" celebrations at the Christmas break from work, and the "Canboulay" commemoration of emancipation on the first day of August, as well as in wakes for the dead.[98]

The "Native Baptists" in Jamaica seemed to be one particular problem, with their independent congregations under popular or self-appointed religious leaders. George Liele, Thomas Swigle and Moses Baker's communications with church authorities in Britain had brought Baptist Missionary Society personnel to the island. This ensured an organized body of Baptist churches with international associations, under the guidance of ministers who received a measure of recognition by governments and by other missionaries. Uneasy relationships followed between mission related Baptists and "native" Baptists, since the latter tended to incorporate African beliefs and practices into the worship and life of their communities.[99] Similar tendencies existed among the Baptist churches in Trinidad.

African religious traditions included belief in a great but remote creator-God – a belief that paved the way for Africans to welcome the monotheism of Christianity.[100] This foundation was combined with a considerable pantheon of subordinate divinities related to natural phenomena such as earth, water, sky and plant growth. These divinities were connected with religious rites practiced in out of the way places. For example the Yoruban thunder-god Shango came to be well known in Trinidad and in some other territories as well.[101] Other beliefs which remained in the African community concerned the importance of dreams, and of communication with the spirits of deceased ancestors who had power to affect the lives of the living. Drumming, dancing, use of herb medicines, amulets, exorcism, and other forms of healing were practised.[102] Much feared was sorcery, believed by the authorities to be directed against the whites, although the activities of the "obeah-man" were mainly aimed against other blacks, and "Myalism" was directed to the protection of people from evil forces. The concern to control the evil spirits which affect human life remained with many who had accepted Christianity.[103]

These religious practices were opposed by colonial governments as well as churchmen, but not as effectively as before. They emerged as a more noticeable factor in Caribbean society. For the churches this was a challenge to study and understanding, as well as definition of the essentials of the Christian faith. These traditions also suggested the relevance for Christian life of a spiritual worldview that denies the distinction of sacred and secular, associates everyday experience with religious faith, and affirms the importance of community life.

Such study was hardly undertaken in colonial times but has become common in more recent years, by sociologists and later by religious scholars. African religious traditions have continued to be part of the environment within which the West Indian Church has been shaped, not only in the late colonial period seen in the next chapter, but up to the present day.[104]

Indentured Immigrants and the Churches (1834–1868)

At the time of emancipation, the members of the plantocracy feared for their labour supply, especially where land was available for settlement, notably in the less developed sugar colonies of the Southern Caribbean.[105] As early as 1834 some European workers (German, British and Portuguese, the latter mostly from the Azores and Madeira) were brought in by private contract to Jamaica, Trinidad and British Guiana. As time went on, other small groups were procured: French, Maltese, Chinese, "free" and "liberated" West Africans, black workers from North America and (to Trinidad and British Guiana) from the smaller islands. The Portuguese and Chinese did not remain long on the estates, preferring to go into small business. Others, being few in number, gradually blended into the community and into whatever church connection they chose.[106]

In 1838 a boatload of indentured workers arrived in British Guiana from India, and the "East" Indians proved to be the most permanent and the most numerous new labour force in the following decades. They began to arrive in 1845 in Trinidad and (in lesser numbers) to Jamaica, and immigration was renewed to British Guiana. After a few years, some came also to Grenada, St Lucia, St Vincent and St Kitts.[107]

The adjustment of indentured workers into West Indian society was a difficult one. On the one hand there was the natural concern of the ex-slaves, and of missionaries who had worked among them as well as the Anti-Slavery Society in Britain, that these new arrivals would depress wages and stand in the way of opportunity for the freed people. This opposition kept their numbers low in all but the newer sugar colonies of the southern Caribbean. On the other hand it was some time before it became clear that many Indians would choose to remain after their five- to ten-year period of indenture was completed. They were therefore regarded at first as transients, and educators and churches paid little attention to their needs.

These Indians arrived after a long and dangerous sea voyage under arduous conditions. Then, being brought to do the work formerly done by slaves, they suffered from traditional attitudes on the part of managers and overseers towards their field and factory workers. Discipline was administered "not by the whip but by the jail". Housing was provided by the plantation in cheap barracks, with little privacy and space. Family life suffered in these conditions, especially as the proportion of women to men among the immigrants was low.[108] It is true that the period of servitude was limited, families were not separated by sale, and children did not inherit the status of slaves. Yet, like the indentured white servants of the seventeenth century, the Indians suffered under a system of forced labour. However, unlike those earlier contract workers, they were isolated from the dominant society by language, culture and religion. Nor was it easy, because of their race, for even enterprising individuals to blend into the dominant society after emerging from their years of separate existence on the estates.

In British Guiana the Methodists took note of the arrival of the East Indians as early as 1848 and in 1852 a missionary with experience in Sri Lanka came to work with them until he died the following year. Seven years later the Revd Henry Bronkhurst replaced him, and laboured for many years in a special mission to the Indians.[109] Although this man did not himself win a great number of converts, in time there came to be in Guyana a number of East Indian Methodists.[110] In 1862 the Church of England also began a special mission to the Indians under E.H. Bhose from Bengal, with the purpose of building a distinctive Guianese East Indian Anglican community which would retain Indian culture. This goal was not achieved.[111]

In Trinidad one of the earliest efforts to meet East Indian needs was in relation to orphan children. In 1857 the "Coolie Orphan Home and Industrial School" at Tacarigua was opened by the Church of England with financial support from government. Initiative for this came from two Anglican planters, one of whom, William Burnley, had also sent a missionary to work among the Indians in the neighbourhood of his Orange Grove estate.[112]

An extensive mission concentrated on East Indians was begun by Canadian Presbyterian missionaries in 1868, as will be narrated in the next chapter.

Economic and Religious Discontent, Crown Colony Government and Disestablishment

Disestablishment of the Church of England in and about 1870 in the West Indies has often been seen as a kind of unexpected result of the Morant Bay uprising of 1865, which led to adoption of crown colony government just before Gladstone's election on the issue of Irish Church Disestablishment. The reasons for it were sought

in "the larger arena of Imperial politics, not within the circle of West Indian politics".[113] Such factors, in addition to the Irish question, included the Clergy Reserves
controversy in Canada, the withdrawal of appointment of colonial bishops after the
Colenso affair, and the pressure for disestablishment in Great Britain seen in the
Scottish Disruption and the activities of the "Society for the Liberation of Religion
from State-Patronage and Control".[114] No doubt these movements abroad had their
weight. Need for financial economy, both in Britain and the Caribbean, played a
part. But also, the Colonial Office was aware of dissatisfaction in Trinidad, the Windward Islands and the Bahamas, as well as in Jamaica.

In Trinidad, as has been told, the Ecclesiastical Ordinance of 1844 had
established and generously endowed the Church of England in that colony.
Presbyterians, Baptists and Roman Catholics protested the Ordinance, and conflict
boiled up frequently between the new Anglican establishment and the Catholics.
Peace was found only with the repeal of the Ordinance in 1870, under pressure
from the imperial government.[115] In the Windward Islands there was unhappiness
among Methodists, Moravians and Roman Catholics with the ecclesiastical *status
quo*.[116] In the Bahamas the move for disestablishment came to a head in 1869 within
the Assembly, on nonconformist initiative. In spite of opposition from the
Legislative Council the move was successful.[117]

In the early 1840s in Jamaica, as noted above, William Knibb and others had
openly attacked the privileges of the established Church. In 1844 petitions from
the Presbyterians and the "Independents" (that is, the Congregationalists) as well
as the Baptists had asked the Assembly for its disendowment.[118] However, after
Knibb's death the mantle fell ultimately to George William Gordon who as a member
of Assembly proposed a motion for disestablishment, thus adding to his
unpopularity with governors and whites. Ironically, what Gordon had sought was
accomplished after the events of 1865, which included his tragic and lawless
execution.[119]

Economic distress reached a climax in the 1860s, with poverty and
unemployment aggravated by drought and official insensitivity. Disturbances broke
out in St Vincent in 1862, but the more well-known turmoil took place in Jamaica.
There George William Gordon as an active political and religious figure and friend
of the people drew public attention to the poverty and suffering in the island. Also
Revd E.B. Underhill, secretary of the Baptist Missionary Society, who had recently
visited the West Indies, warned in what came to be widely circulated as "the
Underhill Letter" of the serious conditions of society, several months before they
exploded in violence. Finally the pent-up tradition of protest, especially among
the poor in Native Baptist congregations, resulted in the Morant Bay rebellion of
1865. In the confusion which followed, the plantocracy concluded that the only
solution to their dilemma was to yield control to London. The Jamaica Assembly

called upon Her Majesty to prescribe a new form of government.[120] Crown colony status was accepted in the West Indies, except in Barbados and the Bahamas.

On Colonial Office recommendation, disestablishment and disendowment of the Church of England took place in the crown colonies, on the ground that it included only a minority of the population – the reason that had led the Bahamian Legislature by local initiative to the same decision there. Barbados, where in fact a large majority was Anglican, chose to retain establishment. Concurrent endowment of several churches was continued or introduced in some territories.[121]

This social and political crisis had had the unexpected consequence of ending Church establishment and endowment. By a devious route the West Indies came to accept the idea of denominational equality, and to recognize the fact of religious pluralism.

11

The Late Colonial Period (1870–1962)

The year 1870, with official recognition of religious pluralism, was also the threshold of the late colonial period. Crown colony government was now both politically and psychologically dominant – although ultimately yielding to pressures for democracy and independence.[1]

For the churches also the attitude of overseas dependence prevailed. Seemingly satisfied with the formal end of slavery, and after the difficulties of the 1840s, 1850s and 1860s, church members and clergy for the most part accepted crown colony government as the necessary way of providing a measure of justice and the minimum needs of society. They indulged in little political questioning, or even deep concern for the problems of a free society, such as labour conditions, unemployment and poverty. Church leaders (many of them expatriates) had a comfortable relationship with colonial officials and foreign-owned business. Their minds and hands were busy with maintenance and extension of the work of the Church, social service to needy families and individuals, and the establishment and upkeep of denominational schools. All in all, the pattern of church life as it was in 1870 remained remarkably unchanged through nine decades.

The life of the Church, nevertheless, was altered by changes in the demographic and cultural pattern. African and some Amerindian religious traditions, along with the newly arrived religions of Asia, presented an opportunity for neighbourly relationships as well as evangelism.

During the nineteenth century some other Christian denominations appeared to join with the church bodies already established. In the new century, the influence of the United States, after its expansionist movement, increased in the Caribbean. As European colonialism declined, the slowly perceived vacuum attracted a new sort of religious (as well as economic and cultural) relationship with North America. One result was a still greater diversification of the ecclesiastical scene.

Meanwhile the attempts of "older" churches to move from "missions" to independent churches, or to indigenous leadership and control, were only partially successful. Expatriate leadership was largely accepted, in spite of efforts to improve theological education. In 1962 trained clergy were still drawn to a great extent from abroad.

Not only was there immigration into the West Indies but movement outwards as well. People in search of employment moved to other parts of the Caribbean area, and later to Britain and North America. Would Church members in this diaspora find expression for their faith in these new environments? Also, would missionary outreach to Africa and elsewhere, begun in earlier decades, be continued?

While the shape of the West Indian Church reflected the denominational mosaic of Europe and North America, the ecumenical movement made little impression here during the colonial period. However a few pioneer moves pointed forward to significant advances following independence.

Demography, Culture and Religion

In slave society the social pattern had been mainly a combination of African and European elements, there being few Amerindians remaining. By the 1830s, blacks and whites and people of colour were to be found, in various proportions, in all the churches, although much social stratification remained in practical terms. Meanwhile the process of creolization – the mutual modification of African and European cultures – was continuing.

African religious traditions continued to be influential. Not only did groups such as Shango and Rada in Trinidad, Kumina and Revivalism in Jamaica, and the "Jordanites" in British Guiana attract many, but some members and/or local leaders from the "orthodox" denominations retained ideas and practices that had come originally from West Africa.[2]

After the abolition of the slave trade in 1807, direct influence from Africa had been largely cut off although "free Africans" were occasionally released from slave ships of other nations. After emancipation, however, one group of labourers that were brought to the British Caribbean consisted of free workers from parts of West Africa. They had a renewing influence by way of transplantation of African religious ideas and practices across the ocean.[3]

Syncretism, resulting from the co-existence of African religious tradition and Christian churches, is of two kinds, depending on whether the particular environment is Roman Catholic or Protestant.[4]

Where the Roman Catholic Church was predominant, a characteristic pattern of folk religion was that rituals and beliefs concerning African divinities quietly came to be identified with Catholic saints. In Trinidad, for instance, orisha worship identified the personality and powers of the Yoruban god of thunder and lightning with those of St John. Other divinities were associated with other saints, the Holy Ghost or even Satan. Rites such as drumming, blood sacrifices, and "spirit possession" appeared less challenging to the faith of the Church by the introduction of traditional Christian elements.[5]

In this category may be compared the syncretism of Roman Catholic with indigenous Amerindian religion, in which ancient Mayan gods became identified with Roman Catholic saints in Central America, including parts of Belize.[6]

In predominantly Protestant surroundings, on the other hand, the names and invocation of the African gods were avoided, and usually Christian saints were not mentioned. Nevertheless ideas and practices from African tradition were used. Here Jamaica's Native Baptists and later Revivalist groups such as Bedwardism and Revival Zion were characteristic.[7] In Trinidad, St Vincent and Barbados, the Spiritual Baptists (Shouters) held to a Christian emphasis, although mutual borrowing from African practices also took place.[8] A variation was that of the "independent" Baptist churches in Trinidad, among those descended from the early "American" Company Villages, which moved away from the help of the Baptist Missionary Society during and after the 1840s. Among the causes of tension between them and the "London Baptist" churches was their desire to "perpetuate the Africanism in their worship". This included the requirement of having an acceptable dream before being approved for baptism, certain customs connected with wakes for the dead, and a distinctive type of music.[9]

In the twentieth century another but quite different spokesman for the African connection arose in the person of Marcus Garvey, a Jamaican who developed a philosophy anticipating in some ways the movements of liberation theology, including black theology. Although Garvey insisted that his United Negro Improvement Association encompassed people of many denominations, one of his followers, the Revd George Alexander McGuire, founded the African Orthodox Church in the USA, which also endeavoured to spread to the Caribbean. Another church body, the Ethiopian Orthodox Church was welcomed to Jamaica in 1970 in line with growing interest in the African-Christian connection.[10]

Garvey's idea of "a return to Africa" had unintended results among adherents of the later Rastafarian movement. Although the Rastafari religion uses many biblical texts it reinterprets them, criticising the Christian churches.[11]

The Roman Catholic Church had considerable cultural diversity within its membership. With its foundation in the former French colonies and Trinidad, it had added immigrants from Europe and Latin America, including refugees from the Haitian Revolution – especially in Jamaica, British Guiana, and British Honduras.[12] Peons from Venezuela, crossed over to Trinidad from time to time. They were of mixed Spanish, African and Amerindian origin. Others were Maronite Christians from Lebanon (often called Syrians). The Catholic Church also grew by conversion of immigrants from Asia (Chinese and Indian), as well as of local residents.[13]

The adjustment of new elements, such as French and Spanish-speaking people, to the British colonies raised tensions from time to time. These had to do with linguistic and cultural as well as religious differences, sometimes with political and colour overtones. Two examples of these problems (mentioned in previous chapters) were the Fédon rebellion in Grenada, and the hard feelings between French creole Roman Catholics and Anglicans in Trinidad over the 1844 Ecclesiastical Ordinance. Even when, in the latter case, the problem was relieved by Anglican disestablishment and concurrent endowment, pressure was continuing for the Catholic Church to bring in English-speaking rather than French clergy. For this purpose it was found that Irish priests and bishops (who were bilingual) suited the need admirably, and in fact with few exceptions the bishops and archbishops in Trinidad were Irish. The transition to English-speaking priests was virtually complete by the time of Archbishop Flood (1887–1907), and as the educational system was organized under government oversight, the language of instruction in Catholic secondary schools was changed from French to English.[14]

Another demographic and cultural variant was that of the immigrants from South Asia, introduced in the previous chapter. The faiths which came with them had the advantage of the sacred writings of Hinduism, and the Qur'an of Islam, as well as the oral and cultural traditions of the people themselves. For these reasons there was resistance to Christian preaching, and theological argument was common. For some people of Hindu background however, who were accustomed to a variety of deities and beliefs, it was not uncommon to acknowledge Jesus Christ as another *avatar* (divine incarnation), and this could be a form of syncretism. For Muslims no mingling of belief was possible, although they shared the religious tolerance of Caribbean society.[15]

Due to the close contact of people of different religious allegiances, considerable mutual borrowing of customs took place over time. For example many East Indians were attracted to Roman Catholic religious practices such as pilgrimages to (and religious blessings at) the church at Mount St Benedict in north Trinidad, and to the celebrations of the "Sipari Mai" connected with the black Virgin at the church of La Divina Pastora in Siparia, a town in the South. Belief in obeah (an African form of the international phenomenon of sorcery) spread to some extent among East Indian people, especially in rural communities. Influence in the opposite direction was not unknown, as with East Indian ideas in the Guyanese Jordanite movement.[16]

In certain respects East Indian culture had effects upon Christian customs, notably in one group, the "Canadian Mission" Presbyterians of the Southern Caribbean. We turn now to the story of what became to some extent an East Indian church.

East Indians in the Churches

An important new development in the shaping of the West Indian Church began in 1864 when the Revd John Morton, a Presbyterian minister from Nova Scotia, made a four-month visit to Trinidad in order to recover from a bout with diphtheria. There he "wandered about the sugar estates, and was particularly drawn to the East Indians, of whom there were then about 20,000 in the island".[17] Anxious that they might learn of the Christian gospel, Morton appealed first to the Presbytery of Trinidad, in which sat three Scottish United Presbyterian ministers together with one from the Free Church, to ask for a missionary from Scotland to the East Indians. He later approached the United Presbyterian Church of the United States, which (as already noted) had briefly carried on mission work among the African freed people. Finally he made an appeal to the Board of Foreign Missions of his own church, the Presbyterian Church of the Lower Provinces of British North America.[18]

The outcome was that John Morton himself, with his wife and infant daughter, arrived in Port-of-Spain in January 1868 as the first Canadian missionaries in the Caribbean. In 1870 a second missionary couple, the Revd and Mrs Kenneth Grant, started work in San Fernando.[19]

Settled at Iere Village, on the site donated to them by the earlier American mission, the Mortons immediately initiated five methods which proved vital to their undertaking: (i) the learning of the culture and language of the Indian people; (ii) the establishment of schools; (iii) the recruitment and training of local leaders for schools and churches; (iv) recognition of the importance of going to the new village settlements established by people who had finished their indenture; and (v) special attention to work among women and girls.

(i) A knowledge of the commonly used Hindi (and some Urdu), the Mortons realized, was the key to communication with the people. This they and the other early missionaries undertook with thoroughness. Preaching, church services, teaching and personal conversation in Hindi (as well as in English) were essential to the work of the mission, until well after the indenture system came to an end in 1917. In the religious education period of denominational schools, in the training of schoolteachers and catechists, in night schools open to adults, and in the nurturing of girls for a Christian domestic life, Hindi was used and taught. At first, printed materials were obtained from India, but in time Morton acquired a Hindi printing press in Tunapuna and produced a book of prayers, a hymn-book, and a supplement to the monthly *Trinidad Presbyterian* magazine.[20] By friendship with the East Indian people in their new country through their own language, by familiarity with their ancient writings and by specializing their work in this one cultural community, these Canadian missionaries were able to do what other churches had not succeeded (and on the whole did not later succeed) in doing: they began to bridge the gap between the ancient traditions of India and the Western creole community with its British educational system.

(ii) The combination of education and evangelism used earlier by other churches in the West Indies was employed by the "Canadian Mission", although with fewer numerical results in terms of new Christians. The Trinidad community was awakening slowly to the reality that most of the Indian workers were electing to remain, rather than to return to their home country, after their period of indentureship.

In Iere Village on 23 March 1868 the Mortons started the first school, "with three little children on our doorstep". By the end of the month there were twenty-one on roll. A Sabbath School also was opened. In January 1869 Morton presented to the British governor, Sir Arthur Gordon, "a scheme for the education of Indian children at the expense of Government". In 1871 the first state assisted school for East Indian children was opened in San Fernando. This was an acknowledgement by the authorities of the fact that almost no Indian parents were willing to send their children to the existing "ward schools".[21]

(iii) Fortunately already in 1869 an Indian teacher for the Iere Village school was obtained in the person of Charles Clarence Soodeen, the first of a long line of teachers who with the missionaries laid the foundations and continued the work of the "Canadian Mission" school system, and who shared also in the leadership of the church.[22]

PHOTOGRAPHS BY GEORGE ADHAR

Charles Soodeen *Revd Babu Lal Bihari*

In the work of evangelism and pastoral care, as well as schools, the missionaries were aided by talented leaders from the East Indian community. Several lay pastors (known as catechists) were enlisted while the Mortons were still at Iere Village. Another early and outstanding leader was Babu Lal Bihari, who in 1882 became the first ordained local minister. A man of experience in Indian religion, he came into contact with the Christian message through Kenneth Grant, became his language teacher, and over many years was a trusted colleague in evangelism, church organization, and theological teaching in Trinidad, and also in missionary work in St Lucia and Grenada. Scores of other local church workers, paid and unpaid, served during the decades following. As time went on, many of them emerged as community leaders, and some in political life.[23]

(iv) Many of the indentured workers after completing their contract obtained land off the estates. Most became small farmers. Others went into trade or business, or, later, became educated for the professions. In what seemed a providential development, the pattern of settlement was extended by Governor Arthur Gordon about the same time that the Mortons arrived in Trinidad. He facilitated the purchase of crown lands in various locations, some near the sugar estates and some in remote areas. Beginning in 1869, many predominantly Indian villages sprang up throughout the island, often by ribbon development along country roads.

The settlers grew vegetables, sugarcane (which they sold to the estates), and in low-lying areas planted rice. In other places they cultivated cocao and coffee. The missionaries visited these areas, preaching and establishing schools. Through the schools they encouraged both education and good agricultural methods. Teachers and catechists lived in the villages, sharing the community life, forming Sunday schools and gathering congregations. The mission realized the importance of these small rural settlements, unlike other denominations which built regional churches, expecting people to travel to them.[24]

(v) Special work among women and girls was begun by Sarah Morton and other missionary wives. Later single women missionaries were appointed,

PHOTOGRAPH BY GEORGE ADHAR

Deborah Talaram

first as school teachers and then (as agents of the Woman's Missionary Society in Canada) to give special care for all needs of women and girls.[25]

Meetings for women as well as house to house and hospital visiting enabled these missionaries to form friends among the people. They tried to provide an alternative to child marriages, starting a "Home for the protection and training of Indian girls", at first in Tunapuna and Couva, and in 1932 centralized as the Iere Home in Princes Town. Many of the girls who had lived in these homes became wives of pastors and other Christian leaders and themselves shared in the work of the church. One was Deborah Talaram, the first of a noble succession of "Bible Women" (and later "women evangelistic workers") who moved about among women in a way comparable to that of the pastors and teachers. The mission also pioneered post-primary education for East Indian girls by founding Naparima Girls' High School in 1912. In 1931 it went on to add a vocational school for girls (the Archibald Institute).[26]

Geographically the activities of the "Canadian Mission" (CM) had begun in the southern part of the island, in the area of the Naparimas where there was a concentration of sugar estates. San Fernando and "the Mission", (that is, Savanna Grande, in 1880 named Princes Town) were the early centres from which began to radiate the schools and congregations under catechist leadership. These were followed in 1871 by Couva in the midwest. In 1881 the Mortons moved to Tunapuna, carrying the outreach to the north. A fifth centre was projected later at Guaico, near Sangre Grande. Trinidad was thus divided into five areas or "fields" around these locations, which were occupied whenever possible by "field missionaries".[27] These men provided supervision in each area, working with catechists, teachers in the church-related schools and later with local ordained ministers, who provided day to day leadership in the many villages throughout the island. Slowly this "Canadian Mission" became indigenized as the Presbyterian Church in Trinidad.

Outreach from Trinidad to East Indians in other British colonies was, with the exception of St Lucia, the result of contacts from Presbyterian churches of Scottish background. Ultimately, with the exception of British Guiana, Indian converts in such territories became integrated into already existing churches.

In Grenada the Revd James Muir, who had come to the island from Scotland in 1883, took the initiative of asking for assistance in reaching the more than twelve hundred East Indians who were in Grenada at that time. In 1884 Kenneth Grant and Lal Bihari introduced two Indian workers for this purpose. These were followed by a number of Trinidad-based Hindi-speaking catechists to serve the three rural communities of Gouyave, Samaritan and Belair.[28]

Work in St Lucia began on the initiative of a convert in Trinidad, named Jageshwar, who had gone to that island as an interpreter with the civil service. He began to witness to his new faith among East Indian people. An appeal was made to the mission in Trinidad, resulting in the sending (1886) of George Sadaphal, the first of a number of teacher-catechists to establish school and church work. One outstanding worker, John Neehall, served for twenty years from 1895 in this island. After the early cessation of Indian immigration to St Lucia and decline of their population in the island, an agreement was made about 1916 with the Methodist Church to continue the work that had been thus started, among those who remained.[29]

The Presbyterian Church in Jamaica in 1892 sent to the Trinidad mission a request for East Indian workers, and two years later Simon Siboo and Jonathan Rajkumar Lal responded. As time went on more catechists followed, and in some cases young Indian men (and their wives) from Jamaica were sent for training at the Theological College in Trinidad and returned to their home island to serve the church.[30] Then, as the use of the Hindi language diminished, the East Indian Christians became integrated into the larger Presbyterian Church in Jamaica, and some into other churches.

In British Guiana, however, the outcome was different. Here a more extensive mission, and later Church, somewhat similar to that in Trinidad, retained a distinctive place in the ecclesiastical scene. The beginning came from individuals in the local Church of Scotland who formed a Presbyterian Missionary Society in 1860. They later turned attention to promoting work among East Indians. John Morton, invited by the local Presbytery, visited the colony in 1880 and made a report. The Missionary Society applied to the Presbyterian Church of Canada for missionaries. The first to be sent out in 1884, the Revd John Gibson, spent a year in Trinidad to study the Hindi language and familiarize himself with the methods used by the Canadian Mission. Unfortunately he died of yellow fever three years after beginning similar work in Guiana.[31]

The mission only became permanently established in 1896, with the arrival of the Revd James B. Cropper who for forty years became such a prominent figure that even after his time it was often referred to as "the Cropper Church". About 1880 the government had begun to provide free land and encourage workers who had completed their indenture to settle in unoccupied areas (notably in those suitable for rice growing) rather than to return to India. Cropper, who supported this policy, was appointed as "Superintendent of East Indian Settlement" by the government, but after some years went back to full time church work.[32]

Another leader who served there from 1912 to 1927 (as well as many years with the mission in Trinidad) was the Revd James Scrimgeour. He was employed in educational work, both in the Berbice High School and in the theological training of catechists. In this period also Niamat Khan, a Trinidadian catechist, served for twelve years in the Upper Corentyne. Several other missionaries and local catechists, teachers and other lay people made this era a high point in church growth and education. It was, however, followed by a period of difficulty and discouragement due to financial shortages, sickness of missionaries, the church union controversy in Canada, and other problems.[33]

The year 1917 brought the indenture system to an end. With no more contract labourers arriving in the West Indies, and with the schools as well as official and community practice favouring English, the use of the Hindi language gradually diminished. The teaching of Hindi in the religious education period in "CM" schools became less frequent, as English became the common language of society. While for almost half a century Presbyterian catechists and some other leaders continued to be able to converse with the older people in their traditional language, the holding of church services in Hindi had virtually ceased by the 1950s.

PHOTOGRAPH BY GEORGE ADHAR

Susamachar Presbyterian Church (nineteenth century)

Many Presbyterian church buildings in Trinidad and Guyana have Hindi names. The occasional singing of *bhajans* also remains as a noticeable expression of East Indian culture. These Hindi Christian hymns originating in India have been very popular, and some English hymns and evangelistic songs have been translated into Hindi (in India, or in the Caribbean itself).[34]

In certain other respects Indian culture was reflected in the customs of the Presbyterian Church in the Southern Caribbean. For a time something like the type of community consultation and local government known as the panchaiyat had been used in the churches, until it gave place to the formal "Session" (that is, the Presbyterian committee of elders in the congregations). The strength of the resultant eldership probably owes something to the panchaiyat tradition (and perhaps also that of the family *guru*). The religious gatherings known as the *bhagwat* and the *puja*, and the (Muslim) *kitab*, were adapted in Christian circles as the "prayer meeting", where a member invites family and neighbours for a Christian service or "Thanksgiving" led by the minister, elder or other lay preacher, followed by a common meal. The larger regional gathering of the *mela* (also involving a common meal) was adapted for special occasions such as church conferences and Good Friday celebrations. The Indian *katha* took the form of the "Jesu Katha" in which the story of Jesus was sung to Indian music as worship and evangelism.[35]

Although the most distinctive outreach to the Indian people in the Caribbean was through the "Canadian Mission", a large number also became members of other churches.[36]

Some four years after John Morton arrived in Trinidad, the newly appointed Anglican bishop, Richard Rawle, came to the island. Being much concerned about the East Indian and Chinese people he endeavoured to reach them himself but realized that he was too old to learn the Hindi language. His attempts to obtain workers who knew it were largely unsuccessful.[37] About the same time an effort was made in Jamaica by the Church of England to reach some of the East Indians in Clarendon but for similar reasons this was discontinued. The concern was revived by the Jamaica Missionary Society in 1894 with more personnel but without many converts.[38] Around the same period an Anglican Indian mission was organized in Trinidad.

In British Guiana the Salvation Army opened work among the East Indians (1896), largely under the leadership of a Scottish officer, Captain Alexander Alexander, who took the name of Ghurib Das ("servant of the poor") and dressed in Indian fashion. After 1918 the Lutheran mission in British Guiana (mentioned below) reached many Indians.[39]

Over the years many East Indians moved to the Roman Catholic, Anglican or other Churches, on an individual or family basis or through their children attending church-related schools. Some of these primary schools were purposely provided to serve communities where Indian children were in need of education.[40]

The "Older" Denominations

By the 1870s the mosaic of the West Indian Church had been set in place from many overseas countries and denominations: from Catholic Spain, Anglican England and Catholic France, later from Central European (and English) Moravian missions, Methodist preachers and missionaries, African American Baptists and later English Baptist missionaries, from London Missionary Society Congregationalists, from Presbyterian missionaries of the nonestablished churches in Scotland, and in the postemancipation period, from American missions of Congregationalists and Disciples of Christ, and the Presbyterian "Canadian Mission".[41]

Two other groups had an early presence in the Caribbean, the Society of Friends (founded by Quakers from England) and the (Dutch) Lutheran congregation in Berbice, which later acquired an American missionary connection. From all these sources arose what may be called the "older churches" of the West Indies.[42] To be included also are two denominations which came to the West Indies in the later nineteenth century, namely the African Methodist Episcopal Church and the Salvation Army, and also the small groups of "Brethren". These are introduced in the present section, before proceeding in the next to describe a large number of "newer" bodies, mostly of American origin.

Quaker Meetings had gradually died out in the West Indies in the eighteenth century.[43] They reappeared in Jamaica as a result of news reports about the Morant Bay crisis. Quakers from the American mid west initiated a mission to the island and in 1883 Evi Sharpless from the Iowa Yearly Meeting started work in remote areas in Cedar Valley in Portland parish and on the north-east coast. This mission emphasized educational as well as religious work, reaching some of the East Indian people among others.[44]

The Lutheran Church in British Guiana consisted of one struggling congregation in Berbice, founded in 1743. It was a sort of planters' church, but after emancipation there was some outreach to the African population. With an occasional and tenuous supply of ministers from the Lutheran congregation in Amsterdam, this church was kept alive by its Dutch lay leadership for over a century. In 1878 Revd J.R. Mittelholzer, a local man who had been ordained by the London Missionary Society in 1872, became the pastor and began new work, including some among the Amerindians. He established a formal connection with the Evangelical Lutheran Synod of East Pennsylvania (1890), but this did not involve financial aid until after Mittelholzer's death in 1913. At that time, when an appeal for a minister went to that body, the church in British Guiana became a mission of the American church, as will be described below. The scope of its mandate came to include both creole and East Indian people, setting a good example of an interracial church.[45]

John Robert Mittelholzer

The African Methodist Episcopal (AME) Church had its origin in the newly formed United States, as early as 1787. Richard Allen had led a group of black followers out of St George's Methodist church in Philadelphia, because of discriminatory treatment from its white leadership. Similar problems existed in other mixed congregations, and Allen's group initiated a movement for the formation of what came to be called the Black Churches. In 1816 the AME Church was founded, with Allen as its first bishop.[46] Shortly afterward in New York a similar movement formed the AME Zion Church.[47]

Since most churches in the West Indies including the Methodist Church were already predominantly African in membership, it might seem that there would have been no felt need for Black Churches in the West Indies. However there was attraction in the idea of a church entirely under African rather than white (and usually expatriate) leadership. There came to be a significant African Methodist Episcopal presence in several parts of the West Indies. In the 1850s the Conference of the AME Church in Canada had become a separate organization under the name of the British Methodist Episcopal Church. It was this group which in the 1870s and 1880s started work in Bermuda and in St Thomas (then a Danish colony), in Trinidad and in Demerara. These later came under the care of the AME Church in the United States.[48] In 1892, on the initiative of the Bermuda Conference, activity began in Barbados. Two pioneers were in fact Barbadians who had become AME ministers abroad (in Bermuda and in Tennessee respectively). One of these, the Revd Reuben Sealey, served for twenty-three years before his death. Jamaica and other Caribbean territories gained AME churches. In 1920, three years after the purchase by the United States of the Danish Virgin Islands, the denomination entered St Croix and established two congregations there. In the Bahamas, Guyana and the Virgin Islands the AME Zion Church opened work.[49]

The Salvation Army had originated in England in the 1860s, as a breakaway from the Methodist Church because of William and Catherine Booth's dissatisfaction with what they felt was the parent church's lack of complete dedication to the gospel. Somewhat similar to the American holiness churches (mentioned below) in respect of cherishing the Wesleyan "holiness" doctrine and spirit, this body assumed its characteristic "Army" form in 1870. Initiated by the preaching in Kingston of Mrs Agnes Foster ('Mother' Foster) who had been born a slave near Port Royal, and by Mr and Mrs Raglan Phillips in Westmoreland, the Salvation Army became officially established in Jamaica in 1887. It spread to British Guiana (1895), Barbados (1898) and Trinidad (1901). Territorial Headquarters, established first in Barbados, were moved to Jamaica in 1902. As throughout the world, "the Army" carried on much social service work. Its spread here was also due in part to reaching people who felt rejected by the other more "respectable" churches, and because it acted early to involve a significant number of local personnel as officers, along with those from abroad. The music of the Army bands was also attractive.[50]

For some time groups of "Brethren" had appeared in the West Indies. Census figures of Jamaica in 1871 include 447 "Bible Christians and Plymouth Brethren". In Barbados there were 754 Brethren by 1891. A Brethren Church was founded in Trinidad in 1900.[51] Although there are various groups that use the name "Brethren" and most would not wish to be described as a "denomination", it is probably correct to consider the largest number to be connected with the "Plymouth" Brethren, who had their origin in Ireland and Plymouth (England) about 1828–30. Some of their theological teachings (for example regarding personal holiness and the imminent Second Coming of Christ) bear comparison with the "newer" bodies to be considered in the following section.

"Newer" Denominations from North America

By the later decades of the nineteenth century the evangelization of the people of the English-speaking Caribbean seemed to have been more or less completed (with the exception of course of the East Indian community). This part of the world was considered, both here and abroad, as a Christian region. Schools did much to create this conception. The strength of the churches depended on schools as well as on worship and preaching. When new denominations later came from abroad, they were able to build on the foundation of the existing churches and schools, by persuading members or adherents of the older denominations to change their allegiance, or by winning former pupils of Christian schools (or government schools which reflected the Christian orientation of British education). "Conversion" to a new church would now be due, most often, to a new kind of religious experience and acceptance of different doctrines, and a new understanding of what it means to be "Christian". Other people might simply be drawn to a different style of worship or way of living, or to an attractive congregational fellowship.

In order to understand why new missionaries and lay people felt called to preach a new type of Christian faith in the West Indies, it is necessary to consider the American historical background of a number of movements and denominations which spread to the Caribbean, largely in the twentieth century. Here, in interaction with local leadership, they created a multiplicity of new churches and related organizations. By the time of independence – and even more since then – the shape of the Church in the English-speaking Caribbean was increasingly reflecting the pluralistic style typical of the United States.

Long before the break of the North American colonies from the British Empire, their religious life had already reached an advanced stage of diversity. The "Independent" Pilgrims and Calvinist Puritans who left England and founded the northern colonies in the seventeenth century were critics (outside and inside the

Church of England respectively) of Anglican orthodoxy. The radical Protestant appeal to scripture, rather than tradition, and a willingness to accept new ecclesiastical and theological ideas, characteristic of American Christianity ever since, took root in the early colonies. "Established" churches, that is, the Church of England in some southern colonies and Congregationalism in New England, were challenged, especially in Pennsylvania and New York, by independent British groups (notably Baptists, Quakers and Presbyterians) and by other religious bodies (such as Lutheran and Reformed) introduced by European immigration. The Great Awakening of the eighteenth century had put new life into all communions that were open to its evangelical appeal. The newer but rapidly increasing Methodists were soon to be organized as a Church. Growing pluralism was demanding a new concept: "separation of church and state". This became institutionalized in the constitution of the new republic. Religious freedom, already widespread, was encouraged by this policy.

At the beginning of the 1800s a "revival" of evangelistic campaigning broke out. It came to be known as the Second Great Awakening. This led in some circles to the preaching of new doctrines or doctrinal emphases, and to the multiplication of new "denominations".[52]

The more spectacular ("Western") aspect of this Second Awakening is often dated from a "camp meeting" revival at Cane Ridge, Kentucky in 1801. The ferment of the movement lasted through the first three decades of the new century, and its effects continued long afterward. In the frontier districts of the American West various kinds of religious novelty were welcomed, including preaching and indoctrination by itinerant and sometimes unlettered evangelists, large regional mass meetings where people camped for several days, and appeals for personal decision. The movement appeared also in urban centres in the Eastern states, where "protracted meetings" became common. Evangelistic preaching, the singing of gospel hymns and emphasis on conversion became prevalent in much of Protestant church life. As time went on, the more conservative churches dissociated themselves from the emotional evangelism of these frontier and urban revivals, but the nation as a whole was inspired to greater religious zeal.[53]

At this period also the "home missionary" movement was stirring the churches. Great energy was exerted to spread Christian life, work and education during American expansion into the new western states. This enterprise was abetted by the optimism connected with the atmosphere of "Manifest Destiny" as the frontier of the new republic moved westward across the continent. Moreover the international movement to send missions to the non-Christian world was growing in North America as well as in Europe.[54]

In the preceding chapter it was told how one group, "the Disciples of Christ", came to Jamaica in the postemancipation era. This church had arisen early in the Second Great Awakening as the "Christian" movement led by Barton Stone, who had been instrumental in organizing the above-mentioned Cane Ridge camp meeting. He subsequently withdrew with others from the Presbyterian Church in Kentucky, in search of a non-sectarian fellowship based solely on the New Testament. This body in 1832 joined with another with similar aims in neighbouring Ohio, known as "Reformers" or "Disciples", in which Scotch-Irish leaders, Thomas and Alexander Campbell and Walter Scott were prominent. The union was called the Christian Church (Disciples of Christ). Its purpose was to unite all Christian people around the simple beliefs and practices of the early Church. This was perhaps the earliest, but not the only, instance of a new denomination resulting from the desire to transcend older denominational divisions on the basis of New Testament Christianity.[55]

A second group which originated later in the Western Revival (already noted because it played a part in the church history of Jamaica) was the company of students from Oberlin College, who first came to that island as Congregational missionaries in 1839. This institution in Ohio was founded in 1833 as part of the westward movement of evangelism and Christian education. It was linked with the name of Charles Finney, a noted evangelist, and with the idealism of the drive for the abolition of slavery in the United States. In a curious way two movements in the story of American revivalism and reform became associated when the Oberlin graduate Julius Beardslee later espoused the teachings of the Disciples and returned to found the Disciples of Christ in Jamaica.[56]

As time went on the American "Second Awakening" developed startling innovative tendencies and produced increasing divisiveness and sectarianism. The 1830s have been called "the era of controversy".[57]

One notable variety of this religious ferment was the Adventist movement. Although there are earlier instances in Christian history when expectations of the imminent return of Christ played a prominent part in the life of groups of believers, perhaps its most spectacular expression was that among followers of William Miller, who were persuaded that biblical prophecies promised this event in 1843 or 1844. When this did not take place as anticipated, a less specific premillenial expectation remained alive in the minds of many, both in small Adventist bodies and in some other Christian denominations as well. One important group, the Sabbatarian Adventists, developed a unique interpretation about the heavenly nature of Christ's coming in 1844, combining with it a requirement to observe the Sabbath according to the Old Testament standard. They later added a programme of health reform as a religious duty. This group was organized as a denomination in 1863 under the name of the Seventh-Day Adventists.[58]

By 1874 they began to send missionaries outside the United States. In the English-speaking Caribbean their doctrines were spread by colporteurs and lay converts in the 1880s and 1890s. By the opening years of the new century, churches had been established in almost all the territories. Membership became particularly high in Jamaica. Schools, both primary and secondary, and training colleges with associated agricultural and industrial activities were instituted in Jamaica and in Trinidad. In some territories medical clinics or hospitals were built and operated.[59]

Other American denominations whose roots can be traced to the Second Great Awakening are more "orthodox" than the Seventh-Day Adventists. The earlier of these came from the holiness movement. Later and at the beginning of the twentieth century came those of pentecostalism.[60]

New emphasis on the need for Christian holiness began as early as the 1830s and 1840s in the United States (and to some extent in other countries). The doctrine of Sanctification which had been a prominent emphasis of the Wesleyan heritage was revived, and enlarged upon, by many Methodists, and by others who sought a deeper dedicated faith. Holiness was understood as a "Second Blessing" subsequent to Justification, as the believer sought greater perfection in the Christian life. After the Civil War an undenominational "National Camp Meeting Association for the Promotion of Holiness" advanced the movement. By the end of the century this concern had given rise to several new ecclesiastical bodies described as "holiness churches".[61] In the twentieth century some of them, including the Church of God, the Church of the Nazarene, the Pilgrim Holiness and the Wesleyan Churches, sent missionaries to the Caribbean.

"The Church of God Reformation Movement" dating from the 1880s, became separately organized in 1906 and was centred in Anderson, Indiana. Led by Daniel S. Warner, this movement sought to reform the Christian Church by rejecting all "sectarian" labels and seeking a restoration of the New Testament pattern of personal holiness and church life. The first appearance of this Church of God in the West Indies was in Trinidad in the same year, when George H. Pye and two others started work. Two years later George Olson and his wife and daughter arrived in Jamaica. They served there for forty-six years. Work in other territories followed, either with missionaries or local evangelists. The West Indies Bible Institute was established in Trinidad and the Jamaica Bible Institute in that island, for the training of leaders.[62]

Another major holiness denomination, beginning in the USA in 1895 with a strong Wesleyan tradition, was the Church of the Nazarene. In the British West Indies the first District Superintendent, James Hill, came to Barbados and Trinidad in 1926. A pioneer with him was a Barbadian, Miss Carlotta Graham, who had attended Eastern Nazarene College in the United States and was ordained in 1931. The Nazarene Training College was opened in Trinidad.[63]

Two other holiness bodies which originated from American Methodist backgrounds became established in the West Indies: the Pilgrim Holiness Church and (especially in western Jamaica) the Wesleyan Church.[64]

The twentieth century development of pentecostalism extended the holiness movement with the addition of an emphasis on the baptism of the Holy Spirit, and the practice of "speaking in tongues". Usually dated from the Los Angeles revival in humble beginnings at the Azusa Street Mission in 1906, it received attention from people far and near and led to a spectacular spread in many parts of the world.[65] Several pentecostal denominations from North America began work in the West Indies during the colonial period.

The Church of God (centred in Cleveland, Tennessee) sent missionaries to the Bahamas in 1910 and to Jamaica during World War I. It had been one of the first American denominations to adopt the practice of speaking with tongues.[66] In time those affiliated with this group in the Caribbean took the name *New Testament* Church of God.

The Pentecostal Assemblies of Canada, with headquarters in Toronto, started work in Trinidad in 1924. A training college, the West Indies School of Theology, was located in northern Trinidad.[67] The Assemblies of God (of the United States) began work in Jamaica through Cyril Huckerby who settled in Spanish Town in 1937 and organized several Pentecostal churches.[68]

The Church of the Open Bible (which had its origin in the Foursquare Gospel organization of Aimee Semple MacPherson of California) began work in Trinidad in the 1950s. This was intended at first as a mission to East Indians, but attracted many others as well.

Two other major movements in American Protestantism should be mentioned as spreading their influence in the West Indies, either through particular American based churches or through wider interdenominational contacts:

(i) The interdenominational organized mass evangelistic campaigns of Dwight L. Moody and Ira Sankey in the latter decades of the nineteenth century, and those of the twentieth century such as Billy Sunday and Billy Graham, spread popular gospel hymns and methods of evangelism to the Caribbean as to other parts of the world.

(ii) The Fundamentalist movement which climaxed in the 1920s began as a doctrinal struggle against "modernism" within the older Protestant churches in the United States. This controversy had comparatively little direct impact in the West Indies, where the older churches in any case tended to be theologically conservative. Fundamentalist teachings critical of the traditional churches were however carried to the Caribbean by some of the newer American bodies.

It is impossible to name all the missions and locally initiated congregations or groups of congregations which directly or indirectly have drawn inspiration from these American movements.[69] To provide a comprehensive description of their doctrines and practices, which vary from church to church, would be still more difficult. Some or all of the following characteristics however may be found among them in various combinations:

- simplicity and freedom of worship, with active participation of the congregation (including women) by singing, clapping, "Amens", prayers, and "testimonies";
- evangelistic preaching, frequently leading up to an altar-call, and personal evangelism;
- stress on the Bible as the inerrant Word of God;
- emphasis on conversion and also subsequent experience of "holiness" and/or baptism by the Holy Spirit, in some cases evidenced by speaking in tongues;
- adult or believers' baptism, usually by immersion;
- faith healing, and sometimes fasting;
- the requirement of simple living and "separation from the world", as by rejection of jewelry, smoking, drinking, dancing, cards and movies;
- expectation of the imminent Second Coming of Christ;
- church organization varying from congregational to presbyterian to episcopal (the latter with scant regard for the doctrine of "Apostolic Succession" in ordination);
- a tendency to criticize older churches as "cold" or doctrinally unsound.[70]

These American-related missions or churches were widespread in the West Indies by the 1930s and increasingly thereafter. It has been suggested that one reason for this was the growing political aspiration to democracy and resistance to the colonial connection with Great Britain. Informality of worship and participation by the people in the local congregation was a form of protest against churches associated in the minds of many with expatriate-dominated colonial culture.[71]

There is a tendency of many of the American-related groups to refer to themselves, and to others of similar beliefs, as "evangelicals". This creates some confusion especially in the Caribbean, where the older churches had long used this term in a different way. For example, prior to the founding of the Caribbean Conference of Churches in 1973, the Federal Council of Evangelical Churches in Trinidad included several denominations (other than the Roman Catholic and Anglican) by analogy with the "Free Church Federal Council" in England. The Constitution of the Union Theological Seminary (1954–67) founded in Jamaica by Methodist, Presbyterian, Moravian, Congregational and Disciples churches, sought "to maintain by its terms the doctrines of the Evangelical Faith as an essential part of Seminary training".[72] Because of this ambiguity, we avoid employing the term "evangelical" in its narrower American usage, preferring "newer" or some other word, according to the context.[73]

The holiness and especially the pentecostal bodies, in the Caribbean as in the United States, have frequently divided among themselves, ostensibly over doctrinal differences and also over leadership. Various "indigenous" congregations and denominations with new names have sprung up. Sometimes American missionary support has come to the aid of such groups which were in need of spiritual fellowship, ecclesiastical approval, assurance of greater permanence, or financial help.[74]

Following practices used in the United States, and in line with custom in the West Indies, the holiness and pentecostal churches established educational institutions, including secondary schools in some territories.[75]

Some scholars have assumed that the worship services of the pentecostal bodies are particularly suited to the African temperament and religious tradition. There may be some resemblances between the feeling of pentecostalism and that of African traditional worship. However, large numbers also of East Indians in Trinidad and Guyana, including preachers and church leaders, are found in these denominations.[76] Moreover, pentecostalism has spread in all continents among people of many cultures. If this kind of religious expression can be said to have a special appeal, it may be to those who have less wealth and education.[77]

Indigenization and Moves towards Independence

In the colonial era each communion had its particular problems, especially those of finance and personnel, during the slow movement towards indigenous adaptation. Dominant personalities (often expatriate) sometimes stood in the way of change; sometimes they promoted it. Overseas missionary societies could direct decisions, and often they favoured "devolution" and their own withdrawal. The disestablishment of the Church of England, the increasing influence of the United States, the effects of two world wars and the introduction of air travel, required major changes. The founding of the University College (later the University) of the West Indies opened the way for scholarship and professional training within the region. These events encouraged more local control in both state and church.

Such pressures produced some unexpected and paradoxical results. The following survey of denominations utilizing a similar order to that of the last chapter's section on "The Growth and Formation of the Churches" gives some examples of forward and occasionally backward movements in the growth of an indigenous West Indian Church.

The Church of England experienced the crisis of disestablishment and disendowment in the different colonies at various dates beginning in 1869.[78] It found itself one church among many, although still with much of its traditional prestige in the community. In some cases endowment lingered on, such as where the stipends of incumbent clergy were continued till their death.[79]

In Jamaica in 1870 Bishop Courtenay called a synod to deal with the new situation, especially the loss of government income. Initial fears proved unfounded, although the 1870s were a period of somewhat painful adjustment. Notable leadership came from a young clergyman, Enos Nuttall, who had had experience with voluntary church support in the Methodist system, and who has been spoken of as "the Moses of the Anglican Church of Jamaica". Nuttall was chosen bishop in 1880 and gave epochal leadership. He became primate of the West Indies (1893–97) and then archbishop until his death in 1916.[80]

When the Barbados Assembly in 1870 declined to disestablish the Church, new dioceses were necessary for neighbouring colonies which did so. Trinidad became a see under Bishop Rawle. The Windward Islands followed in 1877, although for fifty years sharing a bishop with Barbados. In 1883 a separation was made of British Honduras, which nevertheless was still served until 1891 by Bishop Nuttall. Neighbouring Central American countries were included in this diocese until by 1957 they had all been transferred to the Protestant Episcopal Church of the USA.[81]

The churches in the colonies became more aware of their worldwide and regional connections. Caribbean bishops were present at the first Lambeth conference (1867) and advocated continuance of such conferences. (The next was in 1878.) After an episcopal conference in 1873, West Indian provincial synods (consisting of bishops only) met, sometimes in the Caribbean, sometimes in London. The Province of the West Indies was constituted in 1883, electing Bishop William Piercy Austin as the first primate. At the Lambeth Conference of 1897 it became an Archdiocese. The West Indian churches were kept close to their English connection through their bishops, by a preponderance of English clergy and by cultural orientation.

REPRODUCED BY COURTESY OF THE NATIONAL LIBRARY OF JAMAICA

There had been reluctance in the postemancipation era to train and ordain coloured or black clergy, and in later years promotion for them was slow. Nevertheless there were gradual moves toward indigenization. Local election and consecration of bishops began to take place. Although most bishops came from England in colonial times there were three West Indians, W.W. Jackson (1868), C.J. Branch (1882) in the Leeward Islands, and the first of African ancestry, P.W. Gibson in Jamaica (1956). Local preferences, for example in liturgy, came to be recognized. Constitutions were drawn up for the various territories, with laymen playing an increasing part in ecclesiastical

Rt Revd Percival William Gibson

affairs. In 1959 for the first time the provincial synod met with three houses of bishops, clergy and laity.[82]

The Roman Catholic Church was heavily dependent for leadership (bishops, clergy, and lay workers including nuns) on Ireland (Trinidad), England (Guyana, Barbados), the United States (Jamaica, Belize), Canada (Guyana, St Vincent, the Bahamas), and also France and Belgium. Many religious orders were represented, such as Jesuits, Dominicans and Benedictines. Not until well into the twentieth century, with the opening of theological seminaries in Trinidad and in Jamaica, was there much sign of change in the direction of local leadership.

From 1956 new organizational changes took place. The original archdiocese of Port-of-Spain and diocese of Roseau, dating from 1850, were subdivided into several dioceses, centred in Kingston, Montego Bay, Belize, Nassau, Castries, St George's and Georgetown. In 1957 the Antilles Episcopal Conference, with two Provinces of Port-of-Spain and Kingston (and another for the French territories) was constituted. In 1967 Kingston became an archdiocese.[83]

The Methodists, soon after emancipation, had begun to experience pressure from the Wesleyan Methodist Missionary Society and the British Conference, for the West Indian Church to become self-supporting. However the decline of the optimism of the postemancipation period, the difficulties of communication among the scattered Caribbean colonies, the general poverty and the scarcity of higher education left such hopes in abeyance. At the same period a secession (1837–64) of the "Jamaican Wesleyan-Methodist Association", based on the feeling of coloured leaders that they were not accepted as equals for the ministry, had weakened the Methodist community.[84]

Control of the mission remained in London. Nevertheless the hope of autonomy and self-support was not forgotten, and the late 1870s were a time of consultation and debate as to the possibility of a free-standing West Indian conference. How could the Caribbean – an overseas area which had been one of the earliest places of Methodist history, from the days of Nathaniel Gilbert – be delivered from dependence on the Missionary Society in Britain? The correspondence of some missionaries with the "home" church revealed considerable fear that lay people here did not have the education and experience to manage business affairs. Another problem was the small number of locally trained ministers. It was decided at first (by the Missionary Committee in London) that a necessary preliminary was the strengthening of the local base (in circuits and quarterly meetings) in each territory, and that time was needed for this. Then in 1883 the policy was abruptly changed – again in London – to establish a West Indies Conference similar to that of Canada, Australia and South Africa. In the Caribbean there was some support from the Jamaica District, but little in the smaller colonies.[85]

From 1884 to 1903 two Methodist Caribbean Conferences held authority: Western (Jamaica and Haiti) and Eastern (Lesser Antilles, Trinidad and British Guiana).

Until 1891 they both operated under the superintendency of the Revd George Sargeant. The Bahamas and Honduras – whose communications with London were regular, but with the other colonies almost non-existent – were not included. A triennial General Conference was set up to give oversight to the two Annual Conferences, but its legislation was subject to the approval of the British Conference. The General Conference however could not afford to meet after 1894.[86]

The first seven-year period (1883–91) of this constitutional arrangement was seemingly successful. Growth in membership was recorded. New chapels were built and new missions founded in St Lucia, St Thomas and Panama. Yet causes of ultimate failure were ominously gathering: growing debt, depression in the sugar industry, widespread poverty among laity and also among the ministers, natural disasters, difficulties of ministerial staffing (both local and expatriate), the smallness and cost of an increased number of district meetings as well as the General Conference, and the expense of schools (notably two high schools in Jamaica, York Castle and Barbican, and Coke College in Antigua). Finally in 1903 both the Western and Eastern Conferences pleaded to be taken back into a mission relationship with the British church. This reversal took place in January 1904.[87]

By the time of the Bicentenary of Caribbean Methodism (1960) new arrangements concerning finances, the coming of air travel, much improved education of the body of church members, and the development of theological education, had altered the circumstances of the Church so that success could be assured. Then in 1967 the Methodist Church of the Caribbean and the Americas (MCCA) was formed, with seven Districts (Guyana, Haiti, Honduras, Jamaica, the Leewards, Panama/ Costa Rica, and the South Caribbean). The Bahamas became the eighth district in the following year.[88]

The Moravians began an early move from mission to Church, initiated by the Unity (that is, worldwide General) Synod of 1848. The Jamaica Revival of 1860–61 gave hope of further progress. The General Synod and Conferences in St Thomas (1879) set forth plans for two provinces (one in Jamaica and one in the Eastern West Indies), with a schedule for the gradual reduction of mission grants, to end in 1890. This goal was not reached, but by 1914 the West Indies was covering nine-tenths of its expenses.[89]

While plans were going ahead for the older missions to become churches, new work in the southern Caribbean was beginning, mainly among Moravian immigrants from the small islands. A mission in Demerara, with its base among Moravians from Barbados, was founded in 1878 by African Barbadian pioneers (notably the long-serving Henry Moore). For somewhat similar reasons a Swiss missionary, Marc Richard was sent to Trinidad in 1890. Trinidad was added to the Eastern West Indies Province, but Demerara was left as a small province on its own. For some decades also (1905–60) a mission was carried on in Santo Domingo.[90]

The first West Indian provincial synods were held in 1899. At the same time the General Synod was wrestling with the worldwide financial problems of the missions. Ten years later the subject of debate was whether to set the goal of establishing "Native Churches", that is, entirely independent Moravian Churches where the missions had laid the foundations. Among these the West Indies, dating from 1732, was the longest established mission area. In 1914, following the World Missionary Conference of 1910, the Unity Synod reaffirmed its three goals of evangelism, international unity and ecumenical co-operation. The highest authority, however, still lay in the General meeting in Herrnhut.[91]

During the years of World War I the Unitas Fratrum, with its headquarters in Germany, was rent asunder by the fighting. This had a decentralizing effect on the Church. The West Indian synods, each with its Provincial Elders' Conference (Governing Board) assumed full autonomy. The small Province of Demerara likewise carried on, being unique in having no missionaries from abroad. The mission in Nicaragua was transferred from Herrnhut to the American Moravian Missionary Society. After the war endowment funds invested in Germany were lost at the time of inflation. Mission support shifted from Germany towards Great Britain. Later as the British Church after World War II became weaker, the Eastern West Indies Province (but not Jamaica) was transferred in 1953 to the United States. Thus the indigenization of the Church, and in particular the decentralization of its international structure, was pushed forward by two world wars. Finally, the importance of the Caribbean was recognized by the holding of the Unity Synod in Jamaica in 1974.[92]

The African Methodist Episcopal Church had a long struggle in the Caribbean. Organized into episcopal districts which were based on the United States, and with boundaries that changed from time to time, the people rarely saw their bishops until in 1940 the Caribbean and South America became a district on its own (the sixteenth). About the same time air travel improved communication. Finally in the time of Bishop Frederick Talbot (a native of Guyana, appointed in 1972) the district became very active.[93]

Presbyterianism had advanced in Jamaica to a synod in 1849, with four (later five) Presbyteries. This created an increasingly autonomous Presbyterian Church of Jamaica. Church of Scotland congregations (for example, Falmouth and Kingston) in due course united with the synod.[94]

In Trinidad the four Scottish ministers welcomed the Canadian ministers into their Presbytery on their arrival. The Canadians, however, controlled the mission to East Indians under the firm hand of their mission council. After the formation of a mission council in British Guiana in 1903 there was a loose connection between the missions in the two territories, both subordinate to the Foreign Mission Board of the Presbyterian Church of Canada.[95]

In the 1920s "Canadian Mission" Presbyterian work in Trinidad and British Guiana became separated. Division within the "mother church", the Presbyterian Church of Canada, at the time of the formation of the United Church of Canada (1925), resulted in new relationships in the Caribbean. The mission in Trinidad became associated with the United Church and the one in British Guiana with the (continuing) Presbyterian Church in Canada.[96]

Meanwhile in Trinidad some of the local leaders, such as ministers and teachers, were seeking greater independence from missionary control. A petition to the Mission Board in Canada in 1900, a protest against the appointment of the Revd Harvey Morton (son of John the pioneer) to succeed his father as field missionary in Tunapuna, and another petition in the later 1920s, finally led to the reorganization of the Presbytery of Trinidad with local ministers and elders fully represented in accordance with Presbyterian polity. The first local moderator was the Revd Charles D. Lalla, one of the leaders in this movement for local authority. The Mission Council, however, remained powerful, and this renewed local protest in the 1940s, after which more control (including that over the denominational schools) was given to the Presbytery. In the 1950s the term "field missionary" was changed to "field secretary" and the "CM schools" became "Presbyterian". The church became fully independent and self-supporting during the 1970s in terms of both personnel and finances. In British Guiana a somewhat similar transition to local control took place later than in Trinidad (because the mission itself had started later). There the Presbytery was formed in 1945.[97]

The Presbyterian Church in Grenada had begun as the "Scots Kirk" in 1830–31. As already indicated, this congregation was augmented by three rural churches with the help of East Indian catechists from the "Canadian Mission" in Trinidad. Ultimately in 1955 contact was made with the Trinidad Church and for some years the churches in the two islands were united.[98] In 1961 a synod of the Presbyterian Church in Trinidad and Grenada was formed. After two decades of this relationship, however, Grenada withdrew to become an independent Church.

In British Guiana the "Church of Scotland" Presbyterians had a history going back to 1816 when St Andrew's Kirk in Georgetown was founded. The dwindling Dutch Reformed Church, with its similar Calvinist theological tradition, officially ended in 1871, handing over some sacramental vessels to the Kirk.[99]

The "Canadian Mission" Church in British Guiana, as we have seen, with its East Indian constituency, dates from late in the nineteenth century. The result has been the existence of two quite separate churches, one originally "Scottish" and now largely "creole" in membership, the other mainly East Indian. About the time of independence, these became known as the "Presbytery of Guyana" and "The Guyana Presbyterian Church" respectively.[100]

In 1957 the Presbyterian Churches of Jamaica, Grenada, Trinidad and British Guiana held a "Consultative Assembly" in Trinidad, and this led to a series of periodical meetings of the Caribbean Assembly of Reformed Churches (including Congregationalists as well as Presbyterians). This organization had however no administrative powers, although occasionally it facilitated transfer of ministerial personnel from one territory to another.[101]

The Lutheran Church in Guyana is an unusual case of a church becoming a mission. As already noted, after the death in 1913 of the Revd J.R. Mittelholzer, the congregation approached the East Pennsylvania Synod of the Evangelical Lutheran Church of the USA to ask for a minister. The Board of Foreign Missions of the General Synod of that Church – and later the United Lutheran Church of America – assumed responsibility for "the New Amsterdam Mission" and according to custom began dealing with it through its missionaries. Church work immensely increased, with the opening of a special outreach to East Indians under the leadership of catechist Charles Bowen in 1918, and with educational and other work. This was the situation until 1943, the two hundreth anniversary of the founding of the first Lutheran congregation, when the Evangelical Lutheran Church in British Guiana was constituted. Even thereafter the control of subsidies meant that the newly formed Church remained heavily dependent on the American Church.[102]

The London Missionary Society began early to encourage its churches in British Guiana and Jamaica to become independent, and by 1874 started to withdraw its missionaries. Congregational unions were formed in Jamaica in 1877 and in British Guiana three years later.[103] Afterward in view of difficulties, there was a partial restoration of support from Britain under the care of the (Congregational) Colonial Missionary Society.[104]

The Baptists had been pioneers in self-support and self-government. In Jamaica, after declaring independence from BMS financing, they had first formed the Jamaica Baptist Missionary Society (JBMS) to deal with missionary outreach to Africa, and then in 1849 the Jamaica Baptist Union. The JBU combined two earlier unions (West and East), to handle Jamaican church affairs. These organizations in principle gave control of church affairs to the people in Jamaica, although the BMS and its English ministers still held great prestige. However certain English missionaries found themselves in tension in some congregations (notably in Spanish Town) with others speaking for the local people. Then the Morant Bay rebellion brought a conservative movement in the JBU and the BMS. As Calabar Theological College graduated more and more ministers, leadership by the 1880s came into the hands of Jamaicans. Finally the only English ministers were theological tutors at Calabar.[105]

The Baptists in Trinidad had long carried on without benefit of missionaries until they obtained a connection with the BMS in the 1840s. Missionaries served in the South until 1896 when the BMS withdrew from the Caribbean in order to concentrate on work in Africa. Then in 1946 the Society resumed aid to Trinidad to assist in church development and education.[106]

The American-based holiness and pentecostal churches early moved toward self-support and self-government. Bible schools recruited and trained local leaders and preachers. In some cases this training was combined with the learning of a trade so that students could be self-supporting.[107]

In summary it may be said that in all denominations there was an orientation towards church traditions in Great Britain, Europe, or North America, through the presence of expatriate leadership, financial aid, colonial culture, travel abroad, and the sense of identity within "denominations". In some territories there was a shift to an American church connection.[108] Along with these conservative influences, there has been positive, if variable, progress towards an indigenous West Indian Church.

Education and Theological Training

An adequate programme of education was essential for indigenous development of the churches, as well as an expression of Christian service to society.

The education system in the West Indies had begun with the churches and missions. Schools for the ex-slaves and their children, and later schools for children of indentured immigrants, were initiated by them. Secondary schools and teacher-training colleges were often church-connected.[109] Clergy and lay church members were frequently engaged in teaching and in the management of primary and secondary schools, and in some places teacher training and theological colleges. The contribution of the Church to education is incalculable. The absence of a local university until 1948, however, was a serious hindrance for society as a whole. It was also an obstacle to the development of indigenous lay and ministerial leadership for the churches.

The setting up of theological education was originally the responsibility of each denomination. Codrington College (which after many delays, had responded to the need under Bishop Coleridge) during the later colonial period became affiliated with Durham University (1875) in the time of Bishop Mitchenson. For several years beginning in 1955, the College came under the care of an Anglican order from England, the Community of the Resurrection. At the time of the negotiations in the 1960s for the establishing of an ecumenical theological institution in Jamaica (the United Theological College of the West Indies), it was decided in 1970 that Codrington, with its long history and a somewhat Anglo-Catholic theological position, should continue as before.[110]

In Jamaica, following some earlier attempts to institute clergy training, Bishop Enos Nuttall soon after his consecration opened a divinity school (1882), later called St Peter's College. Like Codrington College, an arrangement was made in 1888 for affiliation with Durham University. St Peter's continued to train clergy through the decades and joined in the United Theological College of the West Indies when it was formed in 1966.[111]

In the Roman Catholic Archdiocese of Port-of-Spain the Seminary of St Jean Vianney and the African Martyrs was founded in 1943 with three Trinidadian candidates for the priesthood. Located adjacent to the Benedictine Monastery on Mount St Benedict, it was the result of the concern of Archbishop Finbar Ryan for the training of local clergy. Students soon came also from other eastern Caribbean islands and from Guyana and Suriname. Its new building was opened in 1961, just in time for the new era of political independence. Another centre of theological education, the Holy Ghost Missionary College at Arima, was by this time working with the Seminary.[112] In Jamaica St Michael's Seminary was opened in 1952 by Bishop McEleney. After some years in a rural setting overlooking the city of Kingston, it moved to a site at Mona adjacent to the University and the United Theological College of the West Indies.[113]

In the mission churches theological education was developed through three phases: (i) personal tutoring of catechist-preachers by the missionary in connection with the work of the local station; (ii) the establishment of secondary schools ("colleges") on a denominational basis at which, along with others, church workers could be tutored in theological subjects; (iii) interdenominational co-operation among theological schools. The first two phases had already begun in the postemancipation period. The third phase came much later, not until the twentieth century. During this phase the aspiration towards university-level (or at least post-secondary) training was always present, although it took still longer to implement.

During the second phase, the Baptists in Jamaica had opened Calabar Theological College in October 1843 near Rio Bueno. In 1868 it moved to East Queen Street in Kingston and was headed by the Revd David J. East for thirty-four years. Later it continued in different Kingston area locations while moving into closer co-operation with other denominations in theological education.[114]

The Presbyterians, having founded the Montego Bay Academy (1844), appointed a succession of theological tutors through the following decades who were located in various centres. In 1937 they began to co-operate with the Methodists at Caenwood in Kingston.[115]

The Moravians in Jamaica made repeated attempts to provide training, first with the Teacher Training College at Fairfield with which a theological school was associated from 1876 to 1888. In the eastern Caribbean a theological college was opened in 1885 at Niesky in St Thomas, and later (1900) moved to Buxton Grove in Antigua. Financial difficulties ultimately frustrated these efforts.[116]

The Methodists in 1876 established York Castle High School for Boys and Theological College in St Ann's, Jamaica. It became indebted and had to be closed after twenty-one years. Another beginning for ministerial training was made at Murcott Lodge (1913–18) during which shared teaching with Calabar College was initiated; this was a significant start for the "third phase" of co-operative theological training. In 1928 the Methodists acquired the Caenwood property in Kingston which step by step became a centre for co-operative ministerial training until the formation of the United Theological College of the West Indies in the 1960s.[117]

The "Canadian Mission" Presbyterians in Trinidad opened a Theological College in 1892 for the training of catechists who in many cases were later ordained as ministers.[118] In British Guiana the CM Presbyterians similarly began Bethel College in 1942. The Lutherans also had a Catechist Training School from 1947 to 1957.[119]

The pattern of ministerial training for the various American missions in the West Indies was taken from the system of Bible schools and colleges of the United States, and kept academic connections with that country.[120]

The third phase of theological education – interdenominational co-operative training – emerged just before World War I. In 1909 two visiting Baptist leaders recommended to the "Free Churches" of Jamaica a plan for a United College of theological training. The idea was finally taken up in 1913 after a visit from the Methodist New Testament scholar Dr J.H. Moulton in 1912. Two churches, Baptist and Methodist, carried on a co-operative arrangement of theological training for about twenty-five years. In 1928 the Methodist Church, in order to improve this arrangement with Calabar College, acquired the property at Caenwood in Kingston. Then in 1937 the Presbyterians established St Colme's College on the same site and began working with the other two churches. Moravians, Congregationalists and also the Society of Friends participated in this movement toward joint training.[121] The Disciples of Christ, after at first sending students to the United States, joined in 1949 with the others at St Colme's.[122]

At the time of the opening of the St Colme's Hostel at Caenwood (1955) the co-operative arrangement of Methodist, Presbyterian, Moravian and Disciples Churches was organized as Union Theological Seminary (UTS). UTS continued the arrangement with the Baptists at Calabar College and this was known as United Theological Colleges.[123]

In the late 1950s the Presbyterian Church in Trinidad (after a period of sending theological students to Canada) decided for training within the Caribbean at Union Theological Seminary, after providing the first year of study in Trinidad. Then in 1959 during the Principalship of the Revd J.F. Seunarine, the Presbyterian Theological College in San Fernando was renamed St Andrew's Theological College, to signify its intention to open its doors to students of all denominations. By 1962 it began receiving resident and non-resident pre-theological students, as well as providing lay training courses for students from other churches.

In 1959 negotiations began towards the formation of an interdenominational theological institution to be located next to the University of the West Indies at Mona. Union Theological Seminary, Calabar College and St Peter's College, together with nine co-operating Churches from West Indian territories as far away as Guyana supported the plan. In 1966 the United Theological College of the West Indies (UTCWI) opened with new buildings on a site next to the UWI campus. Concurrently negotiations with the University were in process for the establishment of a Licentiate and later a BA degree in Theology, to be bestowed on the basis of examinations under the University.[124]

About the same time the Missionary Church Association in Jamaica in co-operation with leaders of other denominations in Jamaica and the Caribbean, most of them related to American missions, founded (1960) a theological college under the "evangelical" name in Kingston, known as the Jamaica Theological Seminary.[125]

Thus, appropriately, co-operative theological education for the churches of the West Indies reached new goals in the decade of independence. This took place also, more and more, under local rather than expatriate leadership.

West Indians Abroad

From early days adventurous West Indians (and people from the British Isles) had moved to the Western Caribbean and Central America in search of a livelihood. The Belize area, the Bay Islands and the Moskito Coast have been mentioned as places where groups of such people provided a nucleus for church activity. Towards the end of the nineteenth century, when workers were needed for construction work on the inter-ocean canal, Panama and neighbouring Costa Rica became a magnet for Jamaicans and other West Indians. The SPG began work in Panama in 1883 and in Costa Rica in 1896. Bishop Nuttall was much involved in outreach to Central America.[126] About the same time Baptist work began in Costa Rica and later in Panama, supported by the JBMS. The JBMS also in 1883 took over the field in Haiti which had been started by the English society.[127] The Salvation Army began in 1904 at Cristobal and Colon to serve canal workers. Three years later it extended its work to Costa Rica.[128] The Methodists also entered this area, including a mission among the Valiente Indians in Panama.[129]

Migration of West Indians to Great Britain in considerable numbers began a little before the end of the colonial period. At first it was assumed by the older churches that the members of the British-based churches would integrate with the same denominations in Great Britain. But because forms of worship, culture and race were different, this proved disappointing in practice. In the case of those of Pentecostal background there had not been British-based missions in the West Indies. Pentecostal churches sprang up in Britain on the initiative of West Indian leaders. People who were familiar with these churches "at home" and many others who were seeking a Christian church of a more charismatic type than that of historic British denominations, joined with them.[130]

For similar reasons churches were founded among West Indian immigrants to the USA and Canada.

Outreach to Africa and Asia

West Indian Christians of European race could assume that the culture and religion of their "homeland" was Christian. But what of Africans and East Indians who had become Christian in the Caribbean as a result of missionary work here?   They retained a consciousness of their origins even as they accepted the Christian faith. This concern is found as early as George Liele who proudly spoke of his church members as "Ethiopian Christians".[131]

The last chapter told how West Indian missions to Africa began in the early 1840s because of concern led by British clergy such as Knibb, Waddell, and Rawle, but eagerly supported by West Indians such as the Jamaicans who went to Fernando Po and Nigeria, and those from the diocese of Barbados who went to the Rio Pongas area.

The West Indian African Mission continued through the late colonial period. Its base remained in Barbados, but the Jamaica Church through the Home and

Foreign Missionary Society also contributed to it from 1861 to 1869. With the disendowment of the Church of England, it became difficult to continue this, until in 1889 regular grants were resumed, and in 1896, the Revd and Mrs W.A. Burris were sent from Jamaica to West Africa, where they served until 1925. As time went on it became necessary to seek help from the SPG, and an English committee was formed to support the mission. Later there came an invitation for the training and sending of Jamaican missionaries to Nigeria in connection with CMS work in that country. A number of Jamaicans responded over the following decades, and gave valuable service.[132]

Revd and Mrs W.A. Burris

REPRODUCED BY COURTESY OF THE NATIONAL LIBRARY OF JAMAICA

In 1887 the Congregationalists in Jamaica contributed a teacher and his wife, Mr and Mrs J.H.E. Hemans, to work for many years with the London Missionary Society "on the shores of Lake Tanganyika" in Central Africa.[133]

Many Caribbean men went abroad as soldiers of the West India Regiment, among them some members of the Salvation Army who in this way found themselves in West Africa. They appealed to their church at home to send personnel there. As a result a group of ten Jamaican officers (and seven wives) were commissioned in 1920 to establish what proved to be a successful work in Nigeria.[134]

East Indian Christians had a strong tradition tying them to their country of origin. Some wanted to share the gospel with their motherland and there were occasional contacts between the Caribbean and India. Certain individuals from the Presbyterian Church in Trinidad went back to India and became evangelists there, notably Benjamin Balaram and John Netram.[135] In later times Indian Christian personnel visited Trinidad as fraternal church workers. In the 1950s, at the request of the Moravian Church, two Trinidadian Hindi-speaking evangelists, the Revd Joseph Doman and the Revd James Radhakissoon, served for a time in Suriname.

Co-operation among the Churches

During the eighteenth and nineteenth centuries there was some co-operation among missionaries, and with certain of the other clergy. However the dependence on ex-patriate personnel was not helpful toward close relations among the churches. These leaders had not grown up in the Caribbean. They had come out with a purpose to benefit their particular denomination, and they usually returned to their homeland after a limited period of service.[136] There was nevertheless co-operation among churches with reference to education, where there were common interests in relation to governments regarding the denominational schools. There were also periodic pulpit exchanges, and joint or at least parallel statements on moral issues by Ministerial Associations and Councils of Churches in some colonies.[137]

In spite of the number of "missionaries" in the West Indies, the ecumenical worldwide consultative body known as the International Missionary Council largely ignored the Caribbean. It was considered to be a Christian area. Then in the 1930s Merle Davis, its researcher on the economic and related problems of "the younger churches", made a visit here and issued two reports, one on Jamaica and one on Trinidad.[138] One result was the formation of the Jamaica Christian Council in 1941 with constituent churches as Anglican, Baptist, Church of God (Anderson), Congregational, Disciples of Christ, Methodist, Moravian, Presbyterian, Salvation Army, and the Society of Friends.[139]

One form of ecumenical co-operation which became common in the later years of the colonial period was that of joint evangelistic efforts. Some were sponsored by Ministerial Associations. One notable project was undertaken by the Jamaica Christian Council: the All-Island Evangelistic Campaign of 1950 under the theme "Christ for Jamaica".[140] A number of other evangelistic crusades on an interdenominational basis were held in Trinidad and elsewhere, especially in the 1950s and 1960s. Some of these were supplied with preachers from the USA, such as the Latin American Mission and the Billy Graham organization. In other cases West Indian evangelists, including Ephraim Alphonse and Wingrove Taylor, gave the leadership.

Improvement of intra-Caribbean travel by air, and the founding of the University College of the West Indies (1948) began to pave the way for closer relations among Caribbean churches. However in the formation of this university there was little participation by the churches as such, as was traditionally the case in earlier foundations in Europe, the United States and Canada. This was in part due to lack of financial resources, but the pattern of external ecclesiastical dependence was another reason.

In Jamaica a small movement toward church union began in 1927.[141] By 1952 this was finally expedited with the formation of a Church Union Commission by Congregational, Methodist, Moravian and Presbyterian bodies. Later the Disciples joined in. This commission played an important part in the formation of the Union Theological Seminary mentioned above. In terms of actual church union one early result was the consummation in 1965 of a merger of the Presbyterian and Congregational churches to form the United Church of Jamaica and Grand Cayman.[142]

The year 1954 marks the beginning of Caribbean-wide consultation and co-operation within the worldwide Ecumenical Movement. In that year a representative of the International Missionary Council made a "journey" through the area and published a report of his observations. In 1957 a "Caribbean Consultation" met in Puerto Rico.[143] This led to the setting up of the Caribbean Council for Joint Christian Action (CCJCA) and publication of the "Christian Living Series" of Sunday school lessons, which became widely used throughout the English-speaking Caribbean. Significant programmes of ecumenical co-operation followed, including what was known as CADEC (Christian Action for Development in the Eastern Caribbean). Several interdenominational study seminars and consultations took place during the 1960s on theological education, "Religious and Social Study", missions in the Southern Caribbean, and family life. Other developments came soon after Independence, including a widely representative Caribbean Ecumenical Consultation for Development (CECD) at Chaguaramas (1971) and the formation of the Caribbean Conference of Churches (CCC) in 1973. This regional Church council was the first in the world where the Roman Catholic Church was an integral part of the ecumenical body from the beginning. It included also the United Protestant

Church of Curaçao and Bonaire and the Moravian Church in Suriname from outside the English-speaking territories, precursors of the multilingual extension of its mandate.[144]

Ecumenical co-operation was not only within the Caribbean. Several West Indian churches became members of the World Council of Churches (WCC), and many of their representatives participated in WCC Assemblies and other international meetings. West Indian personnel served officially from time to time in the work of the World Council.[145]

In these ways, before and during the closing years of the colonial period, the West Indian Church was preparing to play its part in the age of independence, and also in the ecumenical movement in the world as a whole.

12

Conclusion

Some outstanding topics in this account of the shaping of the West Indian Church may now be summarized.

Socio-denominational Characteristics

When church history is considered from a sociological point of view, some denominational differences have been attributed to class, national and racial diversities, to immigrant cultures or sectional attitudes.[1] Older but still famous is Troeltsch's distinction between the "church-type" and the "sect-type" of Christian development.[2] Are such analyses relevant in the West Indies?

Two words of caution are in order. First, care has to be taken in applying categories borrowed from abroad to the different circumstances here. For one thing, most denominational differences were brought to the Caribbean from Europe and North America and are quite irrelevant in the local setting.[3] Secondly, the longer each tradition has existed in the Caribbean the more it has changed within itself. Some statements which may be made of Roman Catholics, Anglicans or Quakers, for example, are true of one period but not of another. With these reservations, some socio-ecclesiastical categories may be helpful in describing the development of the West Indian Church.

The Roman Catholic tradition belongs, here as elsewhere, to the "church-type". Its comprehensiveness and aspiration to universality, its corporate and sacramental conception of religion, its institutional and hierarchical organization, its acceptance of society as it is and co-operation with the state wherever possible, its accommodation of "sect-type" groups within its own borders, as religious orders or otherwise – all are found in the Caribbean.

Yet Catholicism in the Caribbean has a long history of change. It began in a late medieval form. The Age of Faith had been reinforced in the Iberian Peninsula by the Reconquest. Feudal and crusading ideas jostled with Renaissance humanism during the first sixty years of Spanish Catholic monopoly in America. A Catholic reformation of the Spanish Church, associated with the names of Cardinal Ximénes and later Ignatius Loyola, did much to equip it and particularly its religious orders for active missionary outreach and church building. But most obvious of all, Spanish Catholicism was closely tied to the crown and identified with national interest. Although papal supremacy was not questioned in theory, from the time of Ferdinand and Isabella the Spanish monarchy asserted its national and lay authority over the Church in no uncertain terms. This Spanish pattern of Catholicism survived in Jamaica until 1655 and Trinidad until 1797, although in the latter it was modified by a French influx after 1783.[4]

In the seventeenth century French Catholicism came to the Lesser Antilles. As in Spain the Church was subservient to royal power, but less spectacularly so. It too had been invigorated religiously by a Catholic revival. This tradition shaped the spiritual life of French St Christopher, the Windward Islands and also Trinidad, prior to their coming under British rule.

In early Spanish and French Catholic culture a hierarchical conception of society rooted in classical philosophy and feudal tradition shaped the attitudes of most Catholics to the Amerindians and the African slaves in their midst. The responsibility of church and state, and especially of the religious and secular clergy, to baptize and instruct the Indians and the Africans in the Christian faith, was recognized. They were then a part of the Church, but the subordinate position of encomienda labourers or slaves was not affected. At best there was paternalistic concern on the part of the master towards his bondservants.

Under British rule, the Roman Catholic Church had to accept its place as one denomination among others, but it retained its comprehensive outlook. For historical reasons there were national associations (Spanish, French and Irish) with the past but these gradually diminished as others, especially African, became influential. Thus the Church (although sometimes marked in practice by national, class or colour distinctions) has held within its fold all who are baptized and has sought to include all. Then in the course of time, hierarchical social conceptions were modified to accord with emancipation and the growth of democracy.

The Church of England, although it had become "Protestant" during the Reformation, retained the Catholic aspiration to comprehensiveness (at least within the English nation and empire) and respect for an ordered hierarchical society as well as ecclesiastical structure. But the growth of Puritanism in the Church, and of Separatism and new sects outside it, placed a heavy strain upon its unity. In the colonies this established Church was further diverted from its ideals by slavery and by the lack of a local episcopacy. As a result, for more than a century and a half it became a national and class church of the English plantocracy. The Catholic policy of inclusion of the slaves in the Church, even in a subordinate social position, was rarely followed.

The competition of nonconformist missionaries, a slowly awakening Anglican conscience, and finally the appointment of bishops for the West Indies in 1824, effected a change in the Church of England. Just before and after emancipation, many thousands of African members were added to the Church through an active programme of religious teaching, pastoral contact, and schools. Its membership now became predominantly non-white, although bishops and clergy long continued to be English or white West Indian.

Disestablishment (except for Barbados) was a further crisis for the Anglican Church. Now one denomination among many, it nevertheless retained the prestige of association with the ruling power. It remained a "church-type" body with a certain English and perhaps upper class bias.

Other national Protestant Churches – the Dutch Reformed (in the Guianas and the Netherlands Antilles), the Lutheran (in the Danish islands) and the Church of Scotland (in British Guiana and some other colonies) – played only a small part in the shaping of Christianity in the Caribbean. The Dutch Church tended to be a class church of merchants and planters. The Danish and Scottish Churches made more effort to reach the slaves but their outreach was smaller than that of the nonconformist evangelical missions.

We turn now from the "church-type" and "national" bodies to what may be called "the churches of the unprivileged".[5]

In West Indian life there has been a succession of missionary bodies which have shown special concern to bring the Christian gospel to disinherited people: the African slaves, the people of colour, the freedmen, the indentured labourers and the later rural and urban proletariat. These bodies usually had a base in the less privileged churches or sects of Europe and North America. Outstanding among them are the Quakers, the Moravians, the Methodists, the Baptists, the Scottish Secession or Free Church missions, the London Missionary Society and the American Missionary Association (largely Congregational), the Disciples of Christ, and the "Canadian Mission" Presbyterians. Coming onto the scene after the majority of the population had been Christianized, yet continuing the concern for the poor, were the African Methodist Episcopal Church, the Salvation Army, and various American groups including the Church of God (Anderson), the Church of the Nazarene, the New Testament Church of God, the Pentecostal Assemblies and others.

All of these bodies are inexplicable apart from their religious zeal. With the exception of the seventeenth century Quakers, all were influenced by the Evangelical Movement. They have common ground also in their sympathy with the poorer classes in their base abroad. They may not, however, be described as "churches of the poor" since most of them include some privileged members of society in the West Indies as well as in their home base.

With these can be compared groups *within* the Catholic and national churches, such as some of the religious orders, the eighteenth century missionaries of the Danish Lutheran Church, and the missionary societies of the Church of England. If all these various evangelically inclined groups be considered together, one may say that here is the most significant movement in the growth of the West Indian Church.

Nothing has been said of "churches of the middle class". If the alleged affinity of Calvinism with the rise of capitalism be believed, it would have to be remembered that the seventeenth century Puritan movement failed as a colonizing factor in the West Indies as spectacularly as it succeeded in the New England colonies. "Bourgeois" entrepreneurial ideas undoubtedly motivated the society of planters and merchants, but these families were hardly inspired by religious doctrine. In more recent times, commercial leaders can be found in various urban churches connected with the Anglican, Roman Catholic, Presbyterian and other denominations. Moreover the tendency of the "churches of the poor" to become more "churchlike" with time, as some members within them become affluent, may be observed in the West Indies as elsewhere.

Again, nothing has been said of the Black church, although there is an African majority in the population, and race and colour undoubtedly play an important part in social attitudes. The African Methodist Episcopal Church has been active in the Caribbean. Some other Black Churches have attempted work, but without great numerical success. This may be in part because they came in late. In part it may be due to limited financial resources.[6]

There are however other national groups in the cosmopolitan West Indies. Are there then "immigrant churches" with special language and cultural needs? Some small immigrant groups have found their place usually in the Roman Catholic Church, like the Lebanese ("Syrians") and the Portuguese, and (by conversion) many of the Chinese.[7]

The immigrant group of East Indians was mainly Hindu and Muslim. Some of them entered the Roman Catholic, the Anglican, the Lutheran, the Pentecostal or other churches on becoming Christian. Others in the "Canadian" Presbyterian churches in Trinidad and Guyana have kept a certain amount of Indian culture, although the use of the Hindi language in church services has become rare.

Finally, the social forces which tended to create new denominations in North America due to sectionalism or the frontier did not exist in the Caribbean. However certain of the churches born on the North American frontier, for example the Disciples of Christ and the holiness and pentecostal churches, have sent missionaries to the West Indies and have established denominations.

Church-State Relationships

How shall the Church be related to the government? This practical question runs through the whole course of Caribbean church history. Over the centuries the answer has been a slow movement "from state-church to pluralism".[8]

The Church in the Caribbean began in the era of rising European nationalism, when it was highly regarded for political as well as religious reasons. Spain's was the first empire and the one in which religion was a strong focus of national unity. Thus the Church appears first in the form of the exclusive Spanish Catholic state church.

This monopoly was challenged by the rival French state, and then by other nations, especially the Netherlands and England. By the seventeenth century non-Spanish colonies had brought religious diversity to the Caribbean. It was usually assumed that religion would be established in each new political realm in the form recognized by the European government concerned. Accordingly, the Church of England was planted in the English colonies, the Roman Catholic Church in the French, and the Dutch Reformed Church (rather weakly) in the trading posts of the Netherlands. But this assumption was modified by new developments: the rise of the Huguenot movement in France, the growth of Puritan groups within and outside the Church of England, and the Dutch policy of religious toleration and emphasis on trade.

It seemed that religious diversity was well on its way. But in fact it was delayed, after the Restoration of Charles II and the established Church in 1660, by the fading out of Puritanism (including Quakerism) in the West Indies. In the French Antilles the Revocation of the Edict of Nantes in 1685 brought persecution and dispersion of the Huguenots.

The movement toward pluralism was resumed in the eighteenth century after the rise of Pietism in Europe and the Evangelical Movement in Britain and North America, and their discovery of the missionary challenge among the slaves of the Caribbean. Lay preachers and missionaries introduced Moravian, Methodist, Baptist, Presbyterian and Congregational churches before emancipation. Their work among the slaves created friction with local Assemblies and government authorities. But the missionaries were supported by the British government in London, which by this time had come to espouse freedom for nonconformist church activity.

During the same period the Roman Catholic Church was accepted in the British colonial empire, and this introduced yet another element in the ecclesiastical picture, particularly in the colonies recently ceded by France and Spain.

With the adoption of nineteenth century crown colony government in most territories, the Church of England was disestablished and financial support from the state was gradually withdrawn. In some cases "concurrent endowment" was continued, but increasingly the policy of separation of Church and state gained ground. Immigration of people from India brought non-Christian religions, especially to Guyana and Trinidad, and the worldwide growth of secularism discouraged formal links between religion and government.

At the same time this trend was checked by the fact that the churches were participating actively in education under the system of denominational schools, and by the reality of the spiritual concern of a majority of the people. Hence religious pluralism and secularism had not, at least at the end of the colonial period, issued in complete separation of church and state. It would be more true to say that in ways varying from territory to territory West Indian governments have recognized and co-operated with the religious bodies in matters of common concern.

Religious Toleration

Complementary to the movement from state church to independent churches there was a step by step broadening of religious freedom.

The express policy of the Spanish Empire was to allow none but reliable Catholics in the American colonies. This was enforced by decree, by control over immigration, and by the Inquisition. Protestants came to the Caribbean during the period of French, English and Dutch challenge to Spain's monopoly either as traders, as raiders of Spanish shipping and ports, as colonists defying the Spanish claim to the whole area, or (in the capture of Jamaica) as conquerors. All of these incursions were regarded by the Spanish authorities not only as illegal actions but as insults by heretics. The attitude on the other side was likewise one of hostility aggravated by religion.

At times, it is true, Catholics and Protestants worked together. French and English jointly occupied St Christopher for most of a century. The common danger they faced from Caribs, Spaniards and possible slave uprisings made religious dispute a luxury. Conditions changed, however, and especially after the Revocation of the Edict of Nantes, co-operation could not go on. French-English imperial rivalry was now compounded by religious difference.

Meanwhile within the Protestant society of the English colonies themselves, tolerance fluctuated with political conditions during the seventeenth century. Such intolerance as there was – for example in the case of the Quakers – had more to do with social and political ideas than with religion. There was widespread lack of zeal in the established Church but nonconformist dissent became rare. To some extent this attitude of indifference was supported by eighteenth century rationalist and empiricist thought.

The growth of religious toleration in official British policy during the eighteenth century is reflected in the changing fortunes of the Roman Catholic Church in the captured colonies. In 1655 in Jamaica and 1713 in French St Christopher, military defeat for Spain and France respectively virtually brought an end to the Catholic Church in these islands for decades. But after the Peace of Paris in 1763 the British policy of toleration for French-Canadian religion spilled over into the ceded islands of the French Antilles. After the capture of Trinidad, a still more co-operative attitude was shown to the Spanish and French Catholics who were there.

In the same era however a new form of intolerance arose within the West Indian society itself, once again more social and political than religious. Nonconformist missions among the slaves alarmed many of the plantocracy. They responded with sometimes violent persecution and legal restrictions, at a time when in most parts of the western world religious freedom was growing. The London government repeatedly overruled these colonial opponents of the missions. Furthermore this resort to persecution intensified the emancipation movement in Britain. After the freeing of the slaves the attempt at repression came to an end.

In the nineteenth and twentieth centuries the growth of the Roman Catholic Church, the increase in the number of Protestant missionary bodies and of their adherents, the continuation of African religious practices, and the entrance of Hinduism and Islam gradually enlarged the scope of religious toleration. Each of these groups was, sometimes grudgingly, accorded recognition. The number of "denominations" taking part in the field of education (including finally some non-Christian bodies), the registration of marriages by a greater variety of religious officers, and (since independence) the recognition of certain non-Christian festivals as public holidays, were among the signs of freedom and greater religious equality.

The Growth of the Church

What were the times of maximum growth of Christianity in the West Indies? The story here is quite different from that of colonial North America, where (apart from Amerindians and African slaves) almost all had some background in Christian Europe – indeed many had crossed the Atlantic expressly to find a place for the free expression of their religious faith. In the Caribbean too, of course, the white settlers brought with them their religion when they came from Spain, Great Britain, Ireland, France or elsewhere. They provided the initial establishment of the Anglican and the Roman Catholic Churches. But after the coming of the sugar economy the whites became a minority of the population. How did the Church spread among the other groups, especially Amerindians, Africans and East Indians?

In the Spanish Empire the religious orders were zealous to baptize and Christianize the aboriginal inhabitants. This was done along with the forced labour of the encomienda system and later by the more humane institution of the reducción or mission, as in Trinidad. Seventeenth century French Catholic orders approached the Caribs of the Windward Islands, and much later Methodist missionaries laboured among them in St Vincent. The effects of this work in the (now) English-speaking islands are very small, since few Amerindians remain. In the mainland colonies of Guyana and Belize however, there are many who are recognized as Christian, both Protestant and Roman Catholic, as a result of nineteenth century missions.

In Spanish and French colonies, in accordance with the policy of Church and government, slaves from Africa were baptized and received into the Church, becoming at least nominally Christian by a continual process, as new slaves were brought in and sold to the planters. Thanks to the religious orders there were usually priests to aid in this work. Where such colonies became British in 1763 and later, the black and coloured population generally remained, with the whites, loyal to the Roman Catholic Church.

On the other hand in the British, Dutch and Danish colonies, the slaves were not welcomed into the Church by their masters, or by the local government authorities, or by the clergy, with few exceptions. It was this large unevangelized group which made the West Indies a "mission field". Nonconformist missionaries, and sometimes lay preachers on the spot, began to reach the slaves under the inspiration of the Evangelical Movement in eighteenth century Germany, England and North America. After the founding of the great Protestant missionary societies in the 1790s the movement gained momentum. The Church of England and some of the island Assemblies began to join in. The period of maximum growth for the Church was the emancipation era, both before and after 1834.

After a slump in the mid century, there followed a longer period of slow increase in church membership extending into the twentieth century. This was, of course, partly related to population growth. Many of the Chinese gradually became Christians, and also a minority of East Indians; many of the latter through the schools and other work of the Presbyterian churches. In the twentieth century the "newer" American denominations and indigenous local congregations have grown rapidly, often at the expense of the "older" churches.

Lay Participation in Church Life

One feature of West Indian church life, common also in other parts of the New World, is the active part played by lay people. In part this is due to the circumstances of pioneer settlement far from the existing Church leadership.

The remoteness of a church hierarchy, especially the lack of any Anglican episcopate until 1824, meant that if there was to be a church at all it would be controlled by lay people. In the West Indies as in Virginia, the lay vestry gained a control over the established Church much greater than in England. This was one deplorable aspect of church life in the slavery era, because these laymen belonged to a vested interest in an exploitative society, maintaining an exclusive church for themselves.

On the other hand, most examples of lay initiative contributed to the extension of the Church. Some of the evangelical churches began with lay rather than ordained: preachers. The names of Leonard Dober, Nathaniel Gilbert, John Baxter, Moses Baker, and the slave Harry in St Eustatius spring to mind.[9] Missionaries encouraged lay participation and lay leadership in their congregations. Day school teachers, lay preachers and catechists were recruited. Sunday school teachers, often untrained, worked zealously. Women appeared as leaders of local congregations, and in some communions as paid "Bible women", deaconesses, or (more recently) as ministers. With the shortage of clergy in all denominations, lay persons had to volunteer to maintain activities and church loyalties, although in some cases the work languished. Certainly if it were not for lay initiative and dedication, the mass movement into the churches before and after emancipation, and the growth in numbers on a more modest scale in later generations, would never have been possible.

Theological Thinking and Social Concern

The attitude of overseas dependence in colonial times weakened the inner life of the Church at the theological level. This was compounded by the materialistic out-look of the plantation culture and the callousness of a society based on slavery and postslavery inequity.

Little or no new theological thought emerged from the West Indian colonies during the colonial period. Any writing was largely the reflection of overseas or European ideas. Most local clergy and lay leaders either did not have the educational stimulus for independent thinking, or were educated abroad and thus schooled in intellectual disciplines and ideas learned there.

During the centuries a few prophetic souls sensed the contradiction between their Christian faith and the exploitative society in which they found themselves, and spoke out in some way against it. This sparse succession of Christian social spokesmen form the exception to the general shortage of theological thinkers, and their publications (or the records of their protests) are more in the nature of tracts for the times than formal scholarship. They began with the Dominican monks who denounced the enslavement of the Amerindians. Here and there in slavery times some challenged the exclusion of the Africans from the Church and began to question the cruelties of slavery, and slavery itself, from the standpoint of Christianity. That they had touched a sensitive issue is proved by the others who undertook to combat their arguments, sometimes quoting the Bible for the purpose.

In the final stages of the anti-slavery agitation, information and concern from a variety of people in the West Indies helped to feed the fires in Great Britain of the movement for emancipation.

After slavery had been abolished, the prophetic note continued, but it was usually less aggressive. In comparison with past evils, the continuing ills of society seemed less disturbing, except of course to the sufferers themselves. Also, it was less clear what the remedy should be, unless it be more and better education. It was here that the Church, and its leading thinkers, gave their chief efforts to serve the community. The work of protest passed, it would seem, to secular or unorthodox religious leaders. Yet – perhaps because of the close association of the Church with the slaves in the emancipation era and its activity in the field of education, and also because of the deep religious feeling of the mass of the people – the agents of protest and radical reform have not as often felt estranged from the Church as in many other countries.

Independence in the Caribbean and other parts of the Third World, new liberation theologies from the Americas and Africa, and the intellectual stimulus of the University of the West Indies have affected social and theological thinking, although there is still tension between prophetic and conservative elements in the churches.[10] Also a marked increase in the number of local leaders (among both the "older" and the "newer" churches) in theological teaching as well as ecclesiastical appointments, and a parallel diminution in the number of expatriates in such positions, facilitates new theological thought.

Pluralism and the Ecumenical Movement

It is undeniable that throughout the world there has been a growing tendency towards religious pluralism, and towards pluralism within the body of Christianity itself. This movement, as we have seen, is allied to the ideal of religious freedom, and to the principle of separation of Church and state. It has an affinity for an individualistic culture, including economic individualism. Its first and most typical expression has been in the United States. Some regard it as natural to the Protestant ethos of the English-speaking New World and of parts of the Old World as well. The West Indies has been deeply influenced by this tendency. In the last few decades of the colonial period and since independence, the increase in the number of missionaries from the newer American churches has contributed to it.

It is less obvious, but also true, that there is a counter-tendency both in the West Indies and elsewhere.[11] It can be called the unitive or ecumenical movement, although the latter term has been so variously used as to be rather ambiguous.

Perhaps in the Caribbean the protracted period of colonialism kept alive for an unduly long time an earlier kind of unitive principle, the idea of an established

Church recognized and favoured by the government. While this died an institutional death with disestablishment, its influence continued in the late colonial period, and even beyond, in attitudes and practices here and there.[12] On the other hand the milieu of colonial dependence could well be blamed for the perpetuation of denominational divisions which had their origin overseas and which were maintained by financial support and personnel from abroad.

The modern Ecumenical Movement, a worldwide phenomenon found both in metropolitan countries and in the Third World, respects the principle of religious liberty and also of freedom of the Church from the state. It co-exists with religious pluralism as a fact, while working for co-operation and closer fellowship among the churches. As an organized movement, in the International Missionary Council and later the WCC, it is a twentieth century development. It had, however, many antecedents in earlier times.

In the West Indies there were early expressions of interdenominational concern and some steps toward co-operation. Informal association among missionaries and some Church clergy and lay Christians, in the interest of bringing the gospel to the slaves, is frequently recorded. The local auxiliaries of the Bible Society have probably been active longer than any other form of organized interdenominational activity. They had individual rather than corporate membership and the same was true of groups such as Ministerial Associations.

The Jamaica Christian Council, however, and similar councils in other territories, were official expressions of the desire for co-operation. The church union movement in Jamaica, leading to the formation of the United Church of Jamaica and the Cayman Islands (1992), which brought together Presbyterian, Congregational and Disciples of Christ traditions from Scottish, English and American origins appears as a pioneering demonstration of West Indian initiative in Christian unity. The most conspicuous flowering of this movement was the 1973 founding of the Caribbean Conference of Churches, with full participation of the Roman Catholic Church as well as the "older" Protestant churches.

The assumption of this study has been that in the final analysis church history can and should be written with a recognition of its original and ultimate unity. This may be a "bias" from the secular historian's point of view. Yet there is much in the long and unfinished story of struggle and development of Christianity in the Caribbean to justify use of the phrase "the shaping of the West Indian Church".

Notes

Chapter 1 Introduction

1. The terms "New World" and "Old World" are of course European misnomers. Cf. Philip M. Sherlock, *West Indian Nations* (Kingston and London, 1973), ch. 2.

2. On the Western hemisphere perspective see: "Conference on the history of religion in the New World during colonial times", *Studies Presented at the Conference* . . . (Washington, 1958); Silvio A. Zavala, *The Colonial Period in the History of the New World* (Mexico, 1962).

3. Cf. William W. Sweet, *The Story of Religion in America* (New York, 1950) and *Religion in Colonial America* (New York, 1942/1965); Sydney S. Ahlstrom, *A Religious History of the American People* (New Haven, 1972); Robert T. Handy, *A History of the Churches in the United States and Canada* (Oxford, 1976); John W. Grant, ed., *A History of the Christian Church in Canada* (3 vols., by Henry H. Walsh [Toronto, 1966], John S. Moir [Toronto, 1972], and John W. Grant [Toronto, 1972]).

4. Sherlock, esp. chs. 6, 7, 11-14, 17, 20, 22. On Africa: Charles P. Groves, *The Planting of Christianity in Africa* (4 vols., London, 1948-1956); Basil Davidson, *Africa: History of a Continent* (London, 1966); G.T. Stride and C. Ifeka, *Peoples and Empires of West Africa* (London, 1971); E. Bolaji Idowu, *African Traditional Religion: A Definition* (London, 1973). On India: Cyril B. Firth, *An Introduction to Indian Church History* (Madras, 1961); Leslie W. Brown, *Indian Christians of St Thomas: An Account of the Ancient Syrian Church of Malabar* (Cambridge, 1956); Murray B. Titus, *Islam in India and Pakistan* (Madras, 1959); John G. La Guerre, ed., *Calcutta to Caroni: The East Indians of Trinidad* (Trinidad and Jamaica, 1974).

5. For example, see Idris Hamid, *In Search of New Perspectives* (Bridgetown, 1971); Sehon Goodridge, *Politics and the Caribbean Church* (Bridgetown, 1971); Ashley A. Smith and M. De Verteuil, *Renewal and Ecumenism in the Caribbean* (Bridgetown, 1972); David I. Mitchell, ed., *With Eyes Wide Open* (Bridgetown, 1973) and *New Mission for a New People* (New York, 1977); Idris Hamid, ed., *Troubling of the Waters* (San Fernando, 1973) and *Out of the Depths* (San

Fernando, 1977); William Watty, *From Shore to Shore: Soundings in Caribbean Theology* (Kingston, 1981); Caribbean Ecumenical Programme, *Towards A Caribbean Theology* (Trinidad, 1981); Ashley Smith, *Real Roots and Potted Plants: Reflections on the Caribbean Church* (Williamsfield, Jamaica, 1984); Kortright Davis, *Emancipation Still Comin'* (Maryknoll, 1990); Caribbean Conference of Churches, *At the Crossroads: African Caribbean Religion and Christianity* (Trinidad, 1995); Howard Gregory, ed., *Caribbean Theology: Preparing for the Challenges Ahead* (Mona, Jamaica, 1995); *Caribbean Contact* (1973-94) and *Caribbean Journal of Religious Studies* (1975–).

6.   Dale A. Bisnauth, *A History of Religions in the Caribbean* (Kingston, 1989) treats the wider religious picture.

Chapter 2 New and Old World Backgrounds

1.   Philip M. Sherlock, *West Indian Nations* (Kingston and London, 1973), ch. 1, incl. map (p. 6). On Caribbean Amerindian religion see Dale A. Bisnauth, *A History of Religions in the Caribbean* (Kingston, 1989), ch. 1.

2.   Areas for Caribs in the islands were reduced as their numbers diminished, until only one such reserve, on Dominica, survived. A glimpse of one small (largely creolized) Carib village is described by E.P. Banks, "A Carib village in Dominica", *Social and Economic Studies* (hereafter SES) 5, no.1 (March 1958): 74-86.

3.   Pane, a Hieronymite friar in Columbus' time (John B. Thacher, *Christopher Columbus* [3 vols., 1904; reprint New York, 1967], I, 79-82, including documents from Peter Martyr, *First Decade*); Breton, a Dominican who worked among the Caribs in the Lesser Antilles in the 17th century (see his *Dictionaire caraîbe-françois* [Auxerre, 1665], *Dictionaire françois-caraîbe* [Auxerre, 1666], *Grammaire caraîbe* [1667; reprint Paris, 1877] and *Petit Catechisme* [Auxerre, 1664]); also Bartolomé de las Casas (see Henry R. Wagner, *The Life and Writings of Bartolomé de las Casas* [Albuquerque, 1967], 200-204, 287-98 re his *Apologética Historia* as an early source book on the Amerindians in the Caribbean area).

4.   William H. Brett's books, especially *The Indian Tribes of Guiana* (London, 1868) and *Legends and Myths of the Aboriginal Indians of British Guiana* (London, 1880) and on the other hand Walter E. Roth, *An Inquiry into the Animism and Folklore of the Guiana Indians* (Washington, 1915) and Audrey J. Butt, "The burning fountain whence it came", SES 2, no.1 (Sept. 1953): 102-16. A Guyanese Anglican priest, himself an Arawak, has worked more recently on the Arawak language: see John P. Bennett and Richard Hart, *Kabethechino: A Correspondence on Arawak* (Georgetown, 1991).

5.   Otto Zerries in Walter Krickeberg et al., eds (trans. Stanley Davis) *Pre-Columbian American Religions* (London, 1968), 258-89.

6.   Zerries, 267, 310-16; Julian H. Steward, ed., *Handbook of South American Indians* (7 vols., Washington, 1946-59) (vols. 3 and 4 re the Caribbean), 4, 3.

7.   Bartolomé de Las Casas, trans. A. Collard, *History of the Indies* (New York, 1971) 155-56; Alan Burns, *History of the British West Indies* (London, 1954), 40, 122.

8. Zerries, 243-52 and books listed in n. 4 above.
9. Zerries, 250, 295-97.
10. Ibid., 290-91.
11. Krickeberg, 60-62; Victor W. Von Hagen, World of the Maya (New York, 1960), 11-16 and passim.
12. Krickeberg, 74-76, 68-69.
13. Ibid., 72, 60; Von Hagen, 131-39, 14-15; Richard E. Greenleaf, Zumárraga and the Mexican Inquisition (Washington, 1961), 18.
14. Donald E. Thompson, "Maya paganism and Christianity: a history of the fusion of two religions", in Munro S. Edmonson et al., eds., Nativism and Syncretism (New Orleans, 1960), 5-32; Sylvanus G. Morley, The Ancient Maya (Stanford, 1958), ch. 11 (183-226), esp. 186.
15. Burns, 49-51; Ephraim Alphonse, God at the Helm (London, 1967), 43-44, and Libro de Adoración Para el uso de los Indios Valientes: Book of Worship for Valiente Indians (Bocas de Toro, Panama, 1934).
16. Douglas M. Taylor, The Black Carib of British Honduras (New York, 1951).
17. Kenneth S. Latourette, History of the Expansion of Christianity (7 vols., New York and London, 1937-45), I, 68-83, 101-8; Stephen Neill, A History of Christian Missions (Harmondsworth, 1971), 26-51; Charles P. Groves, The Planting of Christianity in Africa (4 vols., London, 1948-56), I, ch. 3 (esp. 34-46) and ch. 4; Frederick (van der) Meer and C. Mohrmann, Atlas of the Early Christian World (London, 1958), maps 3-4; 13-14, 18, 22, 36.
18. Latourette, Expansion of Christianity, I, 173-84, 195-216.
19. Williston Walker, A History of the Christian Church (rev. ed., New York, 1959), 123-24, 150-52, 185-212, 257-67;

John R.H. Moorman, A History of the Church in England (London, 1973), 74-114.
20. M. Searle Bates, Religious Liberty: An Enquiry (New York, 1945), ch. 2; Kenneth S. Latourette, A History of Christianity (New York, 1953), 662-69; Moorman, 115-40; Edward Langton, History of the Moravian Church (London, 1956), chs. 1-12 and 20.
21. Neill, 72-77; Latourette, Expansion of Christianity, II, 80-102. Another example of Christianization at the point of the sword is the 13th century campaign of the military order Fratres militae Christi (Knights of the Sword) in the Baltic area, including Courland. This is of interest because of the 17th century attempt of the Duke of Courland, a godson of King Charles I of England, to plant a colony on Tobago near what is still called Courland Bay: Latourette, Expansion of Christianity, II, 199-200; Carlton R. Ottley, The Story of Tobago (Trinidad, 1973), 13-15; Burns, 224, 368, 370, 456.
22. Roland Oliver and J.D. Fage, A Short History of Africa (Harmondsworth, 1966), 68-73; Augsburg Historical Atlas of Christianity (Minneapolis, 1967), map p. 15 (re Muslim expansion); James A. Brundage, ed., The Crusades: Motives and Achievements (Boston, 1964), 56-58 and passim.
23. Samuel E. Morison, trans. and ed., Journals and Other Documents on the Life and Voyages of Christopher Columbus (New York, 1963), 47-48, 130, 276, 383; Thacher, Christopher Columbus I, 177-85 and chs. 32-39; III, App., Docs. 1-5 (643-64); Eric Williams, ed., Documents of West Indian History, Vol. I, 1492-1655 (Port-of-Spain, 1963), Docs. 6, 7 (p. 8).

24. Latourette, *Expansion of Christianity*, II, 8-9, 17-18, 320-38, 348, 352-53; Moorman, 144-47, 173-76.

25. Groves, I, 34-46; Basil Davidson, *Africa: History of a Continent* (London, 1966), 128, 131, 135-42.

26. Davidson, 131-34, 137; Groves, I, 47-51, 72-78, 106-11; Latourette, *Expansion of Christianity*, II, 231-34, 302-4.

27. G.T. Stride and C. Ifeka, *Peoples and Empires of West Africa* (London, 1971), chs. 8 and 20, 51-53, 56-58, 70-75, 116-24; Davidson, 150-56.

28. See Groves, 108-9 re fragmentary evidence of Christian influence in the pre-Muslim history of Ancient Ghana, Songhai and the Hausa states.

29. E. Bolaji Idowu, *African Traditional Religion: A Definition* (London, 1973), esp. ch. 5.

30. Basil Davidson, 71-72, 77; John S. Mbiti, *African Religions and Philosophy* (New York, 1969), 1-5, 103-9; Geoffrey Parrinder, *Africa's Three Religions* (London, 1969), 17-24, 29-38, 67-74; John V. Taylor, *The Primal Vision* (London, 1963; reprint 1965), esp. ch. 8.

31. Mbiti. 29-74, 92-99; Parrinder, 39-46; also Geoffrey Parrinder, *African Traditional Religion* (London, 1954; reprint 1968), 31-43.

32. Mbiti, 75-83; Parrinder, *African Traditional Religion*, 43-54; George E. Simpson, *The Shango Cult in Trinidad* (Puerto Rico, 1965), 100-102. ,

33. Mbiti, 83-91; Parrinder, *African Traditional Religion*, 57-66.

34. Mbiti, 68-71, 166-203; Parrinder, *African Traditional Religion*, 100-134, 144 and *Africa's Three Religions*, 60-65.

35. Mbiti, 110-48; Parrinder, *African Traditional Religion*, 90-99.

36. Cyril B. Firth, *An Introduction to Indian Church History* (Madras, 1961), chs. 1

and 2; Latourette, *Expansion of Christianity*, I, 231-33; II, 280-84; Leslie W. Brown, *The Indian Christians of St Thomas* (Cambridge, 1956), 2-5 and passim.

37. Francis M. Rogers, *The Quest for Eastern Christians* (Minneapolis, 1962).

38. Frances G. Davenport, ed., *European Treaties bearing on the History of the United States and its Dependencies* (4 vols., Washington, 1917), I, 22.

39. J.C. Jha, "The Indian heritage in Trinidad", in John La Guerre, ed., *Calcutta to Caroni* (London, 1974), 6, says that there is evidence of some Christians having come from India, notably from the Malabar coast, but does not give details or source. Cf. ibid., frontispiece map.

40. Murray T. Titus, *Islam in India and Pakistan* (Madras, 1959), esp. 4-8 and ch. 8.

41. William C. Atkinson, *A History of Spain and Portugal* (Harmondsworth, 1960), chs. 1-4.

42. Atkinson, ch. 5.

43. Latourette, *Expansion of Christianity*, II, 218-20, 314.

44. Ibid., II, 220, 315.

45. Ibid.

46. J. Lloyd Mecham, *Church and State in Latin America: A History of Politico-ecclesiastical Relations* (rev. ed., Chapel Hill, 1966), 6-10. For example, the bull of Eugene IV, *Laudibus et honore* (1436): text and translation in William E. Shiels, *King and Church: The Rise and Fall of the Patronato Real* (Chicago, 1961), 275-77, 64-65.

47. Mecham, 10-11. The "Bull of Granada" (*Orthodoxe fidei propagationem*, 1486) is found in Shiels, 277-82, 66-70.

48. Davenport, I, 9–32, includes the texts

and translations of the bulls *Romanus pontifex* (1455) and *Inter caetera quae* (1456). Or see Shiels, ch. 3 (44-60) and 266-75.

49. Joseph Schmidlin (trans. M. Braun), *Catholic Mission History* (Techny, Ill., 1933), 241.

50. Arthur P. Newton, *The European Nations in the West Indies* (London, 1933), 1-5, 18-19; Richard H. Major, trans. and ed., Hakluyt Soc. Works, 1st ser., no. 46, *The Canarien* (London, 1872); Clements R. Markham, trans. and ed., *The Guanches of Tenerife*, Hakluyt Soc., 2nd ser., no. 21 (London, 1907).

51. Leon Lopetegui and F. Zubillaga, *Historia de la Iglesia en la América Española* (Madrid, 1965), 15-19; Juan Friede and B. Keen, eds., *Bartolomé de Las Casas in History* (Dekalb, Ill., 1971), 141, 147, 153-55 (and 211 n. 65).

52. Gomes E. de Azurara, *The Chronicle of the Discovery and Conquest of Guinea*, trans. C.R. Beazley and E. Prestage (2 vols., London, Hakluyt Soc., 1896) I, 39-83; Elizabeth Donnan, ed., *Documents Illustrative of the History of the Slave Trade to America* (4 vols., Washington, 1930-35), I, Doc. 1 (18-41) and Introduction, 1-6.

53. John F. Maxwell, *Slavery and the Catholic Church* (Chichester, 1975), 26-55, esp. 51-52.

54. Roman civil law had recognized capture in war, conviction for crime or debt, voluntary sale of self or children, and birth from a slave mother as providing legal title for slave ownership (ibid., 45-46).

55. Ibid., 52-55; Azurara, 80-83; Arthur Helps, *The Conquerors of the New World and their Bondsmen* (2 vols., London, 1848), I, 28-41.

56. Louis B. Wright, *Gold, Glory and the Gospel* (New York, 1970), passim.

57. Latourette, *A History of Christianity*, 655-57; *History of the Expansion of Christianity*, III, 16-22; Raphael M. Huber, *A Documented History of the Franciscan Order* (Milwaukee, 1944), ch. 32 (443-58).

58. A college would be established from early years in Hispaniola which would attain university status in 1538.

59. Luther's "Ninety-five Theses" were posted in the year that Cardinal Ximénes died, 1517. Queen Isabella had already passed from the scene in 1504, Columbus in 1506 and King Ferdinand in 1516.

Chapter 3 The Spanish Catholic Monopoly

1. Journal of Columbus first voyage (based on Las Casas abstract), in Samual E. Morrison, trans. and ed., *Journals and Other Documents on the Life and Voyages of Christopher Columbus* (New York, 1963), 64-65 (11-12 Oct. 1492) and "Letter to the Sovereigns, Feb.-Mar. 1493", 184.

2. Morison, trans., *Journals and Other Documents*, 64, 65, 70-71, 92, 105, 131, 133, 184, 288; Eric E. Williams, *Documents of West Indian History*, Vol. I 1492-1655 (Port-of-Spain, 1963), Docs. 51 and 52 (53-54).

3. Morison, trans., *Journals and Other Documents*, 65.

4. See Elizabeth W. Loughran, "Did a priest accompany Columbus in 1492?", *Catholic Historical Review* 16 (1930): 164-74, re the absence of clergy on the first voyage.

5. Morison, trans., *Journals and Other Documents*, 132, 138, 153, 179, 186, 265, 281-82.

6. Ibid., 91, 106.

7. "Instructions of the Sovereigns to Columbus for his Second Voyage to the Indies, 29 May 1493 ", in Morison, trans., *Journals and Other Documents*, 203-4, also Williams, *Documents 1492-1655*, Doc. 56 (57-58).

8. Williams, *Documents 1492-1655*, Docs. 50, 54, 55 (54-57), dated 1494, 1495, 1496.

9. Ibid., Doc. 57 (p. 38), dated 1500; Juan Friede and B. Keen, *Bartolomé de Las Casas in History* (DeKalb, Ill., 1971), 148-49; Jalil Sued-Badillo, "Christopher Columbus and the enslavement of Amerindians in the Caribbean", *Monthly Review* (July-Aug. 1992): 71-102.

10. Elizabeth W. Loughran, "The first vicar-apostolic of the New World", |American| *Ecclesiastical Review*, 9th ser., II (Vol. 82, 1930): 1-14; Bartolomé de Las Casas, *Historia de las Indias*, Libro Primo, caps. lxxxi, xcii Augustín M. Carlo and L. Hanke edition (Mexico, 1951), I, 344, 377) (Collard trans., 49).

11. Las Casas, *Historia*, Lib. Prim. cap. cxiii (Collard trans., 60; C/H, I, 436). Las Casas however found that some of the convicts made good.

12. King Ferdinand to Ovando, quoted in Eric E. Williams, *From Columbus to Castro* (London, 1970), 41-42.

13. Clarence H. Haring, *Trade and Navigation between Spain and America in the Time of the Hapsburgs* (Cambridge, Mass., 1918), 104-7.

14. Elizabeth Donnan, *Documents Illustrative of the History of the Slave Trade* (4 vols., Washington, 1930-35) I,14-17; Clarence H. Haring, *The Spanish Empire in America* (New York, 1963), 203; Francis A. MacNutt, *Bartholomew de Las Casas* (New York and London, 1909), 102.

15. Samuel E. Morison, *Admiral of the Ocean Sea* (2 vols., Boston, 1942), II, 166, 298 and notes thereon.

16. Las Casas, *Historia*, Lib. Seg. caps. iii, vi, xiii (Collard trans., 84, 88, 109; C/H, II, 214, 226, 249).

17. Ibid., Lib. Seg. cap. xii (Collard trans., 106-9; C/H, II, 245-49).

18. Williams, *Documents, 1492-1695*, Doc. 58 (58-59); Lesley B. Simpson, *The Encomienda in New Spain* (rev. ed., Berkeley, 1950), Foreword and chs. 1-4; F.A. Kirkpatrick, "Repartimiento-Encomienda", in *Hispanic American Historical Review* 19 (1930): 372-79. The *encomienda* was a "distribution" (*repartimiento*) of Indians, together with land, to Spaniards.

19. *Inter caetera* (3 May), *Eximiae devotionis* (3 May), *Inter caetera* (4 May), and *Dudum siquidem* (26 Sept.). For text, trans. and explanations see Frances G. Davenport, *European Treaties . . .* (4 vols., Washington, 1917), I, 56-83; also William E. Shiels, *King and Church* (Chicago, 1961), 283-87, 78-81; 28-89, 82-84; 289-91, 85-87 and chs. 5, 6. Re concessions to Portugal: ch. 2, n. 48, above.

20. *Inter caetera* (3 May), Davenport, I, 62.

21. J. Lloyd Mecham, *Church and State in Latin America* (rev. ed., Chapel Hill, 1966), 14; Shiels, 294-95, 90-91.

22. Ibid., 313-15, 113-15; 132-33; Mecham, 20. For a detailed description of the royal powers under the *Patronato* see Haring, *The Spanish Empire in America*, 167-69.

23. Las Casas, *Historia*, Lib. Ter. cap. i (Collard trans., 179-81; C/H, II, 432-35). For the text of the bull *Romanus pontifex* (in Spanish and English translations) see Shiels, 316-19, 118-21.

24. Haring, *The Spanish Empire in America*, 170.

25. Mecham, 26; Shiels, 163-68.

26. Las Casas, *Historia.*, Lib. Ter., caps. iii-v (Collard trans., 181-89, esp. 184; C/H,

II, 438-48); Lewis U. Hanke, *The Spanish Struggle for Justice in the Conquest of America* (Boston and Toronto, 1965, 1st pub. 1949), ch. I; Pedro Henríquez-Ureña, *Literary Currents in Spanish America* (Cambridge, Mass., 1945), 15-17.

27. Las Casas, *Historia*, Lib. Ter., cap. viii (Collard trans., 189-92; C/H, III, 455-58); Roland D. Hussey, "Text of the Laws of Burgos (1512-1513) concerning the treatment of the Indians", *Hispanic American Historical Review* 12 (1932): 301-26; Simpson, 31-36.

28. Venancio D. Carro, "The Spanish theological-juridical renaissance and the ideology of Bartolomé de Las Casas", in Friede and Keen, 246-47. Cf. Juan Friede, "Las Casas and indigenism in the sixteenth century", ibid., 126-234, esp. 127-57 on the movement apart from Las Casas involvement.

29. Las Casas, *Historia*, Lib. Seg. cap. liv (C/H, II, 385-86; part trans. MacNutt, 41-42); Henry R. Wagner, *The Life and Writings of Bartolomé de Las Casas* (Albuquerque, 1967), 5-6; Friede and Keen, 72; and esp. Introduction by H.R. Parish in Bartolomé de Las Casas, *The Only Way* (New York, 1992), 13-19. Cf. n. 45 below.

30. Las Casas, *Historia*, Lib. Ter. caps. lxxviii-lxxxi (C/H, III, 89-103; Collard trans., caps. 78-79 only, 206-11); MacNutt, 58-66. Collard and some other historians incorrectly cite the text as "Ecclesiastes".

31. MacNutt, 67-74; Las Casas, *Historia*, Lib. Ter. caps. lxxxiii-lxxxv (C/H, III, 105-14, 122-23;. Collard trans., 212).

32. MacNutt, 93-97; Las Casas, *Historia*; Lib. Ter. cap. xcix (C/H, III, 166-69).

33. Las Casas, *Historia*, Lib. Ter. caps. xix, xxxiii (C/H, II, 496-98, 548-50); Pierre-Gustave-Louis Borde, *The History of the Island of Trinidad under the Spanish Government* (2 vols., trans. from the French 1876-82 ed., Port-of-Spain, 1982), I, 77-83 (and xxiv, item 2).

34. Las Casas, *Historia*, Lib. Ter., cap. lxxxiii (C/H, III, 105-8).

35. Ibid., Lib. Ter. cap. xci (Collard trans., 221-23; C/H, III, 139-41). See also Las Casas's *Brevíssima Relación de la Destrucción de las Indias*, translated in App. I of MacNutt, 375-76; Linda A. Newson, *Aboriginal and Spanish Colonial Trinidad* (London, 1976), 18.

36. Las Casas, *Historia*, Lib. Ter. cap. civ (C/H, III, 187-88).

37. Las Casas, *Historia*, Lib. Ter. caps. cxxx, cxxxii, clvi (Collard trans., 259-62; C/H, III, 276-86, 362).

38. Las Casas, *Historia*, Lib. Ter. cap. clx (C/H, III, 386-88); MacNutt, chs. 11-12 (150-73); M. Giménez Fernández, "Fray Bartolomé de Las Casas: a biographical sketch", in Friede and Keen, 82-85.

39. Robert Ricard, *The Spiritual Conquest of Mexico* (Berkeley, 1966), passim; Latourette, *Expansion of Christianity*, III, 100.

40. Desiderius Erasmus, *Institutio principis Christiani* (1515) and earlier writings, and Thomas More, *Utopia* (1516).

41. Charles Gibson, *Spain in America* (New York, 1966), 68-75.

42. Richard E. Greenleaf, *Zumárraga and the Mexican Inquisition* (Washington, 1961), 26-41.

43. Gibson, 73-74; A. Tibesar, "Latin America, Church in", *New Catholic Encyclopedia* (1967), VIII, 460.

44. Haring, *The Spanish Empire in America*, 179-80; Silvio A. Zavala, *Sir Thomas More in New Spain* (London, 1955); Fintan B. Warren, *Vasco de Quiroga and*

His *Pueblo-Hospitals of Santa Fe* (Washington, 1963); Ricard, ch. 8 (135-54).

45. Translated into English by Francis P. Sullivan, with data by Helen R. Parish as: Bartolomé de Las Casas, *The Only Way* (New York, 1992). It had been published in 1941 in Latin and Spanish, and Lewis U. Hanke, *The Spanish Struggle for Justice in the Conquest of America* (1948; reprint Boston and Toronto, 1965), 72-77 summarized it. See also Wagner, 86-87, 101-2, 265-66; Friede and Keen, 86, 88-89, 314-16.

46. Hanke, *The Spanish Struggle for Justice in the Conquest of America* , 77-82; Wagner, 86-94, 103, 125, 140-42, and 124; B. M. Biermann, "Bartolomé de Las Casas and Verapaz ", in Friede and Keen, 442-84. Some of the Mayas now in Belize came from Verapaz and speak Kekchi, one of its dialects. (Philip M. Sherlock, *Belize* [London, 1969], 67, 92-93.)

47. Text and trans. in MacNutt, App. II (426-31); Lewis U. Hanke, "Pope Paul III and the American Indians", *Harvard Theological Review* 30 (1937): 65-103.

48. Simpson, ch. 10 (123-44).

49. MacNutt, chs. 16-19 (222-76); Friede, and Keen, 170, 176-91.

50. Lewis U. Hanke, *Aristotle and the American Indians* (London, 1959) and *All Mankind is One* (Dekalb, Ill., 1974).

51. Ricard, ch. 4; Haring, *The Spanish Empire in America*, 173; Wagner, 98-100, 103-4.

52. Latourette, *Expansion of Christianity*, III, 108.

53. MacNutt, 98-107; Zavala, *The Defence of Human Rights in Latin America* (Paris, 1964), 58; Eric E. Williams, *From Columbus to Castro* (London, 1970), 43.

54. MacNutt, 105-6, trans. from *Historia*, Lib. Ter. cap. cxxix (C/H, III, 275). The

retraction is found in similar terms also in cap. cii (C/H, III, 177, also trans. MacNutt). For freer translations with more of the context see Williams, *Documents* 1492-1653, Docs. 125, 152 (141, 157-58), also Las Casas, Collard trans., 256-59.

55. There is an immense literature on this subject, for example: Zavala, *Defence of Human Rights*, passim (esp. 58-64); Hanke, *All Mankind is One*, esp. 152-61. On the institution of slavery and the Church, Maxwell, provides what he calls an "interim report" with extensive documentation.

56. Maxwell, 67.

57. Quoted in Zavala, *Defence of Human Rights*, 48-49.

58. Williams, *Documents* 1492-1655, Docs. 153, 155 (158-60, 161-62); Zavala, *Defence of Human Rights*, 49-50; Maxwell, 67-68, 88-89.

59. Cf. Franklin W. Knight, *The African Dimension in Latin American Societies* (New York, 1974), incl. map-charts.

60. Gibson, 75; Tibesar, 461; Ricard, ch. 14 (esp. 228-35).

61. Friede and Keen, 194-205 (esp. 195-96, 205); Tibesar, 452-55; Gibson, 76-78; Shiels, ch. 13 (195-228); R.E. Greenleaf, "Latin America, Church in: The Inquisition", *New Catholic Encyclopedia* (New York), VIII, 462-64; Haring, *The Spanish Empire in America*, 188-89; Fredrick B. Pike, ed., *The Conflict Between Church and State in Latin America* (New York, 1964), 31-77.

62. Hanke, *All Mankind is One*, 120-22; Simpson, ch. 11 ("The tamed encomienda"), 145-58.

63. Modern assessments of the Church in Spanish America from a historical standpoint include: William J.

Coleman, *Latin-American Catholicism: A Self-Evaluation* (New York, 1958); and from a Protestant, W. Stanley Rycroft, *Religion and Faith in Latin America* (Philadelphia, 1958); Shiels, chs. 14-15 re the later stages of the *Patronato*.

64. Haring, *The Spanish Empire in America*, 178-82.

65. Gibson, 83-86; Haring, *The Spanish Empire in America*, 175-78; Tibesar, 457-60.

66. Gibson, 77-80; Haring, *The Spanish Empire in America*, 174-75; Pike, 7-8, 77-88.

67. H.E. Bolton, "The mission as a frontier institution in the Spanish American colonies", *American Historical Review* 23 (1917): 42-61 (a classic summary with examples from North America). J. Fred Rippy and J.T. Nelson, *Crusaders of the Jungle* (Chapel Hill, 1936) is a fuller account for South America: see esp. 3-101, 257-370.

68. Latourette, *Expansion of Christianity*, III, 108; Haring, *The Spanish Empire in America*, 203-6; Williams, *Documents 1492-1655*, Docs. 145, 149-51 (151-57); and his *From Columbus to Castro* (London, 1970), 65-68.

69. Latourette, *Expansion of Christianity*, III, 144; articles on "Peter Claver, Saint" in *New Catholic Encyclopedia*, III, 922-23 and *New Encyclopedia Britannica* (1974), VII, 906-7; Arnold H.M. Lunn, *Saint in the Slave Trade* (New York, 1935), esp. ch. 10 (120-38).

70. Donnan, I, 123-24 (Doc. 20: "Brother Luis Brandaon to Father Sandoval"); Williams, *Documents 1492-1655*, Docs. 154, 156, 157 (160-63).

Chapter 4 Jamaica and Trinidad under Spanish Rule

1. Frank Cundall and J.L. Pietersz, *Jamaica under the Spaniards* (Kingston, Jamaica, 1919) , 34; Philip M. Sherlock, *West Indian Nations* (Kingston and London, 1973), 81, and cf. Cundall and Pietersz, 50.

2. Linda A. Newson, *Aboriginal and Spanish Colonial Trinidad* (London, 1976), 120-23, 184, 190.

3. In 1582 there had been only two priests in Jamaica for some years (Cundall and Pietersz, 14; Francis J. Osborne, *History of the Catholic Church in Jamaica* [Aylesbury, 1977; reprint Chicago, 1988]; chs. 4, 5; For Trinidad see Newson, 119-20).

4. Ferdinand to Diego Colón, 21 June, 1511, quoted by Francis X. Delany, *A History of the Catholic Church in Jamaica* (New York, 1930), 3.

5. Ferdinand to Diego Colón, December 1612 (Cundall and Pietersz, 2.)

6. Joseph Schmidlin (trans. M. Braun), *Catholic Mission History* (Techny, Ill., 1933), 361.

7. See ch. 3, n. 30, above; Las Casas, *Historia*, Lib. Ter. cap. lxxx (C/H, III, 96).

8. Cundall and Pietersz, 6; Delany, 7; Osborne, ch. 4.

9. Cundall and Pietersz, 2-3.

10. Docs. of 29 Jan. 1515 in Delany, 3-5; Osborne, ch. 3.

11. Delany, 11, 15, 18, 20; Cundall and Pietersz, 14; Osborne, ch. 4.

12. Cundall and Pietersz, 6-7, 9, 10-11; Delany, 7-9; Osborne, ch. 3; letter of Peter Martyr 13 June 1525, facs. and trans. in John B. Thacher, *Christopher Columbus* (3 vols., New York, 1904; reprint New York, 1967), I, 30.

13. Cundall and Pietersz, 7, 11-12; Delany, 10; Osborne, chs. 3, 4.

14. Cundall and Pietersz, 12, 13; Delany, 10-11; Francis J. Osborne and Geoffrey Johnston, *Coastlands and Islands* (Mona, Jamaica, 1972), 9; Osborne, ch. 4.

15. Cundall and Pietersz, 4, 5, 8. Las Casas in his *Historia*, which was begun when he was a monk in Española in the 1520s, claims that Jamaica's Spaniards had destroyed the Indians and exacted forced labour while failing to teach them Christianity (Lib. Seg. cap. lvi [C/ H, II, 390-391]) and repeats the accusation in his *Brevíssima Relación*, written for the King in 1542 (Francis A. MacNutt, *Bartholomew de Las Casas* [New York and London, 1909], App. I, 328).

16. Cundall and Pietersz, 20, 22; Osborne, ch. 5.

17. Cundall and Pietersz, 49, 50.

18. Delany, 11, 15, 18; Osborne, chs. 4, 6.

19. Cundall and Pietersz, 14-17; Delany, 12-14; Osborne, ch. 5.

20. This probably means adult male Spaniards. In 1596 the number reported is 120 but in 1611, 523 Spanish men and women and 173 children (Cundall and Pietersz, 18, 34).

21. Cundall and Pietersz, 21-24, 29, 32; Delany, 14; Osborne, ch. 5 (date "1596" [January, O.S.]).

22. Cundall and Pietersz, 22; Delany, 15, and report on the visit of Bishop Juan de las Cabesas Altamirando quoted 15-19 (esp. 16, 18); Osborne, ch. 5. Apparently Cueto was not the only local man. The next abbot reported (1611) that there were "some clergy born in the island with a lot of chaplaincies but these are poor like the people in general" (Cundall and Pietersz, 34). See Osborne, ch. 6.

23. Delany, 15; Cundall and Pietersz, 32; Osborne, chs. 5. 6.

24. Osborne and Johnston, 9; Delany, 20; Osborne, ch. 6.

25. Report of "Abb. Jamaycensis" [Bernardo de Balbuena], 14 July 1611 (Cundall and Pietersz, 34-38).

26. Osborne (1988 ed. only), App. C; summary in Osborne and Johnston, 13-21.

27. Vincent T. Harlow, ed., *The Voyages of Capt. William Jackson, 1642-1645* (Camden Miscellany, XIII, Camden Third Ser. 34) (London, 1923), 18. Cf. Walter Adolphe Roberts, ed., *The Capitals of Jamaica* (Kingston, 1955), 4-5.

28. Cundall and Pietersz, 41; Osborne, ch. 7.

29. Cundall and Pietersz, 42-48; Delany, 20-21; Osborne, ch. 7.

30. Pierre-Gustav-Louis Borde, *The History of the Island of Trinidad under the Spanish Government* (2 vols., trans. from the French, Port-of-Spain, 1982), I, xxiv (item 2), 77-82; Louis A.A. de Verteuil, *Trinidad* (London, 1884), 423; Marie B. Cothonay, *Trinidad: Journal d'un Missionaire Dominicain des Antilles Anglaises* (Paris, 1893), 261-62, 294-97; *New Catholic Encyclopedia*, XIV, 290-91.

31. Gertrude Carmichael, *The History of the West Indian Islands of Trinidad and Tobago* (London, 1961) 21-22, ref. 320.

32. Newson, 73, 102.

33. Royal Appointment quoted in Carmichael, 18-19, ref. 320; Carlton R. Ottley, *An Account of Life in Spanish Trinidad* (Trinidad, 1955), ch. 2.

34. Newson, 73-74; Bernard Moses, *The Spanish Dependencies in South America* (New York, 1914), I, 44-45.

35. Carmichael, 22-23, ref. 320; Ottley, 9-11.

36. Mary Watters, *A History of the Church in Venezuela* (Chapel Hill, 1933), 7. Note: "Guayana" refers to the Spanish empire (or Church) adjacent to the Orinoco; "Guyana" is the former "British Guiana".

37. Claud Hollis, *A Brief History of Trinidad under the Spanish Crown* (Trinidad and Tobago, 1941), 23, 29, 35, 41. The

Ralegh episode, having little effect on the Trinidad Church except to burn down the church building and cause the Franciscan friar to flee, will be considered in the next chapter as an aspect of the conflict with Spain. (Cf. Kenrick S. Wise, *Historical Sketches of Trinidad and Tobago*, II |Port-of-Spain, 1936|, 66, 75.)

38. On the *encomiendas* see Newson, 114, 151-62, esp. 152-53 re their religious aspect. Also Carmichael, 30, ref. 325.

39. Antonio de Berrío had come from New Granada, descending the Orinoco from Bogotá. This may explain the initial church connection of Trinidad. His settlement of this island excited the jealousy of the governor of Margarita who considered it a part of his territory. (Vincent T. Harlow, ed., *The Discoverie of the large and bewtiful Empire of Guiana by Sir Walter Ralegh* |London, 1928|, lxx-xciii and map f. xv; same editor, *Ralegh's Last Voyage* |London, 1932|, 73.)

40. Newson, 109; Watters, 33; Hollis, 69.

41. Newson, 109-10.

42. Hollis, 69, 71; Clarence H. Haring, *The Spanish Empire in America* (New York, 1963), 90.

43. Lionel M. Fraser, *History of Trinidad* (2 vols., Trinidad, 1891-96), I, 163-64; Watters, 31-35.

44. Newson, 109.

45. Carmichael, ref. 325.

46. Hollis, 73-75.

47. Watters, 7-13; J. Fred Rippy and Jean T. Nelson, *Crusaders of the Jungle* (Chapel Hill, 1936), 105-89 (see map between 109 and 110).

48. Fr. Cuthbert, *The Capuchins* (2 vols., London, 1928); Capuchino Buenaventura de Carrocera, *Misión de*

los Capuchinos en Cumaná (3 vols., Caracas, 1968), II, 213 (Doc. 78).

49. Ottley, 23-25.

50. Marc-Aureli Vila, *El Caputxins Catalans a Veneçuela* (Barcelona, 1969), written in the Catalan language, contains a chapter on "Missions a l'illa de Trinitat", 46-54.

51. Newson, 164-65, 171 and App. 4 (258-60); Antonio Caulín, *Historia Corográphica Natural y Evangelica dela Nueva Andalusia* (Madrid, 1779), 121; M.R.P. Baltasar de Lodares, *Los Franciscanos Capuchinos en Venezuela* (3 vols., Caracas, 1929), II, 164-79. Fraylán M. de Rionegro, *Origenes de las Misiones de los PP. Capuchinos en America* (Pontevedra, 1930) gives documents.

52. Ottley, 25; Newson, 163.

53. Newson, 165, 164.

54. Carmichael, 31-32, refs. 326; Newson, 165; Eric E. Williams, *History of the People of Trinidad and Tobago* (Port-of-Spain, 1962), 25-27; Hollis, 68.

55. Newson, 165, 166; Ottley, 29.

56. Hollis, 68; Newson, 166, 167, 129.

57. Rippy and Nelson, 149.

58. For example, at Guayria and Savaneta in 1735, and the new mission at "Mucurapo" in 1749. Newson, 163, 165, 166; Hollis, 68.

59. Newson, 171, 261-62; Ottley, 34.

60. Newson, 220, 260, 183, 221. For various figures on Indian population from 1687 to 1797 see 166, 169-70, 219 and the chart on 221.

61. Hollis, 70-71; Carmichael, 33, ref. 327.

62. Newson, 119-20, 191.

63. Ibid., 179-80, 184; Hollis, 79.

64. Ottley, 116, 121; Carmichael, 363, 368.

65. Newson, 184-88, 189, 191.

66. Ottley, 35; |J. Scott|, "The Discription of Trinidada", in Vincent T. Harlow, ed.,

Colonizing Expeditions to the West Indies and Guiana, Hakluyt Soc. Works, 2nd ser., no. 56 (London, 1925), 125; Cornelis C. Goslinga, *The Dutch in the Caribbean and on the Wild Coast* (Assen, The Netherlands, 1971), 341.

67. Newson, 130-32, 184, 186.
68. The text of the Spanish law is found in translation in Henry B.L. Hughes, "Christian missionary societies in the British West Indies during the emancipation era" (PhD diss., Univ. of Toronto, 1944), II, Appendix 2, 419-28; summary in Williams, 46-47.

Chapter 5 The Monopoly Breached

1. On Reformation and Counter Reformation background: Williston Walker, A *History of the Christian Church* (New York, 1959), 291-401; Latourette, A *History of Christianity*, 697-898; August Franzen, A *Concise History of the Church* (New York, 1969), 254-335 (for a Roman Catholic view); John R.H. Moorman, A *History of the Church in England* (London, 1973), 161-207.
2. Philip A. Means, *The Spanish Main, Focus of Envy* (New York, 1935), 58-59; John H. Parry and Philip M. Sherlock, A *Short History of the West Indies* (London, 1957), 29-30.
3. John T. McNeill, *The History and Character of Calvinism* (New York, 1954), 241-47; Means, 76; Walter A. Roberts, *The French in the West Indies* (New York, 1942), 18, 20; Alan Burns, *History of the British West Indies* (London, 1954), 140.
4. Stefan Lorant, ed., *The New World* (New York, 1965), 5-29, 118, 30-116; Woodbury Lowery, *Spanish Settlements within the Present Limits of the United States: Florida* (New York, 1911), Book I, "The French Colony", 3-207, 333.

5. George R.G. Conway, ed., *An Englishman and the Mexican Inquisition, 1556-1560* (Mexico City, 1927). This contains a reprint of Tomson's account, a translation of the Inquisition record of trial, and (App. I) the Spanish original. (The Sanbenito was the garb of a penitent heretic.)
6. James A. Williamson, *Hawkins of Plymouth* (New York, 1969); and his earler books, *Sir John Hawkins* (Oxford, 1927) (esp. Book II, "The Protestants and the Counter-Reformation", 205-302) and *Sir Francis Drake* (London, 1951); Neville Williams, *Francis Drake* (London, 1973), 12-29; Julian S. Corbett, *Drake and the Tudor Navy* (2 vols., London, 1917), I, 60-73, 151, 154-55, App. A (391-94); cf. Irene A. Wright, ed., *Spanish Documents concerning English Voyages to the Caribbean* (London, 1929), esp. Docs. 9-29 (60-162).
7. Conway, viii-ix, and App. III (155-62) listing Inquisition records in Mexican Archives.
8. Corbett, chs. 5 and 6 (144-90).
9. Cornelis C. Goslinga, *The Dutch in the Caribbean and on the Wild Coast* (Assen, The Netherlands, 1971), 1-16; Roland D. Hussey, "Spanish reaction to foreign aggression in the Caribbean to about 1680", *Hispanic American Historical Review* 9 (1929): 286-302.
10. Goslinga, 47-58; Engel Sluiter, "Dutch-Spanish rivalry in the Caribbean area, 1594-1609", *Hispanic American Historial Review* 28, no. 2 (1948): 165-96.
11. Goslinga, 60; Sluiter, 194-95.
12. Including Hawkins and Drake; see also "A true relation of the voyage undertaken by Sir Anthony Sherley", and "A voyage of Master William Parker", in Richard Hakluyt, *The Principal Naviga-*

tions *Voyages Traffiques & Discoveries of the English Nation* (3 vols., London, 1598-1600), III, 598-603; (reprint, 12 vols., Glasgow, 1903, X, 266-80).

13. Vincent T. Harlow, ed., *The Discoverie of the large and bewtiful Empire of Guiana* (London, 1928), and *Ralegh's Last Voyage* (London, 1942).

14. Goslinga, 73-74, 82-83, 87-99, 89-140.

15. Ibid., 284, and ch. 8 (esp. 194-95).

16. Lorant, 279-80; C.B. Quinn, ed., *The Hakluyt Handbook* (2 vols., London, 1974), passim (for example, I, 3-7, 39-40; II, 461-63, 588-90).

17. First printed in Maine Historical Society, *Documentary History of the State of Maine*, vol. II (Cambridge, 1877) along with introduction (xv-lxi); also in Eva G.R. Taylor, ed., *The Original Writings of the Two Richard Hakluyts* (2 vols., London, 1935), II, Doc. 46 (221-326).

18. Maine Historical Society, 8.

19. Taylor, 217.

20. Maine Historical Society, 14.

21. William W. Sweet, *Religion in Colonial America* (New York, 1965), 3-8 and Louis B. Wright, *Religion and Empire* (Chapel Hill, 1943), 44-49, summarize the *Discourse*.

22. Maine Historical Society, 71-77; V.L. Afanasiev, "The literary heritage of Bartolomé de Las Casas", in Friede and Keen, 555-67 (re the succession of translations of the *Brevíssima Relación* during the 16th and 17th centuries). This work of Las Casas, whose Catholic orthodoxy was never in question, was placed on the Index by the Spanish Inquisition (ibid., 11-12).

23. Hakluyt, *The Principal Navigations Voyages Traffiques & Discoveries of the English Nation* (repr. of 2nd ed., 12 vols., Glasgow, 1903); cf. facs. of 1589 ed. (2 vols.,

Cambridge, 1965); Samuel Purchas, *Hakluytus Posthumus, or Purchas His Pilgrimes* (20 vols., Glasgow, 1905-1907 [first pub. 1625]).

24. Goslinga, 34-42; [William Usselinx], "Memorial to the Dutch States-General on the colonization of Guiana", in *United States Commission on Boundary between Venezuela and British Guiana, Report and Accompanying Papers* (9 vols., Washington, 1897), II, Docs. 9, 10 (27-36).

25. James A. Williamson, *English Colonies in Guiana and on the Amazon, 1604-1668* (Oxford, 1923), 29-149.

26. [John Scott], "The Discription of Guyana", in Harlow, *Colonizing Expeditions to the West Indies and Guiana*, Hakluyt Soc. Works, 2nd ser. no. 56 (London, 1925), 139-40; George Edmundson, "The Dutch in Western Guiana", *English Historical Review* 16 (1901): 640-75; Williamson, *English Colonies in Guiana and on the Amazon*, 64; Goslinga, 81, 412-13, 423, 425, 429-32.

27. William Bradford, *History of the Plimoth Plantation* (facs. ed., Boston, 1896), 55; Williamson, *English Colonies in Guiana and on the Amazon*, 73.

28. Williamson, *English Colonies in Guiana and on the Amazon*, 147-49.

29. John Hilton, "Relation of the first settlement of St Christopher and Nevis", in Harlow, *Colonizing Expeditions*, 10-15.

30. Claud Hollis, *A Brief History of Trinidad under the Spanish Crown* (Trinidad and Tobago, 1941), ch. 7 (41-48); Goslinga, 433-37.

31. [John Scott], "The Discription of Tobago" and "The Discription of Trinidada", in Harlow, *Colonizing Expeditions*, 114-31; Hollis, 53-57;

Goslinga, 437-43; James A. Williamson, *The Caribbee Islands under the Proprietary Patents* (London, 1926) ch. 9 (188-97).

32. Luther K. Zabriskie, *The Virgin Islands of the United States of America* (New York, 1918), 34-35; Isaac Dookhan, A *History of the Virgin Islands of the United States* (St Thomas, 1974), 42-43. St Croix was later inhabited by the French, then after an unoccupied period became part of the Danish West Indies which finally were purchased by the American government.

33. Herbert I. Priestley, *France Overseas through the Old Regime* (New York, 1939), 80-81, nn. 13, 16.

34. Raphael H. Song, *The Sacred Congregation for the Propagation of the Faith* (Washington, 1961), 5-30.

35. Aubrey Gwynn, "The first Irish priests in the New World", *Studies* 21 (1932): 216, 218-19, 222-27. There was also a Memorial in 1631 from an Irishman "Gaspar Chillon" (Jasper Collins of Youghal according to Gwynn) offering to the Spanish government to resettle the Amazon by Irish with the purpose of keeping out the English and Dutch heretics. The offer was not accepted (ibid., 216). Cf. Aubrey Gwynn, "Early Irish emigration to the West Indies (1612-1643)", *Studies* 18 (1929): 380-83; Williamson, *English Colonies in Guiana and on the Amazon*, 96-98, 134-35. See also ch. 6.

36. Frances G. Davenport, ed., *European Treaties* (4 vols., Washington, 1917-37), I, 360, 363 (Art. 3).

37. Williamson, *English Colonies in Guiana and on the Amazon*, 38-39, 55, 60-61, 100, 177 (English, French and Dutch); 72, 133 (English and Dutch); 60, 80, 86-87,

94, 114, 129 (English and Irish); 91 (French and Dutch); 104-5 (Dutch and Irish); 92 (map of English, Irish and Dutch Amazon settlements); 164-65 (Jews and English); Hollis, 44 (English, Irish, French and Flemings at Dutch "New Walcheren"); Goslinga, 82, 410-11, 417 (Dutch and others); 421, 423-25 (Jews and Dutch).

38. Harlow, *Colonizing Expeditions*, 88-89, 139-40; *Dictionary of National Biography* VIII (Oxford, 1921), 1205 ("Harcourt"); Nellis M. Crouse, *French Pioneers in the West Indies* (New York, 1940), 85-92.

39. Cf. Joseph Lecler, *Toleration and the Reformation* (2 vols., New York, 1960), I, 114-42; II, passim.

40. This was demonstrated at the time of the Revocation of the Edict of Nantes later in the century, as will be seen in the next chapter.

41. Paul Reyss, *Étude sur quelques points de l'histoire de la tolérance au Canada et aux Antilles, XVIe et XVIIe siècles* (Geneva, 1907), 29-30, 47-50 and passim.

42. The standard study is Arthur P. Newton, *The Colonizing Activities of the English Puritans* (New Haven and London, 1914).

43. Cf. James J. Parsons, *San Andrés and Providencia: English-speaking Islands in the Western Caribbean* (Berkeley, 1956), 4-13.

44. Philip Sherlock, *Belize: A Junior History* (London, 1969), 40-45.

45. Newton, 37-38 (cf. 21-23, 35-36).

46. Extract of letter of Bell to Sir Nathaniel Rich quoted ibid., 31-34.

47. Ibid., 52-54.

48. Gt. Brit. Public Record Office, *Calendar of State Papers, Colonial Series, America and the West Indies* (many vols., London, 1860–) (hereafter cited as CPSC), I (1574-1660), 147 (10 May 1632), 149

(same date), 181 (19 June 1634), 228, 229 (28 Mar. 1636), 230 (same date, 2 items), 247 (19 Mar. 1637); Newton, 91, 115-16, 119-22, 142, 163-64, 110, 169.

49. Edmund Calamy, *The Nonconformist's Memorial* (2 vols., London, 1775), I, 290-95; Arnold G. Matthews, *Calamy Revised* (Oxford, 1934), 323; CSPC, I, 317 (4 Jan. 13 and 25 Feb. 1641), 319 (25, 29 Mar. 1641); Williamson, *Caribbee Islands*, 190-91; Newton, 254-55, 257, 305.

50. Cf. Newton, 276-78, re the fascination for roving at this time among colonists in general.

51. CSPC, I, 150 (15 May 1632); 187 (30 July 1634).

52. Newton, 114, 118, 121, 229, 256.

53. CSPC, I, 202 (20 Apr. 1635); Newton, 51, 149-50.

54. CSPC, I, 148, 149 (both 10 May 1632); 187 (30 July 1634); 203 (20 Apr. 1635); 226 (26 Mar. 1636).

55. Newton, 275 n. 6.

56. Ibid., 150, 167-208; Clarence H. Haring, *The Buccaneers in the West Indies in the XVII Century* (New York, 1910), 60-62.

57. Ibid., 62-66; Newton, 281-82. This led to France's colonization of the nearby western end of Hispaniola as the colony of St Domingue (now Haiti).

58. See Edward Long, *The History of Jamaica* (3 vols., London, 1774), I, 309-42 (ch. 12, "Of the Dependencies of Jamaica").

59. Frank Strong, "The causes of Cromwell's West Indian expedition", *American Historical Review* 4 (1899): 228-45, esp. 236-42.

60. Thomas Gage, *The English-American, his Travail by Sea and Land: or, A New Survey of the West-Indies* (London, 1648); also

modern eds. with intros. by Arthur P. Newton (London, 1928) and J. Eric S. Thompson (Norman, Okla., 1958).

61. "Some briefe and true observations concerning the West Indies", in John Thurloe, *A Collection of State Papers . . . from the year 1638 to the Restoration* (7 vols., London, 1742), III, 59-61. Gage went as chaplain to Venables' Regiment and died in Jamaica in 1656 (C.H. Firth, ed., *The Narrative of General Venables* [Camden Soc. Pub., new ser., no. 60, London, 1900], 125; Francis J. Osborne, *History of the Catholic Church in Jamaica* [Aylesbury, 1977; 2nd ed. Chicago, 1988], ch. 8).

62. Thurloe's "Account of the negotiations", in Thurloe, III, 761.

63. "A manifesto of the Lord Protector . . . first printed in 1655, translated into English in 1738", in J.A. St John, ed., *The Prose Works of John Milton* (5 vols., London, 1848), II, 333-53.

64. Speech at opening of Parliament 17 Sept. 1656, in Wilbur C. Abbott, ed., *The Writings and Speeches of Oliver Cromwell* (4 vols., Cambridge, MA, 1947), 261-65. See also secret instructions to Venables in Firth, App. A, 107-15.

65. Davenport, II, 94-109, 187-96 (Docs. 55, 65), esp. Articles 8, 38 in 1667 (107, 108; 102, 103) and Art. 7 in 1670 (194).

66. Haring, 66-73 (and passim).

67. Parry and Sherlock, 81-94.

68. Haring, 124-27.

69. Ibid., 73-74; Everild Young and K. Helweg-Larson, *The Pirates' Priest* (London, 1965), 96-97, 154-55.

70. Minister of Port Royal, [Abstract of] "Letters concerning the Earthquake in Jamaica", [dated 22 and 28 July, 1692], in *Gentleman's Magazine* 20 (1750): 213-15.

Chapter 6 Seventeenth Century Colonization and Religion

1. The term Anglican is convenient, although the word was not in use until the 19th century.
2. John R.H. Moorman, A History of the Church in England (London, 1973), 208-26; Williston Walker, A History of the Christian Church (New York, 1959), 402-10; S.T. Bindoff, Tudor England (Harmondsworth, 1966), 225-33, 241-44; Maurice Ashley, England in the Seventeenth Century (Harmondsworth, 1967), 26-34. (The Dutch theologican Arminius affirmed man's free will as well as divine grace.)
3. Babette M. Levy, "Early Puritanism in the southern and island colonies", Proceedings of the American Antiquarian Society 70 (1960): 69-348, esp. 73-91.
4. Latourette, A History of Christianity, 820-31; Ashley, 226-28.
5. Aubrey Gwynn, "Early Irish emigration to the West Indies", Studies 18 (1929): 377-93, 648-63; Father Robert Parsons [in Rome] to Mr Winslade, in Thomas Hughes, ed., History of the Society of Jesus in North America (4 vols., London, 1907-17), Docs. Vol. I, Pt. I, 3-5 (Doc. 1). Cf. Latourette, A History of Christianity, 812-13; Bindoff, 233-41; Ashley, 32-33.
6. Aubrey Gwynn, "Cromwell's policy of transportation", Studies 19 (Dec. 1930): 607-23, and 20 (June 1931): 291-305.
7. Walker, 410-18; Moorman, 226-66.
8. Williamson, English Colonies in Guiana and on the Amazon, 29-149.
9. Charles Leigh to [Privy] Council, Calendar of State Papers, Domestic, 1603-1610 (1857), 127, item 87.
10. "Letter to Sir Olave Leigh", in Samuel Purchas, Purchas His Pilgrimes (20 vols.,

Glasgow, 1905-07), XVI, 319, 323 [orig. ed. IV, 1253, 1255]; cf. "Captain Charles Leigh his voyage to Guiana", ibid., 311 [orig. 1251].

11. "The Relation of Master John Wilson", in Purchas, XVI, 338-51, esp. 340, 343 [orig. ed. 1260, 1262]; Williamson, English Colonies in Guiana and on the Amazon, 29-41.
12. C. Alexander Harris, ed., A Relation of a Voyage to Guiana by Robert Harcourt, 1613, Hakluyt Soc., 2nd ser., no. 60 (London, 1928), 71-73, 77-78, 80-82, 147. Ralegh had advocated missionary work to the Amerindians: [Walter Ralegh or someone writing for him], "Of the Voyage for Guiana", Sloane MSS. 1133, fol. 45, in Robert H. Schomburgk, ed., The Discovery of the Large, Rich and Beautiful Empire of Guiana by Sir W. Ralegh (London, 1848; reprint New York, 1970), App., 135-53.
13. Harris, 54, 55, 56, 127-29.
14. Ibid., 56-61.
15. "Letters Patent to Sir Thomas Gates, Sir George Somers and Others . . . April 10, 1606", in Alexander Brown, The Genesis of the United States (2 vols., Boston, 1890), I, 52-63, esp. 53; "Articles, Instructions and Orders", 20 Nov. 1606, ibid., 65-75, esp. 67-68 (also Peter G. Mode, Source Book and Bibliographical Guide for American Church History [Monasha, Wisc., 1921], 9).
16. "A true and sincere declaration of the purpose and ends of the plantation begun in Virginia", Mode, 9-10 (also Brown, I, 339-40); Harris, 127-31.
17. Outlines of sermon in James S.M. Anderson, The History of the Church of England in the Colonies (3 vols., London, 1856), I, 194, and in Brown, I, 361-75.
18. "Good news from Virginia", excerpts in Hilrie S. Smith, R.T. Handy and L.A.

Loetscher, *American Christianity: An Historical Interpretation with Representative Documents* (2 vols., New York, 1960), I, 45-48.

19. William W. Sweet, *The Story of Religion in America* (New York, 1950), 31-34; James I's Letter to the Archbishops, quoted in Anderson, I, 255-56; John Smith, "The Generall Historie of Virginia . . . 1624", in Edward Arber and A.G. Bradley, eds., *Travels and Works of Captain John Smith* (2 vols., Edinburgh, 1910), II, 520-21.

20. "The barbarous Massacre commited by the Savages on the English-Planters", in Purchas, XIX, 157-64 [orig. ed. IV, 1788-90]; esp. 159-61; Smith, in Arber and Bradley, II, 572-78, 582-83.

21. For example, John Donne's sermon excerpted in Anderson, I, 279-83; J.D., "A publication of Guiana's plantation", ibid., II, 82-85; Williamson, *English Colonies in Guiana and on the Amazon*, 136-40, esp. 138.

22. "Master Stockams Relation", in John Smith, in Arber and Bradley, II, 563-64. Cf. Smith's comment 561-63, 578-82, 584-85; Purchas, XIX, 134-35 [orig. ed. IV, 1179]; Anderson, I, 277-79.

23. "To my very deere and loving Cosen M.G. Minister of the B.F. in London", in Purchas, XIX, 109 [orig. IV, 1771].

24. John H. Lefroy, ed., *Memorials of the Discovery and Early Settlement of the Bermudas* (2 vols., London, 1877-79), I, 691-713 ("Notices of the Clergy") and passim; Levy, 164-200.

25. Smith, Handy, Loetscher, I, 52-53; Edward P. Cheyney, *European Background of American History* (New York, 1904), 290-315.

26. Mode, 12; Bruce, 79-93, 55, 65; Smith, Handy, Loetscher, I, 52.

27. Ibid., I, 52.

28. Wesley F. Craven, *An Introduction to the History of Bermuda* (reprint from *William and Mary Quarterly*, 2nd ser., 17-18 [1937-38]: 125-26). A little later each "Tribe" became a parish (cf. Lefroy, *Memorials*, I, 299).

29. John H. Lefroy, ed., *The Historye of the Bermudaes* (London, 1882, orig. ca. 1622) 229, 283 (cf. Lefroy, *Memorials*, I, 318-21; II, 251-52).

30. Craven, 112 n. 51, 143; Lefroy, *Memorials*, I, 469, 151, App. II (678-86), vol. II, App. IV (588-91); Lefroye, *Historye*, 171-73.

31. Lefroy, *Memorials*, I, 463, 464-70, and passim.

32. "Articles, Lawes, and Orders, Diuine, Politique and Martiall for the Colony in Virginea", in Peter Force, comp., *Tracts and other Papers* (4 vols., Washington, 1836-1846), III, doc. II; also in part in Mode, 10-12.

33. Lefroy, *Historye*, 77-79.

34. Lefroy, *Memorials*, I, 164; *Lefroy*, Historye, 228-29, 282-83; Craven, 143 n. 53. Also "Orders and Constitutions", Lefroy, *Memorials*, I, 182-228, esp. 212-13 ("Ministers") and 220-27 ("Inhabitants").

35. Legislation of March 1624, in Smith, Handy, Loetscher, I, 49-50; Philip A. Bruce, *Social Life in Old Virginia* (New York, 1965), 10-54 on "Popular Religious Feeling" and "Public Morals" in 17th century Virginia. Bruce adds that even late in the century when Anglican influence had clearly replaced Puritan, Sabbath observance for example was still strictly required (35-37).

36. Early narratives in Harlow, *Colonizing Expeditions to the West Indies and Guiana,*

Hakluyt Soc. Works, 2nd ser., no. 56 (London, 1925), 1-4, 18, 25-26; Williamson, Caribbee Islands, 21-25.

37. "Letters Patent . . . 13th September 1625", in Alan Burns, History of the British West Indies (London, 1948), 740 (App. E).

38. Hilton's "Relation", in Harlow, Colonizing Expeditions, 1-3.

39. Jean B. Labat, Nouveau Voyage aux Isles de l'Amerique (Paris, 1722), II, 24-29; IV, 448-49; Nellis M. Crouse, French Pioneers in the West Indies (New York, 1940), 5-6, 39, 214; Joseph Rennard, Histoire religiouse des Antilles francaises (Paris, 1954), 30-32, 41, 74, 188-89, 268-69; Raymond Breton, Grammaire caraibe (Paris, 1871, orig. ed. 1667), esp vii-viii; Petit catechisme . . . Traduit du Francois en la langue des Caraibes insulaires (Auxerre, 1664); Dictionnaire caraibe-francois (Auxerre, 1665); Dictionnaire francois-caraibe (Auxerre, 1666); Pacifique de Provins, Le Voyage de Perse et Breve relation du Voyage des Iles de l'Amerique (1646; reprint Assissi, 1939); D. Gualbert Van der Plas, The History of the Massacre of the Two Jesuit Missionaries in the Island of St Vincent 24th January 1654 (Port-of-Spain, 1954).

40. John Featly, A Sermon Preached to the Nobely-Deserving Gentleman Sir Thomas Warner and the rest of his Companie: Bound to the West Indies. For their Farewell: At St Buttolphs, Aldersgate (London, 1629).

41. |Robert S.| Aucher Warner, Sir Thomas Warner (London, 1933), 46-47; CSPC, I, 15 (item 89); John Featly, The Honor of Chastity: A Sermon (London, 1632).

42. It throws light on the life and theology both of himself and his uncle, Dr Daniel Featley who was for a time a member of the Westminster Assembly (Dictionary of National Biography | 1921|, VI, 1144; John Featley, Featlaei . . .: or, Doctor Daniel Featley Revived |London, 1660|; Robert S. Bosher, The Making of the Restoration Settlement |Westminster, 1951|, 288). John had a brother Henry who was ejected in 1662 (Edmund Calamy, Nonconformist's Memorial |2 vols., London, 1775|, II, 296).

43. Louis B. Wright, Religion and Empire (Chapel Hill, 1943), 87-131, summarizes 19 publications of this kind between 1609 and 1625.

44. Featley, A Sermon Preached, 3, 21-22.

45. Ibid., 32, 34.

46. Memoirs of the First Settlement of the Island of Barbados and the other Caribbee Islands (Barbados, 1741), II.

47. Hilton, "Relation", in Harlow, Colonizing Expeditions, 8-13. Cf. ch. 5, above.

48. Williamson, Caribbee Islands, 38-47, 212-15.

49. ". . . with as ample Royalty and jurisdiction as any Bishop of Durham ever had within the Bishopric of County Pallatine of Durham in England."(Quoted Burns, 262 from the Patent.) In medieval times the Bishop of Durham as a feudal lord had wide authority under the king in a remote area. (Cf. Williamson, Caribbee Islands, 40-41.)

50. James Lord Hay, Earl of Carlisle, "Sr. Thomas Warners Commission for Govr. of St Xt.-phers 29 Sept 1629", Library of Congress transcript from Br. Mus. Egerton Mss. 2395, f. 15-16; Williamson, Caribbee Islands, 87.

51. CSPC, I, 258 (No. 69): Carlisle's appointment of one John Teatley to "the rectory of Palmetor Point, in the island of St Christopher" led to a dispute with another minister. An appeal went to the Privy Council for

redress. Cf. Thomas Lane's appeal to the Archbishop of Canterbury (CSPC, I, 258, No. 70) in the same year (1637), and see below.

52. *Memoirs of the First Settlement of the Island of Barbados* (London 1743; reprint 1891), 11-12.

53. Williamson, *Caribbee Islands*, 90-91.

54. A few "Negroes taken in a prize" arrived with the first colonists in 1627. (John Smith, "The true travels", in Arber and Bradley, II, 906; Nicholas D. Davis, *The Cavaliers and Roundheads of Barbados* |Georgetown, 1887|, 41.) Yet in 1628, 1,400 whites and no blacks were reported in the island; in 1629, 1,800 whites and 50 blacks (Vincent T. Harlow, A *History of Barbados* |Oxford, 1926| App. B, 338).

55. J. Barry deposition, Harlow, *Colonizing Expeditions* 28; cf. witnesses Thompson, Feilding and Astrey, ibid., 26-29.

56. Andrew White, "A Briefe Relation of the Voyage unto Maryland", in Clayton C. Hall, *Narratives of Early Maryland* (New York, 1910), 34.

57. Henry Colt, "Voyage", Harlow, *Colonizing Expeditions* 65-66, 73-74; Williamson, *Caribbee Islands*, 83-88, 91-93.

58. Laud was appointed president in 1634 of a Committee for Plantations "for making laws and orders for government of English colonies planted in foreign parts. With power to impose penalties and imprisonment for offences in ecclesiastical matters; to remove Governors, and require an account of their government; . . . to hear and determine all manner of complaints from the colonies". (CSPC, I, 177, No. 12; cf. 232, Apr. 10, 1936.)

59. CSPC, I, 258-59, No. 70 (6 Oct. 1637); James E. Reece and C.G. Clarke-Hunt,

Barbados Diocesan History (London, 1928), 15-17.

60. Harlow, *Barbados*, App. A, I (331-35); Charles S.S. Higham, "The early days of the Church in the West Indies", *Church Quarterly Review* 92 (1921): 114-16; cf. William W. Manross, *The Episcopal Church in the United States* (New York, 1938), 22-24, which describes the southern mainland colonies but much is true for the West Indies as well.

61. Higham, "The early days of the Church in the West Indies", 107-9, 117, 120.

62. Reece and Clark-Hunt, 17.

63. CSPC, I, 473 (No. 63).

64. Harlow, *Barbados*, 18-19, 25-26; Reece and Clarke-Hunt, 19-20. (The formation of the extra parishes was a gradual process, not a single act of government.)

65. Anderson, II, 60-61; Nicholas Trott, ed., *The Laws of the British Plantations in America, relating to the Church and the Clergy* (London, 1725), 361-62.

66. Anderson, II, 57-58; Trott, 353-54.

67. Anderson, II, 58-60; Trott, 354-56.

68. Higham, "The early days of the Church in the West Indies", 121.

69. Ibid., 121-22; CSPC, 1675-76, No. 570; Joseph Besse, A *Collection of the Sufferings of the People called Quakers* (2 vols., London, 1753), II, 354-65.

70. Richard S. Dunn, *Sugar and Slaves* (New York, 1973), 253.

71. In the Danish West Indies also the governor of St Thomas, a zealous Lutheran, issued orders in 1672 for compulsory church attendance and family prayers, with fines for delinquents (Jens P.M. Larson, *Virgin Islands Story* |Philadelphia, 1950; reprint 1968|, 17-18).

72. Gt. Brit. Statutes, *Two Ordinances of the Lords and Commons Assembled in*

Parliament, *The one dated November 2, 1643, the other March 21, 1645 . . . Whereby Robert Earle of Warwick is made Governor in chief* (London, 1645, photostat Massachusetts Hist. Soc., 1926).

73. Gt. Brit. Parliament, *Journals of the House of Lords* 9, no. 51 (28 Feb. 1646); Harlow, *Barbados*, 31.

74. Richard Ligon, *A True & Exact History of the Island of Barbadoes* (2nd ed., London, 1673), 57-58. (A "shot" is young pig.)

75. Michael Craton, *A History of the Bahamas* (London, 1963), 56-63; "Articles and Orders for the Company of Eleutherian Adventurers" (1647), in Harcourt Malcolm, comp., *Historical Documents relating to the Bahama Islands* (Nassau, 1910), 1-8; Edward D. Neill, "A chapter of American church history", reprint from the *New Englander* (July 1879): 471-86; William H. Miller, "The colonization of the Bahamas, 1647-1670", in *William and Mary Quarterly*, 3rd ser., 2 (1945): 33-46.

76. Harlow, *Barbados*, 48-54; Davis, 137-58.

77. "An Act for the uniting of the Inhabitants of the Island, under the Government thereof", proposed by Thomas Modyford to repeal "coercive Ecclesiastical Lawes, and the penalties thereof", was amended by the Cavalier party to add (inconsistently): "That all and every person or persons who shall goe or come to any Conventicle, or shall labour to seduce any person or persons from repairing to the publick congregation, or receiving of the holy Sacrament shall by any Justice of the peace (upon complaint thereof to him made) be committed to Prison." (Nicholas Foster, *A Briefe Relation of the late Horrid Rebellion* [London, 1650; facs. reprint, London, 1879], 9-12).

78. Foster, 109.

79. Ibid., 110, 40-99, esp. "An Act for the present and future peace of the Island" (to disarm "all the Independent party, non-conformists to the antient Discipline of the Church of England, and all other Sectaries"), 51-56, and the defensive Declaration of Drax's group, denying the charges of sedition, schism, faction and heresy by a statement of faith in Christ and His salvation), 93-94.

80. CSPC, I, 344 (17 Oct. 1650).

81. CSPC, I, 368-69 (26-27 Dec. 1651), 371 (7 Jan. 1652), 388 (Aug.); "The Charter of Barbados, or Articles of Agreement", in Robert H. Schomburgk, *The History of Barbados* (London, 1848), 280.

82. CSPC, I, 380 (3 June 1652).

83. Harlow, *Barbados*, 96-97; P.F. Campbell, *The Church in Barbados in the Seventeenth Century* (Barbados, 1982), 58-59, 166-69 (App. III)

84. Ibid., 59-67; Firth, ed., *Narrative of General Venables* (London, Camden Soc., new ser., no. 60, 1900), passim; John Thurloe, *A Collection of the State Papers* (7 vols., London, 1742), III, esp. 157-59, 249-52, 504-8, 754-55, 681.

85. J. Scott, "The Discription of Barbados" (Br. Mus. Sloane MS. 3662, ff. 62-54), Lib. of Cong. photostat, esp. 60b, 59, 54.

86. Henry Whistler, with the Penn-Venables expedition, comments: "They have that Libertie of contienc which wee soe long have in England foght for: But they doue abus it." ("Extracts from Journal", Firth, App. E, 146.)

87 . Charles S.S. Higham, *The Development of the Leeward Islands under the Restoration* (Cambridge, 1921), 20

88. Text (French) in Burns, App. F (743-44), quoted from Dutertre.

89. Paul Reyss, *Étude sur quelques points de l'histoire de la tolérance au Canada et aux Antilles, XVIe et XVIIe siècles* (Genève, 1907), 66. (Cf. 48 re contrast with French Canada.)

90. CSPC, 1677-80, 572 (No. 1441).

91. Harlow, *Colonizing Expeditions*, 10-11.

92. Thomas Colt, "Voyage", in Harlow, *Colonizing Expeditions*, 87-88.

93. Aubrey Gwynn, "Documents relating to the Irish in the West Indies", *Analecta Hibernica* 4 (1932): 243-49, 278-79; Nellis M. Crouse, *The French Struggle for the West Indies* (New York, 1943), 58-60, 153-54, 188.

94. Aubrey Gwynn, "Early Irish emigration", 648-53, and "The first Irish priests in the New World", *Studies* 21 (1932): 221; John C. Messenger, "The influence of the Irish in Montserrat", *Caribbean Quarterly* 13 (1967): 3-26 (9 re 1678 census: 1,869 Irish, 761, English, 52 Scots, 992 slaves).

95. Andrew White, 37. John Scott a generation later says: "at the west north west end of the Island are thrust together ye poor Catholiques on 2017 Acres of Land planted with Tobacco and some provisions". ("The Discription of Barbados", f. 55.)

96. White, 38-39; cf. "Relatio Itineris in Marilandiam" (Latin version), in T. Hughes, Docs. Vol. I, Pt. I. No. 8, A, 94-107, esp. 101.

97. There is a hint in the Latin version that they were in a hurry for fear of the Spanish fleet. Since this was January 1634, the Catholics from Virginia must have arrived almost as soon as the island was occupied from St Kitts. (Henry Colt reports the place as unsettled in July 1631: Harlow, *Colonizing Expeditions*, 83.) Is this migration in any way connected with the conditions which caused the first Lord Baltimore to have to leave Virginia in 1629 because of his religion? (T. Hughes, Text, I, 279). On relevant legislation in Virginia up to the act of uniformity of 1631 see Sanford H. Cobb, *The Rise of Religious Liberty in America* (New York, 1902), 80-82. Messenger, 6, 8, mentions a post-1644 migration from Virginia (citing an unpublished source by T.S. English). Were there then two periods of movement from that colony, or could the later date be mistaken? Cf. Gwynn, "First Irish priests", 220-21.

98. Pierre Pelleprat, *Relation des Missions des PP. de la Compagnie de Jesus* (Paris, 1655), 37-48; Gwynn, "Early Irish emigration", 656-57 and "First Irish priests", 227-28.

99. Pelleprat, 39-40. While he was there a large number of Caribs attacked the island, plundering, killing and terrorizing the settlers. Pelleprat tells of a comic incident while they were pillaging the Protestant church. One of the Carib leaders found the minister's robe, put it on secretly and emerged with fearful cries to surprise and terrify the other Caribs who believed him to be a *maboya* (devil). (Ibid., 40-41.)

100. Ibid., 41-48.

101. Higham, *The Development of the Leeward Islands under the Restoration*, 41-60; Higham, "The early days of the Church in the West Indies", 109.

102. Gwynn, "Documents", 252-59, and "First Irish priests", 228.

103. CSPC, 1661-68, 187 (No. 664); William J. Gardner, *A History of Jamaica* (London, 1873; reprint 1909), 88; Leonard W. Labaree, *Royal Instructions to British Colonial Governors, 1670-1776* (2 vols., New York, 1935), II, 493-94 (No. 713).

Colonial Governors, 1670-1776 (2 vols., New York, 1935), II, 493-94 (No. 713).

104. Labaree, *Royal Instructions*, 497-98 (No. 724); CSPC, 1685-88, 419 (No. 1404); Francis J. Osborne, *History of the Catholic Church in Jamaica* (Aylesbury, 1977 and Chicago, 1988), ch. 10, 52-58.

105. CSPC, 1685-88, 513 (No. 1653); Higham, "The early days of the church in the West Indies", 123.

106. Labaree, *Royal Instructions*, 494 (No. 714).

107. Reyss, 46-60; Charles W. Baird, *History of the Huguenot Emigration to America* (2 vols., New York, 1885), I, 201-11; Crouse, *French Pioneers*, 205-48, esp. 211-13.

108. Reyss, 61-66; Baird, I, 211-17.

109. Reyss, 64-65; Shelby T. McCloy, *The Negro in the French West Indies* (Lexington, 1966), 15-19.

110. Baird, I, 217-34; Reyss, 66-81; CSPC, 1685-88, 506 (No. 1639).

111. CSPC, 1669-74, 242, 470 (Nos. 591, 1042); Higham, *The Development of the Leeward Islands under the Restoration*, 108; Higham, "The early days of the church in the West Indies", 123-24.

112. So much so that the sincerity of their religion was questioned (*A General Survey of that part of the Island of St Christophers which formerly belonged to France . . . by Mr. R.M.S.B.* [London, 1722], 24-25).

113. Reyss, 70-78; J.H. Lawrence-Archer, *Monumental Inscriptions of the British West Indies* (London, 1875), 76; Labat, I, 325-26, 411-13; IV, 393-97; V, 315-16, 322, 343.

114. Curtis P. Nettels, *The Roots of American Civilization* (New York, 1963), 140-45; Dunn, 110-16.

115. Quoted from one Mr Hanson by Gardner, 89. Richard Hill, a noted 19th century Jamaican layman, has some interesting comments on the decline of Puritanism: *Lights and Shadows of Jamaica History* (Kingston, 1859); cf. his *Address delivered at the Baptist Jubilee* (Jamaica, 1864), 3-5.

116. For example, Mr Grey in Barbados (CSPC, 1681-1685, 60-61, 148 [Nos. 123, 311]; Levy, 296-97; Harlow, *Barbados*, 249); John Oxenbridge in Surinam and Barbados (Calamy, I, 236; Levy, 298-99); Robert Speere and Mr Crow in Jamaica (Gardner, 89-91; Levy, 285); John Coad, *A Memorandum of the Wonderful Providences of God* [London, 1849], 34-35, 97, 99); Solomon Stoddard and Nathanael Williams in Barbados (Levy, 297-98).

117. Coad; Gardner, 89-90; F. Ross Brown, *Mission to Jamaica* (n.p., 1947), 1-4.

118. CSPC, 1685-88, 274-75, 316, 319, 448, 570-71 (Nos. 965, 1128, 1142, 1449, I, 1831, 1832, 1835); Coad, 97; Gardner, 89; Levy, 285-286; Craton, 79-81.

119. Francis Mackemie, *Truths in a True Light* (Edinburgh, 1699); cf. L.P. Bowen, *The Days of Makemie* (Philadelphia, 1885) (a historical novel based on documentary material), esp. 287; Maurice W. Armstrong, L.A. Loetscher, and C.A. Anderson, *The Presbyterian Enterprise* (Philadelphia, 1956), 13-18; Levy, 299.

120. CSPC, 1677-80, 502, 619 (Nos. 1334, 1558); 1699 Addenda, 593 (No. 1113: N. Blake to the King, 1670); 1681-85, 210-11 (No. 444); Rufus M. Jones, *The Quakers in the American Colonies* (London, 1911), 41; Harlow, *Barbados*, 250.

121. William C. Braithwaite, *The Beginnings of Quakerism* (2nd ed., Cambridge, 1955); Hugh Barbour, *The Quakers in Puritan England* (New Haven, 1964).

122. Jones, 26-27, 41-42. Friends were pioneers among Protestants also in the organization and financing of missionary activity overseas: see

(New York, 1950), 5, 157-58.

123. Jones, 28, 71; Besse, II, 291; CSPC, 1669-74, 471 (No. 1044). On Thomas Rous see N.D. Davis, 164, 166, 178.

124. Jones, 26-31, 41, 70-89, *Acts of the Privy Council of England, Colonial*, I, 393-94 (No. 651). Cf. Barbour, 202-33; Alan B. Anderson, "A study in the sociology of religion: the first Quakers", *Journal of Religious History* 9 (1977): 247-62.

125. Jones, 42; Thurloe, VI, 834.

126. Besse, II, 278, 388, and passim.

127. Jonas Langford, A *Brief Account of the Sufferings of the Servants of the Lord called Quakers* (London, 1706) on Antigua; Besse, II, 278-351 (Barbados), 352-66 (Nevis), 366-70 (Bermuda), 370-78 (Antigua), 388-91 (Jamaica); cf. CSPC, 1685-88, 208-9 (No. 742).

128. Besse, II, 279-80; CSPC, 1669-74, 352 (No. 812). A few years later when the French captured Antigua the Quakers there refused to take an oath of allegiance to the French King, thus showing the impartiality of their testimony (Besse, II, 371).

129. Besse, II, 353.

130. Jones, 42 (Henry Fell); Besse, II, 319-22 (Margaret Brewster), 354-55, 356-58, 363-65, 370; Langford, 5.

131. Besse, II, 283, 287, 350.

132. Ibid., II, 352; cf. Barbour, 165-66, 198-99.

133. Levy, 300-307; George Fox, *Journal* (2 vols, Penney ed., Cambridge, 1911), II, 176-258, 425-34; William Edmundson, A *Journal of the Life, Travels, Sufferings, and Labour of Love in the Work of the Ministry* (Dublin, 1715), 52-57, 71-76, 108-11, 279-83, 295-99, 300-307 (re visits of 1671, 1675 and 1683); Thomas Story, A *Journal of the Life* (Newcastle upon Tyne, 1747), 444-45; CSPC, 1693-96, 125-26

(No. 442). Four Quaker meeting-houses are marked on old Barbados maps in St Lucy's, St Peter's, St Thomas's and St Philip's parishes (F. Lucas map in Tony Campbell, *Printed Maps of Barbados* (London, 1965, Plate XXII [No. 51]; Harlow, *Barbados*, f.p. 335). The fifth was in Bridgetown (cf. Dunn. 103-6, esp. 104).

134. In Jamaica the 1692 earthquake was a major blow to the Quakers (Dunn, 44, 183-84, 186-87), and in 1728 only one member was reported in the island. By 1744 there were hardly a hundred Friends even in Barbados (Charles F. Jenkins, *Tortola, A Quaker Experiment of Long Ago in the Tropics* [London, 1923], 5; William C. Braithwaite, *The Second Period of Quakerism* [London, 1919], 618-21). For other glimpses of the 18th century see Story, 433-56 (visits of 1708-9, 1714); Thomas Chalkley, A *Collection of the Works* (Philadelphia, 1749), 33-37, 55-57, 202-7, 223-26, 247, 258-65, 270-74, 319-26, 576-90 (some 21 voyages from 1701 to 1741); Jenkins, re period 1735-80 in the British Virgin Islands. The Quakers reappeared in Jamaica in the 19th century.

Chapter 7 Sugar, Slavery and the Planters' Church

1. Hilary McD. Beckles, *White Servitude and Black Slavery in Barbados, 1627-1715* (Knoxville, 1989); John C. Jeaffreson, ed., A *Young Squire of the Seventeenth Century* (2 vols., London, 1878), I, 255-60; Abbott E. Smith, *Colonists in Bondage: White Servitude and Convict Labour in America, 1607-1776* (Gloucester, MA, 1965), 62-66 and

(Gloucester, MA, 1965), 62-66 and passim; James D. Butler, "British convicts shipped to American colonies", *American Historical Review* 2 (1896): 12-33; Aubrey Gwynn, "Indentured servants and Negro slaves in Barbados (1642-1650)", *Studies* 19 (1930): 279-94.

2. Richard Ligon, *A True and Exact History of the Island of Barbados* (London, 1673), 43-58.

3. Ch. 6, n. 56, above (1634); Ligon, 45-46; Beckles, 71-78; Cf. Richard S. Dunn, *Sugar and Slaves* (New York, 1973), 247.

4. Beckles, 140-67; Smith, 236 and ch. 13 (285-306); John A. Schutz and M.E. O'Neil, "Arthur Holt, Anglican clergyman, reports on Barbados 1725-1733", *Journal of Negro History* (hereafter JNH) 21 (1936): 455 (example of Mr Osborn), 458-59, 461.

5. Nellis Crouse, *The French Struggle for the West Indies* (New York, 1943), 34; Higham, "The early days of the Church in the West Indies", *Church Quarterly Review* 62 (1921): 109; George H. Guttridge, *The Colonial Policy of William III in America and the West Indies* (Cambridge, 1922), 60-61; Smith, 162-74.

6. Smith, 4, 29-34; Frank W. Pitman, *The Development of the British West Indies, 1700-1763* (New Haven, 1917), 50-58; Lowell J. Ragatz, *The Fall of the Planter Class in the British Caribbean, 1763-1833* (New York, 1928), 8-9.

7. Smith, 252-56; Winthrop D. Jordan, "American chiaroscuro: the status and definition of mulattoes in the British colonies", *William and Mary Quarterly*, 3rd ser., 19 (1962): 183-200, esp. 192-200: Elsa V. Goveia, *Slave Society in the British Leeward Islands at the End of the*

Eighteenth Century (Puerto Rico, 1969), 96-101, 214-33, 315-17.

8. Dunn, 74-76, 87; Vincent T. Harlow, *A History of Barbados* (Oxford, 1920), 338-39; Pitman, 369-71.

9. Dunn, 155, 121-23, 127, 141; Pitman, 373 n. 26.

10. Dunn, 110-16, 122-23; Curtis Nettels, *Roots of American Civilization* (New York, 1963), 144, 419. The proportion of Africans in the West Indies was much higher than in the mainland colonies.

11. David B. Davis, *The Problem of Slavery in Western Culture* (Ithaca, 1966), 35-60, 98-101; John F. Maxwell, *Slavery and the Catholic Church* (Chichester, 1975), 38-43, 51-52.

12. Re Dutch and Danish attitudes: Cornelis C. Goslinga, *The Dutch in the Caribbean* (Assen, The Netherlands, 1971), 340-42; Waldemar Westergaard, *The Danish West Indies under Company Rule, 1671-1754* (New York, 1917), 40-41, 158-63. The thesis of Frank Tannenbaum (*Slave and Citizen* [New York, 1946], 42-65, 82-105), that conditions of slaves in the Iberian colonies were much better than in the Protestant ones, with the French somewhere between them, has been challenged and modified by later scholars: Davis, *The Problem of Slavery in Western Culture*, 223-61; Arnold A. Sio, "Interpretations of slavery: the slave status in the Americas", in Allen Weinstein and F. O. Gatell, eds., *American Negro Slavery: A Modern Reader* (New York, 1968), 310-32; Harmannus Hoetink, *Slavery and Race Relations in the Americas* (New York, 1973), 3-9. Cf. Elsa V. Goveia, "The West Indian slave laws of the 18th century", in Goveia and C.J. Bartlett, *Chapters in Caribbean History* 2 (Barbados, 1970), 1-53.

13. Ligon, 50.

14. J. Berkenhead to secretary Thurloe, 17
Feb. 1654/55, in John Thurloe, A
Collection of State Papers (7 vols., London,
1742), III, 159. See Berkenhead also re
five "Indian Christian protestants",
brought from Guiana, who had been
enslaved in Barbados. (Cf. H. Powell
petition in Harlow, Colonizing Expeditions
to the West Indies and Guiana, Hakluyt
Soc. Works, 2nd Ser., no. 56 (London),
1925), 36-38, and depositions 30, 39,
40, 41; Carl and R. Bridenbaugh, No
Peace Beyond the Line [New York, 1972],
29-31.)

15. Davis, The Problem of Slavery in Western
Culture, 98-102, 205, 207-10; Marcus W.
Jernegan, "Slavery and conversion in
the American Colonies", American
Historical Review 21 (1916): 505-7; Edgar
J. McManus, "The Negro slave in New
York", Weinstein and Gatell, 69-70;
John C. Hurd, The Law of Freedom and
Bondage in the United States (Boston,
1858-62), 165-71, 178-94, 209-12, 358;
Helen T. Catterall, Judicial Cases
Concerning American Slavery and the Negro
(5 vols., Washington, 1926-37), I, 1-12,
55-58.

16. CSPC, 1675-76, 335 (No. 784, cf. 783);
Higham, "The early days of the Church
in the West Indies", 113; CSPC, 1677-
80, 590 (No. 1488), item 5.

17. [Edmund Gibson], Two Letters of the Lord
Bishop of London (London, 1727/1729),
repr. in David Humphreys, An Historical
Account of the Incorporated Society for the
Propagation of the Gospel in Foreign Parts
(London, 1730; facs. New York, 1969),
265-66.

18. Jernegan, 506-7; Davis, The Problem of
Slavery in Western Culture, 209, 210;
Hurd, 232, 250 n. 1, 300-301 (also 234-

35, cf. 210 n. 1); Dunn, 243-44, 249-50;
Nicholas Trott, Laws of the British
Plantations relating to the Church (London,
1725), 426. Cf. "A draft of a bill for
converting the Negroes in the
plantations" (about 1708), quoted in
Donald B. Cooper, The Establishment of
the Church in the Leeward Islands
(Stillwater, Okla., 1966), 35-36; also
mentioned in Edward Carpenter,
Thomas Tenison (London, 1948), 356-57,
and his The Protestant Bishop [on Henry
Compton] (London, 1956), 296. But it
seems that this never became law, for
if it had it is hard to see why the legal
experts would have to be consulted
later.

19. CSPC, 1677-80, 611 (No. 1535).

20. CSPC, 1681-85, 25 (No. 59).

21. Morgan Godwyn (or Godwin), The
Negro's & Indians Advocate (London,
1680), 1-3 and passim.

22. CSPC, 1697-98, 518 (No. 955); James E.
Smith, Slavery in Bermuda (New York,
1976), 89. Some Bermudians had in
fact tried to Christianize slaves and in
1669 Governor Heydon had issued a
proclamation denying that this made
them free from their masters (John H.
Lefroy, ed. Memorials of the Discovery and
Settlement of the Bermudas (2 vols.,
London, 1877-79), II, 293-94 (item 12);
cf. 291-92 (item 10). Subsequent slave
revolts may have hardened the
colonists' opposition to their religious
instruction. (Smith, 45-49, 52-56 and
William W. Manross, comp., The Fulham
Papers in the Fulham Palace Library
[Oxford, 1965] 245, 246 [xvii, 45-46, 49-
50, 59-60, 63-64] show that in 1789-92
this opposition remained.)

23. Humphreys, 265, 267-68.

24. CSPC, 1693-96, 448 (No. 1738); cf. Gov.
Stapleton quoted in Higham, "The

early days of the Church in the West
Indies", 127.

25. Humphreys, 262-64.

26. Charles F. Pascoe, comp., *Two Hundred
Years of the* SPG: *An Historical Account . . .*
1701-1900 (London, 1901), 211. (On Le
Jau see Frank J. Klingberg, ed., *The
Carolina Chronicle of Dr Francis Le Jau*
[Univ. of Calif. Pub. in Hist. Vol. 53,
Berkeley, 1956], esp. 4, 10-11, 51;
Carpenter, *Protestant Bishop*, 295-96.) For
other correspondence see Manross,
Fulham Papers, 260, 261-62, 220-21
(xviii, 45-52, 65-70; xv, 80-82, 87-93),
dated 1751, 1788, 1790, 1792 from
Jamaica and the Bahamas.

27. Manross, *Fulham Papers*, 267 (xviii, 157-
60).

28. Note the differences of opinion among
Jamaica clergy about 1724 in Manross,
Fulham Papers, 252-56 (xvii, 185-88, 193-
94, 199-202, 211-35, 236-37, 242-43,
244-45, 246-47); Library of Congress
Transcript, Fulham MSS, Jamaica No.
6; also Commissary J. Knox, Antigua
1732, quoted Cooper, 39 (Manross,
Fulham Papers, 279 [xix, 210-13]); J.
Harry Bennett, Jr, *Bondsmen and Bishops*
(Univ. of Calif. Pub. in Hist. Vol. 62,
Berkeley, 1958) 84-87.

29. Cf. Ligon, 54; "I am of the belief; that
there are to be found among them,
some who are as morally honest, as
Conscionable, as humble, as loving to
their friends, and as loyal to their
Masters, as any that live under the
sun". Cf. also A. Holt to Bp. of London,
21 Dec. 1727, in Schutz and O'Neil,
450-52.

30. Richard Nisbet, *The Capacity of Negroes
for Religious and Moral Improvement
Considered* (London, 1789; facs.
Westport, Conn., 1970), shows

attitudes of a concerned slave owner
of Nevis who undertook to instruct his
own slaves, advocated "melioration",
and anticipated ultimate emancipation. He was a friend and admirer of
Revd James Ramsay, the abolitionist.
(Cf. 76; Goveia, *Slave Society in the British
Leeward Islands at the End of the Eighteenth
Century*, 302 n. 5, 349, 263-69.)

31. Manross, *Fulham Papers*, answers to qu.
7, xiii, xxiii, 226-27 (xv, 203-14,
Barbados), 254-55 (xvii, 211-35,
Jamaica), 274-75, 343 (xix, 116-120,
Leeward Islands and xxxvi, 308,
Displaced Doc., L.I.). For comparative
mainland reports see 172-77 (xii, 41-
84, Virginia), 34-38 (iii, 48-71,
Maryland), 137-39 (ix, 160-71, South
Carolina); Klingberg, *Carolina Chronicle*,
2 and passim).

32. For example: Alfred Caldecott, *The
Church in the West Indies* (London, 1898),
46-70; Henry P. Thompson, *Into All
Lands* (London, 1951), 157-58, 162-63;
George R. Wynne, *The Church in Greater
Britain* (London, 1901), 153-59;
Higham, "The early days of the Church
in the West Indies", 126-29; John H.
Parry and P. Sherlock, *Short History of the
West Indies* (London, 1957) 152; F.R.
Augier, S.C. Gordon, D.G. Hall and M.
Reckord, *The Making of the West Indies*
(London, 1960), 135-36; Pitman, 1-41;
Ragatz, 18-28.

33. For the British (and European)
background in thought and religion in
this period, see Gerald R. Cragg, *From
Puritanism to the Age of Reason* (Cambridge, 1950); and his *The Church and the
Age of Reason* (Harmondsworth, 1960);
S.C. Carpenter, *Eighteenth Century Church
and People* (London, 1959); Norman
Sykes, *From Sheldon to Secker* (Cam-

bridge, 1959); J. Wesley Bready, *England: Before and After Wesley* (London, 1939).

34. Carey Robinson, *The Fighting Maroons of Jamaica* (Kingston and London, 1969), 9-29.

35. Thurloe, III, 753; Edward Long, *History of Jamaica* (3 vols., London, 1774), I, 213-15 (Bk. I, ch. 10, App. [C]); Bridenbaugh, 203.

36. Long, I, 256-57; Thurloe, III, 681; William J. Gardner, *History of Jamaica* (London, 1909) 87-88; CSPC, I, 459 (29 Sept. 1657).

37. CSPC, 1661-68, 6 (No. 22); cf. 5-6 (No. 20).

38. Cf. Archibald P. Thornton, *West-India Policy under the Restoration* (Oxford, 1956), 65-66.

39. CSPC, 1661-68, 261 (No. 882, items 7, 18); Walter A. Feurtado, comp., *Official and Other Personages of Jamaica from 1655 to 1790* (Kingston, 1896), vi-vii; Kit S. Kapp, *The Printed Maps of Jamaica up to 1825* (London, 1968), Plates VIII (1671) and X (1674).

40. CSPC, 1669-74, 305 (No. 704). Cf. Modyford's earlier (1664) report: ibid., 1661-68, 237-38 (No. 810).

41. CSPC, 1669-74, 393 (No. 896). Only Nevis had escaped occupation by the French in the recent war.

42. CSPC, 1675-76, 237 (No. 571); Frank Cundall, *A Brief History of the Parish Church of St Andrew, Jamaica* (Kingston, 1931), 14.

43. CSPC, 1681-85, 6-7 (No. 14). Morgan mentions in the same despatch that a new church building in Port Royal had been opened on the previous 1 January (1681).

44. Other glimpses of the Church in Jamaica in these early days are found in Richard Blome, *A Description of the Island of Jamaica* (London, 1672), 38-41; Henry Houser, *An Exact model or platform of good magistracy: or a sermon preached before the Governour, Council and Assembly at their first meeting at Saint Jago de la Vega, in Jamaica, February 1, 1671* (London, 1673); *The Present State of Jamaica* [anonymous] (London, 1683), 2-3, 47; Sir Thomas Lynch reports (1682, 1683) in CSPC, 1681-85, 313-15, 501 (Nos. 757, 1260).

45. Trott, 409-14, 415-16.

46. CSPC, 1661-68, 29, 57 (Nos. 84, 175); Trott, 356-58 (27 Sept. 1661).

47. Trott, 368-70.

48. Jeaffreson, I, 215; Higham, "The early days of the Church in the West Indies", 109-10; Crouse, 85-101.

49. CSPC, 1669-74, 289 (No. 680).

50. "Answer to inquiries sent to Col. Stapleton", CSPC, 1675-76, 500 (No. 1152, item 14).

51. CSPC, 1669-74, 242-43, 289 (Nos. 592, 680 item 24); Higham, "The early days of the Church in the West Indies, 110-11. Cf. the proposals of the anonymous author of *Virginia's Cure* (1661) in Peter Force, comp., *Tracts and Other Papers* (4 vols., Washington, 1836-46), III, Doc. 15, and contemporary efforts to have a bishop appointed to Virginia (Sykes, 205).

52. CSPC, 1675-76, 238 (No. 571).

53. CSPC, 1675-76, 335, 446, 502 (Nos. 784, 808, 1152 item 30); 1677-80, 103, 158, 174, 212, 245 (Nos. 291, 414, 467, 588, 679); Nelson W. Rightmyer, "List of Anglican clergymen receiving a bounty for overseas service", *Historical Magazine of the Protestant Episcopal Church* (hereafter HMPEC) 17 (1948), 174-75.

54. Charles S.S. Higham, *The Development of the Leeward Islands under the Restoration* (Cambridge, 1921), 212-13, 242-43;

Higham, "The early days of the Church in the West Indies", 112-14; CSPC, 1661-68, 640-41 (No. 1905 item 6); Manross, Fulham Papers, 269 (xix, 1); Trott, 85, 379 (Art. XI). Antigua in 1668 had also provided "for the maintenance of two able orthodox ministers" (Higham, "The early days of the Church in the West Indies", 114). Cf. Stapleton's reports of 1676 and 1678 (CSPC, 1675-76, 500-502 [No. 1152, items 14, 20-22, 29-30]; CSPC, 1677-80, 265-66 [No. 741, item 1]).

55. Trott, 375-79, 391-403, and also 386-87; Manross, Fulham Papers, 269 (xix, 2-5); Higham, "The early days of the Church in the West Indies", 115-17.

56. Bishop [Compton] of London, "Observations regarding a Suffragan for America", in E.B. O'Callaghan, ed., Documents relative to the Colonial History of the State of New York (1856-61) V, 29 (item 4.); refs. to governors' appointments in Schutz and O'Neil, 449, 450, 453, 464; Manross, Fulham Papers, 229, 230, 233, 236, 237 (xv, 247-8, 260-61, 262-63, 264-65; xvi, 2-3, 65-66, 69-70, 83-84, Barbados); ibid. 272, 273, 279, 280, 282, 287 (xix, 44-45, 98-99, 202-3, 210-13, 214-15, 223-24, 267-68; xx, 81-82, Leewards); ibid., 228-29 (xx, 101-2, Leewards and Barbados); ibid., 290, 293 (xx, 132-33, 177-78, Windwards); ibid., 249, 250, 258, 259, 261, 268 (xvii, 107-10, 141-42, 281, 285-86; xviii, 21-22, 45-52, 76-77, 82-83, 84-85, 228-33, Jamaica). Cf. CSPC, 1681-85, 314 (No. 757): "The gentlemen of this parish have asked for Mr. Cooke . . . and I have promised it provided that . . . his salary is raised to 100 [pounds]." Cf. also G. Maclaren Brydon, "The origin of the rights of the laity in the American Episcopal Church", HMPEC

12 (1943): 313-38, esp. 335-38; E. Spencer, "The establishment, government, and functioning of the Church in colonial Virginia", HMPEC 26 (1957): 65-110, esp. 89, 96, 97, 106. These valuable studies of Anglican polity in the colonies (from a mainland viewpoint) in the 17th and 18th centuries must be used with caution if applied to the West Indies.

57. See refs. from Manross, Fulham Papers in note 31, above.

58. Ibid., answers to qu. 6; Pitman, 372 (Barbados, 1724), 379 (Leewards, 1724), 373 (Jamaica, 1722). Population figures (cited by Pitman from governors' reports to the Board of Trade and in the case of Jamaica from Long's History) may be tabulated as follows:

Table 1

	Whites	Blacks
Barbados	18,295	55,206
Antigua	5,200	19,800
St Kitts	4,000	11,500
Nevis	1,100	6,000
Montserrat	1,000	4,400
Jamaica	7,100	80,000
Totals	**36,695**	**176,906**

59. Pitman, 371-73, 375, 378, 380-83.

60. Ibid., 48, 58, 378 and 369-90 (App. I); Harlow, Barbados, 338-39. (Cf. Dunn, 312-13 and Bridenbaugh, 226-27 for the 17th century.)

61. Manross, Fulham Papers, answers to questions 8 and 9.

62. Ibid., answers to questions 16 and 17.

63. Pitman, ch. 1 (1-41); Lowell J. Ragatz, Absentee Landlordism in the British Caribbean, 1750-1833 (London, 1928).

64. Cf. Michael G. Smith, "Some aspects of social structure in the British Carib-

bean about 1820", SES 1, no. 4 (Aug. 1953): 55-79.

65. Gt. Brit., House of Commons, *Papers relating to the West Indies* . . . 1815, 139 and passim. Besides the Church of England these documents contain valuable data on the nonconformist missions and other churches such as the Danish, Dutch and Roman Catholic. Unfortunately there is little ecclesiastical information on Jamaica and none on Trinidad. See also (Revd) Richard Bickell, *The West Indies as they are* (London, 1825).

66. Bickell, passim; cf. George Fox and Morgan Godwyn, mentioned further in ch. 8.

67. This was in fact the original doctrine of Erastus, but its prevalance in the West Indies was not due to this man's teachings but to local circumstances. Cf. *Encyclopedia Britannica* (1972), 8, 670, "Erastus, Thomas".

68. Leonard W. Labaree, *Royal Government in America* (New Haven, 1930), 115-16; Labaree, *Royal Instructions*, 489-90, 491 (Nos. 708, 710).

69. See nn. 73, 87 below re Charles II and James II. In Queen Anne's reign an American episcopate was almost established and she also initiated "Queen Anne's Bounty" to help the colonial clergy.

70. Labaree, *Royal Government*, 3-5, 52-79, 115-20; Winfred T. Root, "The lords of trade and plantations, 1675-1696", *American Historical Review* 23 (1917): 20-41; Thornton, 10-11, 17-20, 134, 146-48, 157-59, 189 n. 1, 210-13.

71. They are thoroughly documented for the period 1670-1776 by Labaree, *Royal Instructions*. Those concerned with "Religion and Morals" are in vol. II, 482-512 (Nos. 694-742). Labaree says

that earlier instructions cannot be standardized (I, xi). However, as shown below, CSPC and other records before 1670 (including the first royal colony, Virginia, as early as 1624) throw some light on the development of policy in the initial stages.

72. Root, 23-27, 36-37; Edward Carpenter, *Protestant Bishop*, 253-62; Labaree, *Royal Government*, 55-56, 420-22, 426-27.

73. O'Callaghan, *Documents*, III, 36, item 10; CSPC, I, 493 (No. 59. I).

74. See note 37, above; CSPC, 1661-68, 81 (No. 259); Manross, *Fulham Papers*, 248 (xvii, 93-94). Cf. similar orders to Gov. William Berkeley of Virginia as early as 1641 and again in 1662 (CSPC, I, 321; 1661-68, 110 [No. 368]; *Virginia Magazine of History and Biography* 3 [1895]: 15).

75. CSPC, 1661-68, 92, 142 (Nos. 309, 489). Willoughby helped to prepare these Instructions (*Acts of the Privy Council, Colonial*, I, 338 [No. 576]; Thornton, 35). They were renewed after his death for his brother William as governor in 1667 (CSPC, 1661-68, 445 [No. 1403]).

76. Labaree, *Royal Instructions*, 483, 482-83 (695, 694). This wording appeared first for Virginia in 1679 (ibid., 483; Arthur L. Cross, *The Anglican Episcopate and the American Colonies* [New York, 1902], 26) and was repeated with variations for a century.

77. Labaree, *Royal Instructions*, 484-85, 486-87, 492 (Nos. 697, 701, 711, cf. 698).

78. Ibid., 489-90 (No. 708).

79. Ibid., 486 (Nos. 699, 700); Carpenter, *Protestant Bishop*, 255-57.

80. Labaree, *Royal Instructions*, II, 487-88 (Nos. 702-4); Church of England. Homilies, *Certain Sermons Appointed by*

the Queen's Majesty to be declared and read by all parsons, vicars, and curates, every Sunday and holiday in their churches (current ed., 2 vols., Oxford, 1683). The Homilies, dating from the sixteenth century, set forth both doctrinal and moral standards for the Church of England, with liberal quotations from Scripture, the Fathers and the continental Reformers. (See ibid., Cambridge, 1850 ed. with editor's preface and notes; *Oxford Dictionary of the Christian Church* [London, 1961], 651; Articles 11 and 35 of the Thirty-nine Articles.)

81. Labaree, *Royal Government*, 117. As early as 1626 Instructions to Gov. Yeardley of the royal colony of Virginia laid on him the duty of "extirpating vice and the encouragement of virtue and goodness".

82. CSPC, 1661-68, 6, 81, 187 (Nos. 22, 259, 664). Among the 27 Acts passed in Modyford's first Assembly was one "against tippling, cursing and swearing", thus bringing Jamaica into the tradition of legislation on conduct (ibid., 261 [No. 882]).

83. Labaree, *Royal Instructions*, II, 503 (No. 728).

84. Ibid., 504-5 (Nos. 729, 730); Labaree, *Royal Government*, 117-18.

85. For example, A. Holt to Bishop of London, 20 Apr. 1725, in *Fulham MSS Transcripts* (Lib. of Cong.), Barbados No. 2 (reprint in Schutz and O'Neil, 447-49).

86. For example, J. Anderson letters (1728-29) to Bp. Gibson re his deprivation by acting governor Mathew of St Christopher for excommunicating a parishioner for desertion and adultery. (Manross, *Fulham Papers*, 277-78 [xix, 162-65,

172-73, 184-87]; [Commissary] W. May to Gibson [1733], ibid., 257 [xvii, 258-59]: "doubts that there is much use in trying to get a law passed against slave concubinage".) Cf. two modern studies of the historical roots in slavery and the plantation system of the social mores and family problems of the West Indies: World Council of Churches, *Sex, Love and Marriage in the Caribbean: Report of the Seminar* (New York and Geneva, 1965); Basil Matthews, *Crisis of the West Indian Family* (Mona, Jamaica, 1953).

87. Dedication "To the King", Morgan Godwyn, *Trade preferred before Religion and Christ made to give place to Mammon* (London, 1685) [iii-vi], including the reference to Charles II on p. [vi]; John Evelyn, *Diary and Correspondence* (London, 1889), II, 245 (16 Sept. 1685). Evelyn notes that the Bishop of Bath and Wells [Thomas Ken], who was present with King James II, "blessed him for" the piety of his "resolution to have them christened".

88. Labaree, *Royal Instructions*, 505-6 (No. 731).

89. CSPC, 1661-68, 92, 111, 131-32 (Nos. 309, 374 [1], 375, 451).

90. CSPC, 1661-68, 187 (No. 664); cf. 180-81 (Nos. 629-32) which throw some light on the emergence of this policy; Gardner, 88-89; Labaree, *Royal Instructions*, 493-94 (Nos. 713, 714); cf. Higham, "The early days of the Church in the West Indies", 120-25. An early "Toleration Act" also was passed in Antigua in 1668 (CSPC, 1661-68, 640 [No. 1902 item (4)]).

91. Trott, 364 (Act of Barbados, 1678); 388-90 (Nevis, 1701); 402-3 (Leewards, 1701); CSPC, 1689-92, 10,

12-13 (Nos. 34, 35, 43, 47); Guttridge, 39; Long, I, 593-95; *Acts of the Privy Council (Colonial)*, IV (1745-66) 73-74 (No. 97: Antigua Act disallowed on technical grounds); Manross, *Fulham Papers*, 282, 283 (xix, 275-76. 278-79).

92. Frances Davenport, ed., *European Treaties bearing on the History of the United States and its Dependencies* (4 vols., Washington, 1917-37), III, 204, 206, 212-13 (Doc. 100, Art. 14, cf. Art. 12). Cf. Articles of Capitulation, CSPC, 1702, 595-96 (No. 968), Arts. iii and x.

93. *General Survey of that part of the Island of St Christopher's* . . . (London, 1722). In 1727 there was "a French church in St Christophers using the Anglican rite" (Manross, *Fulham Papers*, 276 |xix, 150-51|). A description of the Church of England in St Kitts after the whole island became British is found in a letter of J. Anderson, 15 July 1720, in Arthur F. Winnington-Ingram, *The Early English Colonies* (London, 1908), 138-42 (cf. Manross, *Fulham Papers*, 272 |xix, 54-55|). He mentions the French church in Basseterre which had been burnt during the war but which he hoped to rebuild with the help of "a contribution from England" for use by the Church of England. Cf. also David L. Niddrie, "An attempt at planned settlement in St Kitts in the early eighteenth century", *Caribbean Quarterly* 5 (Jan. 1966): 3-11.

94. Labaree, *Royal Instructions*, 434-35, 437-39 (Nos. 622, 623, 626, 627, 628); II, 498-99 (No. 725); Henry H. Walsh, *The Church in the French Era: From Colonization to the British Conquest* (Toronto, 1966), 192-93, 199.

95. Davenport, IV, 93, 95, 86-87 (Doc. 150, Arts. 4, 9; cf. Doc. 148, Arts. 2, 8); Labaree, *Royal Instructions*, 431-33

(Nos. 618-20); II, 496-97 (Nos. 720-23) and cf. II, 499-503 (Nos. 726-27).

96. William Gordon of Barbados (James S. Forsyth, *The Life of William Gordon* |MA thesis, Univ. of Texas, 1952|, I); James Knox of Antigua (Manross, *Fulham Papers*, 276, 279 |xix, 146-47, 210-13, 216-19|), 288 (xx, 92-93).

97. Original Minute Book quoted by the Revd A. McTavish in connection with 150th Anniversary of Scots Kirk, Jamaica; W.A. Fraser, "The Church of Scotland in British Guiana", *The Caribbean Presbyterian* 1 (1958): 30-31; Caldecott, 83-84.

98. Labaree, *Royal Instructions*, 506-7 (No. 733); Labaree, *Royal Government*, 118-20.

99. Labaree, *Royal Instructions*, 507 (Nos. 733, 734); 839-40 (Grenville letter 14 Dec 1752).

100. The classic treatment of this question is Cross, *The Anglican Episcopate*, which is supplemented by Carl Bridenbaugh, *Mitre and Sceptre* (New York, 1962). The Introduction of Manross, *Fulham Papers* (xi-xxii) provides a brief summary. An importment gap, left by these United States-oriented studies, is filled by J. Harry Bennett Jr, "The SPG and Barbadian politics, 1710-1720", HMPEC 20 (1951): 190-206 and Forsyth.

101. Cross, 12-18; Manross, *Fulham Papers*, xiv; Gt. Brit., PRO, *Calendar of State Papers, Domestic Series* (many vols., London, 1857 etc.) Charles I, VI (1633-34, 225 |No. 2|, Oct. 1633). Cf. 74-75 (No. 64), 153 (No. 29) and later docs., on 317, 318, 324-25, 364, 413, 447, 449-50, 545. This document refers to English merchants in the United Provinces and by logical extension to

the American colonies. Laud had no opportunity to make this firm.

102. Cross, 22-25. As mentioned above, the Council of Barbados in 1661 appealed not to London but to Canterbury for help in finding clergy for their parishes. CSPC, 1661-68, 29 (No. 84); cf. Manross, *Fulham Papers*, 336 (xxxvi, 3-10).

103. See nn. 42, 51, above; Cross, 23.

104. CSPC, 1675-76, 337 (No. 789); Manross, *Fulham Papers*, 336 (xxxvi, 11-12); Carpenter, *Protestant Bishop*, 253-54.

105. O'Callaghan, *Documents*, III, 253; CSPC, 1677-80, 117-18 (Nos. 337-39); Carpenter, *Protestant Bishop*, 255-56; Cross, 26-27.

106. CSPC, 1677-80, 176, 590 (Nos. 475, 1488); Carpenter, 259-60, 261-62.

107. CSPC, 1677-80, 117-18, 176, 469 (Nos. 338-39, 475, 1264); Labaree, *Royal Instructions*, 489-90 (No. 708); Manross, *Fulham Papers*, 336 (xxxvi, 13-14, 15-16). Cf. n. 72, above.

108. Manross, *Fulham Papers*, xviii-xix, 253 (xvii, 207-8); 259, 261, 268 (xviii, 5-6, 45-52, 228-33); 282 (xix, 267-68); Long, II, 235-36; Bryan Edwards, *History, Civil and Commercial of the British Colonies in the West Indies* (5 vols., 5th ed., London, 1819, facs. ed. New York, 1966), I, 265.

109. CSPC, 1677-80, 590 (No. 1488); 1681-85, 60, 197-98 (Nos. 123, 414).

110. *Fulham MSS Transcripts* (Library of Congress), Barbados No. 29, 3 Nov. 1725, 13 (Manross, *Fulham Papers*, 228-29 [xv, 227-32]); Forsyth, 38-40; cf. Harlow, *Barbados*, 241-59 re Dutton.

111. Manross, *Fulham Papers*, 250-51 (xvii, 141-42, 147-48) and passim to 260-61 (xviii, 37-38, 53-54); 281-84 (xix, 245-

46, 247-48, 263-64, 275-76, 278-79; xx, 5-6, 9-10, 11-12).

112. *Fulham MSS Transcripts*, Barbados No. 29. 13-14 (Manross, *Fulham Papers*, 228-29 [xv, 227-32]); Forsyth, 40-44; Bp. Robinson's Commission, 7 Mar. 1715/16, Manross, *Fulham Papers*, 222 (xv, 137-38).

113. Bennett, "The SPG and Barbadian politics, 1710-1720", 192-200; Forsyth, 1-31; Manross, *Fulham Papers*, xvi-xvii.

114. Bennett, "The SPG and Barbadian politics, 1710-1720", 195-96. The second bishop was to be located in Jamaica, assisted financially by the allotment to the SPG of 550 acres of Roman Catholic Church lands on St Christopher conquered from the French.

115. Manross, *Fulham Papers*, 222 (xv, 129-32, 133-34, 135-36); Bennett, "The SPG and Barbadian politics, 1710-1720", 196-200.

116. Manross, *Fulham Papers*, xvi, 225 (xv, 201-2).

117. Manross, *Fulham Papers*, 222-23, 225-26, 228 (xv, 139-40, 141-42, 143-48, 184-85, 201-2, 217-22); Labaree, *Royal Government*, 116-17; Bennett, "The SPG and Barbadian politics, 1710-1720", 200-203; Forsyth, 45-73. Cf. comments of Gov. Worsley (Lowther's successor), Manross, *Fulham Papers*, 229, 230 (xv, 243-44, 257-58).

118. Trott, 413, 379; Manross, *Fulham Papers*, 260-61 (xviii, 23-26, 39-44, 45-52); Sherlock's Report 1759, O'Callaghan, *Documents*, VII, 368. Cf. Manross, *Fulham Papers*, 221 (xv, 100-117, 120-21 [Bahamas, 1795]).

119. Trott, 379; Manross, *Fulham Papers*, 249, 251, 257 (xvii, 105-6, 147-48, 272-73); 263-65 (xviii, 97-99, 100-101, 102-3, 107-8, 112-21, 125).

120. Edwards, I, 265. This is lifted almost word for word from Long's account of the Jamaica clergy (II, ch. 10, 234-40, esp. 235-36).
121. *Fulham MSS Transcripts*, Barbados, Nos. 1, 29; Manross, *Fulham Papers*, 224, 228 (xv, 163-64, 168-69, 217-22, 227-32); Cross, App. A, docs. IV, 1-3 (279-82).
122. Cross, App. A, docs. V and VI (283-309) and ch. 3 (52-87, esp. 53-55); Manross, *Fulham Papers*, 337-38 (xxxvi, 61-112); Labaree, *Royal Instructions*, 490-91 (No. 709); Bennett, "The SPG and Barbadian politics, 1710-1720", 205-6; Forsyth, 73-79.
123. Sherlock's Report, O'Callaghan, *Documents*, VII, 360-69; Edward F. Carpenter, *Thomas Sherlock* (London, 1936), 191-230; Cross, 58-59, 112-38, 245-47; Bridenbaugh, *Mitre and Sceptre*, 53, 90-115.
124. Cross, chs. 6-9, 11; Bridenbaugh, *Mitre and Sceptre*, passim.
125. Cross, ch. 10. Cross, ignoring the West Indian colonies entirely (except for Gordon's letter re the historical background of the Bishop of London's authority), fails to appreciate the strength of the doubts among Anglican laymen (and some clergy as well) about the establishment of an American episcopate. These doubts concerned church discipline, disturbance of ecclesiastical functions already secularized in the colonies, and the financial cost. Cf. the quotation from the *Virginia Gazette*, 4 July 1771, included in *An Address from the Clergy of New York and New Jersey to the Episcopalians of Virginia*, re-quoted by Cross (237-38); Bridenbaugh, *Mitre and Sceptre*, 208, 315-23.
126. Manross, *Fulham Papers*, 284 (xx, 11-12; cf. 5-6, 9-10); cf. also 283 (xix, 280).
127. O'Callaghan, *Documents*, V, 29-30.
128. Cf. *Dictionary of National Biography*, XVII, 23-26 ("Robinson, John"). (I find no full-length biography of this bishop.)
129. Manross, *Fulham Papers*, 240 (xvi, 185-86, 195-96); 264, 267, 269 (xviii, 104-5, 157-58, 159-60, 242); 289-90, 293 (xx, 118-19, 179-80, 188-89); cf. 294 (xx, 202-3, Bp. Howley in 1818). Porteous was not timid about disciplining clergy in England: cf. Robert Hodgson, *The Life of the Right Reverend Beilby Porteous* (London, 1812), 142-48, 266-74.
130. A. Holt to Bp. of London (Fulham Mss. Barbados, No. 128, 21 Dec. 1727) printed in Schutz and O'Neil, 450-52.
131. Some of these are mentioned in J. Harry Bennett Jr, "The Society for the Propagation of the Gospel's plantations and the emancipation crisis", in *British Humanitarianism*, edited by Samuel C. McCulloch (Philadelphia, 1950), 23-27.
132. In a series of monographs originating at the University of California, including Frank J. Klingberg, "British humanitarianism at Codrington", JNH 23 (1938): 451-68; Frank J. Klingberg, ed., *Codrington Chronicle* (Univ. of Calif. Pub. in Hist. No. 37, Berkeley, 1949); Bennett, *Bondsmen and Bishops*, and his articles "The SPG and Barbadian politics, 1710-1720", and "The Society for the Propagation of the Gospel's plantations and the emancipation crisis".
133. Vincent T. Harlow, *Christopher Codrington, 1668-1710* (Oxford, 1928), 1-109.
134. William O.B. Allen and E. McClure, *Two Hundred Years: The History of the*

Society for Promoting Christian Knowledge,
1698-1898 (London, 1898; reprint
1970), 1-61, 224-57; Thompson, 3-34;
Hans Cnattingius, *Bishops and Societies:*
A Study of Anglican Colonial and
Missionary Expansion (London, 1950), 7-
27, 38-44; The Society for the
Propagation of the Gospel in Foreign
Parts, A *Collection of Papers, Printed by*
order of the Society (London, 1706);
Humphreys.

135. As first pub. by SPG in Pascoe, 197;
Harlow, *Christopher Codrington,* App. A,
218; Nina Langley, *Christopher*
Codrington and his College (London,
1964), f.p. 17 (facs. of MS at Bodleian
Library).

136. William Gordon, A *Sermon Preach'd at*
the Funeral of the Honourable Colonel
Christopher Codrington (London, 1710);
John A. Schutz, "Christopher
Codrington's will: launching the SPG
into the Barbadian sugar business",
Pacific Historical Review 15 (1946): 192-200;
Harlow, *Christopher Codrington,* 147-214.

137. Humphreys, 236-39; Frank J. Klingberg, *Anglican Humanitarianism*
(Philadelphia, 1940), 121-31;
Klingberg, *The Carolina Chronicle of Dr*
Francis Le Jau, 1706-1717 (Univ. of
Calif. Pub. in Hist. Vol. 53, Berkeley,
1956), 7, 19, 22, 24, 26, 50, 52, 57, 69,
76-77. SPG Letters "A" Series (mfm of
MSS. letter-books 1702-1737,
available at Toronto Univ. Lib.,
and in transcript at Library of Congress)
contain extensive correspondence
from both Neau and Le Jau, beginning with Letter CVI (Neau to Hodges,
10 July 1703).

138. [William Fleetwood], A *Sermon Preached*
before the Society for the Propagation of the
Gospel in Foreign Parts . . . by the Right

Reverend Father in God, William Lord
Bishop of St Asaph (London, 1711,
reprinted in Klingberg, *Anglican*
Humanitarianism, 195-212) (quotation)
211.

139. Klingberg, *Anglican Humanitarianism,*
203-12; SPG *Documents Transcripts,*
Letters [A6] CXIV, Irvine to Bp. of
London, 14 July 1711 (349) and CXV,
Woodbridge to the Secry, 25 Augst
1711 (353).

140. Klingberg, *Codrington Chronicle,* 87, 88-
89; Bennett, *Bondsmen and Bishops,* 75-78.

141. Bennett, "The SPG and Barbadian
politics, 1710-1720", passim; Forsyth,
17, 46-78; Bennett, *Bondsmen and*
Bishops, 78-79.

142. Bennett, *Bondsmen and Bishops,* 79-87;
Klingberg, *Codrington Chronicle,* 88-98;
James E. Reece and C.G. Clark-Hunt,
eds., *Barbados Diocesan History* (London,
1928), 122-23 (catechists and
chaplains as known to the writers
when this official history was
published: this list can now be
supplemented from transcripts and
microfilms of the SPG archives).

143. Humphreys, 245-49; Klingberg,
Codrington Chronicle, 87-88. With this in
view Bishop Gibson's *Two Letters* had
been publicized in 1727 (see n. 17).

144. Bennett, *Bondsmen and Bishops,* 82-94.

145. Ibid., 88-96.

146. Ibid., 84-85 (re John Hodgson), 94-95,
100, 125 (re Bp. Porteous); [SPG],
Twelve Anniversary Sermons preached before
the Society for the Propagation of the Gospel
(London, 1845), Sermon X (by
Porteous); Klingberg, *Anglican*
Humanitarianism, 46-48; [Robert]
Hodgson, 85-91. This passage in
Hodgson's biography of Bp. Porteous
was cited by William E.H. Lecky, A

History of England in the Eighteenth Century (8 vols., 5th ed. rev., New York, 1891), II, 17, and the false deduction drawn that the SPG "absolutely declined" to give Christian instruction to their slaves. Eric E. Williams, *Capitalism and Slavery* (Chapel Hill, 1944), 42, uncritically repeats this, giving it wide currency. As we have seen the Society tried to provide Christian instruction almost continuously since 1711. The particular methods proposed by Porteous in 1783 were indeed rejected at the time but within a generation something like them were put into effect. (Bennett, *Bondsmen and Bishops*, 94-95, 100-105, 111.)

147. Bennett, *Bondsmen and Bishops*, 91, 96-99 and ch. 10 (esp. 106-11); Klingberg, *Codrington Chronicle*, 96, 99-103.

148. Carpenter, *Thomas Tenison*, 348-50; Harlow, *Christopher Codrington*, 213.

149. Thomas H. Bindley, *Annals of Codrington College, 1710-1910* (London, 1911), chs. 1-3; F.A. Hoyos, *Two Hundred Years: A History of the Lodge School* (Barbados, 1945); Klingberg, *Codrington Chronicle*, 106-18; Bennett, *Bondsmen and Bishops*, 1-10; Lloyd Braithwaite, "The development of higher education in the West Indies", SES 7 (1958): 7-9; Langley, 28-45.

150. Michael Craton, *A History of the Bahamas* (London, 1963), chs. 10, 11 (100-121); Manross, *Fulham Papers*, 216-19 (xv, 4 to 68-69). The documents mention also a lay reader Samuel Flavell (ibid., 217, 219 [xv, 33-34, 62-63]). A church was built in New Providence, with a slave gallery, inspired by Dr Thomas Bray's concern

for the conversion of slaves (ibid., 217, 218 [xv, 19-20, 43-44]).

151. Henry B.L. Hughes, *Christian Missionary Societies in the British West Indies* (2 vols., Univ. of Toronto PhD thesis, 1944), I, 126-27; Manross, *Fulham Papers*, 218 (xv, 70-71 to 74-75); cf. ibid., 217, 219 (xv, 29-30, 31-32, 68-69); population figures from Craton, 116. SPG aid had been mooted in Phenney's time (Manross, *Fulham Papers*, 216, 217 [xv, 7-8, 23-24]).

152. Hughes, I, 127-30; Manross, *Fulham Papers*, 220 (xv, 76-77).

153. Hughes, I, 130-35; Craton, 162 and population charts 166.

154. Frank J. Klingberg, "The efforts of the SPG to Christianize the Mosquito Indians, 1742-1785", HMPEC 9 (1940): 305-21; Ellis, 88-89; Long, III, 597; Church in the Province of the West Indies (hereafter CPWI), *Centenary Brochure* (1983), 54. In 1898 an Anglican church was consecrated by the Bishop of Honduras at Bluefields, Nicaragua (Klingberg, 320 n. 65). Meanwhile the Moravian Church opened a successful mission among the Moskitos, as will be seen in ch. 10.

155. CPWI, 42; Narda Dobson, *A History of Belize* (Trinidad and Jamaica, 1973), 159-60.

Chapter 8 The Evangelical Movement and the Slaves

1. This statement requires qualification in the 18th century. The Moravians, led by the Lutheran Zinzendorf, endeavoured to work with the existing established Churches (Lutheran, Anglican or Dutch Reformed). In England they operated first as an

Anglican "Religious Society", and in 1749 an Act of Parliament recognized them as "an ancient Protestant Episcopal Church". (Joseph E. Hutton, "The Moravian contribution to the evangelical revival in England, 1742-1755", in Thomas F. Tout and J. Tait, *Historical Essays* |London, 1902|, 423-52.) Similarly the Methodist Societies, led by an Anglican clergyman John Wesley, were regarded as a movement within the Church of England, although frowned upon by many. In the West Indies the founders of Methodism, the Gilberts and even Thomas Coke, were hardly "nonconformists" at the time.

2. On the evangelical movement see: Gerald R. Cragg, *The Church and the Age of Reason* (Harmondsworth, 1960) 100-106, 141-56; Dale W. Brown, *Understanding Pietism* (Grand Rapids, Mich., 1978); Koppel S. Pinson, *Pietism as a Factor in the Rise of German Nationalism* (New York, 1968), Introduction (11-29); Maximia Piette, *John Wesley in the Evolution of Protestantism* (London, 1937); W.B. Selbie, ed., *Evangelical Christianity: its History and Witness* (London, 1911).

3. A shift in terminology is of significance here. Religious "instruction", usually in doctrine and morals, was the characteristic approach of such as were concerned for the Christianizing of the slaves in established-Church circles (for example, the letters of Bishop Gibson of 1727, the Codrington estates catechists, the "Jamaica curates" (Henry B.L. Hughes, *Christian Missionary Societies in the British West Indies* |PhD thesis, Univ. of Toronto, 1944|, II, 416-18); cf. also |Thomas Coke|, *Extracts of the Journals of the late Rev.*

Thomas Coke (Dublin, 1816), 146 (Gen. Matthews), 146 (John Rae), 149, 199 (the Nesbitts of Nevis), 197 (Mr Carew). Even the 17th century Quakers, assuming that slaves belonged to "the family", had proceeded in terms of their "instruction". The evangelicals, on the other hand, characteristically spoke in terms of "the preaching of the gospel", or its equivalents (Coke, *Extracts*, 85, 123, 126, 146, 193, 194, etc.). Their primary concern was with a personal experience of Christ. (Cf. Benjamin LaTrobe, *A Succinct View of the Missions Established among the Heathen by the Church of the Brethren* |London, 1771|, 3-5; Joseph E. Hutton, *A History of Moravian Missions* |London, 1923|, 178-81.) Thomas Coke in the West Indies preached repeatedly on the "new birth" and "life" (*Extracts*, 125, 153, 214; 92, 212). The evangelicals did, however, go on to "instruct" their converts (ibid., 92, 197).

4. Thomas Coke, the "father of Methodist missions", who is usually critical of the Roman Catholic Church, nevertheless expresses admiration for the French missionaries of the early days (A *History of the West Indies* |3 vols., Liverpool, 1808-11|, II, 326-27) and for Catholic work among the Amerindians of Trinidad (*Extracts*, 115).

5. William Kellaway, *The New England Company, 1649-1776* (London, 1961), 1-16, 41-61.

6. Edmund Calamy, *Nonconformist's Memorial* (2 vols., London, 1775), I, 236; Gustaf Warneck, *Outline of a History of Protestant Missions* (Edinburgh, 1903), 50-51; George G. Findlay and W.W. Holdsworth, *The History of the Wesleyan Methodist Missionary Society* (5 vols.,

London, 1921-24), I, 29. Surinam in 1667 became the Dutch colony of Suriname.

7. Rufus M. Jones, *Quakers in the American Colonies* (London, 1911), 43; Margaret E. Hirst, *Quakers in Peace and War* (New York, 1923), 307; Warneck, 32-37; James A. Scherer, ed., *Justinian Welz* (Grand Rapids, 1969).

8. Cf. Richard B. Schlatter, *Social Ideas of Religious Leaders, 1660 to 1688* (Oxford, 1940), 81-86, 236, 68-72.

9. Richard Baxter, *A Christian Directory* (London, 1673), part II, ch. 14, tit. 2 (557-60), cf. "Advertisements", |1|.

10. George Fox, *A Collection of Many Select and Christian Epistles* (London, 1698), 117, Epistle 153 (New York, 1975 facs. repr. of Philadelphia, 1831 ed., I, 144-45 |vol. 7 of *The Works of George Fox*|).

11. G.F. |George Fox|, *Gospel Family-Order, being a Short Discourse concerning the Ordering of Families, both of Whites, Blacks and Indians* (Barbados, 1671; reprint 1701), 3-23, esp. 3, 16, 23. Cf. Fox, *A Collection . . .*, Epistle 293 ("To Friends in Barbadoes", dated 1672), 326-27: 1831/1975 ed., II, 43-44 (vol. 8 of *The Works*).

12. Ibid., Epistle 355 ("To Friends in America, concerning their Negroes and Indians", 1679), 427 in 1698 ed.; II, 160-62 in 1975 ed. (vol. 8 of *The Works*).

13. Letter "For the Governour of Barbados, with his Council and Assembly, and all others in power . . .", in Fox, *Journal* (Penney, ed., Cambridge, 1911), 197-202; A.C. Bickley, *George Fox and the Early Quakers* (London, 1884), App., Note H, 399-402.

14. George Fox, *To the Ministers, Teachers, And Priests (So called, and so Stileing your Selves) in Barbadoes* (London, |1672|), p. |3|.

15. Morgan Godwyn, *The Negro's and Indians Advocate* (London, 1680), and *Trade preferr'd before Religion* (London, 1685), also *A Supplement to the Negro's and Indians Advocate* (London, 1681), and *The Revival: or Directions for a Sculpture describing the extraordinary Care and Diligence of our Nation, in publishing the Faith among Infidels in America, and elsewhere* (one-page broadside, London, 1682). Cf. *Dictionary of National Biography* (1911 ed.), VIII, 62, and 56-58.

16. Godwyn, *The Negro's and Indians Advocate*, 4-7, esp. 6.

17. Ibid., 20-39, esp. 36; 57-58.

18. Ibid., 61-78, 27-28.

19. Ibid., 111 |127|-35, 40-41, 81-84, 84-85. Godwyn quotes an unnamed "Preacher" in Barbados and also Richard Ligon in support of his views (76-78, 102-4).

20. Ibid., 153-55.

21. Ibid., 160, 164-65.

22. Godwyn, *Trade preferred before Religion*, 26-27, 17.

23. The microcard copy of Godwyn, *The Negro's and Indians Advocate* from Midwest Inter-Library Center is made from Cotton Mather's copy and numerous marginal markings indicate careful reading. Dedications to Bishop Sheldon (Godwyn, *The Negro's and Indians Advocate*) and James II (Godwyn,*Trade preferred*), by a man from an episcopal family, could not escape notice. By two moderate nonjuror clergymen, Henry Dodwell and Francis Brokesby, Godwyn's prophetic writings were cherished and his concern renewed a generation later for the attention of the newly formed SPG shortly before Codrington's bequest fell into its lap.

(Francis Brokesby, *Some Proposals towards Promoting the Propagation of the Gospel in our American Plantations* [London, 1708]: this work includes "A Brief Account of Religion in the Plantations . . . represented by Morgan Godwyn" and an appeal to the recently chartered Society.)

24. Joseph Besse, A *Collection of the Sufferings of the People called Quakers* (London, 1753), II, 306-8.

25. Nicholas Trott, ed., *Laws of the British Plantations . . . relating to the Church* (London, 1725), 366-68; Besse, A *Collection of the Sufferings*, II, 308-9; CSPC, 1675-76, 331 (No. 773), 363-64 (No. 851), 377-78 (No. 890).

26. Besse, II, 324-25. This legislation remained on the statute books until 1812 when it was finally repealed, "there being in fact no Quakers in Barbadoes". (Gt Brit., House of Commons, *Papers* [published 1815], No. 1 Barbadoes, 2: Gov. Beckwith to the Earl of Liverpool.)

27. Besse, II, 309-11, 349-50, says: "By this Act several of the said People were great Sufferers", but produces details only for the case of Ralph Fretwell "who was prosecuted for eighty Negroes being present at a meeting in his House", and Richard Sutton "for thirty Negroes being present at a Meeting", mentioning also one Lewis Morris as a sufferer.

28. Ibid., II, 278-90, 314-18, 330-33, 337-40, 342-43.

29. Henry J. Cadbury, the Quaker historian, who did extensive research in Barbados, has little to report from that location (or indeed elsewhere) in his article, "Negro membership in the Society of Friends", JNH 21 (1936):

151-213. Cf. Thomas E. Drake, *Quakers and Slavery in America* (New Haven, 1950), 18 re Alice Curwen (a Quaker missionary) rebuking a Barbados Quaker for *not* allowing her converted slaves to attend meeting.

30. Alfred Neave Brayshaw, *The Quakers* (London, 1946), ch. 12 (175-98).

31. John H. Overton, *Life in the English Church* (1660-1714) (London, 1885), 207-16.

32. Williston Walker, *History of the Christian Church* (New York, 1959) 444-49, and cf. n. 2, above.

33. Hans Cnattingius, *Bishops and Societies* (London, 1952), 7, 19, 38-39. Cf. ch. 7, above, re Le Jau, Neau and Post, and n. 42, below, re Tranquebar.

34. CSPC, 1699, 424 (No. 766); Leonard W. Labaree, *Royal Instructions to the British Colonial Governors*, 1670-1776 (2 vols., New York, 1935), II, 505-6, 506-8 (Nos. 731, 733-35).

35. Codrington to William Popple, May 1699, as quoted in Charles S.S. Higham, "The Negro policy of Christopher Codrington", JNH 10 (1925): 150-53. Cf. CSPC, 1699, 253 (No. 458) and Vincent T. Harlow, *Christopher Codrington*, 1668-1710 (Oxford, 1928), 123. (Transcription of extracts from this significant letter differs in minor details in these three places.)

36. William Gordon to SPG, 25 July 1710, SPG Documents Transcripts [A6], 69-74 (No. xxviii); Charles F. Pascoe, comp., *Two Hundred Years of the* SPG (London, 1901) 157; Harlow, *Christopher Codrington*, 212.

37. See CSPC, 1699, 337-38 (No. 628); Higham, "Negro policy", 152.

38. CSPC, 1701, 720-21 (No. 1132); Higham, "Negro policy", 152-53.

39. |George Berkeley|, A *Proposal for the Better Supplying of Churches in our Foreign Plantations, and for Converting the Savage Americans to Christianity, by a College to be Erected in the Summer Islands*, repr. in Alexander C. Fraser, ed., *The Works of George Berkeley* (Oxford, 1871), III, 213-31; Arthur A. Luce, *Life of George Berkeley, Bishop of Cloyne* (London, 1949), 94-114, 136-52; Lloyd Braithwaite, "Development of higher education in the West Indies", SES 7, no. 1 (March 1958): 1-5, 62; cf. Berkeley's 1732 sermon in |SPG|, *Twelve Anniversary Sermons* (London, 1845), and in Fraser, III, 233-51.

40. Edward Langton, *History of the Moravian Church* (London, 1956), esp. chs. 7-11 (55-90) and ch. 20 (147-62); Brown, 15-34; Stephen Neill, *A History of Christian Missions* (Harmondsworth, 1971), 227-38; John B. Holmes, *Historical Sketches of the Missions of the United Brethren* (London, 1827); Hutton, *Moravian Missions*, esp. 3-55, 117-25; Hutton, "The Moravian contribution".

41. Langton, 11-62. For their tradition of missionary concern see A. Molnar, "The Czech reformation and missions", in Aubrey Abrecht, ed., *History's Lessons for Tomorrow's Mission* (Geneva, 1960), 130, 132-35; John T. Hamilton, *History of the Missions of the Moravian Church* (Bethlehem, Penn. 1900), 2; Hutton, *Moravian Missions*, 14 note.)

42. Langton, 63-97; Hutton, *Moravian Missions*, 9-11. Lutheran pietism also had a background of missionary concern in the work of Spener, Francke, the Danish College of Missions and the pioneers in Tranquebar (1706), Ziegenbalg, Plütschau, and Gründler. Zinzendorf met these pioneers in Francke's home,

and had even planned at one stage to go to India as a missionary himself (ibid., 4-8, 13-14).

43. Leupold came out later and died in St Croix (Hutton, *Moravian Missions*, 38, 48). Fuller details concerning the origin of the mission to the West Indies, the departure of Dober and Nitschmann from Herrnhut, and pioneer beginnings in St Thomas are told in LaTrobe, 15-16; Christian G.A. Oldendorp, *Geschichte des Mission der evangelischen Brüder auf den caraibischen Inseln S. Thomas, S. Croix und S. Jan* (2 vols., Barby, 1777), II, Bk. i; |Religious Tract Society|, *Missionary Records, West Indies* (London, 1837), 1-14; Hamilton, 3-6; Hutton, *Moravian Missions*, 15-38. Hutton prints translations from key documents (17-21), including Dober's letter in which he wrote: "If another Brother will go with me, I am ready to become a slave myself."

44. Cf. John H. Buchner, *The Moravians in Jamaica* (London, 1854), 37-59, 16-23; |Society for the Furtherance of the Gospel|, *Retrospect of the History of the Mission of the Brethren's Church in Jamaica* (London, 1854), 4.

45. Hutton, *Moravian Missions*, 38-41; G.G. Oliver Maynard, *A History of the Moravian Church, Eastern West Indies Province* (Port-of-Spain, 1968), 7-10. Martin was ordained by letter by David Nitschmann, who had been made a Moravian bishop in 1735 for the overseas missions after returning to Herrnhut from St Thomas (Hutton, *Moravian Missions*, 168-69).

46. Holmes, 297-301 (including translations of petitions to the King of Denmark, 299 n.); LaTrobe, 16; Religious Tract Society, 16-18;

Hamilton, 8-9; Hutton, *Moravian Missions*, 43-46. See also Jens P.M. Larsen, *Virgin Islands Story* (Philadelphia, 1968), 66-69, Larsen, a Lutheran, had access to Danish sources.

47. Even the discovery by a "missionary superintendant" after arrival in the Caribbean that his missionary was in jail was repeated in the case of Thomas Coke and Matthew Lumb in St Vincent some 60 years later! (Coke, *Extracts*, 191-95; *West Indies*, II, 271-72.)

48. Holmes, 297, 301-31; Religious Tract Society, 18-43; Hamilton, 9-10; 36; Hutton, *Moravian Missions*, 39, 48-49.

49. Hamilton, 63, 62; cf. Larsen, 70.

50. Hamilton. This historian gives the figure of 127 deaths in the Danish islands in the first 50 years. Hutton (*Moravian Missions*, 49) makes it 160 in St Thomas alone. Cf. Buchner, 14-15, on the high mortality and early retirement rate in the first century of work in Jamaica.

51. Holmes, 312-22 for accounts of Benjamin, Cornelius and Nathaniel; Religious Tract Society re Rebecca (27) and Abraham (41-43); cf. Maynard, 126-29, esp. re David Mingo (9, 10, 127), and (again) Brother Abraham and Sister Rebecca (127-28).

52. Waldemar Westergaard, *Danish West Indies under Company Rule* (New York, 1917), 159; Larsen, chs. 7-8 (74-101), esp. 84-86 on relations between Lutheran and Moravian missions and the Danish government, also 82-83 re the beginning of the Roman Catholic Church on the Danish islands (as a result of the baptism of escaped slaves in Puerto Rico who were subsequently returned to their owners only on condition of priests being allowed to establish Catholic religious services for them).

53. Holmes, 230-45; Hamilton, 14, 38-42; Hutton, *Moravian Missions*, 117-20. Cf. William H. Coleridge, A *Sermon, preached in the Abbey-Church, Westminster* (London, 1842), 29 n. 6 (a comment by the Anglican Bishop of Barbados on this effort to reach the aborigenes). Three other stations connected with this Moravian mission to the Amerindians – Sharon, Ephraim and Hope – were located within the territory of Suriname. The entire mission was finally abandoned in 1808.

54. Holmes, 331; Buchner, 24; Hutton, *Moravian Missions*, 51; Hutton, "The Moravian contribution", 425.

55. [Soc. for the Furtherance of the Gospel], *Retrospect . . .*, 4; Buchner, 37; S.U. Hastings and B.L. MacLeavy, *Seedtime and Harvest* (Jamaica, 1979), 16-17.

56. Buchner, 27-28, 39, 36; LaTrobe, 17-18.

57. Holmes, 335, quoting a document of 1804 which cites the church register for this figure.

58. Buchner, 36. On the first decades see further: Holmes, 331-36; Buchner, 25-59, including quotations from George Caries' diary (28-30) and extracts from Minutes of Conference (40-41).

59. Charles G. McCrie, *The Moravian Missions* (London, 1883), 1-2; Douglas L. Savory, "The quincentenary of the Moravian Church and the relations between it and the Church of England", *Quarterly Review*, no. 612 (April 1957): 151-57. See n. 1. above.

60. Edward Long, *History of Jamaica* (3 vols., London, 1774), II, 297-300.

61. Buchner, 32-34 (Jamaica); Holmes, 343 (Antigua) and 355 (Barbados); Maynard, 80 (St Kitts).

62. |Society for the Furtherance of the Gospel|, *Retrospect . . .*, 2; Holmes, 342-43. Long, II, 430 opines that "those systems, which are set off with abundance of enthusiastic rant and gesticulation, would operate most powerfully on the Negroes; such as Quakerism, Methodism, and the Moravian rites", rather than "our established church . . . founded on the principles of reason, and therefore adapted only to rational minds". Bryan Edwards however lauds Moravian missions in Antigua (*History, Civil and Commercial, of the British West Indies* |5th ed., 5 vols., London, 1819; reprint New York, 1966|, I, 487-95).

63. LaTrobe, 18; Holmes, 338-39; Maynard, 29-30.

64. Religious Tract Society, 44-50, esp. quotation of Braun's letter to Rowland Hill, 27 July 1785; Holmes, 339-42; Maynard, 30-34; Hutton, *Moravian Missions*, 53-54.

65. Braun to Rowland Hill (Religious Tract Society, 49): "Our time we have here, we spend to the poor negro, and we are provided by our brethren at home, for all our necessary matters outwardly, and when we ever lay on a new place, our dear brethren at home, that is in Germany and America, subscribe by collection from the congregation everywhere, for the heathen missions, and by them we are supported for building, and our outward wants." See Hutton, *Moravian Missions*, 53-54; Oliver W. Furley, "Moravian missionaries and slaves in the West Indies", *Caribbean Studies* 5 (July 1965): 3-16.

66. Quakers and Moravians shared a testimony for peace and against oaths. However, not only Moravians but Baptists and Methodists were assisted by individual Quakers. About 1787 Isaac Lascelles Winn, a Quaker, invited the Baptist preacher, Moses Baker, to teach his slaves at Crooked Spring, thus opening evangelical work in north Jamaica (Ernest A. Payne, "Baptist work in Jamaica before the arrival of the missionaries", *Baptist Quarterly*, new ser., 7 |1934|: 22). Mrs Lilly, a Quaker lady, in 1789 and 1790 actively supported Dr Coke both in Santa Cruz and in Tortola (Coke, *Extracts*, 123, 150). However there was hesitation in English Quaker circles about co-operating with Methodists (Catharine Phillips, *Reasons why the people called Quakers cannot so fully unite with the Methodists in their missions to the Negroes in the West Indian Islands and Africa* |London, 1793|).

67. LaTrobe, 18-19; Holmes, 353-55; Hutton, *Moravian Missions*, 54-55; Maynard, 58-62; C. F. Aldersley, "Two centuries of work in Barbados", in Moravian Church in Barbados, *Bi-Centenary Brochure* (Bridgetown, 1965), 9-11.

68. Elsa V. Goveia, *Slave Society in the British West Indies at the end of the 18th Centurty* (Puerto Rico, 1969), 272 n. 4, cites early sources which give 1774 or 1775 as the date of founding of the St Kitts mission. Holmes, 359, gives 1777 but indicates that invitations to begin work had preceded this. Maynard, 79, seems to clarify the question by recording Gardiner's meeting with Benjamin LaTrobe and John Wallin in England in 1774, adding that Bishop Martin Mack of St Croix then visited St Kitts and reported favourably to the Mission Board. The first missionaries

arrived at Basseterre on 14 June 1777. (Cf. Hutton, *Moravian Missions*, 55.)

69. Holmes, 359-60; Hutton, *Moravian Missions*, 55; Maynard, 79-82.

70. Excerpts from letter of Mary Leadbetter to her brother (1759) in A. Deans Peggs, "The beginning of Methodism overseas", in |Methodist Church in the Bahamas|, *Bicentenary Souvenir* (Nassau, 1960), 2-3; and from letter of Nathaniel Gilbert to John Wesley (10 May 1760), ibid., 3; and in George E. Lawrence and C. Dorset, *Caribbean Conquest* (London, 1947), 20; John Wesley, *An Earnest Appeal to Men of Reason and Religion* (Bristol, 1744) and Wesley's *Journal*, 17 Jan. 1758 and 29 Nov. 1758 (N. Curnock, ed. |8 vols., London, 1909-16|, IV, 247-48, 292); Edgar W. Thompson, *Nathaniel Gilbert, Lawyer and Evangelist* (London, 1960), 1-12; Findlay and Holdsworth, II, 29-30.

71. Thompson, 14-27, including Gilbert's letter of resignation as Speaker (1769), 24; Findlay and Holdsworth, II, 30-31.

72. Coke, HWI, II, 428-32 (incl. Baxter to Wesley letters); Findlay and Holdsworth, II, 31-34; |Methodist Church, Jamaica District|, *For Ever Beginning* (Kingston, 1960), 40-41; Methodist Archivist (Jamaica), mimeographed transcript of financial statement re building of chapel (1785) showing Mary Gilbert and Sophia Campbell as collectors of money, and signed by Barry C. Hart, a coloured planter active in the evangelical work; Frank Baker, "The Origins of Methodism in the West Indies", in *London Quarterly and Holborn Review* (Jan. 1960) and "Francis Gilbert and Methodist ordination", *Proceedings of the Wesley Historical Society*, 27, Pt. 7 (Sept. 1950): 146-48.

73. Coke, *West Indies*, II, 431-36; Findlay and Holdsworth, II, 34-36.

74. This realignment was not immediate. For example, Methodism maintained North American connections for a time: the 1784 Baltimore Conference made John Baxter an "elder" and assigned an American preacher, Jeremiah Lambert, to work in Antigua (he died before sailing). Dr Coke's personal contacts with both the United States and the West Indies maintained a kind of liaison for many years (John Vickers, *Thomas Coke, Apostle of Methodism* |London, 1969|, 98-99 and passim). When however an appeal for help went from the Bahamas to the Virginia Methodist Conference in 1797, it was left to the British connexion to take up the matter (ibid., 299).

75. On the Great Awakening in general, see Kenneth S. Latourette, *A History of Christianity* (New York, 1953), 957-63; Walker, 464-67; Curtis P. Nettels, *Roots of American Civilization* (New York, 1963), 481-84; Wesley M. Gewehr, *The Great Awakening in Virginia, 1740-1790* (Durham, NC, 1930).

76. Whitefield made seven visits to North America 1738-70 but never reached the Caribbean. He did spend nine weeks in Bermuda in 1748. See John C. Pollock, *George Whitefield and the Great Awakening* (Garden City, New York, 1972); |George Whitefield|, *A Letter . . . to a Reverend Divine in Boston; Giving a Short Account of his late visit to Bermuda* (Philadelphia, 1748, facs. ed. 1927); David Benedict, *A General History of the Baptist Denomination in America and Other Parts of the World* (New York, 1848), 701-4, 722-23).

77. William L. Lumpkin, *Baptist Foundations in the South* (Nashville, 1961), 1-20.

78. Ibid., 21-59; Gewehr, 106-37; Reba C. Strickland, *Religion and State in Georgia in the Eighteenth Century* (New York, 1939), 118-19. Daniel Marshall founded the first organized Baptist Church in Georgia, not far from Augusta in 1772 (letter of Abraham Marshall [son of Daniel] in John Rippon, ed., *Baptist Annual Register* (4 vols., London, 1790-1802), I (1793), 544-45; Robert A. Baker, *A Baptist Source Book* (Nashville, 1966), 16-22).

79. Lumpkin, 108, 149, 90-91; Gewehr, 235-50; cf. Strickland, 179-82. Some years later, during the Revolutionary period, Methodist itinerants followed the same policy.

80. Clement H.L. Gayle, *George Liele: Pioneer Missionary to Jamaica* (Kingston, 1982); "An account of the life of Mr David George", in Rippon, I, 473-84, esp. 474-77 re Silver Bluff and George Liele; Walter H. Brooks, "The priority of the Silver Bluff Church and its promoters", JNH 7 (1922): 172-96. (David George, later pastor of Silver Bluff Church, was converted under Liele's influence.)

81. Letter of George Liele, 18 Dec. 1791, in Rippon, I, 332-34; "Account of the life of David George", as preceding note, 476-77; Henry Holcolme, *The First Fruits, in a Series of Letters* (Philadelphia, 1812), 63; David Benedict, *A General History of the Baptist Denomination in America and other parts of the World* (2 vols., Boston, 1813), II, 189-213; Gayle, 8, 10, 14; Kenneth Coleman, *The American Revolution in Georgia, 1763-1789* (Athens, Ga., 1958), 145-46, 312; Michael Craton, *History of the Bahamas* (London, 1962), 160-72.

82. Liele letter 18 Dec. 1791 (as n. 81), 336; J. Clarke letter, 22 Dec. 1792, in Rippon, I, 541 (cf. JNH I [1916]: Documents, 73, 83); Brooks, 193-94; John W. Davis, "George Liele and Andrew Bryan, pioneer Baptist preachers", JNH 3 (1918): 119-27, esp. 120.

83. Liele letter 18 Dec. 1791 (as n. 81), 334-37 (JNH I [1916]: 71-75); Davis, 120-23. Benedict (n. 81 above) also quotes Liele letters.

84. Liele letters 18 May 1792 and 12 Jan. 1793, and S. Cooke letter 26 Nov. 1791, in Rippon, I, 343-44, 541-42, 338-39 (JNH I [1916]: 80-81, 84, 77-78); Payne, incl. text of the Covenant (with Biblical references noted but not given in full as in the original), 24-26.

85. T.N. Swigle letters, [1800], 1 May 1802, 9 Oct. 1802, in Rippon, III (1798-1801), 212-14 and IV (1801-2), 974-75, 1144-46: the second and third of these three letters are reprinted in JNH I (1916): Documents, but not the 1st (I, 88-89, 90-92); Payne, 23-24; Davis, 121-22.

86. Swigle letters of 1802 (see preceding note); Payne, 22-23; Davis, 121-22.

87. Swigle letters of [1800] and 1 May 1802 (see n. 85); Payne, 24; Horace O. Russell, *Foundations and Anticipations: The Jamaica Baptist Story, 1783-1892* (Columbus, Ga., 1993), 9-19 (re pre-BMS period).

88. Findlay and Holdsworth, I, 14-16; Vickers, 131-39; cf. Thomas Coke, *An Address to the Pious and Benevolent, proposing an Annual subscription for the support of missionaries* (London, 1786).

89. Coke, *Extracts*, 76-83; Coke, *West Indies*, II, 437; Findlay and Holdsworth, II, 37.

90. Coke, *Extracts*, 84-89; Coke, *West Indies*, II, 350-53; Findlay and Holdsworth, II, 37-39.

91. Coke, *Extracts*, 89-90; Coke, *West Indies*, II, 56-58; Findlay and Holdsworth, II,

39-40 (esp. quotation 39 tracing the invitation to open work in St Kitts to persons converted in Antigua in Nathaniel Gilbert's time).

92. Coke, *Extracts*, 90-93; Findlay and Holdsworth, II, 40-41.

93. They were also the first to establish a permanent mission in Tobago in 1817 (Findlay and Holdsworth, 220-23), although pioneer attempts had been made by the Moravians in 1790 and 1799 (see below).

94. See Findlay and Holdsworth, II, 174-75 re the formation and changes of Methodist Districts in the Eastern Caribbean, 1806-1921.

95. See below on the first three of these; Findlay and Holdsworth, II, 166-68 (on St Barts); 168-70 (Anguilla); 170-72 (St Martin). The Moravian missionary Samuel Watson made an exploratory visit to Montserrat from Antigua as early as 1790, but he died soon afterward and it was never possible for the Brethren to follow this up (Rippon, I, 378-80; Maynard, 163-64).

96. Coke, *Extracts*, 100-104, 142; *West Indies*, II, 134-50.

97. Within a few years some of them began to migrate to the mainland of what later became British Honduras. On the Methodist Carib mission in St Vincent see Coke, *Extracts*, 104-15, 143; *West Indies*, II, 259-69 (also 178-248 for Coke's account of the Black Caribs and the Carib war).

98. Coke, *Extracts*, 116, 192; *West Indies*, II, 350-58.

99. Coke, *Extracts*, 116-24, 148-50, 198-99; *West Indies*, II, 441; III, 12-15, 50-53, 110-13, 168-71.

100. Coke, *Extracts*, 124-27, 153, 158-60; *West Indies*, I, 413-17.

101. Coke, *Extracts*, 141-64, 189-217; *West Indies*, I, 420-25; II, 65-75.

102. Coke, *Extracts*, 200-202. Of that figure only 240 were in Jamaica, and it was not for about twenty years that membership figures from this largest island began to increase rapidly. Coke reports 520 in 1804 (*An Account of the Rise, Progress, and Present State of Methodist Missions* [London, 1804], 30). William Brown, *The History of Missions . . . Since the Reformation* (2 vols., Philadelphia, 1820), II, 139, shows figures only in the hundreds from 1792 to 1811. Findlay and Holdsworth, II, 82-83, says that a twelve-fold multiplication took place in eight years ending in 1819 when there were 6,540, adding that Jamaica was now second only to Antigua in terms of numbers. Duncan, 156, reports an increase from 2,700 to 9,076 in the years 1815 to 1823.

103. In view of Roman Catholic strength in this island, no missionary was appointed until 1820 (Coke, *Extracts*, 117, 147-48, 202; *West Indies*, II, 409; Findlay and Holdsworth, II, 172).

104. Coke, *Missions*, [30]; Manross, *Fulham Papers*, 221 (xv, 87-93); Coke, *West Indies*, III, 200-202; George Lester, *In Sunny Isles* (London, 1897), 15-16; Alan Betteridge, "The spread of Methodism through the Bahamas", in [Methodist Church in the Bahamas], *Bicentenary Souvenir*, 10. Coke himself did not visit the Bahamas.

105. Trinidad, Guyana and St Lucia were still, in 1793, under Spanish, Dutch and French rule respectively. Belize remained an English settlement on officially Spanish territory at least until 1798 but Coke was already aware of its need (*Extracts*, 221-22).

106. In addition to *Missions, Extracts* and *West Indies* already cited, other examples are: A *Continuation of* Dr Coke's Journal (London, 1787), on his first visit to the West Indies; *Statement of the Receipts and disbursements for the support of the missions . . . in the West Indies* (London, 1794).

107. Vickers, chs. 17, 18 (261-86).

108. Coke, *Extracts*, 85, 86, 87, 90, 91, 101-3, 116, 125, 144-46, 154, 156, 215; Peter Duncan, A *Narrative of the Wesleyan Mission to Jamaica* (London, 1849), 32-34, 121-23. The first Methodist "class" formed by William Hammett in Kingston in 1789 included eight members, five of whom were "free blacks and natives of America", and of the three whites one was a Scotswoman who had spent some time in the mainland colonies before 1783 (ibid., 10-14). Similarly George Liele had an English soldier as well as American blacks in his Kingston congregation (Rippon, I, 334 [JNH I (1916): 72]).

109. Coke, *Extracts*, 144, 195, 197; Duncan, 126, 128-29, 200; Swigle letter 1 May 1802, Rippon, IV, 974 (JNH I [1916]: 88); Thomas Rowland, *Memoirs of the late Rev. Isaac Bradnack* (London, 1835), 26.

110. Buchner, 42-43, 46-47 (Jamaica); Maynard, 10 (Danish), 34-37 (Antigua).

111. Maynard, 82-86 (St Kitts), 62-64 (Barbados).

112. Coke, *West Indies*, II, 174-77; Holmes, 451-52; Maynard, 98-102 (cf. 62-63); [Moravian MSS at Montgomery Church, Tobago], *History of the Commencement and Progress of the Brethren's Mission in the island of Tobago,* [1857?], 1-4 (incl. quotations from Bro. Church).

113. Moravian General Synod returns of 1789 gave 6,690 for the Danish West Indies, 6,820 for the British (Hutton, *Moravian Missions*, 202). (See Tables 2 and 3.) (For the BWI a round figure of 30,000 evangelicals.)

114. Population figures (many of them estimates) in Edwards, may be collated shown in Table 4. Edwards adds that the Jamaica population had increased (as of 1797) and that loyalist immigration from America to the

Table 2 (*See n.* 113)

Antigua (1799)	11, 000	(Maynard, 37)
St Kitts (1800)	2,000	(Hutton, *Moravian Missions*, 55)
Barbados (1800)	150	(Maynard, 64)
Jamaica (1800)	150	Estimate: cf. Hutton, 207; Osborne and Johnston, *Coastlands and Islands*, 50)
Total	13,300	

Table 3 (*See n.* 113)

Danish islands (1794)	9, 345	(Maynard, 10; but there were more by 1800)
Moravians in the Caribbean at least	22, 495	
Methodists (1803-4)	14, 376	(Coke, *Missions*: see n. 104 above)
Baptists (1802)	2, 010	(Swigle letter Oct. 1802 in Rippon, IV, 1145-46)
Total	38, 881	

Table 4 (*See n.* 114)

	Whites	Free Coloured Negroes	Free Black Slaves	Date of figures and page no. [vol.1]
Jamaica	30,000	10,000	250,000	"at this time (1791)", 284
Barbados	16,167	838	62,115	1786, 346
Grenada	1,200	1,115	23,926	"this time", 1787, 1785, 386-407
St Vincent	1,450	–	11,853	"last return" 428
Dominica	1,236	445	14,967	"last return" 444
St Kitts	4,000	300	26,000	"present", 467
Nevis	600	–	10,000	"present", 470
Antigua	2,500	–	37,000	1774, 485
Montserrat	1,300	–	10,000	1787?, 498
Virgin Is.	1,200	–	9,000	1787, 504
Bahamas	2,052	–	2,241	1773, 515
Total	64,923	12,698	457,902	

Bahamas had added to the numbers there. He also mentions "20 to 30 families" of Caribs in Dominica (1,420); the Maroons in Jamaica (1,400 in 1791, 284) and Black Caribs in St Vincent (2,000 in 1763). The last two groups suffered exile before the end of the century.

115. Latourette, A *History of Christianity*, 1031-35. It is interesting that the earliest and most widespread evangelical missionary agencies in the West Indies, the Moravian and the Methodist, both operated for about thirty years (1731-60 and 1784-1813

respectively) under the almost single-handed leadership of pioneers (Zinzendorf and Coke) in newly formed church bodies (the Herrnhut *Unitas Fratrum* and the Methodist Confer-ence): Hutton, *Moravian Missions*, 167-86; Vickers, 131-72; Findlay and Holdsworth, I, 36-55.

116. Hughes, I, 261-62; Manross, *Fulham Papers*, 286-87 (xx, 86-87, 88); Henry B. Foster, *Rise and Progress of Wesleyan-Methodism in Jamaica* (London, 1881), 6-8 re Richard Munn (who died within a few weeks). On the origin of the Slave Conversion Society from the redirec-

tion of the Boyle bequest, see Bielby Porteous, A *Letter to the Governors, Legislatures, and Proprietors of Plantations, in the British West-India Islands* (London, 1808); Robert Hodgson, *The Life of . . . Bielby Porteous* (London, 1811; reprint 1821), 111-16; William Brown, 532-33.

117. It did receive support, however, from well-known figures who also worked with evangelical bodies, such as Wilberforce, Hannah More, and in the West Indies the Revd J.M. Trew (Hughes, I, 269-70, 257).

118. Manross, *Fulham Papers*, 293 (xx, 179-80); cf. p. 240 (xvi, 195-96).

119. Hodgson, 222-25; Thomas Clarkson, *History of the Rise, Progress and Accomplishment of the Abolition of the African Slave Trade by the British Parliament* (2 vols., Philadelphia, 1808; reprint London, 1968), I, 223-24, 226, 236; Folarin O. Shyllon, *James Ramsay, the Unknown Abolitionist* (Edinburgh, 1977), 18-20.

120. Manross, *Fulham Papers*, 240 (xvi, 199-94); Incorporated Society for the Conversion and Religious Instruction and Education of the Negroe Slaves in the British West India Islands, *Report From July to December* 1823 (London, 1824); Alfred Caldecott, *The Church in the West Indies* (London, 1898), 87; Hughes, I, 262-68.

121. William Brown, *History of the Christian Missions of the Sixteenth, Seventeenth, Eighteenth and Nineteenth Centuries* (3 vols., London, 1864), I, 437 n. 1; Coke, West Indies, I, 443-44; George Robson, *Missions of the United Presbyterian Church: The Story of our Jamaica Mission with Sketch of our Trinidad Mission* (Edinburgh, 1894), 25-26; Findlay and Holdsworth, I, 443-53.

122. Paul B. Beatty Jr, *A History of the Lutheran Church in Guyana* (South Pasadena, Calif., 1970), 3-29; Dale A. Bisnauth, A *Short History of the Guyana Presbyterian Church* (Georgetown, 1979), 10-11.

123. Findlay and Holdsworth, II, 274-75, 211-13.

124. Until 1814 in Tobago, 1825 in Trinidad. See Thomas Adam, *The Missionary's Appeal to the Religious Public* (London, 1824); Richard Lovett, *The History of the London Missionary Society, 1795-1895* (2 vols., London, 1899), II, 315-18.

125. Lovett, II, 319-39.

126. John Wray letter, quoted in Lovett, II, 338. In Berbice Wray had responded to Governor Murray's disapproval of such teaching by saying that he would continue with it unless officially forbidden (ibid., II, 330).

127. Findlay and Holdsworth, II, 275-85.

128. Ibid., II, 213-20; cf. n. 124 above; Eric E. Williams, ed., *Documents on British West Indian History, 1807-1833* (Port-of-Spain, 1952), 241, 243-44 (docs. 370, 374, 376, 377, 378).

129. Gertrude Carmichael, *History of the West Indian Islands of Trinidad and Tobago* (London, 1961), 136.

130. *Trinidad Baptist Messenger* 23 (Aug.-Sept. 1948): reprint of an article first published in the *Messenger* in 1929 by Pastor Marcus Mitchell of Fifth Company Baptist Church; "PM for Baptist 150th Anniversary", *Trinidad Guardian*, 17 May 1966. Cf. the following contemporary observers: James McQueen [hostile], *The West India Colonies* (1825; reprint New York, 1969), 164-68; George Truman, J. Jackson and T.B. Longstreth [Quaker], *Narrative of a Visit to the West Indies in 1840 and 1841* (Philadelphia, 1844), 84-108.

131. Adam, 25-27, 40 (text of Woodford's letter 27 Nov. 1819 on 26); Lovett, 318.

132. Cf. nn. 81-87, above; John Clarke,
     Memorials of Baptist Missionaries in Jamaica
     (London and Kingston, 1869), 18-29
     (Baker's account 1803 and letter and S.
     Vaughn's letter 1802, also 68-69) John
     Clark (as distinguished from John
     Clarke, above) in John Clark, W. Dendy
     and J.M. Phillippo, *The Voice of Jubilee*
     (London, 1865), 30-39.

133. Clark, Dendy, Phillippo, 40-48, 141-43
     (Rowe letter, 1 May 1816), 150-51
     (Coultart letter 12 Aug. 1817); *The
     American Baptist Magazine and Missionary
     Intelligencer*, new ser., 3 (1821-22), 384-
     85 (Coultart letter: 20 Dec. 1821);
     Russell, 20-31.

134. Eugene Stock, *The History of the Church
     Missionary Society* (3 vols., London,
     1899), I, 219; Hughes, I, 177. (Re the
     CMS as a separate Evangelical and
     lay-controlled missionary society see
     Stock, I, 64-67.)

135. Cnattingius, 149.

136. Hughes, I, 177. Some of the Gilbert
     family retained allegiance to the
     Church of England (Baker ["Origins of
     Methodism in the W. I."], 16).

137. F.A. Hoyos, *Barbados: A History from the
     Amerindians to Independence* (London,
     1978), 142-43; Hughes, I, 178-79;
     Stock, I, 219.

138. British and Foreign Bible Society, *Fifth
     Report* (London, 1809), 256-58; William
     Canton, *A History of the British and Foreign
     Bible Society* (5 vols., London, 1904-
     1920), I, 255.

139. British and Foreign Bible Society, *Sixth
     Report* (1810), 312-14; *Seventh Report*
     (1811), 112-13.

140. Hughes, 182-86, 210; the Society's
     Ninth Report (1813), 436-39, re the
     scripture distribution and collection of
     money for the Society undertaken by

four rectors of the established Church
in Jamaica.

141. Holmes, 348-49; Maynard, 37, 38.

142. Findlay and Holdsworth, II, 177-81 (St
     Vincent), 185-88 (Grenada), 189-95
     (Barbados), 158-64 (Dominica), 135-37
     (Antigua), 141-45 (St Kitts), 152-54
     (Nevis), 146-50 (Tortola), 155-57 (St
     Eustatius and Saba), 166-68 (St
     Bartholemew); Maynard, 37-41
     (Antigua), 64-65 (Barbados), 86-87 (St
     Kitts); Holmes, 334-64 (Jamaica), 347-
     53 (Antigua), 357-59 (Barbados), 362-
     64 (St Kitts); Buchner, 46-68.

143. Findlay and Holdsworth, II, 192
     (Barbados), 179 (St Vincent), 186
     (Grenada), 234 (Bahamas); Maynard,
     64-65.

144. Findlay and Holdsworth, II, 63-132; cf.
     n. 102, above. Official harassment also
     accompanied the opening of Method-
     ist work in Bermuda at this time (ibid.,
     240-53). See next chapter re persecution.

145. Ibid., II, 225-35; cf. Betteridge, in
     Methodist Church, Bahamas,
     Bicentenary Souvenir, 10-19.

146. Findlay and Holdsworth, II, 168-73.

147. Buchner, 47-53; Clarke, 11-14; Hastings
     and MacLeavy, 24-27.

148. Buchner, 61-62, 65.

149. Maynard, 36; Buchner, 78.

150. As mentioned in ch. 7, n. 65 above, an
     official (though incomplete) survey of
     personnel and church and mission
     membership in the British Caribbean
     as of 1811-12 is found in Gt. Brit.
     House of Commons, *Papers* (1815) passim.

Chapter 9 Other Pre-Emancipation Developments

1. See chs. 5, 6, 7 above.

2. Letter of Richard Challoner (coadjutor

vicar-apostolic of the London District), 1756, in Robert T. Handy, ed., *Religion in the American Experience: The Pluralistic Life* (Columbia, SC, 1972), 22.

3. Challoner's further account (1763) in Hilrie S. Smith, R.T. Handy and L.A. Loetscher, eds., *American Christianity* (2 vols., New York, 1960), I, 303. Bishop Challoner had become vicar-apostolic in 1758. Like the Anglican bishop of London he had a general responsibility for his Church in the overseas colonies (cf. ibid., 300). The only change in this report as far as the older colonies are concerned is that the clerical personnel in Montserrat are now stated as "three or four Irish missionaries". Tobago is said (incorrectly) to be "without inhabitants".

4. Thomas Atwood, *History of the Island of Dominica* (London, 1791), iii, 216-18; Eric E. Williams, *Documents on British West Indian History*, 1807-33 (Port-of-Spain, 1952), 227-28 (Doc. 345).

5. Leonard W. Labaree, *Royal Instructions to the British Colonial Governors*, 1670-1776 (2 vols. New York, 1935), I, 433-34 (No. 621).

6. Manross, *Fulham Papers*, 289-92 (xx, 108-11, 134-37, 138-39, 165, 166-67, 169-70); Alan Burns, *History of the British West Indies* (London, 1954), 505-7; Raymund P. Devas, *The Island of Grenada* (1650-1950) (Barbados, 1964), 68, 71-73, 106-8; Raymund P. Devas, *Conception Island, or the Troubled Story of the Catholic Church in Grenada* (London, 1932), 35-54. (By 1790 Dominica, St Vincent and Tobago had been separated from Grenada.)

7. Franco-English rivalry, the spread of French Revolutionary ideas, and colour prejudice also contributed to this event. Cf. Devas, *Island of Grenada*, 74-155 and *Conception Island*, 97-104; Manross, *Fulham Papers*, 298 (xx, 160-61).

8. Cf. Manross, *Fulham Papers*, 290 (xx, 120-21); Atwood, 216-18, 259-60; cf. 126, 130 (Arts. VI, XIV of Articles of Capitulation 1778) and 142-44; Basil E. Cracknell, *Dominica* (Newton Abbott, 1973), 73; Charles Jesse, *Outlines of St Lucia's History* (Castries, 1970), 29-33.

9. Atwood (218) writing in 1791, notes that the French priests in Dominica continued to be "appointed by superiors in the island of Martinique; to the goverment of which island, and to the laws of their own nation, they consider themselves to be responsible".

10. Joseph Rennard, *Histoire religieuse des Antilles francaises* (Paris, 1954), 315-28, 438-39; Jesse, 31, 32; B.H. Easter, *St Lucia and the French Revolution* (Castries, 1969), 1-19.

11. Atwood, 259-60; Louis A.A. De Verteuil, *Trinidad* (2nd ed., London, 1884), 172; cf. R.L. Guilley, "Roman Catholicism in the Caribbean", in Caribbean Conference of Churches, *Handbook of Churches in the Caribbean* (Barbados, 1973), 34.

12. See ch. 4 re earlier diocesan connections of Trinidad, under Spanish rule, with Santa Fe de Bogota and then Puerto Rico, before the erection (1790) of the see of Guayana. Cf. Lionel M. Fraser, *History of Trinidad* (2 vols., Trinidad, 1891-96), I, 163-64.

13. Mary Watters, *History of the Church in Venezuela* (Chapel Hill, 1933), 34, 31, 60, 54-55, 65, 90.

14. Fraser, I, 163-64; II, 106-112, 120-25, 157-59; Gertrude Carmichael, *History of the West Indian Islands of Trinidad and Tobago* (London, 1961), 127-34, 374;

Eric E. Williams, *History of the People of Trinidad and Tobago* (Port-of-Spain, 1962), 70-74 (n.b. important documents in the text of above refs.); Rennard, 356-59.

15. Only by a despatch of 1824 did it become explicit that Woodford was also the "Head of the Church of the United Kingdom" in the colony, although he had already assumed such authority and had engaged in some controversy with the sole Anglican rector, the Revd J.H. Clapham, on the subject of church government (Carmichael, 130-31). As governor of a crown colony, also, his power was unchecked by an elected assembly.

16. Cf. Williams, *Documents, 1807-33,* 33, 36 (Docs. 32, 34); R. Proesmans, "Notes on the slaves of the French", in Dominica (Government), *Aspects of Dominican History* (Dominica, 1972), 163-72; C.A. Goodridge, "Dominica: the French connection", in ibid., 151-62.

17. Manross, *Fulham Papers,* 293, 289-90 (xx, 188-89, 112-13, 114-15, 118-19, 120-21, 124-26, 130-31).

18. George G. Findlay and W.W. Holdsworth, *History of the Wesleyan Methodist Missionary Society* (5 vols., London, 1921-24), II, 158 (Dominica), 184, 188-89 (Grenada), 211-20 (Trinidad); Cracknell, 73; Joseph Marryat, *An Examination of the Report of the Berbice Commissioners* (London, 1817), 101-7 re Catholic slaves in Grenada.

19. See ch. 8. The vicar-apostolic in London complained that the "Monserrato" Catholics "have no consideration or solicitude for their negroes", in spite of their Irish missionaries (Challoner reports cited [nn. 2, 3 above] in Handy, 22, and Smith, Handy and Loetscher, I, 305). Moravian visitor to Montserrat, Richard Watson, reported in 1790 that "there are many Roman Catholics, even among the white people: but those with whom I became acquainted, did not seem to possess any enmity against the other denominations", and that some blacks had asked him to preach to them, "adding, that they had no body to instruct them, since the Romish priests, who had baptized many of them, had been absent above three years". (John Rippon, ed., *Baptist Annual Register* [4 vols., London, 1793-1802], I, 380, 379.) Elsa V. Goveia, *Slave Society in the British West Indies at the End of the 18th Century* (Puerto Rico, 1969), 267, cites an official document of about the same time reporting that the two "regular clergy" had responded to Bishop Porteous's letter of 1788 by attempting to begin conversion of the slaves, "with what success it is impossible yet to ascertain". Whether this effort was because their work was less heavy, as Goveia suggests, or from rivalry with the Roman priest, or out of missionary zeal, would be difficult to say.

20. The British islands became more aware of this *Code Noir* after the accession of the ceded islands, and even in distant Jamaica Edward Long published an English translation and thought it worthy of partial imitation (Edward Long, *History of Jamaica* [3 vols., London, 1774], III, App. 1, 921-34). In spite of this law – which was itself harsh enough: see articles XI-XIII, XV-XXI, XXVIII, XXX-XXXIX, XLII-XLVI (ibid., 924-32) – slavery in

practice was cruel in the French islands as everywhere else (Elsa V. Goveia, "The West Indian slave laws of the 18th Century", in Goveia and Bartlett, *West Indian Slave Laws/New Balance of Power* [Barbados, 1970], 35-39). It was particularly barbaric in St Domingue before the Haitian Revolution (Cyril L.R. James, *The Black Jacobins* [New York, 1963], 6-26).

21. Goveia, "West Indian slave laws", 10-19; Henry B.L. Hughes, *Christian Missionary Societies in the British West Indies* (2 vols., PhD diss., Univ. of Toronto, 1944), II, 215, 222-25; 419-28 (translation of chs. 1, 7 and 12 of Spanish Slave Code given in I, 224-25); II, 429-62 (Trinidad Order-in-Council 1824); James Stephen, *The Slavery of the British West India Colonies Delineated* (2 vols., London, 1824-30), I, 267-68; William L. Mathieson, *British Slavery and its Abolition* (London, 1926), 34-38, 148-58.

22. Local church records date from this year (Francis X. Delany, A *History of the Catholic Church in Jamaica* [New York, 1930], 26). In James II's time Father Churchill had briefly been pastor to Catholics (ch. 6 above, and Long, I, 593-95). Challoner in 1756 and 1763 had reported: "In Jamaica there are a few Catholics. Of late, two priests have tried to settle there, but they have not succeeded in doing so" (Handy, 22; Smith, Handy and Loetscher, I, 303); Francis I. Osborne, *History of the Catholic Church in Jamaica* (Aylesbury, 1977; reprint Chicago 1988), chs. 10-13.

23. See ch. 6, above; Deuteronomy 15:12-13; G.F. [George Fox], *Gospel Family-Order* (Barbados, 1671; reprint 1701), 16; *Journal* (Penney, ed., 2 vols., Cambridge, 1911), II, 195; Thomas E.

Drake, *Quakers and Slavery in America* (Gloucester, Mass., 1965), 6.

24. William Edmundson, *Journal* (Dublin, 1715), 71-76; Joseph Besse, *Collection of the Suffering of the People called Quakers* (2 vols., London, 1753), II, 305-9; Drake, 9-10. Cf. David P. Davis, *The Problem of Slavery in Western Culture* (Ithaca, 1966), 306-9.

25. Margaret E. Hirst, *Quakers in Peace and War* (London, 1923), 536-37; Smith, Handy and Loetscher, I, 181-82; cf. Drake, 11-12.

26. A.C. Thomas, "The attitude of the Society of Friends toward slavery in the seventeenth and eighteenth centuries", *Papers of the American Society of Church History*, 1st ser., 8 (1896): 263-99; Drake, 11-84; Davis, *Slavery in Western Culture*, 308-32; Roger Anstey, *The Atlantic Slave Trade and British Abolition*, 1760-1810 (London, 1975), 200-235; cf. David B. Davis, *The Problem of Slavery in the Age of Revolution* (Ithaca, 1975), 213-32.

27. Davis, *Slavery in Western Culture*, 312; Drake, 21-22.

28. Drake, 24, 31. Jonathan Dickenson, a well-known American Quaker, wrote his brother-in-law in Jamaica in 1715 asking him to stop sending slaves to him (ibid., 26). John Farmer, a zealot who was disowned by Quakers for his "disorderly" criticism of Newport slave merchants, nevertheless elicited the action in Rhode Island.

29. Thomas Chalkley, *Collection of the Works* (Philadelphia, 1749), 272-73. He was not the only visiting Friend in the island at the time (see 272).

30. The dying throes of the West Indian Meetings may be seen in the dates of their last letters to English Meetings

according to the MSS volumes of correspondence in Friends Reference Library, London: Bermuda 1703; Nevis 1707; Jamaica 1708; Antigua 1728; Tortola 1763; Barbados 1764 (Hirst, 314, 322, 325-26). On Quaker migration away from slavery areas, cf. the movements in and from Maryland, Virginia, the Carolinas and Georgia (Drake, 82-83; Stephen B. Weeks, *Southern Quakers and Slavery* |Baltimore, 1896|, vii-viii, 1-2, 198-285, 291, and end map). There were of course other reasons for Friends to leave the West Indies, esp. the pressure to serve in the militia contrary to their pacifist principles (Long, II, 297).

31. Ralph Sandiford, A *brief Examination of the Practice of the Times* (1729; reprint New York, 1969), i-ii; cf. x; Drake, 39-43; Davis, *Slavery in Western Culture,* 320-21; Anstey, *Atlantic Slave Trade,* 203.

32. Drake, 43-46; J.G. Whittier's "Appreciation" in John Woolman, *Journal* (London, 1898), 14-17; Davis, *Slavery in Western Culture,* 321-25, incl. n. 59 on the time of the Lays' stay in Barbados.

33. Woolman, 252-62. He went instead to England, where he died.

34. Ronald S. Crane, "Suggestions toward a genealogy of the 'Man of Feeling' ", and "Anglican apologetics and the idea of progress", in *The Idea of the Humanities and Other Essays Critical and Historical* (2 vols., Chicago, 1967), I, 188-213, 214-87; Frank J. Klingberg, "The evolution of the humanitarian spirit in eighteenth century England", *Pennsylvania Magazine of History and Biography* 66 (1942): 260-78, and other writings of Klingberg; Davis, *Slavery in Western Culture,* 348-64; Anstey, *Atlantic Slave Trade,* 126-41.

35. Francis Hutcheson, A *System of Moral Philosophy* (|1755|, repr. in vols. 5 and 6 of his *Collected Works* |1969 7 vols., facs. ed. 1969|), V, i-xxxviii (Preface by H. Leechman), 69, 101, 19-20.

36. Wylie Sypher, "Hutcheson and the 'Classical' theory of slavery", JNH 24 (1939): 263-80 (esp. 275-79); Hutcheson, V, 299-303; cf. VI, 199-212; Anstey, *Atlantic Slave Trade,* 98-102, 117-19; Davis, *Slavery in Western Culture,* 374-78, 433.

37. Anstey, *Atlantic Slave Trade,* 102-6, 119-23; Davis, *Slavery in Western Culture,* 374, 400-421, 428-33, and 391-400, 432-33, 368, 457 re conservative tendencies in Voltaire, Montesquieu, Burke, Turgot and Jefferson.

38. David B. Davis, "New sidelights on early anti-slavery radicalism", in *William and Mary Quarterly,* 3rd ser., 28 (Oct. 1971): 585-94; Anstey, *Atlantic Slave Trade,* 109-10, 112-15, 107-9, 110-12, 119.

39. Wylie Sypher, *Guinea's Captive Kings: British Anti-Slavery Literature in the XVIIIth Century* (Chapel Hill, 1942), passim.

40. Pub. Philadelphia 1762, London 1768. Cf. earlier items, Epistle of 1754 to Philadelphia Yearly Meeting (George S. Brookes, *Friend Anthony Benezet* |Philadelphia, Univ. of Pennsylvania Press, 1937|, 80-82, 475-77); and Benezet's *Observations On the Inslaving, Importing and Purchasing of Negroes* (Germantown, 1759) which includes extracts from the London Yearly Meeting Epistle of the same year. Later writings (cited below) excerpted Sharp, Montesquieu, Godwyn and Warburton. See also Brookes, 76-109.

41. Brookes, 318-21, 387, 365-67, 438-39, 418 (cf. 308, 314, 319); Anthony

Benezet, *Letters* |in "Documents" section|, JNH 2, no. 1 (Jan. 1917): 83-95; |Richard Baxter|, *Baxter's Directions to Slave-holders revived* (Philadelphia, 1785), |incl. Benezet letter|.

42. On the way the SPG sermons illustrate the thinking of 18th century leaders of "Anglican humanitarianism", to use Klingberg's phrase, see *Twelve Anniversary Sermons Preached before the Society for the Propagation of the Gospel in Foreign Parts* (London, 1845); Frank J. Klingberg, *Anglican Humanitarianism* (Philadelphia,1940), 11-48 and repr. sermons 193-249; Edgar L. Pennington, "The SPG anniversary sermons 1702-1783", HMPEC 20, no. 1 (Mar. 1951): 10-43.

43. Klingberg, *Anglican Humanitarianism*, 39 n. 88 and 35-36.

44. William Warburton, A *Sermon Preached before the Incorporated Society for the Propagation of the Gospel in Foreign Parts* (London, 1766) repr. in *Twelve Anniversary Sermons*, and in Klingberg, *Anglican Humanitarianism*, 235-49 (this quotation 246-47).

45. Brookes, 272-73, 417-18. Benezet also wrote an undated letter (presumably at the same time) to Archbishop Secker (ibid., 273-74). Cf. James Ramsay, *Objections to the Abolition of the Slave Trade, with Answers* (London, 1788; reprint Miami, 1969), 32-34 ("Object. 10 and 11").

46. Klingberg, *Anglican Humanitarianism*, 30 n. 63, 39; J. Harry Bennett, Jr, *Bondsmen and Bishops* (U. of Calif. Pub. in Hist. 62, Berkeley, 1958), 90. Cf. Sharp's comment on Green's sermon in a letter to the Bishop of Peterborough (Brookes, 88; Granville Sharp, *Memoirs* |London, 1820|, 196).

47. Sermon reprinted in *Twelve Anniversary Sermons*. See below re Porteous's commendation of James Ramsay's *Essay.*

48. J.H. Bennett, Jr, "The Society for the Propagation of the Gospel's plantations and the emancipation crisis", in Samuel C. McCulloch, ed., *British Humanitarianism* (Philadelphia, 1950), 15-29, esp. 23-28 re the 1827-31 controversy involving the *Observer*, the Revd John Riland and the SPG.

49. Folarin O. Shyllon, *Black Slaves in Britain* (London, 1974), passim; Sharp, 12-14, 25-94.

50. Sharp, 95-118, 183-90; Shyllon, 125-40; Brookes, 86-89.

51. John Wesley, *Thoughts upon Slavery* (London, 1774), 33, 35, 49.

52. John Wesley, *Journal* (8 vols., London, 1909-16), V, 445-46 (12 Feb. 1772); Anthony Benezet, *Some Historical Account of Guinea* (1st pub. 1771; reprint London, 1968); Brookes, 84-86, 318. Thomas Clarkson some years later was helped in writing his Latin *Essay* by this same book of Benezet (Thomas Clarkson, *The History of the Rise, Progress and Accomplishment of the Abolition of the African Slave Trade* |2 vols., Philadelphia, 1808; reprint London, 1968|, I, 207-9; cf. 164-77).

53. John Wesley, "A Serious address to the people of England, with regard to the state of the nation", reprinted in *Works* (7 vols., New York, 1853), VI, 339, 341; John A. Vickers, *Thomas Coke, Apostle of Methodism* (London, 1969), 94; J. Wesley Bready, *England: Before and After Wesley* (London, 1939), 225-29.

54. Thomas Coke, *Extracts of the Journals* (Dublin, 1816), 61-74.

55. Coke, *Extracts*, 95; Samuel Drew, *The Life of Rev Thomas Coke, LL.D.* (New York,

1818), 133-39; Vickers, 94-98, 169-72; Davis, *Slavery in the Age of Revolution*, 202-8.

56. Adam Smith, *An Inquiry into the Nature and Causes of the Wealth of Nations* (1776; reprint New York, 1937), 545, 547-49, 553-55, 558-59, 567-74, 576-77, 580-83, 595; Eric E. Williams, *Capitalism and Slavery* (Chapel Hill, 1944), 107.

57. Smith, 80-81, 365-66; Williams, *Capitalism and Slavery*, 5-6; Davis, *Slavery in Western Culture*, 426-33.

58. Cf. Davis, *Slavery in Western Culture*, 150-64; Davis, *Slavery in the Age of Revolution*, 48-83.

59. Anstey, *Atlantic Slave Trade*, Parts 2 and 3 (91-235).

60. One remarkable exception is recorded: in Jamaica in 1774. A debating society discussed whether the slave trade was compatible with natural law, morality and sound policy. The negative won! (Thomas Southey, *Chronological History of the West Indies* [3 vols., London, 1827], II, 420-21; Lowell J. Ragatz, *The Fall of the Planter Class* [New York, 1928; reprint 1963], 242, 30-31.) This happened in the context of alarm in Jamaica over the disproportion of blacks and whites in the colony and an attempt to reduce this by taxing slave imports (which was disallowed by the imperial government).

61. Ragatz, 9-14, 21-23.

62. For example, the historians Edward Long, Bryan Edwards and George Wilson Bridges. Cf. Elsa V. Goveia, *A Study on the Historiography of the British West Indies to the end of the Nineteenth Century* (Mexico, 1956).

63. Goveia, *Slave Society*, 268; A. Holt to Bishop of London, Barbados 1725: "the generality of the people here cheapen Religion what they can, & fondly embrace such anonymous

Books as are written against it" (Fulham MSS Transcript [L.C.] Barbados, No. 2, 2, also John A. Schutz and M.E. O'Neill, "Arthur Holt, Anglican clergyman, reports on Barbados, 1725-1733", JNH 21 [1936]: 448). Manross, *Fulham Papers*, gives examples: Robert Davidson, St Christopher, 1734: "Unitarian and Deistic views are held by many", 280 (xix, 275-76); Francis Byam, Antigua, 1744: "Deists have some representation but have not grown very strong", 282-83 (xix, 275-76); Charles Rose, Antigua, 1749-50 (3 letters) alleges Deism prominent, 283-84 (xix, 283-86; xx, 2-3). In 1791 Coke, facing a somewhat hostile audience in Kingston, Jamaica, addressed a sermon "partly to the Deists, partly to the Socinians, and partly to the Arians" (*Extracts*, 161).

64. Folarin O. Shyllon, *James Ramsay, the Unknown Abolitionist* (Edinburgh, 1977), 1-3. Reid's "common sense" philosophy was open to religious thought (Alexander C. Fraser, *Thomas Reid* [Edinburgh, 1898]; Anstey, *Atlantic Slave Trade*, 177-78, 198).

65. Shyllon, *James Ramsay*, 3-7.

66. Ibid., 3-5, 7-9, 16-17. It is interesting that this combination of medical and religious work is the same as Codrington had in mind when he made his will.

67. Shyllon, *James Ramsay*, 5, 7-12, 14-16; Manross, *Fulham Papers*, 285-89 (some 22 documents by or about Ramsay and another clergyman Edwin Thomas indicating the controversial atmosphere of these years in St Kitts).

68. Shyllon, *James Ramsay*, 12-13, 17-124, incl. 18-19 re Porteous's 1783 sermon

commending Ramsay's *Essay* before its publication; James Ramsay, *An Essay on the Treatment and Conversion of African Slaves in the British Sugar Colonies* (London, 1784) and *An Inquiry into the Effects of Putting a stop to the African Slave Trade and of granting Liberty to the Slaves in the British Sugar Colonies* (London, 1784); *An Answer to the Reverend James Ramsay's Essay on the Treatment and Conversion of Slaves in the British Sugar Colonies* by Some Gentlemen of St Christopher (Basseterre, 1784); [James Tobin], *Cursory Remarks upon the Reverend Mr Ramsay's Essay* (London, 1785); [J. Ramsay, ed.], *A Letter from Capt. J.S. Smith to the Rev Mr Hill, on the State of the Negroe Slaves To which are added an Introduction and Remarks on Free Negroes, &c, by the editor* (London, 1786); James Ramsay, *A Letter to James Tobin, Esq., late member of His Majesty's Council in the island of Nevis* (London, 1787); James Ramsay, *Objections to the Abolition of the Slave Trade, with Answers* (London, 1788; reprint Miami, 1969); James Ramsay, *An Address on the Proposed Bill for the Abolition of the Slave Trade* (London, 1788); Richard Nisbet, *The Capacity of Negroes for Religious and Moral Improvements Considered* (London, 1789; reprint Westport, Conn., 1970), 76. Cf. J.A. Schutz, "James Ramsay, essayist: aggressive humanitarian", in *British Humanitarianism*, 145-65, a [not very perceptive] article which outlines Ramsay's *Essay* and Tobin's counterattack.

69. Ernest M. Howse, *Saints in Politics* (London, 1952; reprint 1960), 12-13, 22-23; Anstey, *Atlantic Slave Trade*, 329.

70. Howse, 13-14, 21-22; Davis, *Slavery in the Age of Revolution*, 184.

71. Howse, passim; cf. also Ford K. Brown, *Fathers of the Victorians: The Age of*

Wilberforce (Cambridge, 1961).

72. For example, Frank J. Klingberg, *The Anti-Slavery Movement in England* (New Haven, 1926); Mathieson (1926); Ragatz (1928), 239-78, 384-99, 408-57 and passim; Reginald Coupland, *The British Anti-Slavery Movement* (London, 1933; reprint 1964); Williams, *Capitalism and Slavery* (1944); Anstey, *Atlantic Slave Trade* (1975); Christine Bolt and S. Drescher, eds., *Anti-Slavery, Religion and Reform* (Folkstone, Kent, 1980); Michael Craton, *Testing the Chains: Resistance to Slavery in the British West Indies* (Ithaca, 1982).

73. Works in preceding note and: Davis, *Slavery in Western Culture* (1966); Roger Anstey, "Capitalism and Slavery: a critique", *Economic History Review*, 2nd ser., 21 (1968): 307-20; Johnson U.J. Asiegbu, *Slavery and the Politics of Liberation 1787-1861* (London, 1969); Laura Foner and E.D. Genovese, eds., *Slavery in the New World* (Englewood Cliffs, 1969); Roger Anstey, "A re-interpretation of the abolition of the British slave trade", *English Historical Review* 87 (1972): 304-32; Davis, *Slavery in the Age of Revolution* (1975); Roger Anstey and P.E.H. Hair, eds., *Liverpool, the African Slave Trade, and Abolition* (Warrington, 1976), esp. 1-3, 9, and essays 8 and 9; Seymour Drescher, *Econocide* (Pittsburgh, 1977).

74. James; Williams, *Documents*, 1807-33, 194 (Doc. 282).

75. Williams, *Documents*, 1807-33, 193-200 (Docs. 279-92), quotation on 200; Ragatz, 384-99.

76. "Remonstrance of the Missionaries of the United Brethren in Jamaica, against the Report of the Committee of the House of Assembly . . . 1832",

quoted in John H. Buchner, *The Moravians in Jamaica* (London, 1854), 100-101; Williams, *Documents*, 1807-33, 238, 239, 242 (Docs. 366, 367, 373) re |London| Missionary Society; Vincent Harlow and F. Madden, eds., *British Colonial Developments 1774-1834, Select Documents* (Oxford, 1953), 549 (ch. 6, doc. 16): (same LMS Instructions, and indicating that these were first given to John Wray in 1807); Wesleyan Methodist Missionary Society, *Statement of the Plan, Object, and Effects of the Wesleyan Mission in the West Indies* (London, 1824) which includes Instructions to missionaries 8-10; cf. 14-16, 20-21; BMS instructions (to William Knibb) quoted in Philip Wright, *Knibb 'the Notorious'* (London, 1973), 31-32.

Goveia, *Slave Society*, 304-10, 323-25, concludes, because of the missionaries' "active endeavour to uphold the moral obligation of subordination", that "far from being a threat to the social order, the increase of the Christian missions was calculated to maintain and strengthen the slave society" (325, 323-24). Some planters may have believed this to be true, but the West Indian plantocracy as a whole remained unconvinced. This book deals with the British Leeward Islands at the end of the 18th century. In a larger and longer context at least, the verdict is questionable (as indeed is suggested on 310).

77. Williams, *Documents*, 1807-33, 242 (Doc. 372).

78. "Report from the House of Assembly, Jamaica, on the injury sustained during the recent rebellion", quoted in Peter Duncan, *Narrative of the Wesleyan Mission to Jamaica* (London, 1849), 312, also in R.W. Smith, "Slavery and Christianity in the British West Indies", *Church History* 19 (1950): 171-86 (citation 185).

79. Williams, *Documents*, 1807-33, 184 (Doc. 259); Coke, *West Indies*, III, 25-26 (re class meetings).

80. Williams, *Documents*, 1807-33, 239-40 (Doc. 368); cf. the attitude of the Colonial Office in disallowing such legislation (ibid., 226, 228 |Docs. 343, 347|).

81. Ibid., 229, 234-35 (Docs. 347, 357, 358); Richard Watson, *A Defence of the Wesleyan Methodist Missions in the West Indies* (London, 1817), 53-62; George Blyth, *Reminiscences of Missionary Life* (Edinburgh, 1851), 67-68 re Presbyterian petition for change of market day to Saturday dismissed as "worse than the Baptists". Then certain Evangelical curates sent a similar petition and received an even angrier response: these were the planter church's own clergy. William Knibb wrote the BMS Secretary (July 1831) complaining that church members were being kept from the means of grace, because they had to buy and sell for their owners on Sunday. Knibb had told them not to obey their masters in this matter, "How would you act?" he enquired (Wright, 66).

82. Cf. ch. 8, n. 126 above; Richard Lovett, *History of the London Missionary Society* (2 vols., London, 1899), II, 337, re Governor Murray's threat to banish John Smith if he taught a negro to read, and Williams, *Documents*, 1807-33, 205 (Doc. 302) for Murray's denial of this to Bathurst; Watson, *Defence*, 140, which notes that education for those considered "the lower classes" in

England was also encountering opposition at the time; Blyth, 84-86; Joseph E. Hutton, A *History of Moravian Missions* (London, 1923), 211-13; G.G. Oliver Maynard, *History of the Moravian Church*, E.W.I. *Province* (Port-of-Spain, 1960), 130; John H. Hinton, *Memoir of William Knibb, Missionary in Jamaica* (London, 1849), 45-68 – Knibb spent his first four years in Jamaica in school work; John Clark, W. Dendy and J.M. Phillippo, *Voice of Jubilee* (London, 1865), 140, 150-51, and John Clarke, *Memorials of the Baptist Missionaries in Jamaica* (Kingston, 1869), 70, re earlier schools of John Rowe (1814) and James Coultart (1817).

83. Revd W. Austin, minister of St George's Chapel, Demerara, 1822: "The marriage of slaves is a thing unheard of in this colony, and I humbly conceive this Holy Institution to be altogether incompatible with the state of slavery under existing laws and regulations" (Williams, *Documents*, 1807-33, 236 |Doc. 360|; cf. 235, 41, 229 |Docs. 359, 42, 347|); Watson, *Defence*, 23-30. Blyth, 47-48, tells of asking permission to marry (or have the rector marry) four couples: the four men were flogged and Blyth himself charged with holding meetings with the slaves after sunset.

84. Watson, *Defence*, 142-43; Blyth, 74-77. The Methodist Brownell wrote from the Virgin Islands to a friend in England: "Fornication, adultery, and neglect of all religion, are reigning sins in this region". The letter came to be published, and this was reported back to Tortola. The missionary was assaulted, brought before a grand jury, imprisoned for a time, and had to

leave the island (Coke, *West Indies*, III, 126-27, 130-32 |letter quoted 126|).

85. Coke, *West Indies*, III, 443; Williams, *Documents*, 1807-33, 242 (Doc. 371); cf. 231 (Doc. 350); Wright, 44-47, 52-54 re case of Sam Swiney.

86. Williams, *Documents*, 1807-33, 241 (Doc. 370).

87. Marryat, 102.

88. For example, the Methodist Resolutions of 1823 (mentioned below); A *Catechism of Certain Moral, Social and Civil Duties, Adapted to Existing Circumstances by the Wesleyan Missionaries of Antigua*, Printed by order of the Legislature (Antigua, 1836). This latter appeared in the one colony (apart from Bermuda) which moved directly from slavery to freedom without the Apprenticeship, and where religious influence was strongest. It suggests some anxiety to ensure stability in this time of transition by adapting the religious sanctions used in the old order to the new: "Some men are to rule and others obey; . . . some are rich and others poor – all by the appointment of providence". (Cf. W.L. Burn, *Emancipation and Apprenticeship in the British West Indies* |London, 1937|, 267; Goveia, *Slave Society*, 325.)

89. Robert F. Wearmouth, *Methodism and the Common People of England of the Eighteenth Century* (London, 1945) provides insight into the background not only of Methodist missions but also of Moravians, LMS, Baptist, Scottish Secession and other evangelicals in the pre-emancipation period, as they brought an outlook of hope, personal significance and self-discipline to an oppressed people.

90. Hutton, *Moravian Missions*, 195-97 re C.I. Latrobe and Moravian policy; *Authentic*

Report of the Debate in the House of Commons, June 23, 1825, on Mr Buxton's Motion (London, 1825), 7 (Buxton denies communication with missionaries); Marryat, 101 re John Wray's opposition to slavery although teaching obedience to slaves – "this equivocal doctrine"; J. Rowe letter 1 May 1816, quoted Clark, Dendy and Phillippo, 141-43 re accusations of communication with Wilberforce (at time of Registry Bill); Watson, *Defence*, 144-45; *An Authentic Copy of the Minutes of evidence on the trial of John Smith, a missionary, in Demerara* (London, 1824), 54, re Smith's admission of his aversion to slavery; Blyth, 54-56, 68.

91. Watson, *Defence*, 111-29; *Authentic Copy of the Minutes* (see preceding note); David Chamberlin, *Smith of Demerara* (London, 1923), 56-57, 59-60, 64, 66, 80-81, 92, 101; Blyth, 57-58, 60-61; Wright, 69-70, 73, 100-101, 103, 108; William Knibb, *Colonial Slavery: Defence of the Baptist missionaries from the charge of inciting the late rebellion in Jamaica* (London, 1832); Buchner, 88-96, 105-7 re trial of Moravian Henry Pfeiffer.

92. Buchner, 85-88, 97, 102-5; Blyth, 62-63; Duncan, 289-93.

93. Watson, *Defence*, 152 re texts missionaries dared not quote, such as "If the Son shall make you free, ye shall be free indeed". The story of Moses and the Exodus would also give food for thought. Cf. Eugene D. Genovese, *Roll, Jordan, Roll* (New York, 1974), 161-93, 232-55 (for example 254: "When the black slaves of the New World made [Christianity] their own, they transformed it into a religion of resistance – not often of revolutionary defiance, but of a spiritual resistance that

accepted the limits of the politically possible"); Duncan, 310-11 (observations [1832] of A.H. Beaumont, former editor of *Jamaica Courant*, now a supporter of Amelioration).

94. Williams, *Documents*, 1807-33, 201 (Doc. 294), from C.O. 111/39, Gov. Murray to Bathurst, 24 Aug. 1823.

95. Williams, *Documents*, 1807-33, 245 (Doc. 381).

96. Clarke, 101-2, 107; Wright, 76-80; Edward K. Brathwaite, *Nanny, Sam Sharpe and the Struggle for People's Liberation* (Kingston, 1977), 21-26, 30; Mary Turner, *Slaves and Missionaries* (Urbana, 1982), 150-52, 199-200, 202; Craton, 299-301, 321.

97. Quoted by Charles S. Horne, *The Story of the L.M.S., 1795-1895* (London, 1895), 147-48.

98. William J. Shrewsbury, *Sermons preached on several occasions in the island of Barbados* (London, 1825), sermons VII and VIII. While this missionary's style of preaching doubtless had a great deal to do with the hostility he encountered, these discourses were obviously considered by their author to be normal Christian teaching, and were printed "that the world may judge of the character and tendency of those Doctrines which the Wesleyan missionaries preach in the West Indies" (p. vi). Presumably other preachers were less abrasive, and perhaps had fewer whites in their audience: at any rate it was not until 1832 that other Methodist chapels were destroyed.

99. Ibid., 211-12, 216-33.

100. Ibid., 251, 266-67, 272-75.

101. Manross, *Fulham Papers*, 258-59 (xvii, 282-83, 287-92; xviii, 1-2, 5-6); *Minutes*

of the proceedings of the trial of an action for defamation . . . Bayley, Wentworth, Esq. vs. Donaldson, the Rev Colin (Kingston, 1808); Manross, Fulham Papers, 267 (xviii, 157-66).

102. Charles Peters, Two sermons, preached at Dominica, on the 11th and 13th April, 1800; and officially noticed by His Majesty's Council in that island (London, 1802); Fulham MSS Transcripts, Dominica, No. 34; Manross, Fulham Papers, 293 (xx, 175-76); Goodridge, 156.

103. See the following chapter re W.S. Austin of Demerara who defended LMS missionary John Smith in 1823, also re the Revd W.M. Harte and H.J. Leacock in Barbados (1827) who had support from the newly arrived bishop, W.H. Coleridge.

104. Rippon, I, 334 (JNH 1 [1916]: 71); Clark, Dendy and Phillippo, 31-32.

105. Coke, Extracts, 125-26 (re Kingston, 1789); Extracts, 147; West Indies, II, 442-43 (Antigua, 1790); Extracts, 160-63; West Indies, I, 422-24 (Spanish Town, Port Royal, 1791); Extracts, 212-15 (Montego Bay and Falmouth 1793).

106. Coke, Extracts, 142; West Indies, II, 143-56. (In Barbados opposition contin-ued, and in 1801 the chapel was closed for a time.) Extracts, 158; West Indies, I, 420-22; Duncan, 14-18, 39-40 (Jamaica); Extracts, 163-64 (St Vincent); letter of Brownell, 12 May 1797, quoted West Indies, III, 21-22.

107. Mob violence against Methodists in England (mostly in the 1740s, 1750s and 1760s) was recent enough that missionaries would be none too surprised by it (Wearmouth, 141-64).

108. Coke, Extracts, 91-93, 118-20, 148-49, 189-91 (text of the law 118); Findlay and Holdsworth, II, 40-41, 45-46, 50-

51, 54-55, 155-56.

109. Coke, Extracts, 191, 193-95, 203-4; Rippon, I, 561; Coke, West Indies, II, 271-80 (law 274-75); Findlay and Holdsworth, II, 55-56.

110. Coke, West Indies, II, 356-57. At this period Victor Hughes had stirred French Revolutionary ideas and violence in neighbouring Guadeloupe, St Vincent and Grenada (Easter, 9-11).

111. Rippon, III, 368; Coke, West Indies, III, 240-48; Joshua Marsden, Narrative of a Mission to Nova Scotia, New Brunswick and the Somer's Islands (Plymouth-Dock, 1816), 114-70 (text of Act 122-23); James E. Smith, Slavery in Bermuda (New York, 1976), 189-205.

112. Duncan, 43-66; Coke, West Indies, I, 441-59; Fulham MSS Transcripts (L.C.), Jamaica Nos. 151-56; Manross, Fulham Papers, 265-66 (xviii, 126-41).

113. Duncan, 67-103, esp. documents 73-75, 76-77, 81-83; Coke, West Indies, II, 3-33; Findlay and Holdworth, II, 73-82; Williams, Documents, 1807-33, 225-26, 227 (Docs. 340-42, 344).

114. Lovett, II, 321-32.

115. Findlay and Holdsworth, II, 215-17, 186, 179-81 (cf. also II, 153 re Nevis, where the missionary was called to serve in the militia); Alan Betteridge, "The spread of Methodism through the Bahamas", in Methodist Church, Bahamas, Bicentenary Souvenir (Nassau, 1960), 11; Joseph Marryat, Thoughts on the Abolition of the Slave Trade (London, 1816); Watson, Defence (1816, replying to Marryat); Marryat, More Thoughts, occasioned by two publications (London, 1816); Marryat, Examination of the Report of the Berbice Commissioners (London, 1817); Marryat, More Thoughts still on the State of the West India Colonies (London,

1818). Cf. Williams, *Documents*, 1807-33, 196-97, 183 (Docs. 285, 286, 287, 257).

116. Lovett, II, 333-39; letter of Smith quoted Chamberlin, 28-42.

117. Williams, *Documents*, 1807-33, 236-37 (Doc. 362).

118. Turner, 132-78; Coke, *Extracts*, 190-91; *West Indies*, II, 149; Findlay and Holdsworth, II, 120; Buchner, 62-63; James M. Phillippo, *Jamaica, its Past and Present State* (London, 1843), 347-67; Duncan, 196, 256-60 and 303-4 (the case of Henry Williams), 299-303; Henry Bleby, *Death Struggles of Slavery* (London, 1853), 64-82, 88-103, 316-23.

119. See Coke, *Extracts*, 86-90, 102-3, 146, 149-50, 197, 499, 204-5; George Robson, *Missions of the United Presbytarian Church* (Edinburgh, 1894), 26, 30. Such help seems to have been lacking for the Methodists in Jamaica, where their work was mostly confined to the towns during the period now under review (cf. Findlay and Holdsworth, 93-120). In 1824 however, H.T. de la Beche invited Methodists to his area (Hilton S. Airall, *The Origins of Methodism in Clarendon* [Kingston, 1960], 6-10).

120. Cf. Turner, 19-30.

Chapter 10 Emancipation and After

1.   Eric E. Williams, *Documents on British West Indian History*, 1807-33 (Port-of-Spain, 1952), 201, 202 (Docs. 294, 296, 298); London Missionary Society, *Report of the Proceedings against the late Rev J. Smith of Demerara* (London, 1824); cf. the earlier *Authentic copy of the Minutes of Evidence on the trial of John Smith, a missionary, in Demerara* (London, 1824), which was incomplete; *The Missionary Smith, Substance of the debate in the House of Commons on Tuesday the 1st and on Friday the 11th of June, 1824* (London, 1824); Alfred Caldecott, *The Church in the West Indies* (London, 1898; reprint 1970), 88-89; Richard Lovett, *A History of the London Missionary Society* (2 vols., London, 1899), II, 336-54, 356; William L. Mathieson, *British Slavery and its Abolition* (London, 1926), 146-47; David Chamberlin, *Smith of Demerara* (London, 1923), 76-77, 91, 94.

2.   Williams, *Documents*, 1807-33, 246 (Doc. 384); cf. 245-48 (Docs. 382, 383, 385, 387, 388, 390); Royal Gazette [Barbados], *Extracts* (11 to 18 June 1825) pub. as a pamphlet by Alex. Aikman Jr, 1825; *An Authentic Report of the debate in the House of Commons, June 23, 1825, on Mr Buxton's motion relative to the demolition of the Methodist chapel and mission house in Barbadoes, and the expulsion of Mr Shrewsbury* (London, 1825); *Substance of the debate in the House of Commons . . . respecting the destruction of the Methodist chapel in Barbadoes* (London, 1825); John V.B. Shrewsbury, *Memorials of the Rev William J. Shrewsbury* (London, 1869); Jabez Marrat, *In the Tropics* (London, 1876), 31-37.

3.   Peter Duncan, *A Narrative of the Wesleyan Mission to Jamaica* (London, 1849), 156-67; George G. Findlay and W.W. Holdsworth, *History of the Wesleyan Methodist Missionary Society* (5 vols., London, 1921-24), II, 84-88; Alexander Barclay, *A Practical View of the Present State of Slavery in the West Indies* (London, 1825/1826), App. II (449-56: text of the Resolutions); Francis J. Osborne and G. Johnston, *Coastlands and Islands* (Mona, Jamaica 1972), 69-

71; Henry B.L. Hughes, *Christian Missionary Societies in the BWI* (2 vols., PhD thesis, Univ. of Toronto, 1944), II, 337-43.

4. W.L. Burn, *Emancipation and Apprenticeship in the British West Indies* (London, 1937), 88-104, 118; [Thomas F. Abbott] for the Baptist Mission Committee, *Narrative of certain events connected with the late Disturbances in Jamaica* (London, 1832); *Facts and Documents connected with the Late Insurrection in Jamaica* (n.p., 1832); *A Narrative of Recent Events connected with the Baptist Mission in this island* (Jamaica, 1833); Henry Bleby, *Death Struggles of Slavery* (London, 1853); Duncan, 268-62; John H. Buchner, *The Moravians in Jamaica* (London, 1854), 84-114; George Blyth, *Reminiscences of Missionary Life* (Edinburgh, 1851), 56-82; Hope M. Waddell, *Twenty-nine Years in the West Indies and Central Africa* (London, 1863), 50-84; John H. Hinton, *Memoir of William Knibb* (London, 1849), 111-89; William F. Burchell, *Memoir of Thomas Burchell* (London, 1849), 177-236, 246-87; Francis A. Cox, *History of the Baptist Missionary Society* (2 vols., London, 1842), II, 78-216, esp. 150-52.

5. *Jamaica Courant*, 3 Mar. 1832 quoted in Duncan, 287-88 (also in *Facts and Documents* [n. 4, above], 31-32); Burn, 95; cf. *Christian Record*, new ser., 1831-32 (published by certain evangelicals in Jamaica).

6. Richard R. Madden, *A Twelvemonth's Residence in the West Indies, during the transition from slavery to apprenticeship* (Philadelphia, 1835), II, 5-8; Buchner, 114, 122-24; Joseph Sturge and T. Harvey, *The West Indies in 1837* (London, 1838; reprint 1968); Waddell, 144, 146;

[Baptist Missionary Society], *Freedom in Jamaica; or the first of August, 1838* (London, 1838); James M. Phillippo, *Jamaica its Past and Present State* (London, 1842), 175-79; Hinton, 256-59; reports by Bp. Coleridge (quoted in James E. Reece and C.G. Clark-Hunt, *Barbados Diocesan History* [London, 1928], 38) and by Bp. Lipscomb (in John B. Ellis, *The Diocese of Jamaica* [London, 1913], 75-76). In 1834 in Port-of-Spain on the other hand unruly crowds protested for three days the "Apprenticeship" limitation on their freedom and were quieted only by armed force (Gertrude Carmichael, *History of the West Indian Islands of Trinidad and Tobago* [London, 1961], 186-88).

7. Cf. Hinton, 136-37, 141-57; "Testimony of Rev Richard Watson against Slavery" (1830) in John D. Long, *Pictures of Slavery in Church and State* (Philadelphia, 1857), 407-15. (Watson was Methodist Mission Secretary.)

8. Mathieson, 133-40, 147-48; Caldecott, 89-91; Ellis, 60-61; Reece and Clark-Hunt, 36.

9. Caldecott, 80-81; Roger Anstey, *Atlantic Slave Trade* (London, 1975), 326-29; Mathieson, 18-20. Young had sent a catechist to St Vincent to instruct his own slaves (Manross, *Fulham Papers*, 252 [xx, 163-64]). Elsa V. Goveia, *Slave Society in the British West Indies at the End of the 18th Century* (Puerto Rico, 1969), 190-202 (196 re clause XXVI of 1798 Act); Ellis, 45-46, 55. On official attitudes to religious education see Williams, *Documents*, 1807-33 (in order of date) 232, 33, 233, 234-35, 236, 18, 238 (Docs. 353, 32, 354, 358, 361, 20, 364-65). For one account of baptisms see Buchner, 62-63.

10. George W. Bridges, *The Annals of Jamaica* (2 vols., London, 1827-28), I, 554-57 (quotation 556); Ellis, 56-57; Hughes, , II, 416-18 (text of the Act); Richard Bickell, *The West Indies as they are* (London, 1825), 78-91; Caldecott, 84-85.

11. Charles F. Pascoe, *Two Hundred Years of the* SPG (London, 1901), 752.

12. Williams, *Documents*, 1807-33, 244 (Doc. 377).

13. Thomas R. Baxter, "Caribbean bishops: the establishment of the bishoprics of Jamaica and Barbados and the Leeward Islands, 1824-1843", HMPEC 32 (1963): 192.

14. Baxter, 189-96; Reece and Clark-Hunt, 36-38, 133-36 (Letters Patent re Diocese of Barbados and the Leeward Islands); Ellis, 60-61 (re Diocese of Jamaica); Caldecott, 90-91.

15. Sehon S. Goodridge, *Facing the Challenge of Emancipation: A Study of the Ministry of William Hart Coleridge* (Bridgetown, 1981); Ellis, 61-81; "The first bishop in Jamaica", in The Church in Jamaica in the Province of the West Indies [hereafter cited as CJPWI], *The 150th Anniversary of the Diocese of Jamaica* (Kingston, 1974), 12-13.

16. Baxter, 197-98, 200-201; Reece and Clark-Hunt, 14.

17. Summary of Clergy Act (1825) in Bridges, *Annals of Jamaica*, I, 568-74; Baxter, 204-5; Ellis, 62-64.

18. Revd George Wilson Bridges, who had begun his literary avocation with A *Voice from Jamaica; in reply to William Wilberforce* (London, 1823) and *Dreams of Dulocracy* (London, 1824), expressed the hope in his *Statistical History of the Parish of Manchester* (Jamaica, 1824), 20-21, that the new bishop would prove an ally against the "puritans" (that is, abolitionists and "sectarian missionaries"). When, however, he published the first volume of *Annals of Jamaica* (1827), he was clearly anxious lest Lipscomb be given too much power, 567-68, 574-75. In the second volume (1828) he speaks of "emotions of distrust" concerning the ecclesiastical changes that were taking place, 382-87. In a "Note" (495-96) he accuses the bishop of seeking "possession of the patronage" and of hostility to "the old clergy" (that is, those who owed their appointments to the Duke of Manchester). Bridges indicates the suspicion of the plantocracy of this new appointee of the British government, but his main complaint is that clergy are denied legitimate leave of absence abroad. (Cf. Ellis, 428-29.) See n. 20 below re the Barbados Assembly's suspicions of Bp. Coleridge in the W.H. Harte incident.

19. Caldecott, 92-133; Henry P. Thompson, *Into All Lands* (London, 1951), 166-71; Ellis, 61-62, 65-67, 69, 71-81; Goodridge, 31-54; Reece and Clark-Hunt, 37-39, 70, and 75-129; William H. Coleridge, *Charges delivered to the Clergy of the Diocese of Barbados and the Leeward Islands* (London, 1835) (esp. statistics, and information re state of the Church in 1812, 1825 and 1834, and maps); also other publications of Bp. Coleridge (London, Barbados and Demerara, 1829-1842); Christopher Lipscomb, *An Address Delivered on Laying the First Stone of a new Chapel at Lincoln Estate in the Parish of Westmoreland* (Kingston, 1837); |Rural Dean| Robert Holberton, A *Plain and Practical Discourse on the Duties and Responsibility of the West India Clergy* (Antigua, 1831).

20. Robert H. Schomburgk, *The History of Barbados* (London, 1848), 427-29; Caldecott, 93; Henry Caswall, *The Martyr of the Pongas, being a Memoir of the Rev Hamble James Leacock* (London, 1857), 6-10.

21. Thompson, 167-68, 169-70.

22. John H. Bernau, *Missionary Labours in British Guiana* (London, 1847); William T. Veness, *Ten Years of Mission Life in British Guiana; being a memoir of the Rev Thomas Youd* (London, 1875). After CMS withdrawal the Revd W.H. Brett under the SPG continued Amerindian work (see below).

23. Hans Cnattingius, *Bishops and Societies* (London, 1952), 105, 148-58; cf. also Mary Turner, "The bishop of Jamaica and slave instruction", *Journal of Ecclesiastical History* 26 (Oct. 1975): esp. 363-78.

24. Eugene Stock, *History of the Church Missionary Society* (3 vols., London, 1899), I, 342, 346-47; Ellis, 82. Two articles by J.E. Pinnington, "The Anglican struggle for survival in Jamaica in the period of abolition and emancipation 1825-50", *Journal of Religious History* 5 (1968): 125-48; and "Parties and priorities: the background to the Anglican failure to Evangelize the Negro population of Barbados and Antigua in the years immediately following the creation of the diocese of Barbados", HMPEC 42 (1973): 155-69, treat this time as one of failure in the face of opportunity, because of internal division in the Church and other circumstances. On the other hand Ellis, 66-67, 71, 76-78, points to the important contribution of the CMS at this vital period.

25. David A.G. Waddell, *British Honduras* (London, 1961), 68; Narda Dobson, A *History of Belize* (Trinidad and Jamaica, 1973), 159-60.

26. Caldecott, 99, 118-29; cf. Manross, *Fulham Papers*, 289-93. Henry N. Coleridge (a nephew of the bishop) gives a vivid account in his *Six Months in the West Indies in 1825* (London, 1826) of some aspects of Bp. Coleridge's first visit to his diocese, including the smaller neglected islands Anguilla and Barbuda but not Guiana or the Virgins.

27. Phillippo, published in 1843, admirably reflects the optimism of the first few years after Emancipation. Cf. Robert Young's 1843 visit (Findlay and Holdsworth, II, 352).

28. For the decline of enthusiasm see David King, *The State and Prospects of Jamaica* (London, 1850), 78-213; Edward B. Underhill, *The West Indies: Their Social and Religious Condition* (London, 1862), 252-53, 255, 427-42 (re Jamaica; 5 reports better conditions in St Kitts and other islands); Sibbald D. Scott, *To Jamaica and Back* (London, 1876).

29. Church of England, Diocese of Guiana, *A Journal of the Bishop's Visitation in 1851* (London, 1852); William P. [Austin], A *Charge delivered to the Clergy of the Diocese of Guiana* (London, 1852).

30. Caldecott, 105, 262. In 1872 Trinidad became a diocese under Richard Rawle (who had been principal of Codrington College from 1847 to 1864).

31. The Church in the Province of the West Indies [hereafter cited as CPWI], *This is the CPWI* (Barbados, 1983), 53-55; Michael Craton, A *History of the Bahamas* (London, 1962), 223; William F.H. King, *Addington Venables, Bishop of Nassau* (London, 1877).

32. Lovett, II, 355-59 (Resolution of Feb. 1824 meeting called by Gov. Murray, quoted 356); [William H.] Coleridge, map of "English and Scotch parishes"; Caldecott, 127-29; Paul B. Beatty, Jr, A History of the Lutheran Church in Guyana (Berbice and South Pasadena, 1970), 35; Dale A. Bisnauth, Guyana Presbyterian Church (Georgetown, 1979), 13-14.

33. Fortunato P.L. Josa, The Apostle of the Indians of Guiana (London, 1888); William H. Brett, Indian Missions in Guiana (London, 1851), The Indian Tribes of Guiana (London, 1852), Legends and Myths of the Aboriginal Indians of British Guiana (London, 1880), Mission Work among the Indian Tribes in the Forests of Guiana (London, 1881), and Guiana Legends, Leonard Lambert, ed. (Westminster, 1931).

34. Ellis, 81-98, 147-50. See below re the mission to Africa. Nine decades later (1950) the Society was renamed the Jamaica Church Missionary Society, in part to eliminate the word "Foreign" (CJPWI, 28).

35. Donald Wood, Trinidad in Transition (London, 1968), 191-211; Carmichael, 225-29, 292-93, 427-32. The 16 parishes are listed in The Diocese of Trinidad and Tobago, 1872-1972 (brochure, San Fernando, 1972), 8.

36. John T. Harricharan, The Catholic Church in Trinidad, 1492-1852 (Trinidad, 1981), 105-15; Vincent Leahy, Bishop James Buckley 1820-1828 (Arima, 1980).

37. Osborne, ch. 13; Catholic Church, Jamaica, Centenary Souvenir, 1837-1937 (Kingston, 1937); Hughes, II, 382; Caribbean Catholic Directory (1971), 36.

38. William Clancy, The Catholic Church in British Guiana (London, 1841), 3, 6-7; Raymund Devas, "The adventures of John Thomas Hynes, O.P., 1799 to 1869" (typescript seen 1969); Caribbean Catholic Directory, 29. Clancy mentions still earlier workers: a Spanish priest who visited in 1810, and the French Abbé Du Bos who stayed two years (4-5).

39. William Clancy, Memorial to her Most Gracious Majesty Queen Victoria, and other Documents regarding the Present Condition of the Catholic Church in British Guiana (London, 1841), 4. A priest was assigned to work "a hundred miles in the interior among a Catholic tribe of Spanish Indians, who fled in terror after the slaughter of their padres by the infidel republicans of the Brazils and Venezuela" (Clancy, Catholic Church in British Guiana, 13).

40. Herman S. DeCaires, The Jesuits in British Guiana (London, 1946); Alan Burns, History of the British West Indies (London, 1954), 54, 645. (Famine in Madeira in 1846 brought additional immigrants to the Caribbean.)

41. Francis Shorrocks, "History of the Catholic Church in Barbados during the 19th century", Journal of the Barbados Museum and Historical Society 25 (1958): 102-22; Francis X. Delany, A History of the Catholic Church in Jamaica (New York, 1930), 58-59; New Catholic Encyclopedia (14 vols., New York, 1967), "Bahamas", II, 15.

42. Frederick C. Hopkins, "The Catholic Church in British Honduras 1851-1918", Catholic Historical Review [USA] 4 (1918): 304-5; Delany, 59, 99; Osborne, ch. 19.

43. Williams, Documents, 1807-33, 247-48 (Docs. 387-90); A Declaration of inhabitants of Barbados, respecting the demolition of the Methodist Chapel (Barbados, 1826) [apologetic]; Francis

(Woodie) Blackman, *Methodism 200 Years in Barbados* (Bridgetown, 1988), 25-34; Findlay and Holdsworth, II, 209-10.

44. Ibid., II, 288-99, 430-36; Osborne and Johnston, 180-81; William V. Davidson, *Historical Geography of the Bay Islands* (Birmingham, AL, 1974), 86. From 1840 to 1846 Methodists were also in Grand Cayman (Henry B. Foster, *Rise and Progress of Wesleyan-Methodism in Jamaica* [London, 1881], 59-60), but turned over this work to the Presbyterians (see below).

45. Cf. ch. 9, above; Duncan, 177-79, 181-91, 198-99, 202-21, 237-44; Williams, *Documents*, 1807-33, 248-49 (Docs. 391, 392); Findlay and Holdsworth, II, 86-92, 95-132, 319; Mary Turner, *Slaves and Missionaries* (Urbana, Ill., 1982), 102-47.

46. Findlay and Holdsworth, II, 328, 365 (Jamaica), 340-41; 386-87 (eastern colonies); 351, 370, 372, 391.

47. Findlay and Holdsworth, II, 512, 256-59; Underhill, *West Indies*, 133; Osborne and Johnston, 181-84, 223-24.

48. Buchner, 69-83; Joseph E. Hutton, *Moravian Missions* (London, 1923), 210-13; S.U. Hastings and B.L. MacLeavy, *Seedtime and Harvest* (Bridgetown, 1979), 36-41, 43-45.

49. Kenneth G. Grubb, *Religion in Central America* (London, 1937), 30-31, 90-93; Hastings and MacLeavy, 121; Buchner, 144; H.G. Schneider, *Moskito* (Herrnhut, 1899); Hutton, *Moravian Missions*, 321-45; further information (1968) from Mrs Stephenson (daughter of Moravian bishop of Nicaragua) per Mr Harry Bodden.

50. G.G. Oliver Maynard, *A History of the Moravian Church, Eastern West Indies Province* (Port-of-Spain, 1968), 14-21.

51. Ibid., 41-53 (Antigua), 65-75 (Barbados), 88-95 (St Kitts), 102-12 (Tobago).

52. Chs. 7 and 9, and previous section of this chapter; *Caribbean Presbyterian 1*, no. 1 (1958): 29; Robert Gordon Balfour, *Presbyterianism in the Colonies* (Edinburgh, 1900), 272-73.

53. For the background in Scottish church history, esp. re the choice of Presbyterian church government, the evangelical movement and the divisions of the 18th century and of 1843, see Kenneth S. Latourette, *A History of Christianity* (New York, 1953), 769-74, 1190-94.

54. Blyth, 35-55; Waddell, 15-49; John McKerrow, *History of the Foreign Missions of the Secession and United Presbyterian Church* (Edinburgh, 1867), 245-51 (doc. concerning Presbytery, 250-51); George Robson, *Missions of the United Presbyterian Church* (Edinburgh, 1894), 25-36, 54, 57.

55. It also drew them into a controversy in the 1840s over the leader and ticket system especially as used by most of the Baptist missionaries: *Remonstrance of the Presbytery of Jamaica with the majority of the Baptist Missionaries in that island* (Edinburgh, 1843); see also William G. Barrett, *Baptist Mission in Jamaica: An Exposition of the system pursued by the Baptist Missionaries in Jamaica, by missionaries and catechists of the London Missionary Society* (London, 1842); Samuel Green, [for] Baptist Mission in Jamaica, *A Review of the Rev W.G. Barrett's Pamphlet, entitled a Reply to the Circular of the Baptist Missionary Committee* (London, 1842); Committee of the Baptist Missionary Society, *Remarks on "An exposition of the system pursued by the Baptist Missionaries in Jamaica by missionaries and catechists of the London Missionary Society in that island"*.

(London, 1843). Cf. Wright, 201-9;
Osborne and Johnston, 137-43, 147.

56. Robson, 46-47; McKerrow, 286, 308-10,
356-61; Balfour, 271-75.

57. Robson, 104-17, 133-34; McKerrow,
265-71, 365-66; Underhill, West Indies,
37-38; The Caribbean Presbyterian 1, no. 1:
47-49. Prior to Kennedy's arrival some
Scotsmen had met with the purpose of
claiming government support for a
Presbyterian church "in connection
with the Established Church of
Scotland" (Carmichael, 200-202). This
attempt did not succeed. Then
Kennedy, in line with the "voluntaryist"
principles of the Secession Church,
declined government support either
for building the church or paying the
minister.

58. Robson, 111; Eduardo Moreira, The
Significance of Portugal: A Survey of
Evangelical Progress (London, 1933), 20,
27-28, 33, 37; Balfour, 275-81;
Underhill, West Indies, 19-21; Donald
Wood, Trinidad in Transition (Oxford,
1968), 104-6.

59. Sarah E.S. Morton, John Morton of
Trinidad (Toronto, 1916), 40-41, 42, 49,
56-57; James B. Scouller, Manual of the
United Presbyterian Church of North
America, 1751-1881 (Harrisburg, Penn.,
1881), 604.

60. Lovett, II, 355-75; Beatty, 48; Caribbean Conference of Churches,
Handbook of Churches in the Caribbean
(2nd ed., Bridgetown, 1982), 10-13.

61. George Liele (who came from Georgia)
was an independent self-supporting
preacher who later asked the Baptist
Missionary Society (in England) for help.

62. For the LMS and the Oberliners, see
James Watson and C.A. Wookey,
Jamaica Congregational Churches

(Guildford, Surrey, 1901), 1-24; F. Ross
Brown, Mission to Jamaica: A History of our
Congregational Churches (n.p., ca. 1947),
13-27, 37-44; Lovett, II, 376-88.

63. Lester G. McAllister and W.E. Tucker,
Journey into Faith: A History of the Christian
Church (Disciples of Christ) (St Louis, Mo.,
1976), 15-158. For further details on
the Disciples movement and also on
Oberlin College, see ch. 11 (under
"Newer" Denominations).

64. Agnes Henderson and H.S. Shirley, A
Brief History of the Disciples of Christ in
Jamaica (Kingston, 1959), 8-9; Robert G.
Nelson, Disciples of Christ in Jamaica,
1858-1958 (St Louis, Mo., 1958), 29-60
and
passim; Osborne and Johnston, 120-21.

65. John Clarke, Memorials of the Baptist
Missionaries in Jamaica (London, 1869),
88-113; Edward B. Underhill, Life of
James Mursell Phillippo (London, 1881);
Hinton; Philip Wright, Knibb 'the
Notorious' (London, 1973); W.F.
Burchell; Underhill, West Indies, 430;
Horace O. Russell, Foundations and
Anticipations: The Jamaica Baptist Story
(Columbus, Ga, 1993), 31-57.

66. Underhill, 107-19; Cox, II, 42-43, 48,
50-51, 269-70, 348-49; James J.
Parsons, San Andrés and Providencia
(Berkeley, 1956), 48; Osborne and
Johnston, 222; Inez Knibb Sibley, The
Baptists of Jamaica (Kingston, 1965), 25-
26 (and cf. 23-31).

67. Cf. ch. 8, above. Cox, II, 261-69, 346-48;
Clarke, 124-25 (re Joseph Burton in the
Bahamas); Underhill, West Indies, 16-18,
472-93; Carmichael, 136-37, 230, 252,
270-72. (In the 1950s the "Cowen-
Hamilton" Secondary School was
opened on Moruga Road [Trinidad], in
memory of the two early leaders.)

Table 5 (*See n.* 68)

Church of England	100,000	Jamaica, 40,000
Presbyterian	16,000	Jamaica, 10,000; Guiana, 4,000
Roman Catholic	32,000	Dominica, 10,000 Trinidad, 16,000 St Lucia, 4,000
Wesleyan Methodist	95,000	well dispersed
Baptist	53,000	51,000 in Jamaica
Moravian	26,000	in Jamaica, Antigua, & Barbados

68. Comprehensive Church membership or attendance figures are difficult to obtain and hard to assess in this period. Caldecott, 132 quotes a "Parliamentary paper" about 1870 re church attendance, showing an estimate of 322,000 for the British West Indies. (See Table 5.)

69. Findlay and Holdsworth, II, 320-26; Hastings and MacLeavy, 39-41, 43-44, 91-92; Maynard, 130-37.

70. Frank J. Klingberg, "The Lady Mico Charity Schools in the British West Indies (1835-1842)", JNH 24, no. 3 (July 1939): 291-344. Schools were opened in Jamaica, Grand Cayman and the Bahamas (299-312); Barbados, Trinidad, Tobago, British Guiana (312-28); Antigua, Dominica, St Lucia and St Vincent (328-40). See Maynard, 131 re Mico teacher training in Antigua.

71. British and Foreign Bible Society, *Reports* (London, 1814), 35, and 1817 onwards, annual mention of West Indian Auxiliaries; [Bible], *Emancipation New Testament* (Cambridge, 1834); George Browne, *The History of the British and Foreign Bible Society* (2 vols., London, 1859), I, 158-60; William Canton, *History of the British and Foreign Bible Society* (5 vols., London, 1904-1920), II, 318-32; Waddell, 103-6; [Bible Society], *The substance of a speech delivered by the Rev James M. Phillippo . . . at the reorganization of the St Catherine and St Thomas in the Vale Auxiliary Bible Society* (Spanish Town, 1839). "Bible Thomson" in 1835 inspired what was probably the first ecumenical West Indian Ministerial Association, in the county of Cornwall, with 26 members.

72. H.M. Waddell, 98-99; Buchner, 121; Blyth, 84-86, 98-103.

73. The lengthy and complicated story of the relations of the "denominational" schools to government, interesting though it is, lies outside our present terms of reference.

74. Underhill, *West Indies*, 294-306; Robson, 47, 121; Osborne and Johnston, 150-55; Hastings and MacLeavy, 93-95.

75. Phillippo, 212-13, 477-85; Lloyd Braithwaite, "The development of higher education in the West Indies", SES 7, no. 1 (March 1958): 1-64.

76. Goodridge, 31-54; Schomburgk, App. VI (names of early students).

77. Robson, 47 (re George Miller), 123 (Alexander Renton).

78. Findlay and Holdsworth, 352. See ch. 11 below re York Castle High School.

79. King, 200-201; Maynard, 137.

80. Maynard, 50-51, 72-73, 130-35, 140. Cedar Hall had to be closed for

financial reasons in 1870. In 1854 however this church had added a Female Teacher Training College, which survived for over 100 years.

81. Knibb and Blyth advised them not to accept less than a shilling a day plus housing and provision grounds, or 1s. 6d. if rent was charged. See Hinton, 281-99; Blyth, 87-90; Waddell, 148-51; Osborne and Johnston, 111-12; *Misrepresentations Refuted, or the Triumph of Truth* (St Jago de la Vega [Spanish Town], 1839).

82. Hugh Paget, "The free village system in Jamaica", *Jamaican Historical Review* 1, no. 1 (1945): 31-41, 43-48; Findlay and Holdsworth, 338-41; Wood, 48-49, 95; Beatty, 44-45.

83. F.R. Augier and S.C. Gordon, *Sources of West Indian History* (London and Kingston, 1962), 210-15; Ronald V. Sires, "Negro labor in Jamaica in the years following emancipation", JNH 25, no. 4 (Oct. 1940): 492-96; Philip D. Curtin, *Two Jamaicas: The Role of Ideas in a Tropical Colony, 1830-1865* (Cambridge, Mass., 1955), 109-21.

84. Paget, 41-43; Curtin, 115-16 (Baptist), 114-15 (Methodist); Hinton, 291, 299-302, 309-10, 486-88; Phillippo, 220-29; Blyth, 114-18; Waddell, 152-59; Buchner, 130-31; Hastings and McCleavy, 56-57; Osborne and Johnston, 112-17.

85. Maynard, 47, 110.

86. Lawrence S. Squires, *These Hundred Years . . . The Story of Davyton* (n.p., 1945), 21-27; G. Johnston's revision (typescript, 261-64) of Osborne and Johnston, with data re LMS villages.

87. Wood, 92-96, esp. 94. Also, black "American" ex-soldiers, settled in the "Company Villages", with their own

Baptist lay preachers and churches, were contacted by the BMS in this same decade.

88. Wood, 270-76; Bridget Brereton, *Race Relations in Colonial Trinidad, 1870-1900* (Cambridge, 1979), 9, 138-39, 142, 181; Morton, 122, 315-16.

89. Curtin, 179-81; Swithin Wilmot, "Baptist missionaries and Jamaican politics", in Keith O. Laurence, ed., *A Selection of Papers presented at the Twelfth Conference of the Association of Caribbean Historians* (1980) (St Augustine, Trinidad, 1986), 45-50; Wright, 234-38.

90. Hinton, 491-94 (a speech of William Knibb); *Baptist Herald and Friend of Africa* (1841-44) (periodical); Wilmot, 50-56; Curtin, 181-83; Wright, 236 (re Quaker, Presbyterian and Independents); William H. MacIntosh, *Disestablishment and Liberation* (London, 1972), 25-28 (re "Jamaica dissenters" present in 1844 at the formation of the British Anti-State-Church Association). Oddly, Wilmot and Curtin have inverted "Anti-State-Church" into "Anti-Church-State".

91. Charles P. Groves, *The Planting of Christianity in Africa* (4 vols., London, 1948-56), II, 2-40; Buchner, 136-38; Hutton, *Moravian Missions*, 219. One reason for the teacher-training college at Cedar Hall in Antigua (1847) [see above under Ministerial Training] was the hope that some graduates of this programme might be prepared to go to Africa as missionary workers (Maynard, 131-33).

92. Thomas F. Buxton, *The African Slave Trade and its Remedy* (London, 1840); Edward B. Underhill, *Alfred Saker, Missionary to Africa* (London, 1884), 8-19; H.M. Waddell, 206-17; Donald M. McFarlan, *Calabar: The Church of Scotland*

Mission (London, 1946), 12-13; John A. Parker, A *Church in the Sun* (London, 1959), 69-77.

93. George Mather and C.J. Blagg, *Bishop Rawle: A Memoir* (London, 1890), 52-53 and passim; Church of England, Barbados Church Society, *Proposed Mission from the Church in the West Indies to Western Africa* (Barbados, 1850); [West Indian Mission to Western Africa], *Occasional Paper No. II* (1858); Noel Titus, *Missionary Under Pressure: The Experiences of the Rev John Duport in West Africa* (Barbados, 1983); Caswall, 61-291; A.H. Barrow, *Fifty Years in Western Africa* (London, 1900; reprint New York, 1969).

94. Edward B. Underhill, *The Jamaican Mission in its relation with the Baptist Missionary Society, from 1838 to 1879* (London, 1879); Russell, 58-63; Blyth, 91-92 (self-support declaration by Blyth's Hampden congregation); Findlay and Holdsworth, II, 359-67 (365 re Baptist missionaries having to engage in trade to help support themselves); Lovett, II, 389-96 (LMS 1867 policy of devolution); Maynard, 53, 94, 112 (Moravian moves toward self-support).

95. Osborne and Johnston, 130-34 re details of church growth and decline 1834-70.

96. Findlay and Holdsworth, II, 379-80, 385 (Demerara and Nevis), 374-75 (Jamaica); Hutton, *Moravian Missions*, 224-27; Hastings and MacLeavy, 64-75, 76-90; Underhill, *Life of Phillippo*, ch. 24.

97. Findlay and Holdsworth, II, 374-75; Foster, 127-50, 157-63; Buchner, 144-47; Underhill, *Life of Phillippo*; Russell, 63-68; Curtin, 168-72.

98. Ivor Morrish, *Obeah, Christ and Rastaman* (Cambridge, 1982), 62-66; Wood, 243;

Michael Craton, A *History of the Bahamas* (London, 1962), 188.

99. Buchner, 138-42; Curtin, 32-35; Robert J. Stewart, *Religion and Society in Post-Emancipation Jamaica* (Knoxville, 1992), 110-52.

100. Cf. ch. 2; Dale A. Bisnauth, *Religions in the Caribbean* (Kingston, 1989), 84-86. Monotheism may have been helped also by some Muslim Africans scattered among the slaves (ibid., 82-83).

101. George E. Simpson, *The Shango Cult in Trinidad* (Puerto Rico, 1965); Bisnauth, *Religions in the Caribbean*, 86-89.

102. Ibid., 93-96.

103. Ibid., 89-93, 96; H.M. Waddell, 136-39.

104. Cf. Caribbean Conference of Churches, *At the Crossroads: African Caribbean Religion and Christianity* (Trinidad, 1995).

105. Keith O. Laurence, *Immigration into the West Indies in the 19th Century* (Barbados, 1971; reprint, 1977), 7-8; Wood, 59-65.

106. Laurence, 9-26, 36-39; Wood, 65-68 (re small islanders), 68-80 (Africans), 81-106 (Europeans).

107. Laurence, 19-23, 26; Carmichael, 213-16, 241-43; Wood, 107-14.

108. Brinsley Samaroo in David Dabydeen and B. Samaroo, *India in the Caribbean* (London, 1987), 25-30; Bridget Brereton in John La Guerre, ed., *Calcutta to Caroni* (Trinidad and Jamaica, 1974), 28-32; Eric E. Williams, *History of the People of Trinidad and Tobago* (Port-of-Spain, 1962), 103-10; Wood, 114-20, 277-78.

109. Findlay and Holdsworth, II, 271, 272-73, 377-78, 417.

110. Three congregations in the Southern Caribbean have built churches named "Susamachar" – the Hindi word for "good news" or "gospel". One is

Methodist, in Guyana; one Presbyterian, in Trinidad; and one Moravian, in Suriname.

111. Bisnauth, *Guyana Presbyterian Church*, 17.
112. John T. Harricharan, *The Work of the Christian Churches among the East Indians in Trinidad* (Trinidad, 1976), 21; Carmichael, 280; "The story of St Mary's Children's Home", in *The Diocese of Trinidad and Tobago, 1872-1972*, 55-57).
113. Caldecott, 135. He adds (141-42) that there seemed to be no local pressure for the change, in spite of having mentioned (123) the difficulties in Trinidad over the 1844 Ordinance.
114. MacIntosh, 191-95; S.M. Ingham, "The Disestablishment Movement in England, 1868-74", *Journal of Religious History* [Australia] 3 (1964): 38-60.
115. Cf. nn. 35, 36, above; Louis A.A. De Verteuil, *Trinidad* (London, Paris and New York, 1884), 26-28, 156, 172, 454-63; Anthony De Verteuil, *Sir Louis De Verteuil: His Life and Times* (Trinidad, 1973), 145-61; Augier and Gordon, 233-34 (Docs. 7cd).
116. Ibid., 232-33 (Doc. 7b).
117. Craton, 211, 214, 222, 241-42; MacIntosh, 197-98.
118. Curtin, 182-84; cf. nn. 89, 90 above.
119. MacIntosh, 192 n. 2; Mavis C. Campbell, *The Dynamics of Change in a Slave Society* (Rutherford and London, 1976), 234, 277, 279; Walter Adolphe Roberts, *Six Great Jamaicans* (Kingston, 1951), 49, 24-47.
120. Findlay and Holdsworth, II, 388-89 (re St Vincent); Edward B. Underhill, *A Letter addressed to the Rt. Honourable M. Cardwell, with illustrative documents on the condition of Jamaica* (London, 1865) and also his *The Tragedy of Morant Bay*

(London, 1895); William L. Mathieson, *The Sugar Colonies and Governor Eyre* (London, 1936); Gad J. Heuman, *The Killing Time: The Morant Bay Rebellion in Jamaica* (London, 1994), esp. chs. 3-6 (also 179-80) re the long tradition of protest and religious motivation leading to the rebellion; Stewart, 153-89.
121. Caldecott, 118-29, 134-47.

Chapter 11 The Late Colonial Period

1. Cf. F.R. Augier and Shirley C. Gordon, *Sources of West Indian History* (London, 1962), 109-40.
2. Dale A. Bisnauth, *Religions in the Caribbean* (Kingston 1989), 180 (Kumina), 180-85 (Jordanites); Maureen Warner-Lewis, *Guinea's Other Suns: The African Dynamic in Trinidad Culture* (Dover, Mass., 1991); George E. Simpson, *The Shango Cult in Trinidad* (Puerto Rico, 1965); Ivor Morrish, *Obeah, Christ and Rastaman* (Cambridge, 1982), 49-62.
3. Keith O. Laurence, *Immigration into the West Indies in the 19th Century* (Barbados, 1977), 13-16; Monica Schuler, "Alas, Alas, Kongo": A Social History of Indentured African Immigration into Jamaica (Baltimore, 1980), 32-44; Warner-Lewis, 1-55; George G. Findlay and W. Holdsworth, *The History of the Wesleyan Methodist Missionary Society* (5 vols., London, 1921), II, 373, 387; Donald Wood, *Trinidad in Transition* (London, 1968), 238-43.
4. "Syncretism" has been defined as "the integration (and consequent elaboration) of selected aspects of two or more historically distinct traditions" (Munro S. Edmonson et al., *Nativism and Syncretism* [New Orleans, 1960], 192).

5. Simpson, 17-23, 39-60 and passim; Melville J. Herskovitz and Frances S. Herskovitz, *Trinidad Village* (New York, 1947), 321-39. Cf. Dorothy C. Holland and Julia C. Crane, "Adapting to an industrializing nation: the Shango cult in Trinidad", SES 36, no. 4 (Dec. 1987): 41-66.

6. Edmonson, 5-32. Cf. ch. 2 above.

7. Patrick Bryan, *The Jamaican People* 1880-1902 (London, 1991), 33-66; George E. Simpson, "Jamaican Revivalist cults", SES 5, no. 4 (Dec. 1956): 337 and passim; Roscoe M. Pierson, "Alexander Bedward and the Jamaican Native Baptist Free Church", *Lexington Theological Quarterly* 4, no. 3 (July 1969): 65-76; Morrish, 49-51.

8. Herskovitz and Herskovitz, 167-68, 181-223, 340-45; E.A. Pitt, "Acculturative and synthetic aspects of religion and life in the island of St Vincent and other predominantly Protestant islands and areas of the West Indies and the Caribbean", [repr. from] *Actes du IVe Congrès International des Sciences Anthropologiques et Ethnologiques* (1952), II, 385-90; Simpson, *Shango Cult in Trinidad*, 62-63, 89-92, 106, 113-18; Ezra E.H. Griffith, "The psycho-social development and evolution of the Barbadian Spiritual Baptist Church", *Caribbean Journal of Religious Studies* 13, no. 1 (April 1992): 3-14; Eudora Thomas, A *History of the Shouter Baptists in Trinidad & Tobago* (Ithaca, 1987); C.M. Jacobs, *Joy Comes in the Morning* (Port-of-Spain, 1996).

9. A.B. Huggins, *The Saga of the Companies* (rev. ed., Freeport, Trinidad, ca. 1982), 32, 44, 39-43, 51-52, 56; John Stewart, "Where goes the indigenous Black church?" in Orde Coombs, ed., *Is Massa Day Dead?* (Garden City, New York, 1974).

10. Rupert Lewis and P. Bryan, eds., *Garvey: His Work and Impact* (Mona, Jamaica, 1988), esp. Ernle P. Gordon. "Garvey and Black Liberation Theology", 135-43; and Philip Potter, "The religious thought of Marcus Garvey", 145-63; *The Holy African Orthodox Church* (brochure, Antigua, 1971); Morrish, 95-96 (re Ethiopian Orthodox Church).

11. Bisnauth, 185-93; Morrish, 68-91; Joseph Owens, *Dread: the Rastafarians of Jamaica* (Kingston, 1976).

12. Cf. chs. 9 and 10.

13. Re peons, see Wood, 33-34, 49, 271; Bridget Brereton, *Race Relations in Colonial Trinidad*, 1870-1900 (Cambridge, 1979), 131. Re Chinese: Wood, 160-67; Morrish, 11-12, 96-97. (The Anglican Church welcomed Greek Orthodox "Syrians" in Jamaica (John B. Ellis, *The Diocese of Jamaica* [London, 1913], 145-47).

14. Anthony de Verteuil, *Sylvester Devenish and the Irish in 19th Century Trinidad* (Port-of-Spain, 1986), 38-50, 54.

15. Bisnauth, *Religions in the Caribbean*, 140-64; and *Guyana Presbyterian Church* (Georgetown, 1979), 41-44; J.C. Jha, "The Indian heritage in Trinidad", in John G. La Guerre, ed., *Calcutta to Caroni: The East Indians of Trinidad* (Trinidad, Jamaica and London, 1974), esp. 5-10, 18.

16. Arthur and Juanita Niehoff, *East Indians in the West Indies* (Milwaukee, Wisc., 1960), 151, 153-56. Cf. n. 2, above.

17. J. Morton as quoted in Sarah E.S. Morton, *John Morton of Trinidad* (Toronto, 1916), 5-6.

18. This church was a union (1860) in Nova Scotia of the Scottish Free Church and the Secession Church. The latter had been a pioneer in foreign

missions in the South Pacific. After Canadian Confederation this union (and its overseas missions) became part of the new union (1875) of the Presbyterian Church of Canada (R. Gordon Balfour, *Presbyterianism in the Colonies* [Edinburgh, 1900], 47-48, 51-58, 67-72).

19. Morton, 7-17, 19; Kenneth J. Grant, *My Missionary Memories* (Halifax, 1923), 77-114.

20. Morton, 66-67, 179, 266, 348-49, 424-25, 431-33, 434; Grant, 87-88, 145.

21. Morton, 56-58, 61-62, 64-65, 77, 98-102, 363-66. The ward schools were government schools where the pupils were in fact mostly children of African background.

22. Ibid., 62-63, 259, 455; Canadian Mission Council, *The Canadian Presbyterian Mission to East Indians, Trinidad BWI* (Trinidad, 1911), 14-16; Mission Council of Trinidad, *East Meets West in Trinidad* (Toronto, 1934), 47-48; Anthony de Verteuil, *Eight East Indian Immigrants* (Port-of-Spain, 1989), 55-81.

23. *Canadian Presbyterian Mission to East Indians, Trinidad BWI*, 16-19 (re Revds Lal Bihari and Andrew Guyadeen); Grant, 115-31; *East Meets West in Trinidad*, 45-47, 51; Morton, 79-81, 107-10, 115, 163-69, 270-72, and many other references to East Indian workers; William S. MacTavish, ed., *Reapers in Many Fields* (Toronto, 1904), 127-37, and *Harvests in Many Lands* (Toronto, 1908), 122-31; Hector F. Kemp, *Trinidad Writings* (mimeographed, 1967), 35-37 (Revd Joseph Gibbings), 32 (Samuel Dourga), 33-33a (many other names); Roy G. Neehall, *Presbyterianism in Trinidad: A Study of the Impact of Presbyterianism in the Island of Trinidad in the 19th Century* (STM thesis,

Union Theological Seminary, New York 1958), 75-82; Idris Hamid, *A History of the Presbyterian Church in Trinidad, 1868-1968* (San Fernando, 1980), ch. 3 (99-131).

24. Morton, 122-24, 153-55, 162-63, 166, 169, 316-20, 334-37, 417; Grant, 64-65; Wood, 270-76, 279-80.

25. Morton, 340-57, 447; Grant, 149-51; "Work among women", by Mrs Morton in *Canadian Presbyterian Mission to East Indians, Trinidad BWI*, 19-29; Adella J. Archibald, *The Trinidad East Indian Mission* (Trinidad, 1922); *East Meets West in Trinidad*, 71-90; Mabel Brandow, *The History of our Church Women of Trinidad, 1868-1963* (Altona, Manitoba, 1983).

26. Morton, 357-59; Brandow, passim; Archibald, 5-7; *East Meets West in Trinidad*, 71-90.

27. Archibald, 10-11.

28. Grant, 161-62; Morton, 298-99.

29. Grant, 162-64; Morton, 275-93. John Neehall (ibid., 338, 288-90) was the father of the Revd Roy Neehall, later General Secretary of the Caribbean Conference of Churches.

30. Grant, 166-69; Morton, 301.

31. Bisnauth, *Guyana Presbyterian Church*, 17-18; Charles Alexander Dunn, *The Canadian Mission in British Guiana: The Pioneer Years (1885-1927)* (Thesis, Knox College, Toronto, 1971), 7-38, 87-88; William S. MacTavish, ed., *Missionary Pathfinders* (Toronto, 1907), 223-32 (on Gibson); Grant, 164-66; Morton, 293-98.

32. Bisnauth, *Guyana Presbyterian Church*, 19-28; Dunn, ch. 3 (39-75) and passim; Paul B. Beatty Jr, *A History of the Lutheran Church in Guyana* (Berbice and South Pasadena, 1970), 69-71. Cropper, as a civil servant in St Lucia, had been active in the East Indian mission there prior to taking theological training in Canada.

33. Dunn, chs. 4, 5, 6 (76-206); Bisnauth, *Guyana Presbyterian Church*, 22-24.

34. Morton, 111; John Morton, comp., *Hindi Hymn Book* (Rasalpura, India, several editions). As late as the 1990s a book of *bhajans* in Hindi, with transliteration in English letters and translation into English, was published: Archibald S. Chauharjasingh, ed., *Bhajans of the early Presbyterian Church* (Trinidad, 1991).

35. Charles Alexander Dunn, 60, 83 and his *The Canadian Mission in British Guiana: From Mission to Church 1927-1967* (Thesis, Knox College, Toronto, 1975), 50, 54, 60; Bisnauth, *Religions in the Caribbean*, 160; Bisnauth, *Guyana Presbyterian Church*. 42-43; Neehall, 75.

36. *Census of the Colony of Trinidad & Tobago*, 1946 (Port-of-Spain, 1949), xli (Table D) quotes 1931 census figures of 23,183 Indian Christians:

Roman Catholic	8,469
Church of England	3,946
Wesleyan	160
Presbyterian (Canadian Mission)	10,335
Baptist	61
Moravian	23
Seventh Day Adventists	68
Others	121

Cf. Brinsley Samaroo et al., eds., *In Celebration of 150 Yrs. of the Indian Contribution to Trinidad & Tobago* (2 vols. in 1, Port-of-Spain, 1995), I, 61, 67; also II, 48, 64, re post-independence increased proportion of members in newer churches from North America, and 1990 census distribution of Indian Christians.

37. George Mather and C.J. Blagg, *Bishop Rawle: A Memoir* (London, 1890), 238-39, 241-42, 274-77, 290-301, 316-17; Morton, 211-12.

38. Ellis, 143-44; CJPWI, *150th Anniversary of the Diocese of Jamaica* (Kingston, 1974), 26-27.

39. Doreen Hobbs, *Jewels of the Caribbean: The History of the Salvation Army in the Caribbean Territory* (London, 1986), 45-48; Robert Sandall and A.R. Wiggins, *The History of the Salvation Army* (5 vols., London, 1947-68), IV, 34-35, V, 34; Beatty, 82-84, 89.

40. John T. Harricharan, *The Work of the Churches Among the East Indians in Trinidad* (Trinidad, 1975), 16-20 (re Roman Catholic Church), 21-24 (re Anglican Church).

41. The Dutch Reformed Church in early Guyana, and the short-lived United Presbyterian Mission from the USA in Trinidad, did not leave distinguishable permanent effects.

42. Another possible term "the historic churches" is awkward in frequent use. Some expression is needed to identify denominations that existed both abroad and in the West Indies for many decades, consequently holding a traditional place in society. (In the USA the expression "mainline churches" is often used.) Some indeed would like to consider these older groups as the Churches and categorize others as "sects", much as the nonconformist missions of pre-emancipation years were called "sectarists".

43. Chs. 6; 8 (n. 71); and 9 (n. 30).

44. Gilbert Bowles, *Jamaica and Friends' Missions* (Oskaloosa, Ia., 1900), 49-143; Jamaica Yearly Meeting, *The Society of Friends in Jamaica* (Richmond, Ind., 1962), 13, 19-20 and passim; Ellen Davis, *Friends in Jamaica* (Richmond, Ind., 1943); US Bureau of the Census,

Religious Bodies, 1936 (2 vols., Washington, DC, 1941), II, 698-710.

45. Beatty, 114 and passim; Bisnauth, *Religions in the Caribbean,* 42-43, 45-46.
46. Carol V.R. George, *Segregated Sabbaths: Richard Allen and the Emergence of Independent Black Churches,* 1760-1840 (New York and Oxford, 1973).
47. David H. Bradley, Sr, *A History of the A.M.E. Zion Church, Part I,* 1796-1872 (Nashville, 1956).
48. Charles S. Smith, *A History of the African Methodist Episcopal Church . . . 1856 to 1922* (Philadelphia, 1922; reprint New York, 1968), 27-28, 239, 241, 338-39, 369.
49. Uklyn Hendricks, *The African Methodist Episcopal Church in Barbados* 1892-1980 (CGSRS No. 2, Barbados, 1982); Mrs V.H. Adams-Gordon, "The history of the African Methodist Episcopal Church in the Virgin Islands", *Voice of Missions* (Feb. 1963): 10-11; *Latin-American News Letter,* no. 60 (June 1962): 1. AME work in the non-English Caribbean actually began much earlier, in Haiti in 1826 (Daniel A. Payne, *History of the African Methodist Episcopal Church* [Nashville, 1891; reprint New York, 1968], 64-70).
50. Hobbs, passim; Sandall and Wiggins, IV, 27, 32-33, 36-37, 38.
51. Sibbald D. Scott, *To Jamaica and Back* (London, 1876), 211; Kortright Davis, *Cross and Crown in Barbados* (Frankfurt am Main and New York, 1983), 52; *Trinidad & Tobago Year Book* (1960-61), 238-39. The "Bible Christians" lumped in the 1871 Jamaica census with the "Plymouth Brethren" may have been members of a British group of that name which had seceded from the Wesleyan Methodists (1815-19) and which later (1907) entered the (united)

Methodist Church. Note also that the Moravian Church was known as the *Unitas Fratrum* (United Brethren).
52. Winthrop S. Hudson, *Religion in America* (New York, 1965), 109-17, 120-26, 131-57; Sydney Ahlstrom, *A Religious History of the American People* (New Haven and London, 1972), 415-54; Jerald C. Brauer, *Protestantism in America* (Philadelphia, 1965), 74-88.
53. Hudson, 131-54; Ahlstrom, 429-54; Brauer, 93-101, 106-14.
54. Ahlstrom, 429-71; Hudson, 145-57; Brauer, 133-40.
55. Cf. below re the Church of God. Hudson, 122-24; Ahlstrom, 445-52; Lester G. McAllister and W.E. Tucker, *Journey into Faith: A History of the Christian Church (Disciples of Christ)* (St Louis, 1975), 19-60; Robert G. Nelson, *Disciples of Christ in Jamaica, 1858-1958* (St Louis, Mo., 1958), 27-54.
56. Cf. ch. 10, n. 64.
57. Among unorthodox innovations of the time was the emergence of Mormonism (Hudson, 190-94; Ahlstrom, 501-9).
58. Hudson, 194-97; Ahlstrom, 478-81; Ingemar Lindén, *The Last Trump* (Frankfurt am Main, 1978), 15-138.
59. *Seventh-Day Adventist Encyclopedia* (1974), under entries for various Caribbean territories; Eric J. Murray, *A History of the Seventh-Day Adventist Church in Trinidad and Tobago, 1891-1981* (Trinidad, 1982); J. Merle Davis, *The Church in the New Jamaica* (New York, 1942), 21.
60. Vinson Synan, *The Holiness-Pentecostal Movement in the United States* (Grand Rapids, 1971).
61. Synan, 13-54; John W.V. Smith, *The Quest for Holiness and Unity* (Anderson, Ind.,, 1980), ix-xiii, 15-40.
62. J.W.V. Smith, 43-100, 120-22; also his *A Brief History of the Church of God Reforma-*

tion Movement (rev. ed., Anderson, Ind., 1976), 57-58; David C. Schultz, ed., *Church of God Missions: The First 100 Years* (Anderson, Ind., 1980), 27-29 (Barbados 1912, Guyana 1914, Antigua, St Kitts/Nevis, Grenada and Cayman Islands in early 1930s).

63. Synan, 51, 60, 195; Timothy L. Smith, *Called unto Holiness: The Story of the Nazarenes: The Formative Years* (Kansas City, Mo., 1962), 11-25, 345 and passim; D.I. Vanderpool, *In Their Steps* (Kansas City, Mo., 1956), ch. 11 (re Trinidad), ch. 12 (Barbados); Ruth O. Saxon, *A History of the Church of the Nazarene in Trinidad and Tobago* (thesis, Nazarene Theological Seminary, Kansas City, Mo., 1967), 5-18.

64. They were merged later in the century in the USA, and consequently in the Caribbean, as the Wesleyan Holiness Church.

65. Walter J. Hollenweger, *The Pentecostals* (Minneapolis, 1972; reprint 1977), 21-74 and passim; Synan, 55-215.

66. Charles W. Conn, *Where the Saints have Trod* (Cleveland, Tenn., 1959), 49-79; Synan, 80-83, 119, 133.

67. *Trinidad & Tobago Year Book* (1960-61), 273.

68. Assemblies of God, General Council, Foreign Missions Department, *Jamaica* (pamphlet, Springfield, Mo., ca. 1960).

69. Morrish, 116-18, lists 127 "sects and denominations" in Jamaica. These include 14 of what we have called "the older churches", and a few syncretistic African or "revivalist" groups. But most bear names (for example ten "Church of God" bodies) indicating American origin or inspiration. The other English Caribbean territories could produce similar lists. Cf. Robert W.M. Cuthbert,

Ecumenism and Development (Bridgetown, 1986), 24-25.

70. J.W.V. Smith, *Quest for Holiness*, 29-39, 81-98, 183-99, 326; Hollenweger, 291-451, 457-92; Jamaica Theological Seminary, *Prospectus 1988-1991*, 2-3 ("Statement of Purpose" and "Statement of Faith"); Cuthbert, 17.

71. Ashley Smith, *Pentecostalism in Jamaica: A Challenge to the Established Churches & Society* (Kingston, 1975), 5-6; Mandeville, 1993 ed.), 30.

72. Union Theological Seminary, *St Colme's Hostel: Souvenir of Dedication*, (Kingston, 1955) (hereafter cited as *St Colme's Souvenir*), 3.

73. Cf. Cuthbert, 22, 24-25, and tables (as listed vii), showing statistics of church membership, etc. (selected from *World Christian Encyclopedia*, 1982).

74. One example (known to the writer) was the "Christian General Assembly" headed for many years by an East Indian contractor and preacher Edward Hasmatali in Trinidad. While associated during the 1950s with the United Holy Church of America Inc., a black holiness-pentecostal church (see Synan, 74, 167), he received ordination from a bishop of that body. Later his group of congregations became part of the New Testament Church of God (Conn, 111-12).

75. For example, various Bible Schools; Ardenne High School of the Church of God (Anderson) (Nelson, 135); Church of the Open Bible secondary school in San Fernando.

76. For example, Edward Hasmatali (mentioned in n. 74, above) and most of his preachers, and also the Church of the Open Bible and some indigenous offshoots in Trinidad.

77. This is by no means a criticism: it is recorded that in the days of Jesus "the common people heard him gladly". He also gave thanks that not "the wise and prudent" but "babes" received God's revelation (cf. 1 Cor. 1:17-28). Re the appeal of pentecostal-type congregations in the West Indies, and the importance of local leadership among them, see Ashley Smith.

78. For example, the Bahamas, 1869; Jamaica and Trinidad, 1870; British Honduras, 1872; Antigua and Nevis, 1873; St Kitts and Grenada, 1874. Dominica, the Virgin Islands and Montserrat do not seem to have taken legislative action, and in Montserrat the Church received aid as late as 1905 (CPWI, *Brochure* 1883-1983, 34).

79. Caldecott, 133-49. "Concurrent endowment" in British Guiana was gradually reduced after the clergy list ordinance of 1899 until state aid ended in 1945 (*Caribbean Presbyterian*, 31). In Trinidad and Tobago, "concurrent endowment" continued after Independence.

80. Ellis, 108-12, 121-26; Frank Cundall, *The Life of Enos Nuttall, Archbishop of the West Indies* (London, 1922), 18-28, 221-24, and passim.

81. CPWI, 57, 41-42, 61-63.

82. Caldecott, 153-73; CPWI, 15-21, 32, 49-50; Robert J. Stewart, *Religion and Society in Post-Emancipation Jamaica* (Knoxville, Tenn., 1992), 94-109 (re the reluctance to ordain or appoint black clergy).

83. CCC *Handbook* 1982, 30-31; *Caribbean Catholic Directory* 1971; Osborne, chs. 18, 20-29. See below (nn. 112, 113) re Seminary of St Jean Vianney (1942) and St Michael's Seminary (1952). Some further diocesan changes took place in 1970.

84. Findlay and Holdsworth, II, 399-400, 445-46; Stewart, 74-83 (re the schism).

85. Findlay and Holdsworth, II, 446-52.

86. F. Rought Wilson, *Life of George Sargeant, Wesleyan Missionary and first President of the West Indian Conference* (London, 1901); Findlay and Holdsworth, II, 453-55, 458-59, 462.

87. Ibid., II, 458-73.

88. Hugh Sherlock, *Methodism in the Caribbean with Particular Reference to Autonomy* (Kingston, 1966); CCC *Handbook* 1982, 18.

89. Joseph E. Hutton, *Moravian Missions* (London, 1923), 482-83 (see 463-72 re the system of government in the *Unitas Fratrum* or Moravian Church); S.U. Hastings and B.L. MacLeavy, *Seedtime and Harvest* (Bridgetown, 1979), 61, 106-12; Maynard, 143-55.

90. Hutton, *Moravian Missions*, 388-93, 234-35; Moravian Church in Trinidad, *Diamond Jubilee* 1890-1965 (brochure); Maynard, 116-23.

91. Hastings and MacLeavy, 118, 211-13; Maynard, 152-53; Hutton, *Moravian Missions*, 484-91, 495-502.

92. Hutton, *Moravian Missions*, 503-5, 509-11; Maynard, 155-60; Hastings and MacLeavy, 212-24. The large Moravian Church in Suriname was able to retain its connection with Europe during World War I since the Netherlands was neutral. Also it was largely financed by the Moravian business firm of Kersten & Co. (Hutton, *Moravian Missions*, 250-65, 504, 510-11).

93. Hendricks, 31-35.

94. Robson, 56-57; McKerrow, 321.

95. Morton, 7; Dunn, *Pioneer Years*, 208-10.

96. This division of overseas "mission fields" between these two churches was negotiated far away in Canada.

Since most overseas missionaries were supporters of the union (including all missionaries in Trinidad and almost all in British Guiana), the "continuing" Presbyterians were in danger of being left almost without any "foreign missions" of their own. Without consultation with the people in Trinidad and British Guiana, the two churches in Canada made a settlement which divided the work in the Caribbean. Thus church union in Canada led to church division in the Caribbean. This was an example of ecclesiastical colonialism, and of how church structures in the West Indies have reflected irrelevant denominational developments abroad. See Charles A. Dunn, "The great divorce and what happened to the children", Th.M. paper, Knox College and Toronto School of Theology, 1971, later published as Zander Dunn, same title, in *Canadian Society of Presbyterian History Papers*, 1977, 58-96.

97. Idris Hamid, 144-61; C.D. Lalla, "Address in Aramalaya Church", *Brochure: 75th Anniversary of the Canadian Mission, Trinidad, 1943* (San Fernando, 1943), esp. 21-40; Bisnauth, *Guyana Presbyterian Church*, 28-35, 50-51; Dunn, *Mission to Church*, 108-9, 114-16, 191, 206-7, 258, 271.

98. J.C. MacDonald, "The Church of Scotland in Grenada", *The Caribbean Presbyterian* (1958): 29-30.

99. Bisnauth, *Guyana Presbyterian Church*, 10-14; Beatty, 54.

100. "Histories" of these two churches by W.A. Fraser and A.S. MacDonald in *The Caribbean Presbyterian*, 30-31, 34-38; Bisnauth, *Guyana Presbyterian Church*, 50; Dunn, *Mission to Church*, 92, 261, 321.

101. *The Caribbean Presbyterian*; Caribbean Assembly of Reformed Churches, *Minutes*, 1965, 1967, 1969–.

102. Beatty, 78-106.

103. CCC *Handbook* 1982, 10-13; F. Ross Brown, *Mission to Jamaica: A History of Our Congregational Churches* (n.p., 1947), 45; Charles S. Horne, *The Story of the London Missionary Society* (2nd ed., London, 1895), 170.

104. Brown, 45-63.

105. Edward B. Underhill, *The Jamaica Mission in its relations with The Baptist Missionary Society, from 1838 to 1879* (London, 1879); Inez K. Sibley, *The Baptists of Jamaica* (Kingston, 1965), 23; Horace O. Russell, *Foundations and Anticipations* (Columbus, Ga, 1993), 44-45, 48-52, 58-59, 61, 96-98, 103-6, 113; Stewart, 83-94.

106. Revd W.C. Bell, short histories of Baptist Church in Trinidad (mimeo, 1962, 1966); Huggins.

107. Wilfred Scopes, ed., *The Christian Ministry in Latin America and the Caribbean* (New York, 1962), 146.

108. For example, Nicaragua and the Eastern West Indies Province of the Moravians (n. 92, above) and Central America with the Anglicans (Cundall, 55-56, 163, 192; CPWI, 20).

109. For example, Codrington Grammar School, Calabar College, Montego Bay Academy, York Castle, Naparima College, Naparima Girls' High School; Jamaica Moravian and Baptist, Trinidad Presbyterian and Roman Catholic, teacher training colleges.

110. Nina Langley, *Christopher Codrington and his College* (London, 1964); Anselm Genders, *Codrington College, 1745-1960* (Guildford, 1960); CPWI, 20, 24-26.

111. Cundall, 67, 103; Ellis, 151-55;

Edmund Davis, *Roots and Blossoms* (Bridgetown, 1977), 21-53.

112. *The Seminary of St John Vianney*, 1943-1968 (brochure, Trinidad, 1968).

113. Osborne, ch. 29; United Theological College of the West Indies, *Twenty-fifth Anniversary Souvenir Magazine* (Mona, Jamaica, 1982), 15.

114. Sibley, 16-21; Russell, 103, 134-37.

115. *St Colme's Souvenir*, 4, 6; George Robson, *Missions of the United Presbytarian Church* (Edinburgh, 1894), 47, 60, 71-75, 121. Tutors included the Revd Alexander Renton at Montego Bay, followed by Dr Alexander Robb in Kingston, and at New Broughton the Revds G.B. Anderson and Robert Johnston.

116. Moravian Church, Jamaica, *The Breaking of the Dawn* [by Walter Hark and Augustus Westfall] (London, 1904), 147-50; Hutton, *Moravian Missions*, 227, 232; Hastings and MacLeavy, 58-60, 227-31; Maynard, 137-42; *St Colme's Souvenir*, 6.

117. Findlay and Holdsworth, II, 393, 395-99, 402, 456, 458, 463, 466, 469; *St Colme's Souvenir*, 5; Wilfred Easton, *No Harbour* (London, 1959), 108-16.

118. *East Meets West in Trinidad*, 99-101; Grant, 144-49; Morton, 373-87; Kemp, 33, 33a, 34.

119. Bisnauth, *Guyana Presbyterian Church*, 27-28, 31, 34; Dunn, *Mission to Church*, 85, 149-50, 163, 204, 212, 223, 238; Beatty, 98.

120. Scopes, 146, 149, 152, 156-59, 163-65. Examples: West Indies Bible Institute (Trinidad) and Jamaica Bible Institute of the Church of God; Nazarene Training College, Trinidad; Seventh Day Adventist Colleges, Maracas Valley (Trinidad) and Mandeville (Jamaica); West Indies School of Theology (Pentecostal), Trinidad; Open Bible Institute, Trinidad; Crusaders' Bible School, Trinidad; Pilgrim Holiness Bible Institute, Barbados; [Southern] Baptist Theological Institute, Bahamas.

121. *St Colme's Souvenir*, 9; Nelson, 171-72.

122. Ibid., 172-75; *St Colme's Souvenir*, 7.

123. Caenwood College, *The Methodist Church: Caenwood College, 1928-1949* (1949); Nelson, 171-76.

124. United Theological College of the West Indies and its *Brochure* (2nd ed., Mona, Jamaica, 1968), esp. 5-7; Howard Gregory, ed., *Caribbean Theology: Preparing for the Challenges Ahead* (Mona, 1995), ix-xi.

125. *Jamaica Theological Seminary: Prospectus 1988-1991* (brochure, Kingston, 1988).

126. SPG, *Churchman's Missionary Atlas* (London, 1912), 22; Cundall, 55-57, 58-60, 67-69, 163, 192, 205.

127. Sibley, 27-28, 25-26. At this active period Baptist missionaries were also sent to Cayman Brac and Little Cayman (ibid., 28-29). These smaller islands, it has been said, then became as predominantly Baptist as Grand Cayman was Presbyterian. These Baptist churches later became part of the Jamaica Baptist Union.

128. Sandall and Wiggins, V, 36-37, 39; Hobbs, 184-99.

129. Ephraim Alphonse, *God at the Helm* (London, 1967).

130. John L. Wilkinson, *Church in Black and White* (Edinburgh, 1993); Clifford Hill, "Afro-Caribbean religion in Britain", in Brian Gates, ed., *Afro-Caribbean Religions* (London, 1980), 67-86, esp. 70-71, 74-80; Conn, 252-53; Hollenweger, 187-90.

131. Clement Gayle, *George Liele: Pioneer Missionary to Jamaica* (Kingston, 1982), 3, 24.

132. Ellis, 147-50; CJPWI, *150th Anniversary of the Diocese of Jamaica*, 26-28 (including portraits of some of these Jamaican missionaries).

133. Brown, 48-49.

134. Hobbs, 28-29.

135. Morton, 200-204; C.D. Lalla "Address", in *75th Anniversary* (n. 97 above), 24 (re Benjamin Balaram); John W. Richards Netram, *Will India Become Christian?* (New York, 1930). (Netram was the son of John Netram, a convert of John Morton in Trinidad).

136. Nelson, 164-66.

137. For example, the Christian Social Council in British Guiana, the Federal Council of Evangelical Churches in Trinidad, and the Jamaica Christian Council.

138. John Merle Davis, *The Church in the New Jamaica* and *The East Indian Church in Trinidad* (New York, 1942).

139. Nelson, 166-70. Later the YMCA, the YWCA and the Bible Society became associate members.

140. Jamaica Christian Council, *Christ for Jamaica* (Kingston, 1951): Nelson, 168.

141. Hastings and MacLeavy, 225-27:

142. Nelson, 170-71. The UCJGC in 1992 further merged with the Disciples of Christ in Jamaica, taking the name of The United Church of Jamaica and the Cayman Islands (UCJCI).

143. E.J. Bingle, *Cuba to Surinam* (London, 1955); International Missionary Council, *The Listening Isles* (New York, 1957).

144. Cuthbert, 3, 41-75.

145. The Revd Dr Philip Potter, originally from Dominica, was Associate General Secretary of the WCC (1967-72), then General Secretary (1972-84).

Chapter 12 Conclusion

1. For example, H. Richard Niebuhr, *The Social Sources of Denominationalism* (New York, 1929; reprint 1957).

2. Ernst Troeltsch, *The Social Teaching of the Christian Churches* (trans. O. Wyon) (2 vols., 1931; reprint New York, 1960). Cf. also Elmer T. Clark, *The Small Sects in America* (New York, 1949); S.D. Clark, *Church and Sect in Canada* (Toronto, 1948).

3. Some however assume a new significance for local cultural reasons. There are also indigenous groups. Some stand outside orthodox Christianity. Others can bear comparison to the "Independent Churches" in Africa.

4. See chs. 2, 3,4.

5. Troeltsch's term "sect" is not used here, for some of these denominations retain elements of the "church-type", for example, the practice of infant baptism, episcopacy in the case of the Moravians, and above all their generally co-operative rather than exclusive outlook. Moreover their membership – at least before the mid 19th century, and afterwards in the case of the East Indians – was drawn by missionary outreach to non-Christians, rather than by recruitment from other churches, as often happened with denominations of North American origin.

6. The African churches in the USA arose out of tensions within American churches between white and black members. There blacks are in a minority both in society and in the major denominations. However in the West Indies whites are in the minority.

7. Cf. also the Protestant refugees from Madeira who owed their conversion to a Scottish doctor, the founders of St Ann's congregation in Port-of-Spain (ch. 11).

8. To borrow the phrase, though not the philosophy of history that goes with it, of Franklin H. Littell, *From State Church to Pluralism* (New York, 1962).

9. George Liele had been ordained in the Baptist Church in Georgia, but he had to be self-supporting and in this respect was like a lay person.

10. Cf. ch. 1, n. 6.

11. It is relevant to observe that H. Richard Niebuhr, after studying the phenomena of denominational diversity in the American scene went on to stress the unitive elements in the history of the Church in the United States in *The Kingdom of God in America* (New York, 1937; reprint 1959).

12. For example: the gravitation to the Anglican Church of some persons who found themselves rising in the social and political scale; in Barbados the continuing Anglican establishment until 1970; and in Trinidad and Tobago the production of a "Concordat" between the government and the Roman Catholic Church on the subject of education in 1962.

Select Bibliography

DOCUMENTARY AND OTHER EARLY SOURCES

Acts of the Privy Council, Colonial. *See* Great Britain (Government of).

Arber, Edward, and A.G. Bradley, eds. *Travels and Works of Captain John Smith*. 2 vols. Edinburgh, 1910.

An *Authentic Copy of the Minutes of evidence on the trial of John Smith, a missionary, in Demerara.* London, 1824.

Authentic Report of the debate in the House of Commons, June 23, 1825, on Mr. Buxton's Motion. London, 1825. *See* House of Commons.

Augier, F.R., and S.C. Gordon. *Sources of West Indian History*. London and Kingston, 1962.

Azurara, Gomes E de. *The Chronicle of the Discovery and Conquest of Guinea*. 2 vols. Translated by C.R. Beazley and E. Prestage. London, Hakluyt Society, 1896.

Baptist Herald and Friend of Africa. 1841–44.

|Baptist Mission Committee.| *Facts and Documents connected with the Late Insurrection in Jamaica*. 1832.

Baptist Mission Committee |Thomas F. Abbott|. A *Narrative of Recent Events connected with the Baptist Mission in this island*. Jamaica, 1833.

Baptist Missionary Society. *Freedom in Jamaica; or the first of August, 1838*. London, 1838.

Baxter, Richard. A *Christian Directory*. London, 1673.

Besse, Joseph. A *Collection of the Sufferings of the People Called Quakers*. 2 vols. London, 1753.

Bible Society. *The substance of a speech delivered by the Rev. James M. Phillippo . . . at the reorganization of the St. Catherine and St. Thomas in the Vale auxiliary Bible Society*. Spanish Town, 1839.

Bickell, Richard. *The West Indies as they are*. London, 1825.

Bridges, George W. *Statistical History of the Parish of Manchester*. Jamaica, 1824.

Bridges, George W. *The Annals of Jamaica*. 2 vols. London, 1827–28.

British and Foreign Bible Society Reports. London, 1809, 1810, 1811, 1814, 1817–

Brown, Alexander. *The Genesis of the United States*. 2 vols. Boston, 1890.

Buxton, Thomas F. *The African Slave Trade and its Remedy*. London, 1840.

Calamy, Edmund. *The Nonconformist's Memorial*. 2 vols. London, 1775.

Calendar of State Papers, Colonial (America and the West Indies). *See* Great Britain (Government of). Public Record Office.

Casas, Bartolomé de Las. *See* Las Casas.

Chalkley, Thomas. A *Collection of the Works*. Philadelphia, 1749.

Church of England, Barbados Church Society. *Proposed Mission from the Church in the West Indies to Western Africa*. Barbados, 1850.

Church of England, Diocese of Guiana. A *Journal of the Bishop's Visitation in 1851*. London, 1852.

Clancy, William. *Memorial to her Most Gracious Majesty Queen Victoria, and other Documents regarding the Present Condition of the Catholic Church in British Guiana*. London, 1841.

Clancy, William. *The Catholic Church in British Guiana*. London, 1841.

Clark, John. *Memorials of Baptist Missionaries in Jamaica*. London and Kingston, 1869.

Clarke, John, W. Dendy, and J.M. Phillippo. *The Voice of Jubilee*. London, 1865.

Coad, John. A *Memorandum of the Wonderful Providences of God*. London, 1849.

Coke, Thomas. A *History of the West Indies*. 3 vols. Liverpool, 1808–11.

Coke, Thomas. A *Continuation of Dr. Coke's Journal*. London, 1787.

Coke, Thomas. *An Account of the Rise, Progress, and Present State of Methodist Missions*. London, 1804.

Coke, Thomas. *An Address to the Pious and Benevolent, proposing an Annual subscription for the support of missionaries*. London, 1786.

Coke, Thomas. *Extracts of the Journals of the late Rev. Thomas Coke*. Dublin, 1816.

Coke, Thomas. *Statement of the Receipts and disbursements for the support of the missions . . . in the West Indies*. London, 1794.

Coleridge, William H. *Charges delivered to the Clergy of the Diocese of Barbados and the Leeward Islands*. London, 1835.

Conway, George R.G., ed. *An Englishman and the Mexican Inquisition, 1556–1560*. Mexico City, 1927.

Coleridge, Henry N. *Six Months in the West Indies in 1825*. London, 1826.

CSPC. *See* Great Britain (Government of). Public Record Office. *Calendar of State Papers, Colonial (America and the West Indies)*. London, 1860– (multiple volumes).

Cundall, Frank, and J.L. Pietersz, *Jamaica under the Spaniards*. Kingston, Jamaica, 1919.

Declaration of inhabitants of Barbados, respecting the demolition of the Methodist Chapel. Barbados, 1826.

de Las Casas. *See* Las Casas.

Donnan, Elizabeth, ed. *Documents Illustrative of the History of the Slave Trade to America*. 4 vols. Washington, 1930–35.

Duncan, Peter. A *Narrative of the Wesleyan Mission to Jamaica*. London, 1849.

Edmundson, William. A *Journal of the Life, Travels, Sufferings, and Labour of Love in the Work of the Ministry*. Dublin, 1715.

Emancipation New Testament. Cambridge, 1834.

Featley, John. A *Sermon Preached to the Nobely-Deserving Gentleman Sir Thomas Warner and the rest of his Companie: Bound to the West Indies. For their Farewell: at St. Buttolphs, Aldersgate*. London, 1629.

Firth, C.H., ed. *The Narrative of General Venables*. Camden Society Publications, new series, no. 60. London, 1900.

Fleetwood, William. *A Sermon Preached before the Society for the Propagation of the Gospel in Foreign Parts . . . by the Right Reverend Father in God, William Lord Bishop of St Asaph*. London, 1711. (Reprinted in *Anglican Humanitarianism* by Frank J. Klingberg. Philadelphia, 1940.)

Force, Peter, comp. *Tracts and other Papers*. 4 vols. Washington, 1836–46.

Foster, Nicholas. *A Briefe Relation of the late Horrid Rebellion*. London, 1650. Facs. rpt. London, 1879.

Fox, George. *Gospel Family-Order, being a Short Discourse concerning the Ordering of Families, both of Whites, Blacks and Indians*. Barbados, 1671; reprint 1701.

Fox, George. *To the Ministers, Teachers, And Priests (So called, and so Stileing your Selves) in Barbadoes*. London, 1672.

Fox, George. *A Collection of Many Select and Christian Epistles*. London, 1698; also New York, 1975, facs. rpt. of Philadelphia, 1831 ed., vol. 7 of *The Works of George Fox*.

Fox, George. *Journal*. Edited by Norman Penney. 2 vols. Cambridge, 1911.

Gibson, Edmund. *Two Letters of the Lord Bishop of London*. London, 1727 and 1729. Reprinted in David Humphreys, *An Historical Account of the Incorporated Society for the Propagation of the Gospel in Foreign Parts*. London, 1730. Facs. New York, 1969.

Godwyn, Morgan. *The Negro's and Indians Advocate*. London, 1680.

Godwyn, Morgan. *Trade preferr'd before Religion*. London, 1685.

Great Britain, House of Commons. *Papers relating to the West Indies*. 1815.

Great Britain. House of Commons. *The Missionary Smith, Substance of the debate in the House of Commons on Tuesday the 1st and on Friday the 11th of June 1824*. London, 1824.

Great Britain. House of Commons. *An Authentic Report of the debate in the House of Commons, June 23, 1825, on Mr. Buxton's motion relative to the demolition of the Methodist chapel and mission house in Barbadoes, and the expulsion of Mr. Shrewsbury*. London, 1825.

Great Britain. House of Commons. *Substance of the debate in the House of Commons . . . respecting the destruction of the Methodist chapel in Barbadoes*. London, 1825.

Great Britain (Government of) Public Record Office. *Calendar of State Papers. Colonial Series. America and The West Indies*. London, 1860– (many vols.). Also, *Calendar of State Papers, Domestic; Acts of the Privy Council, Colonial*.

Hakluyt, Richard. *The Principal Navigations Voyages Traffiques and Discoveries of the English Nation*. 3 vols., 2nd ed. London, 1598–1600; 12 vols. Glasgow, 1903.

Hakluyt, Richard. "Discourse of Western Planting". In Maine Hist. Society, *Documentary History of the State of Maine*, Vol. II. Cambridge, 1877.

Hall, Clayton C. *Narratives of Early Maryland*. New York, 1910.

Handy, Robert T., ed. *Religion in the American Experience: The Pluralistic Life*. Columbia, SC, 1972.

Harlow, Vincent T., ed. *The Voyages of Capt. William Jackson, 1642–5*. Camden Miscellany, XIII. Camden 3d series, no. 34. London, 1923.

Harlow, Vincent T., ed. *Colonizing Expeditions to the West Indies and Guiana*. Hakluyt Society, series 2, no. 56. London, 1925.

Harlow, Vincent T., ed. *The Discoverie of the large and bewtiful Empire of Guiana by Sir Walter Raleigh*. London, 1928.

Harris, C. Alexander, ed. A *Relation of a Voyage to Guiana by Robert Harcourt*, 1613. Hakluyt Society, series 2, no. 60. London, 1928.

Hughes, Thomas, ed. *History of the Society of Jesus in North America*. 4 vols. London, 1907–17.

Humphreys, David. *An Historical Account of the Incorporated Society for the Propagation of the Gospel in Foreign Parts*. London, 1730. Facs. New York, 1969.

Incorporated Society for the Conversion and Religious Instruction and Education of the Negroe Slaves in the British West India Islands. Report From July to December 1823. London, 1824.

Labaree, Leonard W. *Royal Instructions to British Colonial Governors*. 1670–1776. 2 vols. New York, 1935.

Labat, Jean B. *Nouveau Voyage aux Isles de l'Amérique*. Paris, 1722.

Langford, Jonas. *A Brief Account of the Sufferings of the Servants of the Lord called Quakers*. London, 1706.

Las Casas, Bartolomé de. *Brevissima Relacion de la Destruycion de las Indias*. Translated in Appendix I of *Bartholomew de Las Casas* by Francis A. MacNutt. New York and London, 1909.

Las Casas, Bartolomé de. *Historia de las Indias*. 3 vols. Edited by Augustin M. Carlo with an introduction by Hanke. Mexico, 1951.

Las Casas, Bartolomé de. *History of the Indies*. Translated [in part, into English] by A. Collard. New York, 1971.

Las Casas, Bartolomé de. *The Only Way*. Translated by Frances P. Sullivan with an introduction by H.R. Parish. New York, 1992.

Lefroy, John H., ed. *Memorials of the Discovery and Early Settlement of the Bermudas*. 2 vols. London, 1877–79.

Lefroy, John H., ed. *The Historye of the Bermudaes*. London, 1882.

Levant, Stefan, ed. *The New World*. New York, 1965.

Ligon, Richard. *A True and Exact History of the Island of Barbadoes*. 2nd ed. London, 1673; repr. 1970.

London Missionary Society. *Report of the Proceedings against the late Rev. J. Smith of Demerara*. London, 1824.

Long, Edward. *The History of Jamaica*. 3 vols. London, 1774.

Maine Historical Society. *Documentary History of the State of Maine*, Vol. II. Cambridge, 1877.

Manross, William W., comp. *The Fulham Papers in the Fulham Palace Library*. Oxford, 1965.

Matthews, Arnold G. *Calamy Revised*. Oxford, 1934.

Minutes of the proceedings of the trial of an action for defamation . . . Bayley, Wentworth, Esq. vs. Donaldson, the Rev. Colin. Kingston, 1808.

Misrepresentations Refuted, or the Triumph of Truth. St Jago de la Vega (Spanish Town), 1839.

The Missionary Smith. Substance of the debate in the House of Commons on Tuesday the 1st and on Friday the 11th of June, 1824. London, 1824. (See Great Britain. House of Commons.)

Mode, G. *Source Book and Bibliographical Guide for American Church History*. Monasha, Wisconsin, 1921.

Morison, Samuel E., tr. and ed. *Journals and Other Documents on the Life and Voyages of Christopher Columbus*. New York, 1963.

Morton, John, comp. *Hindi Hymn Book*. Rasalpura, India, several editions.

O'Callaghan, Edmund B., ed. *Documents relative to the Colonial History of the State of New York*. 10 vols. Albany, 1856–61.

Pascoe, Charles F., comp. *Two Hundred Years of the* SPG: *An Historical Account* . . . 1701–1900. London, 1901.

Peters, Charles. *Two sermons, preached at Dominica, on the 11th and 13th April, 1800; and officially noticed by His Majesty's Council in that island.* London, 1802.

Porteous, Bielby. *A Letter to the Governors, Legislatures, and Proprietors of Plantations, in the British West-India Islands.* London, 1808.

Purchas, Samuel. *Hakluytus Posthumus, or Purchas His Pilgrimes.* 20 vols. 1625; reprint Glasgow, 1905–1907.

Ramsay, James. *An Essay on the Treatment and Conversion of African Slaves in the British Sugar Colonies.* London, 1784.

Ramsay, James. *Objections to the Abolition of the Slave Trade, with Answers.* London, 1788; reprint Miami, 1969.

Religious Tract Society. *Missionary Records, West Indies.* London, 1837.

Rippon, John, ed. *Baptist Annual Register.* 4 vols. London, 1790–1802.

Sandiford, Ralph. *A brief Examination of the Practice of the Times.* 1729; reprint New York, 1969.

Scott, John. "The Discription of Barbados". Br. Mus. Sloane MS 3662 ff. 62–54, Lib. of Cong. photostat.

Shrewsbury, William J. *Sermons preached on several occasions in the island of Barbados.* London, 1825.

Smith, Hilrie S., R.T. Handy, and L.A. Loetscher, eds. *American Christianity.* 2 vols. New York, 1960.

Society for the Propagation of the Gospel in Foreign Parts. *A Collection of Papers, Printed by order of the Society.* London, 1706.

Society for the Propagation of the Gospel. *Twelve Anniversary Sermons preached before the Society for the Propagation of the Gospel in Foreign Parts.* London, 1845.

Story, Thomas. *A Journal of the Life.* Newcastle-upon-Tyne, 1747.

Thacher, John B. *Christopher Columbus.* 3 vols. New York, 1904; reprint New York, 1967.

Taylor, Eva G.R., ed. *The Original Writings of the Two Richard Hakluyts.* 2 vols. London, 1935.

Thurloe, John. *A Collection of State Papers . . . from the year 1638 to the Restoration.* 7 vols. London, 1742.

Trott, Nicholas, ed. *The Laws of the British Plantations in America, relating to the Church and the Clergy.* London, 1725.

Underhill, Edward B. *The West Indies; Their Social and Religious Condition.* London, 1862.

Underhill, Edward B. *A Letter addressed to the Rt. Honourable M. Cardwell, with illustrative documents on the condition of Jamaica.* London, 1865.

Underhill, Edward B. *The Jamaican Mission in its relation with the Baptist Missionary Society, from 1838 to 1879.* London, 1879.

Warburton, William. *A Sermon Preached before the Incorporated Society for the Propagation of the Gospel in Foreign Parts.* London, 1766.

Watson, Richard. *A Defence of the Wesleyan Methodist Missions in the West Indies.* London, 1817.

Weinstein, Allen, and F.O. Gatell, eds. *American Negro Slavery: A Modern Reader.* New York, 1968.

Wesley, John. *Thoughts upon Slavery.* London, 1774.

Wesley, John. *Journal.* Edited by N. Curnock. 8 vols. London, 1909–16.

Wesleyan Methodist Missionary Society. *Statement of the Plan, Object, and Effects of the Wesleyan Mission in the West Indies*. London, 1824.

White, Andrew. "A Briefe Relation of the Voyage into Maryland". In Clayton C. Hall, *Narratives of Early Maryland*. New York, 1910.

Williams, Eric E., ed. *Documents on British West Indian History, 1807–1833*. Port-of-Spain, 1952.

Williams, Eric E., ed. *Documents of West Indian History, Vol.I, 1492–1655*. Port-of-Spain, 1963.

SECONDARY SOURCES

Books and Brochures

Ahlstrom, Sydney. *A Religious History of the American People*. New Haven and London, 1972.

Airall, Hilton S. *The Origins of Methodism in Clarendon*. Kingston, 1960.

Anderson, James S.M. *The History of the Church of England in the Colonies*. 3 vols. London, 1856.

Anstey, Roger. *The Atlantic Slave Trade and British Abolition, 1760–1810*. London, 1975.

Archibald, Adella J. *The Trinidad East Indian Mission*. Trinidad, 1922.

Ashley, Maurice. *England in the Seventeenth Century*. Harmondsworth, 1967.

Assemblies of God, General Council, Foreign Missions Department, Jamaica. Pamphlet. Springfield, Mo., c. 1960.

Atkinson, William C.A. *History of Spain and Portugal*. Harmondsworth, 1960.

Atwood, Thomas. *History of the Island of Dominica*. London, 1791.

Baird, Charles W. *History of the Huguenot Emigration to America*. 2 vols. New York, 1885.

Balfour, Robert. *Presbyterianism in the Colonies*. Edinburgh, 1900.

Barbour, Hugh. *The Quakers in Puritan England*. New Haven, 1964.

Barrow, A.H. *Fifty Years in Western Africa*. London, 1900; reprint New York, 1969.

Beatty, Paul B. Jr. *A History of the Lutheran Church in Guyana*. South Pasadena, 1970.

Beckles, Hilary McD. *White Servitude and Black Slavery in Barbados, 1627–1715*. Knoxville, 1989.

Bennett, J. Harry, Jr. *Bondsmen and Bishops*. University of California Publications in History 62. Berkeley, 1958.

Bernau, John H. *Missionary Labours in British Guiana*. London, 1847.

Bindoff, S.T. *Tudor England*. Harmondsworth, 1966.

Bingle, E.J. *Cuba to Surinam*. London, 1955.

Bisnauth, Dale A. *A Short History of the Guyana Presbyterian Church*. Georgetown, 1979.

Bisnauth, Dale A. *A History of Religions in the Caribbean*. Kingston, 1989.

Blackman, Francis (Woodie). *Methodism: 200 Years in Barbados*. Bridgetown, 1988.

Bleby, Henry. *Death Struggles of Slavery*. London, 1853.

Blyth, George. *Reminiscences of Missionary Life*. Edinburgh, 1851.

Borde, Pierre-Gustav-Louis. *The History of the Island of Trinidad under the Spanish Government*. 2 vols. Translated from the French 1876–82 edition. Port-of-Spain, 1982.

Bowles, Gilbert. *Jamaica and Friends' Missions*. Oskaloosa, Ia., 1900.

Bradley, David H., Sr. *A History of the A.M.E. Zion Church, Part I, 1796–1872*. Nashville, 1956.

Brandow, Mabel. *The History of our Church Women of Trinidad, 1868–1963*. Altona, Manitoba, 1983.

Brauer, Jerald C. *Protestantism in America*. Philadelphia, 1965.

Brereton, Bridget. *Race Relations in Colonial Trinidad, 1870–1900*. Cambridge, 1979.

Brett, William H. *Indian Missions in Guiana*. London, 1851.

Brett, William H. *The Indian Tribes of Guiana*. London, 1868.

Brett, William H. *Legends and Myths of the Aboriginal Indians of British Guiana*. London, 1880.

Brett, William H. *Mission Work among the Indian Tribes in the Forests of Guiana*. London, 1881.

Bridenbaugh, Carl. *Mitre and Sceptre*. New York, 1962.

Bridenbaugh, C., and R. Bridenbaugh. *No Peace Beyond the Line*. New York, 1972.

Brookes, George S. *Friend Anthony Benezet*. Philadelphia, 1937.

Brown, F. Ross. *Mission to Jamaica: A History of Our Congregational Churches*. N.p., ca. 1947.

Brown, William. *The History of Missions . . . Since the Reformation*. 2 vols. Philadelphia, 1820.

Brown, William. *History of the Christian Missions of the Sixteenth, Seventeenth, Eighteenth and Nineteenth Centuries*. 3 vols. London, 1864.

Browne, George. *The History of the British and Foreign Bible Society*. 2 vols. London, 1859.

Bryan, Patrick. *The Jamaican People 1880–1902*. London, 1991.

Buchner, John H. *The Moravians in Jamaica*. London, 1854.

Burchell, William F. *Memoir of Thomas Burchell*. London, 1849.

Burns, Alan. *History of the British West Indies*. London, 1954.

Caenwood College. *The Methodist Church: Caenwood College, 1928–1949*. Jamaica, 1949.

Caldecott, Alfred. *The Church in the West Indies*. London, 1898.

Campbell, P.F. *The Church in Barbados in the Seventeenth Century*. Barbados, 1982.

Canadian Mission Council. *The Canadian Presbyterian Mission to East Indians, Trinidad BWI*. Trinidad, 1911.

Canton, William. *A History of the British and Foreign Bible Society*. 5 vols. London, 1904–20.

Caribbean Catholic Directory, 1971.

Caribbean Conference of Churches. *Handbook of Churches in the Caribbean*. Barbados, 1973; 2nd ed. 1982.

Caribbean Conference of Churches. *At the Crossroads: African Caribbean Religion and Christianity*. Trinidad, 1995.

Caribbean Journal of Religious Studies. Mona, Jamaica, 1975–

Carmichael, Gertrude. *The History of the West Indian Islands of Trinidad and Tobago*. London, 1961.

Carpenter, Edward. *The Protestant Bishop* [re Henry Compton]. London, 1956.

Caswall, Henry. *The Martyr of the Pongas, being a Memoir of the Rev. Hamble James Leacock*. London, 1857.

Catholic Church, Jamaica. *Centenary Souvenir, 1837–1937*. Kingston, 1937.

Chamberlin, David. *Smith of Demerara*. London, 1923.

Chauharjasingh, Archibald S., ed. *Bhajans of the early Presbyterian Church*. Trinidad, 1991.

Church in Jamaica in the Province of the West Indies. *150th Anniversary of the Diocese of Jamaica*. Kingston, 1974.

Church in the Province of the West Indies. *This is the CPWI*. Barbados, 1983.

Cnattingius, Hans. *Bishops and Societies: A Study of Anglican Colonial and Missionary Expansion*. London, 1952.

Conn, Charles W. *Where the Saints have Trod*. Cleveland, Tenn., 1959.

Cooper, Donald B. *The Establishment of the Church in the Leeward Islands*. Stillwater, Okla., 1966.

Corbett, Julian S. *Drake and the Tudor Navy.* 2 vols. London, 1917.

Cox, Francis A. *History of the Baptist Missionary Society.* 2 vols. London, 1842.

Cracknell, Basil E. *Dominica.* Newton Abbott, 1973.

Craton, Michael. *A History of the Bahamas.* London, 1962.

Craven, John Wesley. *An Introduction to the History of Bermuda.* Reprint from *William and Mary Quarterly,* 2nd Ser., 17–18 (1937–38).

Cross, Arthur L. *The Anglican Episcopate and the American Colonies.* New York, 1902.

Crouse, Nellis M. *French Pioneers in the West Indies.* New York, 1940.

Crouse, Nellis. *The French Struggle for the West Indies.* New York, 1943.

Cundall, Frank. *The Life of Enos Nuttall, Archbishop of the West Indies.* London, 1922.

Cuthbert, Robert W.M. *Ecumenism and Development.* Bridgetown, 1986.

Davidson, William V. *Historical Geography of the Bay Islands.* Birmingham, AL, 1974.

Davis, David B. *The Problem of Slavery in Western Culture.* Ithaca, 1966.

Davis, David B. *The Problem of Slavery in the Age of Revolution.* Ithaca, 1975.

Davis, Edmund. *Roots and Blossoms.* Bridgetown, 1977.

Davis, Ellen. *Friends in Jamaica.* Richmond, Ind., 1943.

Davis, Kortright. *Cross and Crown in Barbados.* Frankfurt am Main and New York, 1983.

Davis, Merle. *The Church in the New Jamaica.* New York, 1942.

Davis, Nicholas D. *The Cavaliers and Roundheads of Barbados.* Georgetown, BG, 1887.

DeCaires, Herman S. *The Jesuits in British Guiana.* London, 1946.

de Verteuil, Anthony. *Sir Louis de Verteuil: His Life and Times.* Port-of-Spain, 1973.

de Verteuil, Anthony. *Sylvester Devenish and the Irish in 19th Century Trinidad.* Port-of-Spain, 1986.

de Verteuil, Anthony. *Eight East Indian Immigrants.* Port-of-Spain, 1989.

de Verteuil, Louis A.A. *Trinidad.* London, Paris and New York, 1884; 2nd ed. London, 1884.

Delany, Francis X. *A History of the Catholic Church in Jamaica.* New York, 1930.

Devas, Raymund P. *Conception Island, or the Troubled Story of the Catholic Church in Grenada.* London, 1932.

Devas, Raymund P. *The Island of Grenada (1650–1950).* Barbados, 1964.

Dictionary of National Biography. Oxford, 1921.

The Diocese of Trinidad and Tobago 1872–1972. San Fernando, 1972.

Dobson, Narda. *A History of Belize.* Trinidad and Jamaica, 1973.

Drake, Thomas E. *Quakers and Slavery in America.* Gloucester, Mass., 1965.

Dunn, Richard S. *Sugar and Slaves.* New York, 1973.

Easter, B.H. *St. Lucia and the French Revolution.* Castries, 1969.

Easton, Wilfred. *No Harbour.* London, 1959.

Edmonson, Munro S., et al. *Nativism and Syncretism.* New Orleans, 1960.

Edwards, Bryan. *History, Civil and Commercial, of the British Colonies in the West Indies.* 5 vols. 5th ed. London, 1819. Facs. ed. New York, 1966.

Ellis, John B. *The Diocese of Jamaica.* London, 1913.

Findlay, George G., and W.W. Holdsworth. *The History of the Wesleyan Methodist Missionary Society.* 5 vols. London, 1921–24. (Vol. 2 on West Indies.)

Foster, Henry B. *Rise and Progress of Wesleyan-Methodism in Jamaica.* London 1881.

Friede, Juan and B. Keen, eds. *Bartolomé de Las Casas in History.* Dekalb, Ill., 1971.

Gayle, Clement H.L. *George Liele: Pioneer Missionary to Jamaica*. KinGston, 1982.

Gardner, William J. *A History of Jamaica*. London, 1873; Reprint, 1909.

George, Carol V.R. *Segregated Sabbaths: Richard Allen and the Emergence of Independent Black Churches, 1760–1840*. New York and Oxford, 1973.

Gibson, Charles. *Spain in America*. New York, 1966.

Goodridge, Sehon S. *Facing the Challenge of Emancipation: A Study of the Ministry of William Hart Coleridge*. Bridgetown, 1981.

Goslinga, Cornelis C. *The Dutch in the Caribbean and on the Wild Coast*. Assen, The Netherlands, 1971.

Goveia, Elsa V. *A Study on the Historiography of the British West Indies to the end of the Nineteenth Century*. Mexico, 1956.

Goveia, Elsa V. *Slave Society in the British Leeward Islands at the End of the Eighteenth Century*. Puerto Rico, 1969.

Grant, Kenneth J. *My Missionary Memories*. Halifax, 1923.

Gregory, Howard, ed. *Caribbean Theology: Preparing for the Challenges Ahead*. Mona, Jamaica, 1995.

Groves, Charles P. *The Planting of Christianity in Africa*. 4 vols. London, 1948–56.

Grubb, Kenneth G. *Religion in Central America*. London, 1937.

Guttridge, George H. *The Colonial Policy of William III in America and the West Indies*. Cambridge, 1922.

Hamid, Idris. *A History of the Presbyterian Church in Trinidad, 1868–1968*. San Fernando, 1980.

Hanke, Lewis U. *The Spanish Struggle for Justice in the Conquest of America*. 1949; reprint Boston and Toronto, 1965.

Haring, Clarence H. *The Buccaneers in the West Indies in the XVII Century*. New York, 1910.

Haring, Clarence H. *The Spanish Empire in America*. New York, 1963.

Hark, Walter, and Augustus Westphal. *The Breaking of the Dawn*. London, 1904.

Harlow, Vincent T. *A History of Barbados*. Oxford, 1926.

Harlow, Vincent T. *Christopher Codrington, 1668–1710*. Oxford, 1928.

Harricharan, John T. *The Work of the Christian Churches among the East Indians in Trinidad*. Trinidad, 1976.

Harricharan, John T. *The Catholic Church in Trinidad, 1492–1852*. Trinidad, 1981.

Hastings, S.U., and B.L. MacLeavy. *Seedtime and Harvest*. Jamaica, 1979.

Henderson, Agnes, and H.S. Shirley. *A Brief History of the Disciples of Christ in Jamaica*. Kingston, 1959.

Hendricks, Uklyn. *The African Methodist Episcopal Church in Barbados, 1892–1980*. CGSRS, no. 2. Barbados, 1982.

Herskovitz, Melville J., and Frances S. *Trinidad Village*. New York, 1947.

Heuman, Gad J. *The Killing Time: The Morant Bay Rebellion in Jamaica*. London, 1994.

Hinton, John H. *Memoir of William Knibb*. London, 1849.

Hirst, Margaret E. *Quakers in Peace and War*. New York, 1923.

Hobbs, Doreen. *Jewels of the Caribbean: The History of the Salvation Army in the Caribbean Territory*. London, 1986.

Hodgson, Robert. *The Life of the Right Reverend Beilby Porteous*. London, 1812.

Hollenweger, Walter J. *The Pentecostals*. Minneapolis, MN 1971/77.

Hollis, Claud. *A Brief History of Trinidad under the Spanish Crown*. Trinidad and Tobago, 1941.

Horne, Charles S. *The Story of the London Missionary Society, 1795–1895*. 2nd ed. London, 1895.

Howse, Ernest M. *Saints in Politics*. London, 1952; reprint 1960.

Hudson, Winthrop S. *Religion in America*. New York, 1965.

Huggins, A.B. *The Saga of the Companies*. Rev. ed. Freeport, Trinidad, ca. 1982.

Hurd, John C. *The Law of Freedom and Bondage in the United States*. Boston, 1858–62.

Hutton, Joseph E. *A History of Moravian Missions*. London, 1923.

Idowu, E. Bolaji. *African Traditional Religion: A Definition*. London, 1973.

International Missionary Council. *The Listening Isles*. New York, 1957.

Jacobs, C.M. *Joy Comes In The Morning*. Port-of-Spain, 1996.

Jamaica Christian Council. *Christ for Jamaica*. Kingston, 1951.

Jamaica Theological Seminary. *Prospectus 1988–1991*. Kingston, 1988.

Jamaica Yearly Meeting. *The Society of Friends in Jamaica*. Richmond, Ind., 1962.

Jenkins, Charles F. *Tortola, A Quaker Experiment of Long Ago in the Tropics*. London, 1923.

Jesse, Charles. *Outlines of St. Lucia's History*. Castries, 1970.

Jones, Rufus M. *The Quakers in the American Colonies*. London, 1911.

Josa, Fortunato P.L. *The Apostle of the Indians of Guiana*. London, 1888.

King, David. *The State and Prospects of Jamaica*. London, 1850.

Klingberg, Frank J. *Anglican Humanitarianism in the State of New York*. Philadelphia, 1940.

Klingberg, Frank J., ed. *Codrington Chronicle*. University of California Publications in History 37. Berkeley, 1949.

Klingberg, Frank J. *The Carolina Chronicle of Dr. Francis Le Jau, 1706–1717*. University of California Publications in History 53. Berkeley, 1956.

Krickeberg, Walter. *Pre-Columbian American Religions*. London, 1968.

La Guerre, John G., ed. *Calcutta to Caroni: The East Indians of Trinidad*. Trinidad, Jamaica and London, 1974.

Labaree, Leonard W. *Royal Government in America*. New Haven, 1930.

Langley, Nina. *Christopher Codrington and His College*. London, 1964.

Langton, Edward. *History of the Moravian Church*. London, 1956.

Larson, Jens P.M. *Virgin Islands Story*. Philadelphia, 1950; reprint 1968.

Latourette, Kenneth S. *History of the Expansion of Christianity*. 7 vols. New York and London, 1937–1945.

Latourette, Kenneth S. *A History of Christianity*. New York, 1953.

Laurence, Keith O. *Immigration into the West Indies in the 19th Century*. Barbados, 1971; reprint 1977.

Lawrence, George E., and C. Dorset. *Caribbean Conquest*. London, 1947.

Leahy, Vincent. *Bishop James Buckley 1820–1828*. Arima, 1980.

Lewis, Rupert, and P. Bryan, eds. *Garvey: His Work and Impact*. Mona, Jamaica, 1988.

Linden, Ingemar. *The Last Trump*. Frankfurt am Main, 1978.

Lovett, Richard. *The History of the London Missionary Society, 1795–1895*. 2 vols. London, 1899.

MacIntosh, William H. *Disestablishment and Liberation: The Movement for the Separation of the Anglican Church from State Control*. London, 1972.

MacNutt, Francis A. *Bartholomew de Las Casas*. New York and London, 1909.

MacTavish, William S., ed. *Reapers in Many Fields*. Toronto, 1904.

MacTavish, William S., ed. *Missionary Pathfinders*. Toronto, 1907.

MacTavish, William S., ed. *Harvests in Many Lands*. Toronto, 1908.

Marryat, Joseph. *An Examination of the Report of the Berbice Commissioners*. London, 1817.

Mather, George, and C.J. Blagg. *Bishop Rawle: A Memoir*. London, 1890.

Mathieson, William L. *British Slavery and its Abolition*. London, 1926.

Mathieson, William L. *The Sugar Colonies and Governor Eyre*. London, 1936.

Maxwell, John F. *Slavery and the Catholic Church*. Chichester, 1975.

Maynard, G.G. Oliver. *A History of the Moravian Church, Eastern West Indies Province*. Port-of-Spain, 1968.

Mbiti, John S. *African Religions and Philosophy*. New York, 1969.

McAllister, Lester G., and W.E. Tucker. *Journey into Faith: a History of the Christian Church (Disciples of Christ)*. St Louis, 1976.

McFarlan, Donald M. *Calabar: The Church of Scotland Mission*. London, 1946.

McKerrow, John. *History of the Foreign Missions of the Secession and United Presbyterian Church*. Edinburgh, 1867.

Means, Philip A. *The Spanish Main, Focus of Envy*. New York, 1935.

Mecham, J. Lloyd. *Church and State in Latin America: A History of Politico-ecclesiastical Relations*. Rev. ed. Chapel Hill, 1966.

Methodist Church, Jamaica District. *For Ever Beginning*. Kingston, 1960.

Methodist Church in the Bahamas. *Bicentenary Souvenir*. Nassau, 1960.

Mission Council of Trinidad. *East Meets West in Trinidad*. Toronto, 1934.

Moorman, John R.H. *A History of the Church in England*. London, 1973.

Moravian Church in Barbados. *Bi-Centenary Brochure*. Bridgetown, 1965.

Moravian Church in Trinidad. *Diamond Jubilee 1890–1965*. Trinidad, 1965.

Moravian Church, Jamaica [by Walter Hark and Augustus Westphal]. *The Breaking of the Dawn*. London, 1904.

Moreira, Eduardo. *The Significance of Portugal: A Survey of Evangelical Progress*. London, 1933.

Morrish, Ivor. *Obeah, Christ and Rastaman*. Cambridge, 1982.

Morton, Sarah E.S. *John Morton of Trinidad*. Toronto, 1916.

Murray, Eric J. *A History of the Seventh-Day Adventist Church in Trinidad and Tobago, 1891–1981*. Trinidad, 1982.

Nelson, Robert G. *Disciples of Christ in Jamaica, 1858–1958*. St Louis, 1958.

New Catholic Encyclopedia. 14 vols. New York, 1967.

Newson, Linda A. *Aboriginal and Spanish Colonial Trinidad*. London, 1976.

Newton, Arthur P. *The Colonizing Activities of the English Puritans*. New Haven and London, 1914.

Osborne, Francis J. *History of the Catholic Church in Jamaica*. Aylesbury, 1977; 2nd ed., Chicago, 1988.

Osborne, Francis J., and Geoffrey Johnston. *Coastlands and Islands*. Mona, Jamaica, 1972.

Ottley, Carlton R. *An Account of Life in Spanish Trinidad*. Trinidad, 1955.

Owens, Joseph. *Dread: The Rastafarians of Jamaica*. Kingston, 1976.

Parker, John A. *A Church in the Sun*. London, 1959.

Parrinder, Geoffrey. *African Traditional Religion*. London, 1954; reprint 1968.

Parrinder, Geoffrey. *Africa's Three Religions*. London, 1969.

Parsons, James J. *San Andrés and Providencia, English-Speaking Islands in the Western Caribbean*. Berkeley, 1956.

Payne, Daniel A. *History of the African Methodist Episcopal Church.* Nashville, 1891; reprint New York, 1968.

Phillippo, James M. *Jamaica, its Past and Present State.* London, 1843.

Pitman, Frank W. *The Development of the British West Indies, 1700–1763.* New Haven, 1917.

Ragatz, Lowell J. *The Fall of the Planter Class in the British Caribbean, 1763–1833.* New York, 1928.

Reece, James E., and C.G. Clark-Hunt. *Barbados Diocesan History.* London, 1928.

Rennard, Joseph. *Histoire religieuse des Antilles françaises.* Paris, 1954.

Reyss, Paul. *Étude sur quelques points de l'histoire de la tolérance au Canada et aux Antilles XVIe et XVIIe siècles.* Geneva, 1907.

Rippy, J. Fred, and J.T. Nelson. *Crusaders of the Jungle.* Chapel Hill, 1936.

Robson, George. *Missions of the United Presbyterian Church: The Story of our Jamaica Mission with a Sketch of our Trinidad Mission.* Edinburgh, 1894.

Rowland, Thomas. *Memoirs of the late Rev. Isaac Bradnack.* London, 1835.

Russell, Horace O. *Foundations and Anticipations: The Jamaica Baptist Story, 1783–1892.* Columbus, Ga., 1993.

Samaroo, Brinsley et al., eds. *In Celebration of 150 Years of the Indian Contribution to Trinidad and Tobago.* Port-of-Spain, 1995.

Sandall, Robert, and A.R. Wiggins. *The History of the Salvation Army.* 5 vols. London, 1947–68.

Schomburgk, Robert H. *The History of Barbados.* London, 1848.

Schuler, Monica. *"Alas, Alas, Kongo": A Social History of Indentured African Immigration into Jamaica.* Baltimore, 1980.

Schultz, David C., ed. *Church of God Missions: The First 100 Years.* Anderson, Ind.1980.

Scopes, Wilfred, ed. *The Christian Ministry in Latin America and the Caribbean.* New York, 1962.

Seminary of St John Vianney, 1943–1968. Trinidad, 1968.

Sherlock, Hugh. *Methodism in the Caribbean with Particular Reference to Autonomy.* Kingston, 1966.

Sherlock, Philip M. *West Indian Nations.* Kingston and London, 1973.

Shiels, William E. *King and Church: The Rise and Fall of the Patronato Real.* Chicago, 1961.

Shrewsbury, John V.B. *Memorials of the Rev. William J. Shrewsbury.* London, 1869.

Shyllon, Folarin O. *Black Slaves in Britain.* London, 1974.

Shyllon, Folarin O. *James Ramsay, the Unknown Abilitionist.* Edinburgh, 1977.

Sibley, Inez Knibb. *The Baptists of Jamaica.* Kingston, 1965.

Simpson, George E. *The Shango Cult in Trinidad.* Puerto Rico, 1965.

Smith, Abbott E. *Colonists in Bondage: White Servitude and Convict Labour in America, 1607–1776.* Gloucester, Mass., 1965.

Smith, Ashley. *Pentecostalism in Jamaica: A Challenge to the Established Churches and Society.* Kingston, 1975; Mandeville, 1993.

Smith, Charles S. *A History of the African Methodist Episcopal Church . . . 1856 to 1922.* Philadelphia, 1922; reprint New York, 1968.

Smith, John W.V. *The Quest for Holiness and Unity.* Anderson, Ind., 1980.

Smith, Timothy L. *Called unto Holiness: The Story of the Nazarenes: The Formative Years.* Kansas City, Mo., 1962.

Society for the Furtherance of the Gospel. *Retrospect of the History of the Mission of the Brethren's Church in Jamaica.* London, 1854.

Squires, Laurence S. *These Hundred Years . . . The Story of Davyton.* N.p., 1945.

Stewart, Robert J. *Religion and Society in Post-Emancipation Jamaica.* Knoxville, 1992.

Stock, Eugene. *The History of the Church Missionary Society.* 3 vols. London, 1899.

Synan, Vinson. *The Holiness-Pentecostal Movement in the United States.* Grand Rapids, 1971.

Thomas, Eudora. *A History of the Shouter Baptists in Trinidad and Tobago.* Ithaca, 1987.

Thompson, Edgar W. *Nathaniel Gilbert, Lawyer and Evangelist.* London, 1960.

Thompson, Henry P. *Into All Lands.* London, 1951.

Titus, Noel. *Missionary Under Pressure: The Experiences of the Rev. John Duport in West Africa.* Barbados, 1983.

Truman, George, J. Jackson, and T.B. Longstreth. *Narrative of a Visit to the West Indies in 1840 and 1841.* Philadelphia, 1844.

Turner, Mary. *Slaves and Missionaries.* Urbana, Ill., 1982; reprint Kingston, 1998.

Underhill, Edward B. *Life of James Mursell Phillippo.* London, 1881.

Underhill, Edward B. *Alfred Saker, Missionary to Africa.* London, 1884.

Underhill, Edward B. *The Tragedy of Morant Bay.* London, 1895.

Union Theological Seminary. *St. Colme's Hostel: Souvenir of Dedication.* Kingston, 1955.

United Theological College of the West Indies. *Twenty-fifth Anniversary Souvenir Magazine.* Mona, Jamaica, 1982.

Vanderpool, D.I. *In Their Steps.* Kansas City, Mo., 1956.

Veness, William T. *Ten Years of Mission Life in British Guiana: being a memoir of the Rev. Thomas Youd.* London, 1875.

Vickers, John. *Thomas Coke, Apostle of Methodism.* London, 1969.

Von Hagen, Victor W. *World of the Maya.* New York, 1960.

Waddell, Hope M. *Twenty-nine Years in the West Indies and Central Africa.* London, 1863.

Walker, Williston. *A History of the Christian Church.* Rev. ed. New York, 1959.

Warneck, Gustaf. *Outline of a History of Protestant Missions.* Edinburgh, 1903.

Warner-Lewis, Maureen. *Guinea's Other Suns: The African Dynamic in Trinidad Culture.* Dover, Mass., 1991.

Watson, James, and C.A. Wookey. *Jamaica Congregational Churches.* Guildford, Surrey, 1901.

Watters, Mary. *A History of the Church in Venezuela.* Chapel Hill, 1933.

Wearmouth, Robert F. *Methodism and the Common People of England of the Eighteenth Century.* London, 1945.

Wilkinson, John L. *Church in Black and White.* Edinburgh, 1993.

Williams, Eric E. *Capitalism and Slavery.* Chapel Hill, 1944.

Williams, Eric E. *History of the People of Trinidad and Tobago.* Port-of-Spain, 1962.

Williamson, James A. *English Colonies in Guiana and on the Amazon, 1604–1668.* Oxford, 1923.

Williamson, James A. *The Caribbee Islands under the Proprietary Patents.* London, 1926.

Wilson, F. Rought. *Life of George Sargeant, Wesleyan Missionary and first President of the West Indian Conference.* London, 1901.

Wood, Donald. *Trinidad in Transition.* London, 1968.

Wright, Philip. *Knibb 'the Notorious'.* London, 1973.

Zavala, Silvio A. *The Defence of Human Rights in Latin America.* Paris, 1964.

Articles and Theses

Baker, Frank. "Francis Gilbert and Methodist ordination". *Proceedings of the Wesley Historical Society* 27, pt.7 (Sept. 1950): 146–48.

Baker, Frank. "The origins of Methodism in the West Indies". *London Quarterly and Holborn Review* (Jan. 1960): 6–17.

Baxter, Thomas R. "Caribbean bishops: the establishment of the bishoprics of Jamaica and Barbados and the Leeward Islands, 1824–1843". *Historical Magazine of the Protestant Episcopal Church* 32 (1963): 189–203.

Bennett, J.H., Jr. "The Society for the Propagation of the Gospel's plantations and the emancipation crisis". In *British Humanitarianism*, edited by Samuel C. McCulloch, 15–29. Philadelphia, 1950.

Bennett, J. Harry, Jr. "The SPG and Barbadian politics, 1710–1720". *Historical Magazine of the Protestant Episcopal Church* 20 (1951): 190–206.

Betteridge, Alan. "The spread of Methodism through the Bahamas". In *Methodist Church in the Bahamas, Bicentenary Souvenir*, 10–20. Nassau, 1960.

Braithwaite, Lloyd. "The development of higher education in the West Indies". *Social and Economic Studies* 7, no. 1 (1958): 1–64.

Davis, John W. "George Liele and Andrew Bryan, pioneer Baptist preachers". *Journal of Negro History* 3 (1918): 119–27.

Dunn, Charles Alexander. "The Canadian Mission in British Guiana: the pioneer years (1885–1927)". Thesis, Knox College, Toronto, 1971.

Dunn, Charles Alexander. "The Canadian Mission in British Guiana: from mission to church (1927–1967)". Thesis, Knox College, Toronto, 1975.

Forsyth, James S. "The life of William Gordon". Master's thesis, University of Texas, 1952.

Fraser, Wilfred A. "The Church of Scotland in British Guiana". *Caribbean Presbyterian* 1 (1958): 30–31.

Goodridge, C.A. "Dominica: the French connection". In *Aspects of Dominican History*, Government of Dominica, 157–62. Dominica, 1972.

Goveia, Elsa V. "The West Indian slave laws of the 18th century". In *Chapters in Caribbean History* 2, edited by Elsa Goveia and C.J. Bartlett. Barbados, 1970.

Griffith, Ezra E.H. "The psycho-social development and evolution of the Barbadian Spiritual Baptist Church". *Caribbean Journal of Religious Studies* 13, 1 (April 1992): 3–14.

Guilley, R.L. "Roman Catholicism in the Caribbean". In *Caribbean Conference of Churches, Handbook of Churches in the Caribbean*. Barbados, 1973.

Gwynn, Aubrey. "Early Irish emigration to the West Indies (1612–1643)". *Studies* 18 (Sept. and Dec. 1929): 377–93, 648–63.

Gwynn, Aubrey. "Indentured servants and Negro slaves in Barbados (1642–1650)". *Studies* 19 (March 1930): 279–94.

Gwynn, Aubrey. "Cromwell's policy of transportation". *Studies* 19, no. 1 (December 1930): 607–23 and 20 (June 1931): 291–305.

Gwynn, Aubrey. "Documents relating to the Irish in the West Indies". *Analecta Hibernica*, no. 4 (Oct. 1932): 138–286.

Gwynn, Aubrey. "The first Irish priests in the New World". *Studies* 21 (1932): 213–28.

Higham, Charles S.S. "The early days of the Church in the West Indies". *Church Quarterly Review* 92 (1921): 106–30.

Holland, Dorothy C., and Julia C. Crane. "Adapting to an industrializing nation: the Shango cult in Trinidad". *Social and Economic Studies* 36, no. 4 (Dec. 1987).

Hopkins, Frederick C. "The Catholic church in British Honduras 1851–1918". *Catholic Historical Review* [USA] 4 (1918): 304–14.

Hughes, Henry B.L. "Christian missionary societies in the British West Indies during the emancipation era", 2 vols. PhD diss., University of Toronto, 1944.

Hutton, Joseph E. "The Moravian contribution to the evangelical revival in England, 1742–1755". In *Historical Essays*, edited by Thomas F. Tout and J. Tait, 423–52. London, 1902.

Ingham, S.M. "The Disestablishment Movement in England, 1868–74". *Journal of Religious History* [Australia] (1964): 38–60.

Jernegan, Marcus W. "Slavery and conversion in the American Colonies". *American Historical Review* 21, no. 3 (1916): 504–27.

Klingberg, Frank J. "The efforts of the SPG to Christianize the Mosquito Indians, 1742–1785". *Historical Magazine of the Protestant Episcopal Church* 9 (1940): 305–21.

Klingberg, Frank J. "The Lady Mico Charity Schools in the British West Indies, 1835–1842". *Journal of Negro History* 24, no. 3 (July 1939): 291–344.

Levy, Babette M. "Early Puritanism in the southern and island colonies". *Proceedings of the American Antiquarian Society* 70 (April 1960): 69–348.

Messenger, John C. "The influence of the Irish in Montserrat". *Caribbean Quarterly* 13, no. 2 (June 1967): 3–26.

Neehall, Roy G. "Presbyterianism in Trinidad: a study of the impact of presbyterianism in the island of Trinidad in the 19th century". STM thesis, Union Theological Seminary, New York, 1958.

Paget, Hugh. "The free village system in Jamaica". *Jamaican Historical Review* 1, no. 1 (1945): 31–48.

Payne, Ernest A. "Baptist work in Jamaica before the arrival of the missionaries". *Baptist Quarterly*, New Series 7 (Jan. 1934): 20–26.

Pierson, Roscoe M. "Alexander Bedward and the Jamaican Native Baptist Free Church". *Lexington Theological Quarterly* 4, no. 3 (July 1969): 65–76.

Pitt, E.A. "Acculturative and synthetic aspects of religion and life in the island of St Vincent and other predominantly Protestant islands and areas of the West Indies and the Caribbean". Reprint from *Actes du IVe Congrès International des Sciences Anthropoligiques et Ethnologiques*, 1952, II, 385–90.

Proesmans, R. "Notes on the slaves of the French". In *Aspects of Dominican History*, Government of Dominica, 163–72. Dominica, 1972.

Root, Winfred T. "The lords of trade and plantations, 1675–1696". *American Historical Review* 23 (Oct. 1917): 20–41.

Schutz, John A., and M.E. O'Neill. "Arthur Holt, Anglican clergyman, reports on Barbados, 1725–1733". *Journal of Negro History* 21 (1946): 444–69.

Shorrocks, Francis. "History of the Catholic Church in Barbados during the 19th century". *Journal of the Barbados Museum and Historical Society* 25, no. 3 (May 1958): 102–22.

Simpson, George E. "Jamaican Revivalist cults". *Social and Economic Studies* 5, no.4 (Dec. 1956): 321–442.

Tibesar, A. "Latin America, Church in". *New Catholic Encyclopedia*, vol. 8, 448–69. New York, 1967.

Wilmot, Swithin. "Baptist missionaries and Jamaican politics". In *A Selection of Papers presented at the Twelfth Conference of the Association of Caribbean Historians*, edited by K.O. Laurence, 45–62. St Augustine, 1986,

Zerries, Otto. "Primitive South America and the West Indies". In *Pre-Columbian American Religions*, edited by Walter Krickeberg, 258-89. London, 1968.

Abbreviations Used in Indexes

Abp: Archbishop; AME: African Methodist Episcopal; An: Anglican(s); Ant: Antigua; Bah: Bahamas; Bp: Bishop; Bs: Barbados; Bt: Baptist(s); Bz: Belize; CMS: Church Missionary Society; Co: Congregationalist(s) Ds: Disciples; Gov: Governor; Gr: Grenada; Gy: Guyana; HS: High School; Hu: Huguenot(s); Ja: Jamaica; LMS: London Missionary Society; LC: Lutheran Church; Ll: Leeward Islands; Lu: Lutheran(s); Me: Methodist(s); Mo: Moravian(s); POS: Port-of-Spain Pr: Presbyterian(s); Qu: Quaker(s); RC: Roman Catholic(s); SA: Salvation Army; SK: St Kitts; SV: St Kitts; SPG: Society for the Propagation of the Gospel; Td: Trinidad; To: Tobago; US: United States; VI: Virgin Islands; WI: West Indies

General Index

Index of Persons

Index of Places